To Deneen, Daniel, Kelley, and Ryan, ILYANMWITWWA.

To Deborah, for making time.

Contents at a Glance

Contents

About the Authors

Dave Mark is a longtime Mac developer and author who has written a number of books on Mac and iOS development, including *Beginning iPhone 4 Development* (Apress, 2011), *More iPhone 3 Development* (Apress, 2010), *Learn C on the Mac* (Apress, 2008), *Ultimate Mac Programming* (Wiley, 1995), and the *Macintosh Programming Primer* series (Addison-Wesley, 1992). Dave was one of the founders of MartianCraft, an iOS and Android development house. Dave loves the water and spends as much time as possible on it, in it, or near it. He lives with his wife and three children in Virginia.

James Bucanek has spent the past 30 years programming and developing microprocessor systems. He has experience with a broad range of computer hardware and software, from embedded consumer products to industrial robotics. His development projects include the first local area network for the Apple II, distributed air conditioning control systems, a piano teaching system, digital oscilloscopes, silicon wafer deposition furnaces, and collaborative writing tools for K-12 education. James holds a Java Developer Certification from Sun Microsystems and was awarded a patent for optimizing local area networks. James is currently focused on OS X and iOS software development, where he can combine his deep knowledge of UNIX and object-oriented languages with his passion for elegant design. James holds an Associate's degree in classical ballet from the Royal Academy of Dance.

About the Technical Reviewer

Michael Thomas has worked in software development for over 20 years as an individual contributor, Team Lead, Program Manager, and Vice President of Engineering. Michael has over 10 years experience working with mobile devices. His current focus is in the medical sector using mobile devices to accelerate information transfer between patients and health care providers.

Acknowledgments

This book could not have been written without the support of our wonderful families. Deneen, Daniel, Kelley, Ryan, Deborah, Doug, and Amber, thank you all for everything you've done for us. We truly are lucky men.

Many, many thanks to the fine folks at Apress. Clay Andres started this ball rolling by bringing both Dave and James over to Apress. Steve Anglin is largely responsible for deciding what Apress prints, and we are flattered by his continued conviction in this book. James Markham kept a watchful eye on every paragraph, keeping our message clear and comprehensible. Michael Thomas checked every line of code and symbol to ensure complete accuracy. Any technical errors are ultimately our responsibility, but there are significantly fewer thanks to Michael. Mary Behr dotted our i's, crossed our t's, corrected our spelling, and made sure we used "whom" correctly. If you find this book easy to read, you have Mary's blue pencil to thank. Anna Ishchenko designed our beautiful cover. Last, but certainly not least, we are indebted to Coordinating Editor Jill Balzano who managed to juggle schedules, coordinate editors, track production, and herd two headstrong authors towards a common goal. To all the folks at Apress, thank you, thank you, thank you!

Dave says: A very special shout out goes to James, my incredibly talented co-author. James made many important technical contributions to this book, helping me scrub the prose and the sample code to ensure that it followed the C standard to the letter. He also added many concepts to the book that are vital to any aspiring programmer.

And from James: I am most grateful to David Mark for allowing me the opportunity to contribute to this venerable title. Dave has made learning C engaging and enjoyable for an entire generation of programmers. It's been an honor contributing to that institution. I would also like to extend thanks to Apple's Xcode development team for continually improving one of the finest software development tools in the world.

Introduction

Welcome Aboard

Welcome! Chances are that you are reading this because you love the Mac. And not only do you love the Mac, but you also love the idea of learning how to design and develop your very own Mac programs.

You've definitely come to the right place.

This book assumes that you know how to use your Mac. That's it. You don't need to know anything about programming—not one little bit. We'll start off with the basics, and each step we take will be a small one to make sure that you have no problem following along.

This book will focus on the basics of programming. At the same time, you'll learn the essentials of the C programming language.

In Douglas Adam's book The Hitchhiker's Guide to the Galaxy, the answer to "the Ultimate Question of Life, the Universe, and Everything" is determined to be "42." That answer is, of course, wrong; the correct answer is "C."

The C language is the wellspring of software. The nothing-short-of-miraculous revolution in computing and consumer electronics over the past half century has largely been accomplished using C, languages that are direct descendants of C (Objective-C, C++), or languages designed to work like C (Java, C#). Learn C and the programming world is your oyster.

Note Douglas Adams was a big Macintosh fan.

Once you get through this book, you'll be ready to move on to object-oriented programming and Objective-C—the official programming language of OS X and iOS.

Does this all sound a little overwhelming? Not to worry; in this book, we'll take small steps, so nobody gets lost. You can definitely do this!

Who Is This Book For?

When Dave wrote the very first edition of *Learn C on the Mac* back in 1991, he was writing with college students in mind. After all, college was where he really learned to program. It seems he was way off.

"My first clue that I had underestimated my audience was when I started getting e-mails from fifth graders who were making their way through the book. Fifth graders! And not just one but lots of nine-, ten-, and eleven-year-old kids were digging in and learning to program. Cool! And the best part of all was when these kids started sending me actual shipping products that they created. You can't imagine how proud I was and still am."

Dave was really on to something. Over the years, we've heard from soccer moms, hobbyists, even folks who were using the Mac for the very first time, all of whom made their way through *Learn C on the Mac* and came out the other end, proud, strong, and full of knowledge.

So what do you need to know to get started? Although learning C by just reading a book is possible, you'll get the most out of this book if you run each example program as you encounter it. To do this, you'll need a Mac running OS X (preferably version 10.6.8 or later) and an Internet connection. You'll need the Internet connection to download the free tools Apple has graciously provided for anyone interested in programming the Mac and to download the projects that go along with this book.

Again, if you know nothing about programming, don't worry. The first few chapters of this book will bring you up to speed. If you have some programming experience (or even a lot), you might want to skim the first few chapters, and then dig right into the C fundamentals that start in Chapter 3.

The Lay of the Land

Here's a quick tour of what's to come in this book.

- Chapter 1 shows you how to get the free software tools you'll use throughout this book.
- Chapter 2 explains some of the basics of how computer programs are built.
- Chapter 3 shows you how to embed a series of programming statements into a reusable function, something you can call again and again.
- Chapter 4 adds variables and operators into the mix, bringing the power of mathematical expressions into your programs.
- Chapter 5 teaches you how to watch your program execute, line-by-line, to see that it's doing the right thing, or fix it if it's not.
- Chapter 6 introduces the concept of flow control, using constructs like if, else, do, and while to control the direction your program takes.
- Chapter 7 covers pointers and parameters, two concepts that will add a dramatic new level of power to your programs.
- Chapter 8 moves beyond the simple data types used in the first half of the book, adding the ability to work with more complex numbers along with data types like arrays and text strings.

- Chapter 9 takes a break to show you how to deploy your finished program and use it from the command line.
- Chapter 10 dives even deeper into data and teaches you how to design your own custom data structures.
- Chapter 11 shows you how to save your program's data and read it back in again by introducing the concept of the data file.
- Chapter 12 gives you some techniques for dealing with errors, for when things go wrong.
- Chapter 13 covers a variety of advanced topics—typecasting, unions, recursion, sorting, collections, and much more.
- Finally, Chapter 14 wraps things up and points you to the next step on your journey.

Ready to get started? Let's go!

Chapter 1

Go Get the Tools!

If you want to build a house, you need a solid set of well-crafted tools. Building computer programs is no different. Programming requires a specialized set of *development tools*—basically, programs that make programs.

In the early days of C, you only needed a few, relatively simple tools. As computers have become more sophisticated, so has the universe of development tools. Today, it's not uncommon to employ dozens of programs to create even a "simple" application: editors, compilers, linkers, debuggers, emulators, profilers, analyzers, and more. Add to that list programs that help you find documentation, cross reference your code, record your development history, and, well, it's starting to look like a whole hardware store full of tools!

The good news is that Apple has come to your rescue. Just as Apple has used an elegant user interface to demystify their most sophisticated applications, they've done the same for software developers. (That's you!)

Installing Xcode

Apple's Xcode is a complete hardware store of software development tools, packaged and delivered as a single application. All you have to do is write your program and Xcode will—behind the scenes—direct the scores of individual development tools needed to turn your idea into reality. It would make the Wizard of Oz proud.

> **NOTE:** An application that organizes multiple development tools into a single workspace is called an *integrated development environment* (IDE). Xcode is an IDE.

And getting Xcode into your computer couldn't be easier. The entire Xcode development suite is available from the App Store.

Launch the App Store, go to the Developer Tools category (or just search for "Xcode"), and click to install Xcode, as shown in Figure 1-1. Don't worry if your screen looks a bit different than the figure. Apple is constantly updating Xcode, so there will probably be a new version of Xcode in the App Store by the time this book hits the shelves (or your screen).

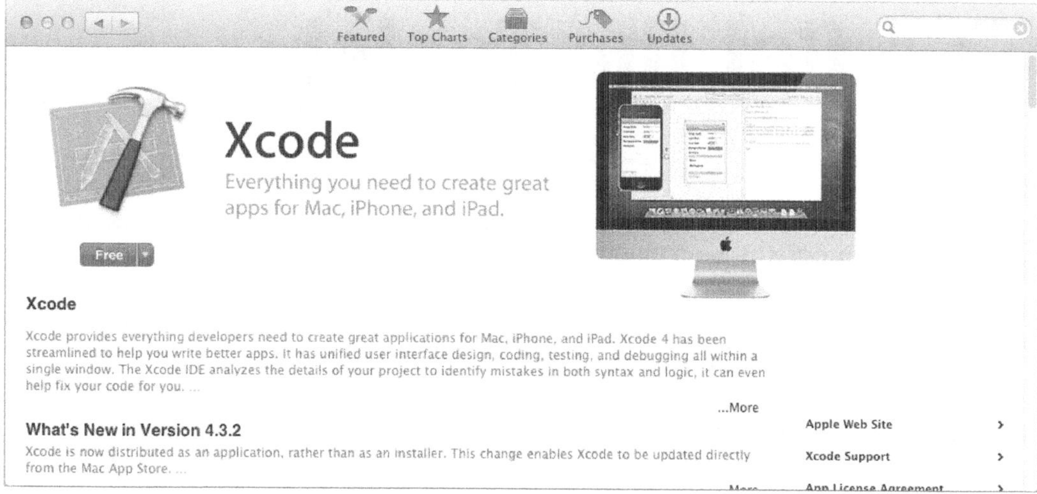

Figure 1-1. *Installing Xcode from the App Store*

That's it! Sit back and wait for Xcode to download and install. And you're going to have to wait awhile, as it's a really big application. So amuse yourself with the rest of this chapter while it downloads. Switch to the Purchases view, at the top of the App Store window, if you want see how the download is progressing.

How much is that IDE in the Window?

Xcode has gone through various prices in the past. Apple really wants you to create great applications and has strived, for the most part, to make its developments tools freely available.

It used to be that Xcode was only available to *registered developers*. Becoming a registered developer usually costs money, so Xcode was "free" only in the sense that the prize inside a cereal box is "free."

For a while, Xcode was priced at $5. As of this writing, Xcode is free in the App Store. Hopefully, it will stay that way.

NOTE: If you're running an older version of OS X and don't have access to the App Store, you can still download an earlier version of Xcode—but we don't recommend it.

The first problem you're going to encounter is how to get your copy of Xcode. As of this writing, you must be a registered developer to obtain an older version of Xcode. Unfortunately, Apple no longer offers free developer registration—largely because Xcode is now available for free in the App Store—so you'll have to pay to register, and that can be expensive. If you *are* a registered developer or have access to Apple's University Program for higher education, you can log into `http://developer.apple.com/` and download the tools.

But your biggest problem is going to be the differences between the current Xcode and older versions. The code examples in this book will still work and make sense, but the commands, windows, features, and controls are all going to be substantially different. You're going to have to figure out a lot on your own.

We certainly don't want to discourage anyone from learning C on the Mac, but we strongly recommend you upgrade to the latest version of OS X so you have access to the latest version of Xcode.

What's a Registered Developer?

So what's a registered developer and do you need to be one? The short answer is "not yet."

Becoming a registered developer grants you access to even more tools and resources than just Xcode. But you don't need any of that to write great applications for OS X or iOS! You don't need it to use Xcode. You certainly don't need to be a registered developer to work through this book (or most other books, for that matter).

You *will* need to become a registered developer if you want to sell, or even give away, your masterpieces on any of Apple's app stores. How cool would that be? You can register at any time, so there's no hurry. When you are ready, visit `http://developer.apple.com/`.

Getting the Projects

While you're still waiting for Xcode to download and install, why not get the project files for this book? Everything you need to create the projects in this book is described in the text, but downloading the finished projects from the Apress web site will save you a lot of typing.

Go to `http://www.apress.com/book/view/9781430245339`. Below the book's description, you'll see some folder tabs, one of which is labeled `Source Code/Downloads`. Click that tab. Now find the link that downloads the projects for this book. Click that link and a file named `Learn C Projects.zip` will download to your hard drive.

Locate the file `Learn C Projects.zip` in your `Downloads` folder (or wherever the browser saved it). Double-click the file to extract its contents, leaving you with a folder named `Learn C Projects`. Move the folder wherever you like.

Using Xcode

Once Xcode has finished installing, launch it as you would any application, from the dock or LaunchPad. When first launched, Xcode will present its startup window (Figure 1-2).

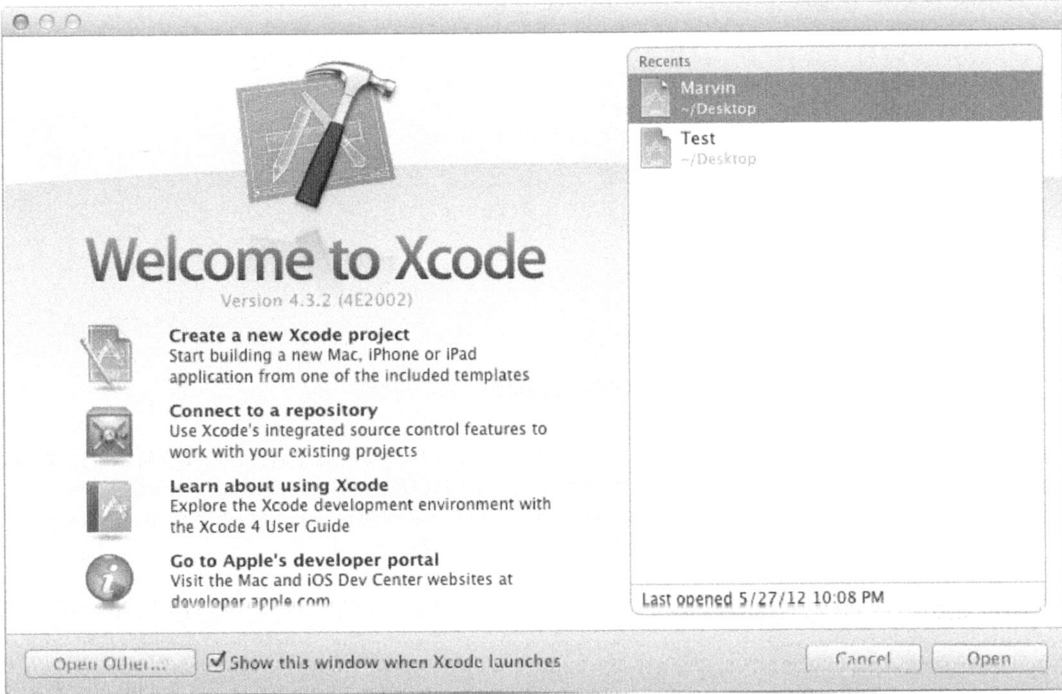

Figure 1-2. *Xcode startup window*

The startup window has convenient buttons that create a new project, reopen a recently visited project, link to the Xcode documentation, and some other stuff we're not going to cover in this book.

Xcode organizes your work around a *project*. A project is a collection of files that ultimately produce a program. It always consists of a *project document* (the icon with the little blueprint) stored inside a folder, as shown in Figure 1-3. That folder is called the *project folder*. You open a project by opening the project document.

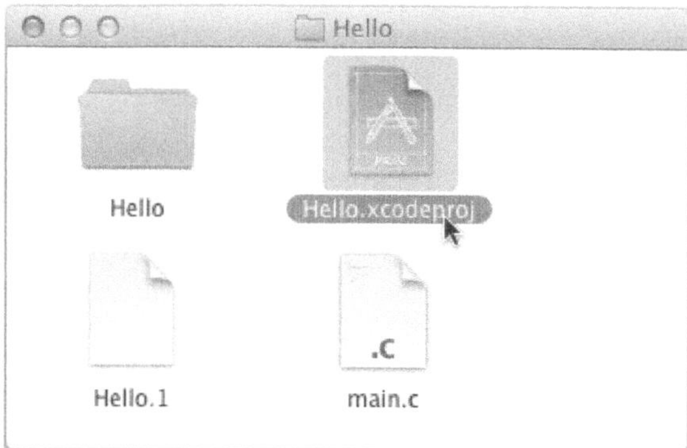

Figure 1-3. *The contents of a simple Xcode project folder*

When opened in Xcode, your project appears in a *workspace window*, as shown in Figure 1-4. The window is full of cryptic settings and seemingly complex controls, but don't worry. Until you get to some really advanced programming, you won't need to fiddle with any of these settings.

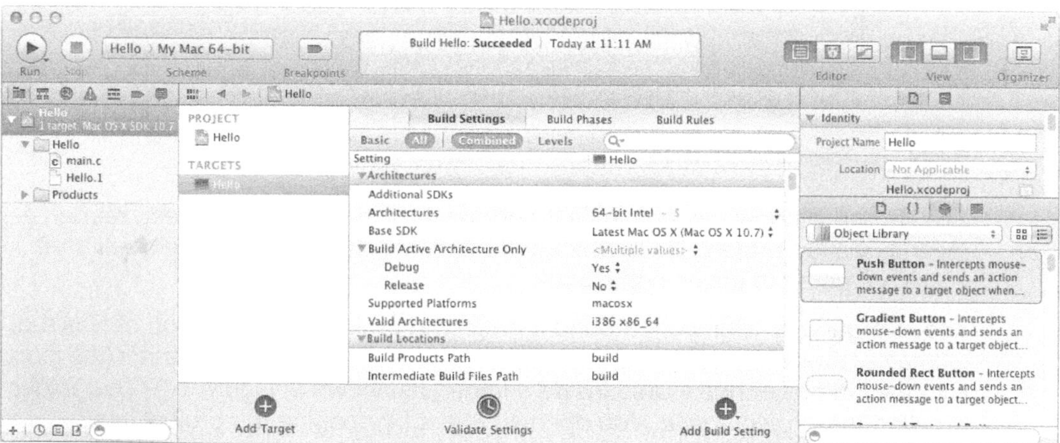

Figure 1-4. *A workspace window in Xcode*

Creating a New Xcode Project

While Xcode still has that "new car smell," let's take it for a quick spin around the block and create a new Xcode project.

To do this, either click on the link labeled *Create a new Xcode project* link in the startup window, or choose File ➤ New ➤ Project from the menubar. You'll be presented with the *new project assistant*, shown in Figure 1-5, which will help you specify the type of new project you want to create.

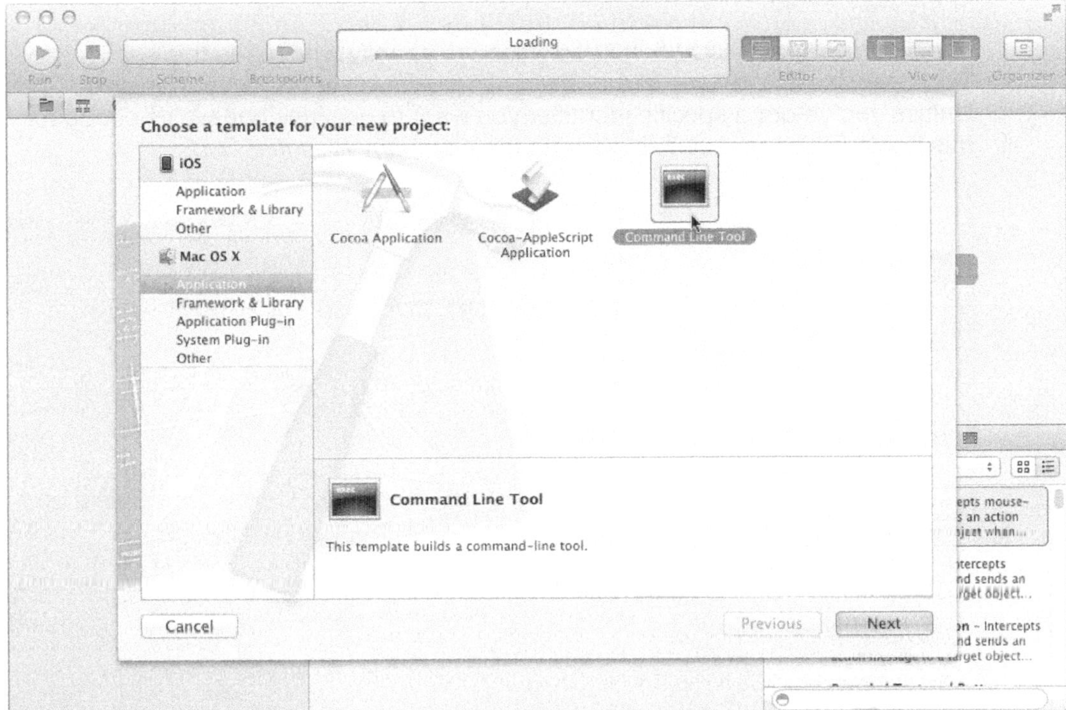

Figure 1-5. *New project assistant*

The left side of the new project assistant lets you choose whether to create a project for iOS (one that will run on your iPhone, iPad, or iPod touch) or for Mac OS X (one that will run on your computer). Select *Application* in the Mac OS X section.

Next, you need to decide the type of Mac OS X application you want to build. In this book, you're going to learn how to build simple, text-only applications that display text in a window, one line at a time. Once you finish this book, you can move on to books that will teach you how to use the skills you've just mastered to build applications that will run on your iOS device or on your Mac with the graphical elements that define those devices.

Select *Command Line Tool* from the templates pane. This is the only project template you'll be using in this book. To complete your selection, click the *Next* button.

The next screen (Figure 1-6) lets you name your new project and specify a few other options. For a command-line tool the options are pretty simple. Enter *Hello* in the *Name* field.

The field *Company Identifier* allows Xcode to specify who made this application. Typically, this is a reverse of a domain name you've set up for your product. Unless you've got a specific identifier you want to use, use one we've set up for this book. Enter *com.apress.learnc* in the *Company Identifier field.*

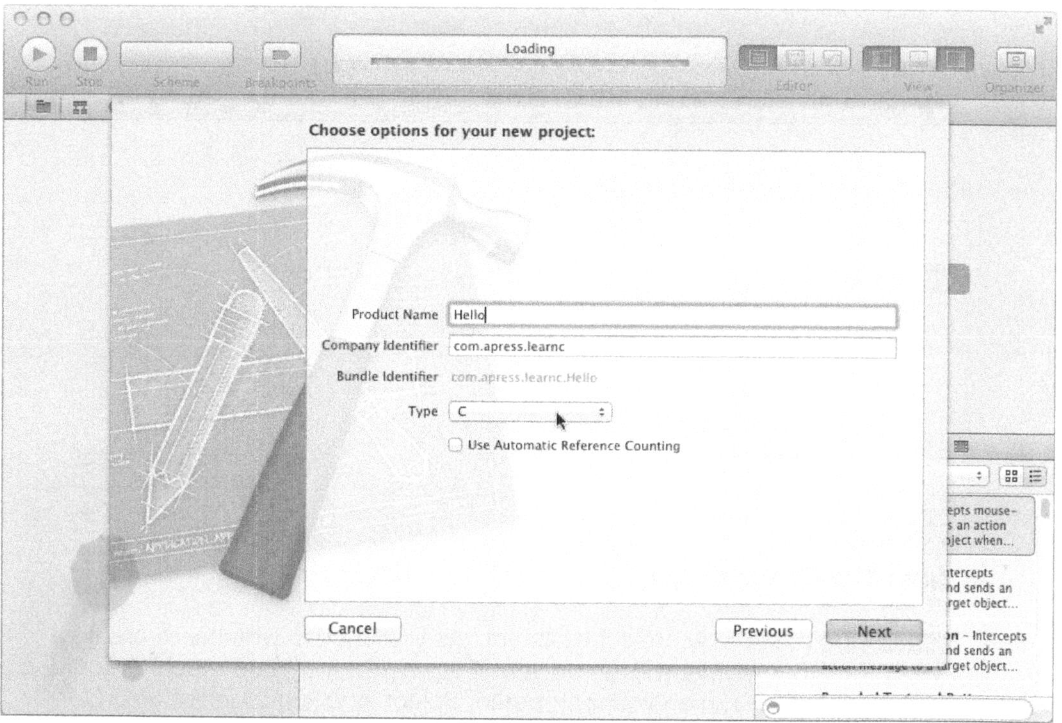

Figure 1-6. *Project template options*

Set the *Type* pop-up menu to *C*, since you'll be writing all your programs in the C programming language.

Automatic Reference Counting doesn't apply to C. Leave the *Use Automatic Reference Counting* checkbox unchecked.

Now that your options are all set, click the *Next* button.

Finally, Xcode will prompt you for a location in which to save your project folder. Though you can save your projects anywhere you like, you might want to first create a master folder, perhaps named *My Learn C Projects*, in which you can store all the projects you create for this book

The Workspace Window

Xcode opens your new project in a workspace window, as shown in Figure 1-7. The workspace window is divided up into panes or views. On the left are the navigators (how you get around your project). In the middle are your editors (where you write and design your application). To edit a file, double-click the file in the navigator and it will appear in the editor. On the right are utilities (inspectors, libraries, help, and such). Any of these views can be hidden as you work. In Figure 1-7, the utilities are hidden for the sake of simplicity.

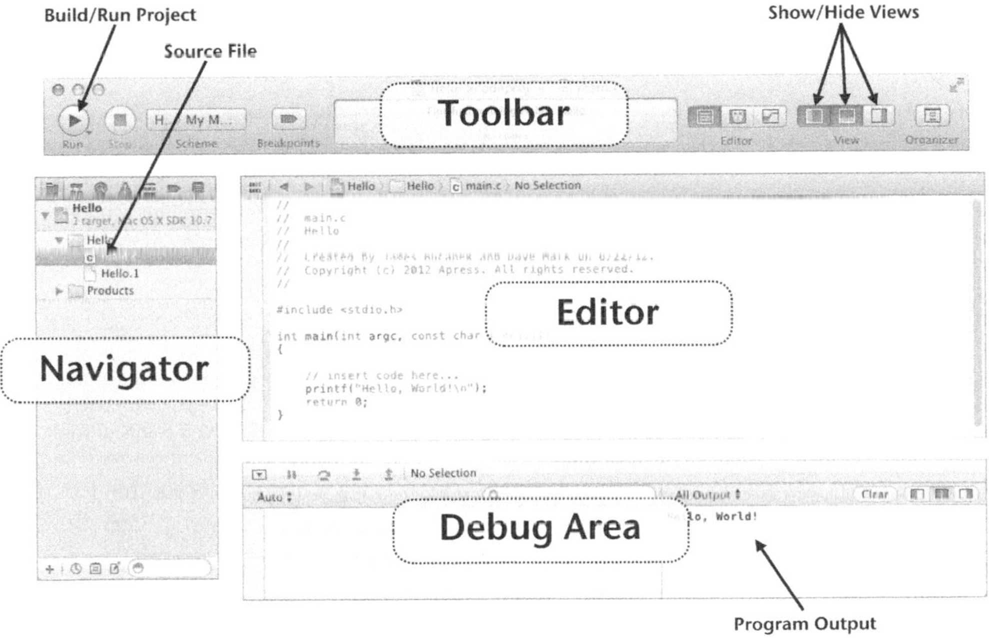

Figure 1-7. *Hello project workspace window*

At the bottom you'll find the debug area, which normally appears only while you're running or testing a program. This is where you inspect your program while it's running and view its output. At the very top is the toolbar. It has buttons and controls for things you commonly do. The big *Run* button at the left will build and run your program, which is what it's all about. Everything in the toolbar is just a shortcut for a command in the Xcode menubar; it doesn't matter which you use.

Running a Project

One really nice thing about Xcode project templates is that they always create a finished project. That is, everything it needs to build and run is ready right from the start. Of course, it won't do anything useful. In fact, it really won't do much of anything at all beyond starting and then stopping again. Changing your project to do something useful is your job.

But don't let that stop you; let's make your new project do nothing! Click the *Run* button (the big *Play* button in the upper left corner of the workspace window). Xcode will assemble all of the parts of your project (a process know as building) and will then execute it.

Don't expect fireworks. The Xcode command-line template makes a project that causes the words "Hello, World!" to appear in the lower right pane (called the *console*), as shown in Figure 1-7.

HELLO, WORLD!

Dennis Ritchie developed the original C language over a period of time between hippies and disco. Years later, he worked with Brian Kernighan to pen a complete description of the language. This version of C became known as *K&R C*.

In their seminal book, the very first example of C (it's on page 6; you can look it up) was a tiny program that caused the words "Hello, World" to appear on a console. And in those days it was probably a Teletype console—a washing-machine–sized mechanical typewriter with roll paper.

Ever since that day, practically every book that explains, teaches, or describes a programming language starts with an example that makes the words "Hello, World" appear somewhere. In the spirit of that grand tradition, we are honor bound to teach you how to make "Hello, World!" appear on your Mac!

Moving On

Believe it or not, you are now ready to learn C on the Mac!

You've installed all of the tools you need to create OS X applications, and you've created, built, and run a brand new application. That's pretty good for one chapter!

The next chapter will take a break from all of this excitement to talk about the software development process in general.

Chapter 2

Programming Basics

Before we dig into C programming specifics, let's spend a few minutes discussing the basics of programming. Why write a computer program? How do computer programs work? We'll answer these questions and look at all of the elements that come together to create a computer program, such as source code, a compiler, and the computer itself.

If you are already familiar with the basics of programming, please feel free to skim through this chapter and, if you feel comfortable with the material, skip on ahead to Chapter 3. The goal here is to get you familiar with the steps involved in creating a running a simple program.

Programming

Why write a computer program? There are many reasons. Some programs are written in direct response to a problem too complex to solve by hand. For example, you might write a program to calculate a value to 5,000 decimal places or to determine the precise moment to fire the boosters that will safely land the Mars Rover.

Other programs are written as performance aids, allowing you to perform a regular task more efficiently. You might write a program to help you balance your checkbook, keep track of your baseball card collection, or lay out this month's issue of *Dinosaur Today*.

Whatever their purpose, each of these examples shares a common theme. They are all examples of the art of programming. Your goal in reading this book is to learn how to use the C programming language to create programs of your own. Before we get into C, however, let's take a minute to look at some other ways to solve your programming problems.

Some Alternatives to C

As mentioned previously, C is one of the most popular programming languages around. There's very little you can't do in C (or in some variant of C), once you know how. On the other hand, a C program is not necessarily the best solution to every programming problem.

For example, suppose you are trying to build a database to track your company's inventory. Rather than writing a custom C program to solve your problem, you might be able to use an off-the-shelf package like FileMaker Pro or perhaps a Unix-based solution like MySQL or PostgreSQL to construct your database. The programmers who created these packages have already solved most of the knotty database-management problems you'd face if you tried to write your program from scratch. The lesson here is this: before you tackle a programming problem, examine all the alternatives. You might find one that will save you time and money or one that will prove to be a better solution to your problem.

Some problems can be solved using the Mac's built-in scripting language, AppleScript. Just like C, AppleScript is a programming language. Typically, you use AppleScript to control other applications. For example, you could create an AppleScript script that gets your daily calendar from iCal, formats it just the way you like it using TextEdit, and then prints out the results. Or you could write a script that launches Safari and opens each of your bookmarked news sites in a separate window. If you can use existing applications to do what you need, chances are good you can use AppleScript to get the job done.

Some applications feature their own proprietary scripting language. For instance, Microsoft Excel lets you write programs that operate on the cells within a spreadsheet. Some word processing programs let you write scripts that control just about every word processing feature in existence. Although proprietary scripting languages can be quite useful, they aren't much help outside their intended environments. You won't find much use for the Excel scripting language outside Excel, for example.

What About Objective-C, C#, C++, and Java?

There is a constant debate as to which programming language is the best one to learn first. Naturally, the C++ people think that C++ is by far the best language to start with. Java, C#, and Objective-C people feel the same way about Java, C#, and Objective-C. But the truth is that all of those languages are based on C. And if you learn C first, you'll have a huge leg up on learning any of them. And when the next C-based language hits the streets, you'll have a leg up on that one, as well.

In a nutshell, C is the best language to start with because many other languages use the vast majority of C's syntax and structure. Objective-C, C++, and Java each start with C and build on C, each in its own unique way. Learning C first is like learning to walk before learning how to run. If you learn C first, you'll have an excellent foundation on which to base your future programming education.

What's the Best Programming Language for the Mac or iOS Devices?

All the programs in this book will run in the console, a simple scrolling text window that is part of Xcode. If you would like to build applications that feature the Mac look-and-feel with buttons, scroll bars, and windows, you'll need to finish this book, then learn Objective-C and Cocoa (for the Mac) or Cocoa Touch (for iOS devices).

Objective-C is a programming language based on C. Everything you learn about C will apply to Objective-C. Objective-C is designed to work with *objects*. Objects are blocks of code that represent parts of your program, such as a scrolling window, an image, or a menu. Cocoa is a vast collection of objects that represent all the elements of the Mac experience. Objective-C was designed to work together with Cocoa and Cocoa Touch.

Learn C, Objective-C, and Cocoa, and you will have everything you need to develop even the most complex Macintosh applications. Learn C, Objective-C, and Cocoa Touch, and you will have everything you need to develop applications designed to run on mobile devices running iOS.

Learn C on the Mac is the beginning of a series of books that will teach you how to build professional Mac and iOS applications. Once you've finished this book, you'll want to dig into *Learn Objective-C on the Mac*, 2nd Edition by Mark Dalrymple, Scott Knaster, and Waqar Malik (Apress 2012). It was designed as a sequel to *Learn C on the Mac* and does a great job taking you from C to Objective-C.

Learn Cocoa on the Mac was written by Jack Nutting, Dave Mark, and Jeff LaMarche (Apress 2010). It completes the cycle, giving you everything you need to build your own scrollable, clickable Mac applications.

If you are interested in building applications that run on the iPhone, iPod touch, or iPad, check out *Beginning iOS 6 Development* by Dave Mark, Jack Nutting, and Jeff LaMarche (Apress 2012). *Beginning iOS Development* was also written as a sequel to *Learn Objective-C*. Instead of focusing on Cocoa, though, it focuses on Cocoa Touch.

So, first, finish this book, and then make your way through *Learn Objective-C on the Mac*. If Mac application design is your goal, next pick up a copy of *Learn Cocoa on the Mac*. If the iPhone, iPod touch, or iPad is your thing, pick up *Beginning iOS Development*.

And that's the road map. Oh, one more thing. You can find each of these books on the Apress web site at `http://www.apress.com`.

The Programming Process

In Chapter 1, you installed the Mac development tools and went through the process of creating a project, which you then built and ran. Let's take a look at the programming process in a bit more detail.

Source Code

No matter their purpose, most computer programs start as *source code*. Your source code will consist of a sequence of instructions that tells the computer what to do. Source code is written in a specific programming language, such as C. Each programming language has its own set of rules (called *syntax*) that defines what is and isn't legal in that language.

Your mission in reading this book is to learn how to create useful, efficient, and, best of all, legal C source code.

If you were programming using everyday English, your source code might look like this:

> *"Hi, Computer! Do me a favor. Take the numbers from 1 to 10, add them together, and then tell me the sum."*

If you want to run this program, you need a programming tool that understood source code written in English. Sadly, computers don't understand English (yet). Instead, you must use a precise language, like C, to explain to the computer exactly what you want it to do. Listing 2-1 is an example of code that sums numbers 1 through 10.

Listing 2-1. *Summing Numbers 1 through 10 in C*

```
#include <stdio.h>
int main (int argc, const char * argv[])
{
	int number, sum;
	sum = 0;
	for ( number=1; number<=10; number++ )
		sum += number;
	printf("The sum of the numbers from 1 to 10 is %d.\n", sum );
	return 0;
}
```

If this program doesn't mean anything to you, don't panic. Just keep reading. By the time you finish this book, this will all make perfect sense.

In case you were wondering, here's what appeared in the console window when we ran this program:

```
The sum of the numbers from 1 to 10 is 55.
```

Want to try this out for yourself? In Chapter 1, you downloaded the project files for the book from the Apress web site. Open the *Learn C Projects* folder on your hard drive. Next, open the folder named *02.01 - Sample*, and double-click the file named *Sample.xcodeproj* to open the project in Xcode.

Figure 2-1 shows the workspace window for *Sample.xcodeproj*. The window is a complex beast, full of incredibly useful tools to help with your programming pursuits. The most important part of the project window (at least for the moment) is the editing pane, the area that allows you to edit your source code.

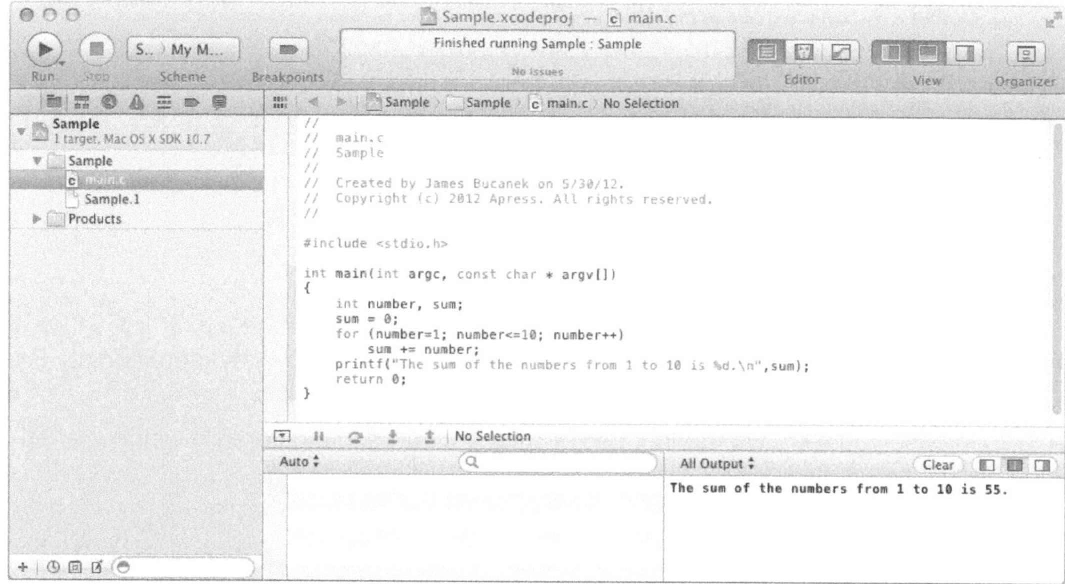

Figure 2-1. *The Sample project workspace*

Run the program by clicking the *Run* button in the toolbar, by choosing the **Project ➤ Run** command, or by typing ⌘R.

The program should build and then run, and the text we showed you previously should appear in the console pane. If you don't see the console pane, choose the **View ➤ Debug Area ➤ Show Debug Area** command.

OK, enough reveling. Let's get back to the programming process.

Compiling Your Source Code

Once your source code is written, your next job is to hand it off to a *compiler*. The compiler translates your C source code into instructions—a sequence of numeric codes—that make sense to your computer. These instructions are known as *machine language* or *object code*. Source code is for you; machine language/object code is for your computer. You write the source code using an editor, and then the compiler translates your source code into a machine-readable form.

> **NOTE:** Don't let the terminology bog you down. Read the rest of this chapter, just to get a basic sense of the programming process, and then move on to Chapter 3. We'll lay out everything step-by-step for you, so you won't get lost.

Think of the process of building and running your program as a three-stage process. First, Xcode compiles all your source code into object code. Next, all the object code in your project is linked together by a program called a *linker* to form your application. That finished application (called an *executable*) is what actually runs on your computer.

Take a look at Figure 2-2. This project contains two source code files, one named `main.c` and another named `extras.c`, as well as an object file named `libc.dylib`. Sometimes, you'll find yourself making use of some code that others have already compiled. Perhaps they want to share their code but do not want to show you their source code. This is the way Apple makes their code available to programmers. They compile the code and save it a special object file called a *library*. Or perhaps you've built a library of code that you'd like to use again and again, but don't want to recompile each time you use the code. By adding a library of pre-compiled code to your project, you can save some time and gain immediate access to a world of solutions.

As it turns out, a library called the C Standard Library comes with Xcode and every other C development environment in the universe. Hmm, that must be why they call it "standard." The C Standard Library comes packed with an incredible number of useful programming bits and pieces that you can use in your own programs. (This library is so commonly used you don't even have to ask Xcode to include it in your project; it just does so automatically.) We'll talk about those bits and pieces as we make use of them throughout the book.

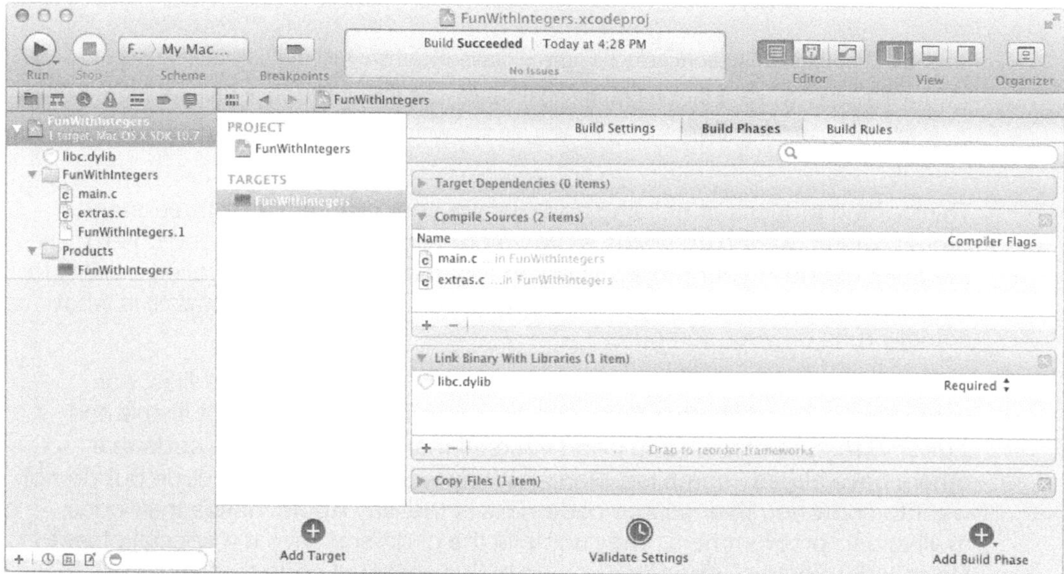

Figure 2-2. *Project with multiple source files*

Building Your Application

Xcode starts by compiling `main.c` and `extras.c` source files, shown in Figure 2-2, turning them into object code. Next, all three object files are linked together by the linker to create a runnable application. The programs in this book were all designed to run in the console window. As you make your way through the rest of the books in this series, you'll learn how to add the rest of the pieces necessary to create applications that can be run from the Finder. For now, Xcode's console will do just fine.

This entire process—turning source code into a finished program—is called a *build*. Xcode's `build` command takes care of all of the details for you. It determines what compilers you need, keeps track of the libraries your code links to, finds a place to store all of the intermediate files created by the compilers and linkers, and keeps those files organized and up-to-date.

The great thing about Xcode is that you'll probably never have to concern yourself with any of these under-the-hood details. You just write your source code and press the *Run* button. Xcode will take care of the rest.

What's Next?

At this point, don't worry too much about the details. The basic concept to remember from this chapter is how your C programs run: they start life as source code and then get translated into object code by the compiler. Finally, all the object code gets linked together to form your runnable application.

Now, let's get to the business of writing your very first C program.

Chapter 3

C Basics: Statements and Functions

Every programming language is designed to follow strict rules that define the language's source code structure. The C programming language is no different. These next few chapters will explore the syntax of C. This chapter focuses on two of the primary building blocks of C programming: statements and functions. In a nutshell, a statement tells the computer to do something. A function is a series of statements.

C Statements

A statement in C is very much like a declarative statement in English; it tells the computer to do something. "Say 'Hello'" and "preheat oven to 350°F" are examples of concise, unambiguous, English statements. Here are two statements in the C language:

```
printf( "Hello!\n" );
temperature = 350;
```

The first statement tells the computer to make the text "Hello!" appear on the console (similar to what you saw in Chapter 2). The second statement tells the computer to assign the value `350` to a variable named `temperature`. C statements end with a semicolon (;), just as English sentences end with a period.

C Functions

A C function is a group of C statements. There are many reasons for organizing statements into a function, but the primary reason for gathering statements into a single function is to make them easily reusable.

A cake recipe consists of many individual steps: “sift flour,” “add eggs,” “preheat oven,” “spread icing,” and so on. By organizing these steps into a larger entity, a recipe, we can now simply say “bake a cake,” instead of repeating all of the individual steps.

Similarly, a C function is a sequence of C statements, the whole of which can be invoked as a C statement. (Read that again, slowly.) You create your own functions in C like this:

```
void SayHello( void )
{
    printf( "Hello!!!\n" );
}
```

You just created a function named `SayHello()`, which does one thing. It consists of a single statement that calls another function, named `printf()`, that outputs a message to the console window.

CONSOLE

Technically, the function `printf()` sends its output to something called *standard output* and Xcode redirects standard output to its console pane. You'll learn more about standard output in Chapter 9 when we discuss the command line. For the moment, just think of `printf()` as a function that sends information to the console.

> **NOTE:** Throughout this book, we'll designate a function by placing a pair of parentheses after its name. This will help distinguish between variable names and function names. For example, the name `doTask` refers to a variable (variables are covered in Chapter 4), while `doTask()` refers to a function.

The printf() function consists of dozens of statements, many of which call other functions, which themselves consist of dozens of statements, many of which call even more functions, and so on—unraveling computer programs can be a lot like peeling an onion. The point is, you don't need to concern yourself with the details of how printf() works, any more than you need to remember all of the steps involved in baking a cake you buy from your local bakery. You order the cake and the chef goes through the steps to bake it. You call the SayHello() function and it goes through the steps to make "Hello!" appear in the console.

Defining a Function

Functions start off with a *function declaration*, in this case:

```
void SayHello( void )
```

A function declaration consists of a *return type*, the *function name*, and a pair of parentheses wrapped around a *parameter list*. We'll talk about the return type and parameter list later. For now, the important thing is to be able to recognize a function declaration and be able to pick out the function's name in the declaration.

Following the declaration comes the *body* of the function. The body is always placed between a pair of curly braces: { and }. These braces are known in programming circles as *left curly* and *right curly*. Here's the body of SayHello():

```
{
    printf( "Hello!!!\n" );
}
```

The body of a function consists of a series of statements. This particular statement calls another function, but there are other kinds of statements, too. As you make your way through this book, you'll learn all of the different kinds of C statements, and what they're used for.

Creating efficient statements will make your programs run faster with less chance of error. The more you learn about programming (and the more time you spend at your craft), the more efficient you'll make your code.

Syntax Errors and Algorithms

When you ask Xcode to compile your source code, the compiler does its best to translate your source code into object code.

As you learn C, you'll find yourself making two types of mistakes. The simplest type, called a *syntax error*, prevents the program from compiling. The syntax of a language is the set of rules that defines what is or is not legal. The compiler will only compile code that properly follows the C language syntax, as defined by the official C standard (C99). If the code you write doesn't conform to these rules, the compiler won't understand what you wrote. When this happens, the compiler complains and won't compile your program. You'll explore several common kinds of syntax errors, and fix them, later in this chapter.

The second type of mistake is a *semantic error*, or a flaw in your program's algorithm. An algorithm is the approach used to solve a problem. You use algorithms all the time. For example, here's an algorithm for sorting your mail:

1. Start by taking the mail out of the mailbox.
2. If there's no mail, you're done! Go watch TV.
3. Take a piece of mail out of the pile.
4. If it's junk mail, throw it away, and go back to step 2.
5. If it's a bill, put it with the other bills, and go back to step 2.
6. If it's not a bill and not junk mail, read it, and go back to step 2.

This algorithm completely describes the process of sorting through your mail. Notice that the algorithm works, even if you didn't get any mail. Notice also that the algorithm always ends up at step 2, with the TV on.

Figure 3-1 shows a pictorial representation of the mail-sorting algorithm, commonly known as a flow chart. Much as you might use an outline to prepare for writing an essay or term paper, you might use a flow chart to flesh out a program's algorithm before you actually start writing the program. Here's how this works.

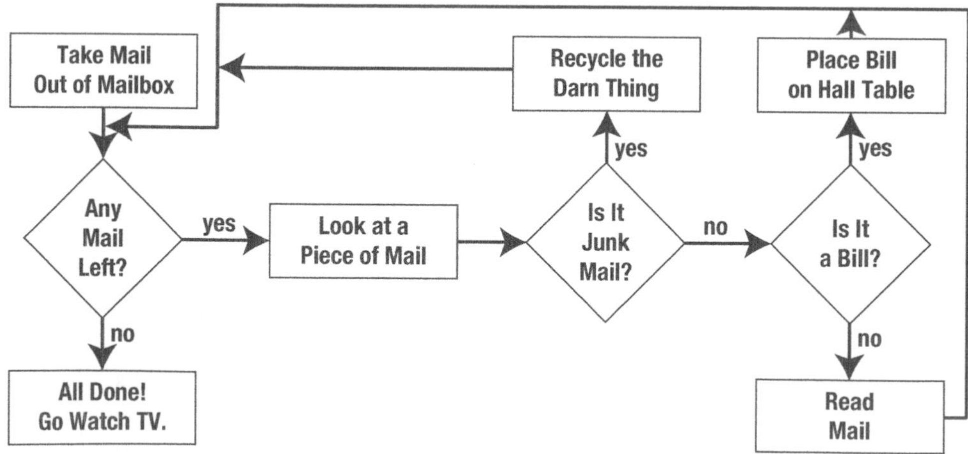

Figure 3-1. *The mail-sorting flow chart*

This flow chart uses two types of boxes. The rectangular box portrays an action, such as taking mail out of the mailbox or recycling the junk mail. Once you've taken the action, follow the arrow leading out of the rectangle to go on to the next step in the sequence.

Each diamond-shaped box poses a yes/no question. Unlike their rectangular counterparts, diamond-shaped boxes have two arrows leading out of them. One shows the path to take if the answer to the question inside the box is yes; the other shows the path to take if the answer is no. Follow the flow chart through, comparing it to the algorithm described previously.

In the C world, a well-designed algorithm results in a well-behaved program. On the other hand, a poorly designed algorithm can lead to unpredictable results. Suppose, for example, you wanted to write a program that added three numbers together, printing the sum at the end. If you accidentally printed one of the numbers instead of the sum of the numbers, your program would still compile and run. However, the result of the program would be in error (you printed one of the numbers instead of the sum) because of a flaw in your program's algorithm.

The efficiency of your source code is a direct result of good algorithm design. Keep the concept of algorithm in mind as you work your way through the examples in this book.

Calling a Function

In Chapter 1, you ran a test program to make sure Xcode was installed properly. The test program sat in a file called *main.c* and consisted of a single function, called `main()`. As a refresher, here's the source code from *main.c*:

```
#include <stdio.h>

int main(int argc, const char * argv[])
{
    // insert code here...
    printf( "Hello, World!\n" );
    return 0;
}
```

Though some parts of this program might seem intimidating, hopefully some parts of it should start to feel familiar.

There's really only one line in this code that you need to focus on at this point, and that's this function call:

```
    printf( "Hello, World!\n" );
```

Though this program does have a few complicated-looking elements, at its heart is a single function call. As far as all the other dangly bits, you can read the "Five Easy Pieces" sidebar, or just ignore them and know that we'll get to them as we go along.

So what does "calling a function" really mean? Basically, whenever your source code calls a function, each of the statements in the called function is executed before the next statement of the calling function is executed.

Confused? Don't worry, you'll get there. Look at Figure 3-2. In this example, `main()` starts with a call to the function `MyFunction()`. This call to `MyFunction()` will cause each of the statements inside `MyFunction()` to be executed, one after the other. Once the last statement in `MyFunction()` is executed, control is returned to `main()`. Next, `main()` calls `AnotherFunction()`. Once the last statement in `AnotherFunction()` is executed, control is again returned to `main()`, and `main()` can then exit with a return code of `0`. When `main()` exits, your program exits. Returning a value of 0 tells whatever program launched your program that all is OK and that your program is done.

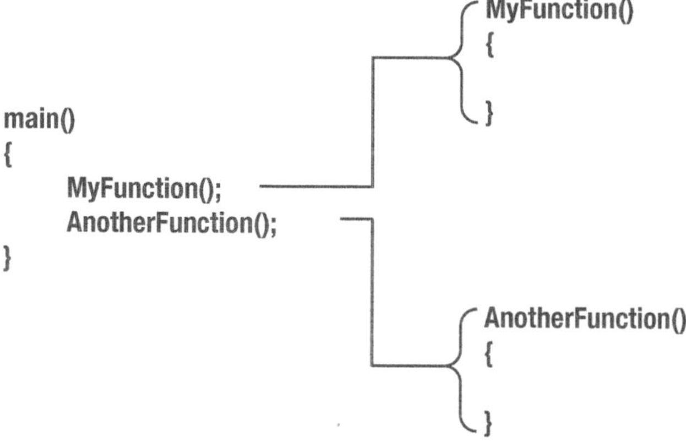

Figure 3-2. *`main()` calls `MyFunction()`. All the statements in `MyFunction()` are executed. Once `MyFunction()` returns, `main()` then calls `AnotherFunction()`.*

Every C program you write will have a `main()` function. Your program will start running with the first line in `main()` and, unless something unusual happens, end with the last line in `main()`. Along the way, `main()` may call other functions which may, in turn, call other functions and so on.

FIVE EASY PIECES

Here's a bit of behind-the-scenes technical detail for folks who want a more complete picture of the source code we just explored. Skim through this explanation and, if it seems a bit fuzzy, come back to it later on. By the time you get to the end of the book, this will all seem pretty straight-forward.

The source code in *main.c* can be broken into five basic pieces. Here's the first piece:

```
#include <stdio.h>
```

In C, any line that starts off with a pound sign (#) is known as a *preprocessor directive*, an instruction that asks the compiler to do something special. This particular directive is called a `#include` (pronounced "pound include"). It asks the compiler to include code from another file on your hard drive as if that code was in this file in the first place. A `#include` file is also known as a *header file* or just plain header. As it turns out, the file *stdio.h* contains all kinds of goodies that you'll use throughout the book. Just ignore this line for now.

Here's the second piece:

```
int main (int argc, const char * argv[])
{
}
```

As discussed a bit earlier, this is the function declaration for the function named `main()`. The curly braces surround the body of the function.

The third piece of this puzzle is this line:

```
// insert code here...
```

Any time the compiler encounters two slashes (//) in a row, it ignores the slashes and anything else on that line. This line of code is called a *comment*. Its only purpose is to document your code and to help make clear what's going on at this point in the program. Comments are a good thing.

The fourth piece is the call to the function `printf()`, which we will focus on in this chapter.

```
printf( "Hello, World!\n" );
```

The fifth and final piece of your program is this line of code:

```
return 0;
```

A return statement in a function tells the compiler that you are done with this function and you want to return. In this case, you want the function to return a value of 0.

Again, don't get hung up on the specifics. It'll all become clear as you go.

Same Program, Two Functions

As you start writing your own programs, you'll find yourself designing many individual functions. You might need a function that puts a form up on the screen for the user to fill out. You might need a function that takes a list of numbers as input, providing the average of those numbers in return. Whatever your needs, you will definitely be creating a lot of functions. Let's see how it's done.

Your first program contained a function named `main()` that passed the text string "Hello, world!\n" to `printf()`. Your next program, *Hello2*, embeds that functionality in a new function, named `SayHello()`.

> **NOTE:** You've probably been wondering why the characters `\n` keep appearing at the end of the text strings. Don't worry; nothing's wrong with your copy of the book. The `\n` is perfectly normal. It tells `printf()` to move the cursor to the beginning of the next line in the text window, sort of like pressing the Return key in a text editor.
>
> The sequence `\n` is frequently referred to as a *newline* character, a carriage return, or just plain return. By including a newline at the end of a `printf()`, you know that the next line you print will appear at the beginning of the next line in the console window.

The Hello2 Project

In the Finder, open the *Learn C Projects* folder. Open the subfolder named *03.01 - Hello2*, and double-click the project file *Hello2.xcodeproj*. A project window with the title Hello2 will appear, as shown in Figure 3-3.

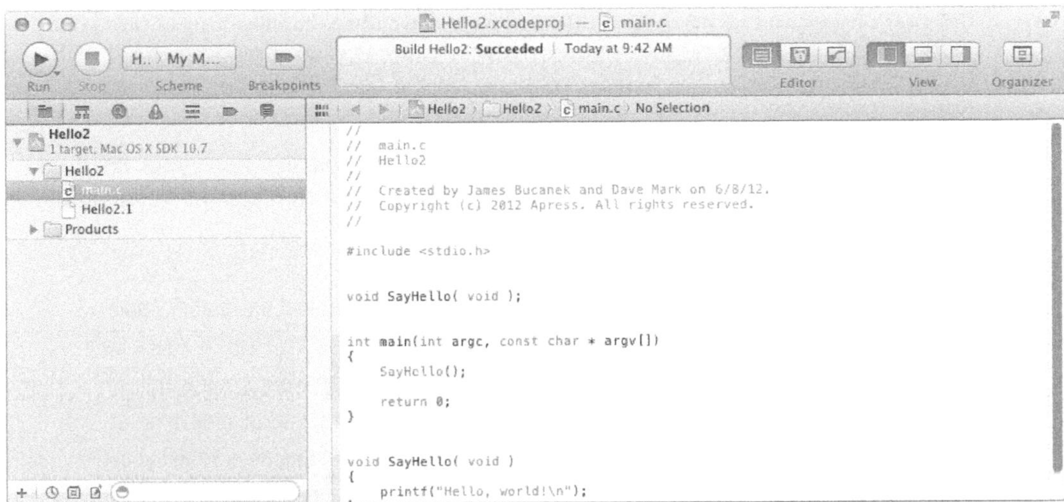

Figure 3-3. *Hello2 workspace window*

The area with the gray background on the top of the project window is called the toolbar. The toolbar contains a variety of convenient shortcuts, which you can customize to some degree.

The area below the toolbar is divided into a series of panes. On the left side of the project window, you'll find the navigator pane. The icons at the top of the navigator pane allow you to navigate to different areas of your project. By default, the project navigator icon should appear. The project navigator lists all the files and folders that make up your project.

The central area is the editor pane and, below it, the debug pane. Select a file in the project navigator and it will open for editing in the editor pane. When you run your project, you'll make use of the debug area. That's where the console lives.

To the right of the editor pane is the utility pane. The utility area lets you customize various elements in your program and is especially useful when you start adding objects to your programs as you move on to Objective-C, Cocoa, and Cocoa Touch.

On the right side of the toolbar, you'll find three sets of controls, labeled *Editor*, *View*, and *Organizer*. The three *View* buttons allow you to show or hide the navigator, debug, and utility panes, as you please. You can't hide the editor pane—that's always there. The commands for switching, revealing, and hiding these panes can all be found in the **View** menu.

Let's take a look at the project navigator. If you don't see the project navigator, with its list of folders and files, on the left side of your workspace window (like the one shown in Figure 3-3), choose **View ➤ Navigators ➤ Show Project Navigator**. Notice the C source code file named *main*.c in the project navigator's list of files. If you click on *main*.c, the source code within the file will appear in the editor pane.

Notice the *Products* folder, below the *Hello2* folder. This is where your finished program (i.e. the "product" of this project) will appear once you've successfully built it. If it's red, your program hasn't been built yet.

> **TIP:** Want to learn more about the rest of the items in the project navigator? Apple has an excellent Xcode manual built right into Xcode. Choose the Help ➤ Xcode User Guide command. The very first page explains the parts of the workspace window, with links that explain each of the various navigators, editors, and utilities in great detail. We'll give you just enough information about Xcode in this book to get you through learning C, but if you ever want to explore Xcode more, just pull up the Xcode User Guide and dig in.

The Hello2 Source Code

Here's the source code from *main.c:*

```
#include <stdio.h>

void SayHello( void );

int main (int argc, const char * argv[])
{
    SayHello();

    return 0;
}

void SayHello( void )
{
    printf( "Hello, world!\n" );
}
```

Let's walk through this line by line. *Hello2* starts off with this line of source code:

```
#include <stdio.h>
```

You'll find this line (or a slight variation) at the beginning of each one of the programs in this book. It tells the compiler to include the source code from the file *stdio.h* as it compiles *main.c*. *stdio.h* contains information you'll need if you are going to call `printf()` in this source code file. You'll see the `#include` preprocessor directive used throughout this book. Get used to seeing this line of code at the top of each of your source code files.

The line following `#include` is blank. This is completely cool. Since the C compiler ignores all blank lines, you can use them to make your code a little more readable. We like to leave two blank lines between functions.

This line of code appears next:

```
void SayHello( void );
```

While this line might look like a function definition, don't be fooled! If this were a function definition, it would not end with a semicolon; it would be followed by a left curly ({) and the rest of the function. This line is known as a *function prototype* or *function declaration*. You'll include a function prototype for every function, other than `main()`, in your source code file.

To understand why, it helps to know that a compiler reads your source code file from the beginning to the end, a line at a time. By placing a complete list of function prototypes at the beginning of the file, you give the compiler a preview of the functions it is about to compile. The compiler uses this information to make sure that calls to these functions are made correctly.

> **NOTE:** Function prototypes will make a lot more sense to you once you get into the subject of parameters in Chapter 7. For now, get used to seeing function prototypes at the beginning of all your source code files.

Next comes the function `main()`. The first thing `main()` does is call the function `SayHello()`.

```
int main (int argc, const char * argv[])
{
    SayHello();
```

At this point, the lines of the function `SayHello()` get run. When `SayHello()` is finished, `main()` can move on to its next line of code. The keyword `return` tells the compiler to stop executing statements and return a value of 0 (zero) to the function that originally called `main()`. We'll talk about return later on. Until then, the only place you'll see this line is at the end of `main()`.

```
return 0;
}
```

Following main() are some more blank lines, followed by the function you created, SayHello(). SayHello() prints the string "Hello, world!", followed by a return, in a window, and then returns control to main().

```
void SayHello( void )
{
    printf( "Hello, world!\n" );
}
```

Let's step back for a second and compare the first program to *Hello2*. In your first program, main() called printf() directly. In *Hello2*, main() calls a function that then calls printf(). This extra layer demonstrates a basic C programming technique: taking code from one function and using it to create a new function. This example took this line of code

```
printf( "Hello, world!\n" );
```

and used it to create a new function called SayHello(). This function is now available for use by the rest of the program. Every time you call the function SayHello(), it's as if you executed this line of code:

```
printf( "Hello, world!\n" );
```

SayHello() may be a simple function, but it demonstrates an important concept. Wrapping a chunk of code in a single function is a powerful technique. Suppose you create an extremely complex function, say, 100 lines of code in length. Now, suppose you call this function in five different places in your program. With 100 lines of code, plus the five function calls, you are essentially achieving 500 lines' worth of functionality. That's a pretty good return on your investment!

Let's watch *Hello2* in action.

Running Hello2

In Xcode, run your program. Do this by clicking on the *Run* button in the toolbar, choosing the **Project ➤ Run command, or pressing** ⌘R. This asks Xcode to compile all of your source files (yes, all one of them), link the object code together to form an executable program, and run that program.

You'll see the debug area appear below your source code. On the right is the console output, as shown in Figure 3-4. If you don't see this, choose the View ➤ Debug Area ➤ Activate Console command or press ⇧⌘C.

Gee, this looks just like the output from Chapter 1's test program. Of course it does; that was the point. Even though you embedded your printf() inside the function SayHello(), *Hello2* produced the same results.

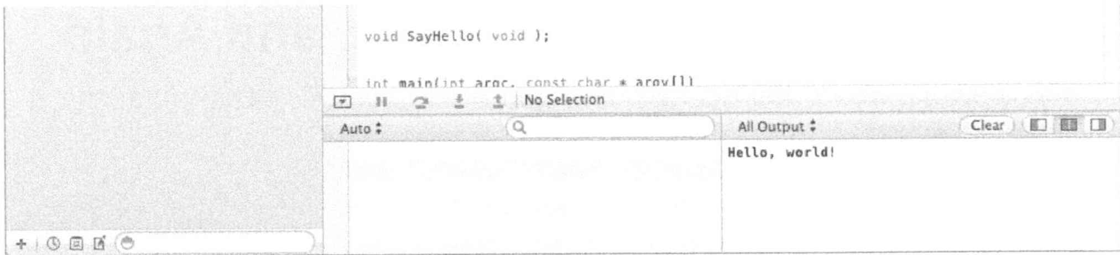

Figure 3-4. *The result of running Hello2*

Before you move on to your next program, let's revisit a little terminology we first touched on at the beginning of the chapter. The pane in the debug area that appeared when you ran *Hello2* is referred to as the *console pane*, or just plain console. There are numerous Standard Library functions designed to send text to the console; you're using `printf()`. The text that appears in the console is known as the program's *output*. After you run a program, you're likely to check the output that appears in the console to make sure your program ran correctly.

THE STANDARD LIBRARY

One element of the C standard that relates directly to our discussion of functions is the Standard Library. The Standard Library is a set of functions available to every C programmer. As you may have guessed, the printf() function you saw in the sample source code is part of the Standard Library, as are tons of other great functions. You'll learn some of the more popular ones as you make your way through this book. Once you get comfortable with the Standard Library functions presented here, dig through some of the Standard Library documentation that you'll find on the Web, just to get a sense of what else is in there.

A number of great sites discuss the Standard Library. One of our favorite resources on the net is the Wikipedia entry for the ANSI C Standard Library (`http://en.wikipedia.org/wiki/ANSI_C_standard_library`). This page is a terrific way to get to know the Standard Library. There's a lot of interesting information here, but the best part is the table titled "C Standard Library headers." It contains a link to each of the Standard Library #include files. Each link takes you to a page that describes the functions included in that particular header file.

For example, click the stdio.h link. Wow, there sure are a ton of functions in this header file. If you scroll down a bit, you'll find a link to a page that describes the Standard Library function printf(). Follow that link, and you'll come to a page that contains just about everything you could ever want to know about printf().

Yeah, it's a bit techie, but it's an invaluable reference resource once you start developing your own code or if you encounter a function in this book and want to know more.

Doing That Again, and Again, and Again

Imagine what would happen if you changed *Hello2*'s version of `main()` so that it read as follows:

```
int main (int argc, const char * argv[])
{
    SayHello();
    SayHello();
    SayHello();

    return 0;
}
```

What's different? In this version, you've added two more calls to `SayHello()`. Can you picture what the console will look like after you run this new version?

To find out, close the *Hello2* project window, and then select **Open** from Xcode's **File** menu. When Xcode prompts you to open a project, navigate into the *Learn C Projects* folder and then into the *03.02 - Hello3* subdirectory, and open the *Hello3.xcodeproj* project file.

When you run *Hello3*, the console pane shown in Figure 3-5 will appear. Take a look at the output. Does it make sense to you? Each call to `SayHello()` generates the text "Hello, world!" followed by a carriage return.

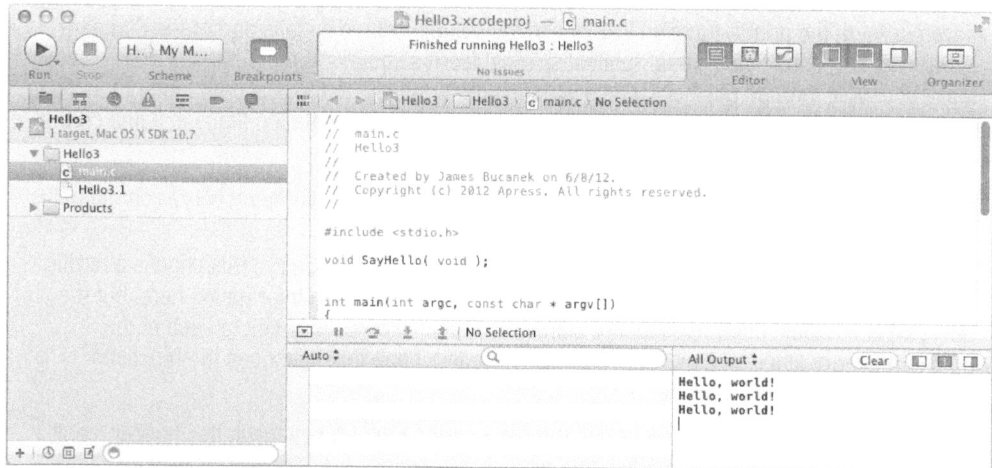

Figure 3-5. *Output from Hello3*

Generating Some Errors

Before you move on to the next chapter, let's see how the compiler responds to errors in your source code. In the Hello3 project window, select *main.c* so the source code appears in the editing pane.

In the source code window, find the `SayHello()` function definition. Note that the definition of a function is where you actually provide the function body. A function declaration does not include curly braces. A function definition does include curly braces. Got it? Good! The function should read

```
void SayHello( void )
{
    printf( "Hello, world!\n" );
}
```

Click to the right of the printf() statement, so the blinking cursor appears just after the semicolon at the end of the line. Delete the semicolon, so the line now reads

```
    printf( "Hello, world!\n" )
```

Remember that in C, a regular C statement ends with a semicolon, and you just left it out. This is like forgetting the period at the end of a sentence Confusing, isn't it? Your source code no longer follows the rules established in the C99 standard. This is called a *syntax error*. Look back at your source code. It should look like the window in Figure 3-6.

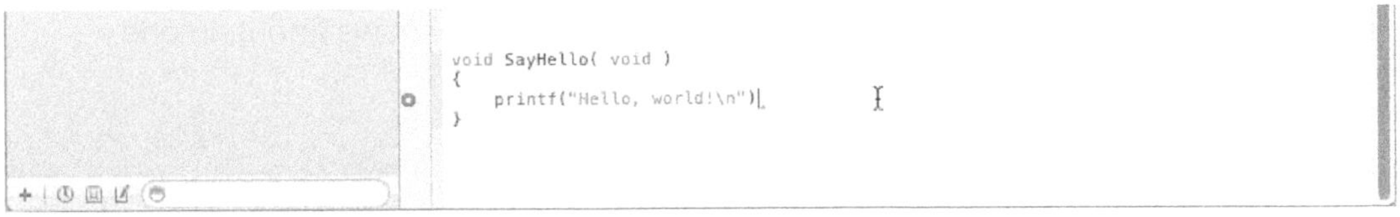

Figure 3-6. *Xcode detects a syntax error*

While you are typing, a group of elves—OK, technically Xcode's "live issues" checker—is constantly re-evaluating your source code to see that meets all of the requirements for correct C syntax. If it doesn't, it immediately puts an error (or warning) indicator in your editing window at, or near, where it thinks the problem is.

Fixing the Problem

Click on the error indicator in the gutter, and your window will look something like Figure 3-7.

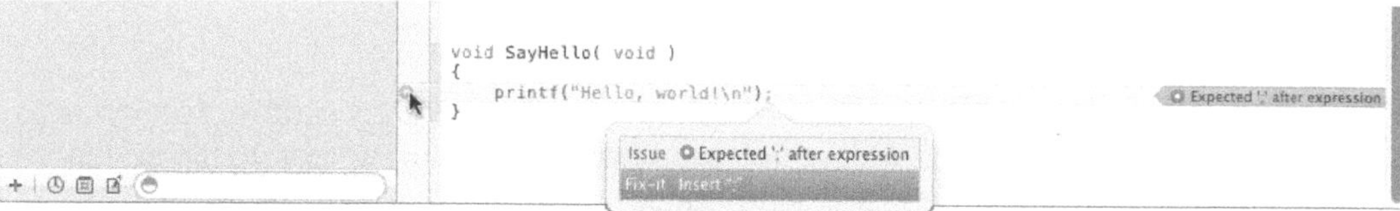

Figure 3-7. *Issue detail and Fix It suggestion*

Clicking on an issue in the gutter displays additional information about the problem, or at least Xcode's interpretation of what it thinks the problem is—we'll get to that in a moment.

In this case, Xcode correctly determined that you omitted the semicolon required at the end of a C statement. It even includes a *Fix It* button that offers to correct the problem for you. Double-click the *Fix It* button, and Xcode inserts the required semicolon, and the issue disappears.

Before the days of automatic syntax checking, programmers wouldn't discovers errors like this until they tried to compile their source code. If you give those elves a well-deserved break (by turning off "live issues" feature in the Xcode preferences), you won't find out about these kinds of problems until you compile your code. Leave the semicolon out and try to run (**Project ➤ Run**) your program again. It doesn't run. Instead, you receive a "Build failed" message and the error, once again, appears in your source code. You'll also see the error in the output of the latest build log (**View ➤ Navigators ➤ Show Log Navigator**) and in the *issues navigator* (**View ➤ Navigators ➤ Show Issue Navigator**). The issues navigator keeps a running tab of all of the problems Xcode has knows about, in one convenient location.

Getting Close

"Close only counts in horseshoes and hand grenades," as the old saying goes. Someday they might add "compilers" to that list.

Let's try a different kind of mistake. This time, go to the function definition (not the declaration, right?). Add a superfluous semicolon at the end of that line, so your code now looks like this:

```
void SayHello( void );
{
```

A new issue indicator should appear in the gutter of your editing pane. Click on it, as shown in Figure 3-8.

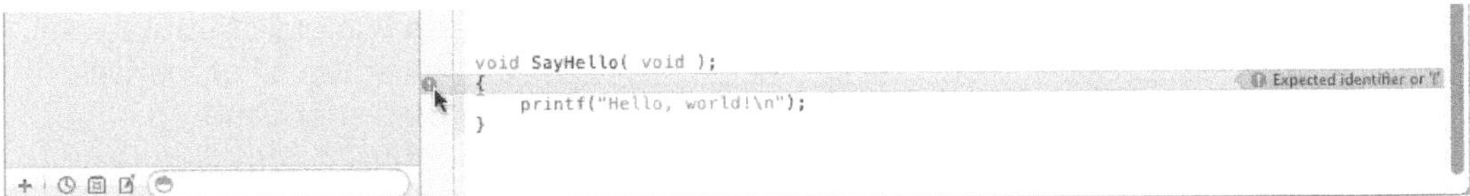

Figure 3-8. *Another syntax issue*

This time the error message is "Expected identifier or '('". That doesn't sound very helpful, and there's no *Fix It* button this time.

A lot of times the compiler can't tell you what's wrong with your code, only that it doesn't follow the rules for the C language. In this case, the compiler looks at the first line of the function and assumes it's a function declaration—remember that a declaration ends in a semicolon, while a definition contains a function body. The compiler can't know that what you did was add an extra semicolon where it doesn't belong. It only knows there's a function declaration followed by something else that shouldn't be there.

The take-away message is that the compiler can't always tell you exactly what the mistake is, or even exactly where it is. Start by looking for a problem immediately before where the compiler complains. In some cases the actual mistake will be someplace else entirely, even in another source file. With some experience, and a little practice, you'll get good at figuring out what the problem is and how to fix it.

Speaking of which, delete that stray semicolon so everything compiles again. You've got other kinds of mistakes to make!

C is Case Sensitive

Another very common mistake results from the fact that C is a *case-sensitive language*. In a case-sensitive language, there is a difference between lowercase and uppercase letters, which means you can't refer to `printf()` as `Printf()` or even `PRINTF()`.

Let's try this out. Double-click "printf" in your source code to select it, engage the Caps Lock on your keyboard, and type "PRINTF". Whoa! What happened? Does your screen look like Figure 3-9?

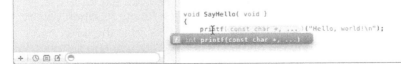

Figure 3-9. *Xcode's auto-completion offering the correct function name*

Those Xcode elves are hard at work again, trying to keep you out of trouble. As you typed the letters "P" "R" "I" "N" "T" "F", Xcode looked up all of the valid function names (that it knows about) that begin with those letters and immediately listed them below where you are typing. It quickly narrowed in on the only function that it thinks is valid here, which is `printf()`. If you pressed the return key, or kept typing, Xcode would change what you actually typed ("PRINTF") into what was correct ("printf").

If Xcode gives you more than one choice (type the function name again, but this time start with "get"), use the mouse or arrow keys to select one, or continue typing more letters of the function to narrow down the choices. To dismiss Xcode's auto-completion suggestion, press the Esc key. So if you type "P" "R" "I" "N" "T" "F" Esc, you'll get "PRINTF()". As discussed, PRINTF() isn't a function, so a warning now appears in your code, as shown in Figure 3-10.

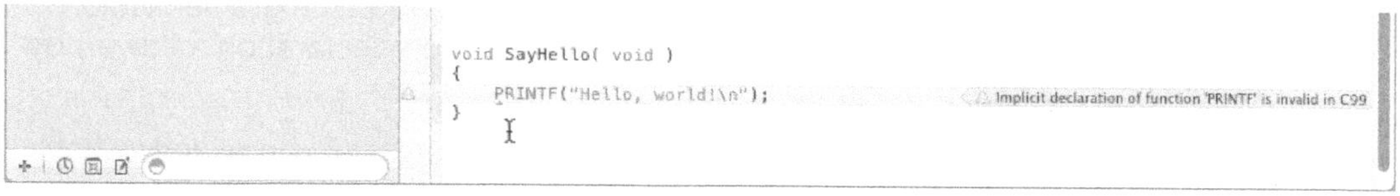

```
void SayHello( void )
{
    PRINTF("Hello, world!\n");        Implicit declaration of function 'PRINTF' is invalid in C99
}
```

Figure 3-10. *An unrecognized function name warning*

This time the issue is a warning instead an error. So what's the difference? An error is something the compiler knows is wrong. In other words "I (the compiler) can't make any sense of what you typed." An error will prevent your program from compiling.

A warning, by contrast, is something the compiler suspects is wrong, but can interpret anyway. In other words "I think that this code is probably wrong, but you're the programmer and you're a lot smarter than me, so I'll do what the code says anyway." A warning will not prevent your program from compiling. It *may* prevent it from linking or running. Or it maybe that it's exactly what you meant to write, the code is 100% correct, and the compiler is just being a nervous Nelly. But to be honest, that's unlikely. Try to avoid writing code that generates warnings.

In this particular case, the reported problem is "Implicit declaration of function 'PRINTF' is invalid in C99." Translated into English, it means that you never gave the compiler a declaration for a function named `PRINTF()`, either by `#including` a file where it was declared, or by declaring one yourself like you did for `SayHello()`. And that's correct, because there is no such function! When you try to build this program, it will compile but then fail to link because the linker can't connect your request to call a function named `PRINTF()` with any known function that's actually been written.

The wording, and the reason it's a warning and not an error, has to do with the history of C. Originally (K&R) C didn't require you to first declare a function before you called it. You just wrote `PRINTF("Hello")` and the compiler *assumed* there was a function named `PRINTF()` somewhere and would compile your code without any errors. This resulted in thousands of programmers writing thousands of programs that would compile OK, but then wouldn't run because they'd mistyped the name of a function somewhere. The ANSI and ISO organizations decided this wasn't good and it would be much better if you had to explicitly declare every function before you called it. That way, if you did mistype the name of a function, the compiler could catch it immediately. And now, the mystery of that `SayHello()` declaration at the beginning of your file is solved!

Change `PRINTF()` back to `printf()` and let's continue.

Exploring Xcode's Built-In Manuals

Before we move on to the next chapter, let's take a minute to explore an incredible resource built-in to Xcode: the Documentation browser. The Documentation browser puts the entire set of Mac, iOS, and Xcode technical documentation at your fingertips. To bring up the Documentation browser, either click on the Organizer button on the right edge of the toolbar, or select **Help ➤ Documentation and API Reference**, as shown in Figure 3-11.

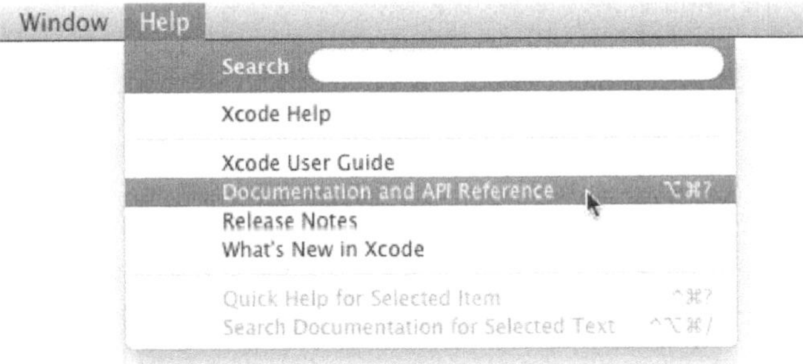

Figure 3-11. *Opening the documentation browser to the API reference*

The documentation browser (Figure 3-12) is like having a library of technical manuals at your fingertips. Wait, it *is* a library of technical manuals at your fingertips! The written material available through Xcode is vast, and—just like your local library—you'll probably never read it all. But if you want to know what a particular function does, you need help getting started using a new technology, or you would like some advice on how to design the application icon for your iOS app, it's all right there.

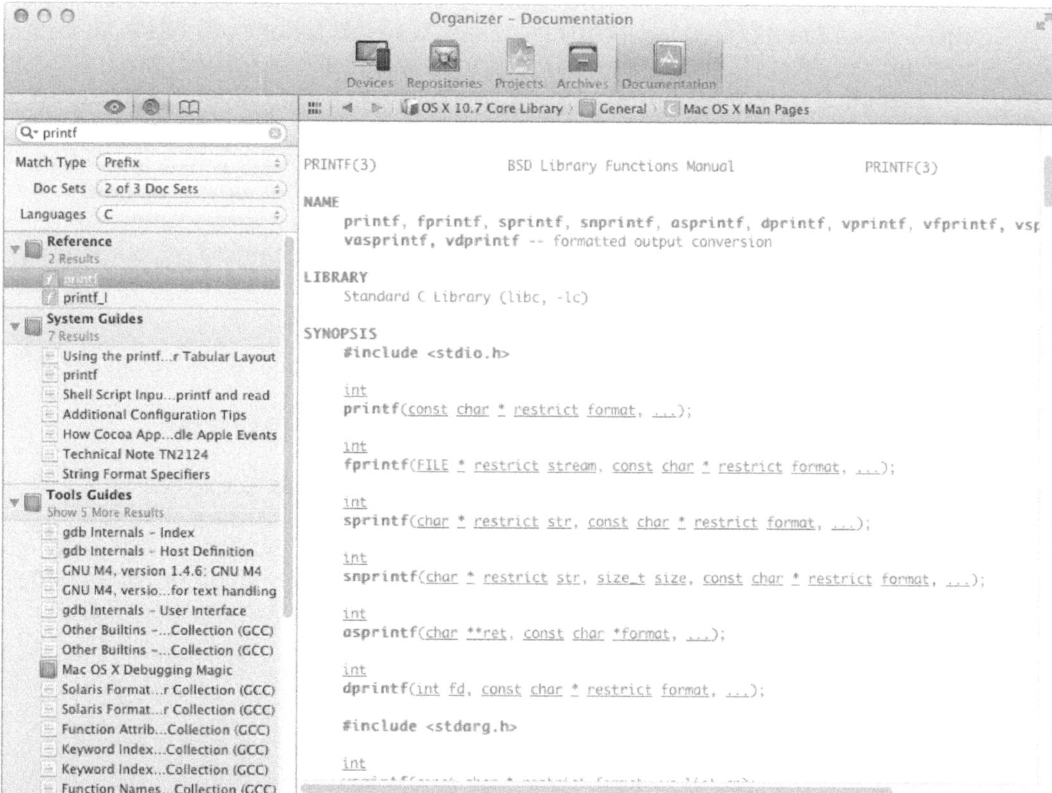

Figure 3-12. *Documentation browser*

Notice the set of search options, just below the search field, as shown in Figure 3-12. If you don't see the options, click on the magnifying glass icon on the left side of the search field and select ***Show find options*** from the popup menu that appears.

We recommend starting out by setting *Match Type* to `Prefix`, *Doc Sets* to Mac *`OS X Core Library`* and *`Xcode Developer Library`* `(select the latest version of each)`, and set *Languages* to *`C`* and leave all other languages unchecked. This will make it easy to search for functions and will filter out a lot of information that's not relevant while you're working through this book.

To look up a Standard Library function, type the beginning of the function name into the search field and press Return. All of the relevant matches will appear below. Click on one to see its documentation (see Figure 3-12 again).

Getting Help Quickly

As you make your way through the book, you'll frequently find yourself looking up functions in the documentation browser. There is, however, a really easy way to look up functions right from your source code. Let's give that a try.

Open up one of your Xcode projects. To find the definition of `printf()`, you could open the documentation browser, type in "printf," press Return, click on the search results, and read the documentation. Or, you could simply hold down the Option key and click once on the word `printf` in your source code, as shown in Figure 3-13.

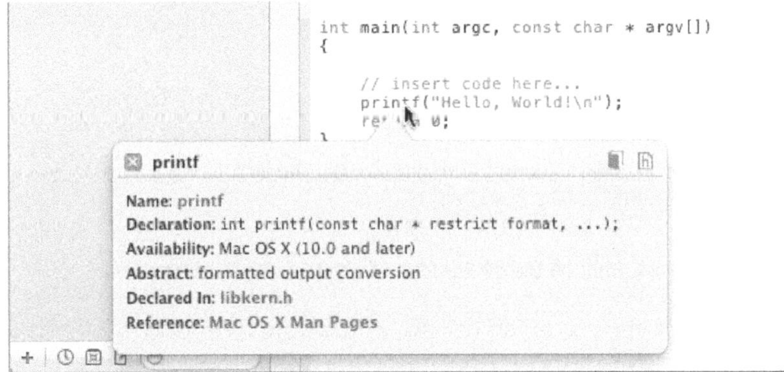

Figure 3-13. *Contextual help*

Option-clicking on a function name will pop up an abbreviated synopsis of the function's purpose, parameters, and return value. How convenient is that? If that's not enough information, you can get to the full documentation either by clicking on the tiny book icon in upper right corner of the pop-up window, or you can skip the pop-up and go right to the full documentation window by option-double-clicking the function name.

What's Next?

Congratulations! You've made it through basic training. You know how to open a project, compile your code, and even fix a syntax error or two. You've learned about the most important function, `main()`, and how to declare and define your own functions. You've also learned a little about `printf()`, the console, and the Standard Library.

Now you're ready to dig into the stuff that gives a C program life: variables and operators.

CHAPTER 3 EXERCISE

Open the project ***Hello2.xcodeproj***, and edit ***main.c*** as instructed in each step. Then, describe the error that results.

1. Change the line
   ```
   SayHello();
   ```
   to
   ```
   SayHello(;
   ```
2. Change things back. Now, change the following line
   ```
   int main(int argc, const char * argv[])
   ```
   to
   ```
   int MAIN(int argc, const char * argv[])
   ```
   Try to build your project.
3. Change things back. Now, delete the left curly brace after the line, like so:
   ```
   int main(int argc, const char * argv[])
      SayHello();
   ```
4. Change things back. Now, change the declaration of `SayHello()` from
   ```
   void SayHello( void );
   ```
   so it reads
   ```
   void SAYHELLO( void );
   ```

Chapter 4

C Basics: Variables and Operators

At this point, you should feel pretty comfortable using Xcode. You should know how to open a project and how to edit a project's source code. You should also feel comfortable running a project and (heaven forbid) fixing any syntax errors that may have occurred along the way.

On the programming side, you should recognize a function when you see one. When you think of a function, you should first think of `main()`, the function that gets called to start your program. You should remember that functions are made up of statements.

With these things in mind, you're ready to explore the foundation of C programming: *variables* and *operators*. Variables and operators are the building blocks you'll use to construct your program's statements.

An Introduction to Variables

A large part of the programming process involves working with data. You might need to add together a column of numbers or sort a list of names alphabetically. The tricky part of this process is representing your data in a program, which is where variables come in.

Variables can be thought of as containers for your program's data. Imagine a table with three containers sitting on it. Each container represents a different variable. One container is labeled cup1, one labeled cup2, and the third cup3.

Now imagine you have three plastic numbers. Place one number inside each of the three containers. Figure 4-1 shows a picture of what this might look like.

Figure 4-1. *Three cups, each one labeled and each with its own value*

Each cup represents a different variable.

Now imagine asking a friend to reach into each cup, pull out the number in each one, and add the three values together. You can ask your friend to place the sum of the three values in a fourth container created just for this purpose. The fourth container is labeled sum and can be seen in Figure 4-2.

Figure 4-2. *Four cups, one of which is the sum of the other three*

This is exactly how variables work. Variables are containers for your program's data. You create a variable and place a value in it. You then ask the computer to do something with the value in your variable. You can ask the computer to add three variables together, placing the result in a fourth variable. You can even ask the computer to take the value in a variable, multiply it by two, and place the result back into the original variable.

Getting back to the example, now imagine that you changed the values in cup1, cup2, and cup3. Once again, you could call on your friend to add the three values, updating the value in the container sum. You've reused the same variables, using the same formula, to achieve a different result. Here's the C version of this formula:

```
sum = cup1 + cup2 + cup3;
```

Every time you execute this line of source code, you place the sum of the variables `cup1`, `cup2`, and `cup3` into the variable named `sum`. At this point, it's not important to understand exactly how this line of C source code works. What is important is to understand the basic idea behind variables. Each variable in your program is like a container with a value in it. This chapter will teach you how to create your own variables and how to place a value in a variable.

Working with Variables

Variables come in a variety of flavors, called *types*. A variable's type determines the type of data that can be stored in that variable. You determine a variable's type when you create the variable (we'll discuss creating variables in just a second). Some variable types are useful for working with numbers. Other variable types are designed to work with text. In this chapter, we'll work strictly with variables of one type, a numerical type called `int`, short for "integer" (eventually, we'll get into other variable types). A variable of type int can hold a numerical value, such as 27 or –589.

Working with variables is a two-stage process. First you create a variable; then you use the variable. In C, you create a variable by declaring it. Declaring a variable tells the compiler, "Create a variable for me. I need a container to place a piece of data in." When you declare a variable, you have to specify the variable's type as well as its name. In our earlier example, we created four containers. Each container had a label. In the C world, this would be the same as creating four variables with the names `cup1`, `cup2`, `cup3`, and `sum`. In C, if we want to use the value stored in a variable, we use the variable's name. We'll show you how to do this later in the chapter.

Here's an example of a variable declaration:

```
int    myVariable;
```

This declaration tells the compiler to create a variable of type int (remember, ints are useful for working with numbers) with the name `myVariable`. The type of the variable (in this case, int) is extremely important. As you'll see, variable type determines the type and range of values a variable can be assigned.

Variable Names

Here are a few rules to follow when you create your own variable names:

1. Variable names must always start with an uppercase or lowercase letter (A, B, . . . , Z or a, b, . . . , z) or with an underscore (_).

2. The remainder of the variable name must be made up of uppercase or lowercase letters, numbers (0, 1, . . . , 9), or underscores.

These two rules yield variable names like `myVariable`, `THIS_NUMBER`, `VaRiAbLe_1`, and `A1234_4321`. Note that a C variable may never include a space or a character like an ampersand (&) or asterisk (*). These rules must be followed.

> **TIP:** While the compiler will allow you to begin a variable name with an underscore (_) character (as in `_myVar`), you shouldn't. Apple reserves all names that begin with a single underscore. There are situations where variable names that you've created can be confused with private variable names that Apple has created. In these cases, Apple promises to use names that start with a single underscore. If you stick to using names that *do not* start with an underscore, there won't be any confusion.
>
> Similarly, the compiler itself reserves all names that begin with two underscores, as in `__func__`. You and Apple both promise not to use names that begin with two underscores. These kinds of informal agreements between programmers, operating system developers, and compiler engineers are called *programming conventions*. We'll tell you about conventions you need to know about as we go. And in case you missed it, you just learned one.

However, these rules do leave a fair amount of room for inventiveness. Over the years, different groups of programmers came up with additional guidelines (also known as conventions or style guides) that made variable names more consistent and a bit easier to read.

As an example of this, Unix programmers tended to use all lowercase letters in their variable names. When a variable name consisted of more than one word, the words were separated by an underscore. This yielded variable names like `my_variable` or `number_of_puppies`.

Another popular convention stems from a programming language named Smalltalk. Instead of limiting all variable names to lower case and separating words with an underscore, Smalltalk used a convention known as InterCap, where all the words in a variable or function name are stuck together. Rather than include a special, separating character, each new word added to the first word starts with a capital letter. For example, instead of `number_of_puppies`, you'd use `numberOfPuppies`. Instead of `my_variable`, you'd use `myVariable`. When the first character is lowercase, the style is called camelCase. (Get it? The "humps" are in the middle.) Function names follow the same convention, but start with a capital letter, giving us function names such as `SmellTheFlowers()` or `HowMuchChangeYouGot()`.

Which convention should you use? For now, we'll follow the InterCap convention described in the previous paragraph. But as you make your way through the programming universe, you'll encounter different naming conventions that vary from language to language and environment to environment.

As mentioned in Chapter 3, C is a case-sensitive language. The compiler will cough out an error if you sometimes refer to `myVariable` and other times refer to `myvariable`. Adopt a variable naming convention and stick with it. Be consistent!

The Size of a Type

When you declare a variable, the compiler reserves a section of memory for the exclusive use of that variable. When you assign a value to a variable, you are actually modifying the variable's dedicated memory to reflect that value. The number of bytes assigned to a variable is determined by the variable's type. You should check your compiler's documentation to see how many bytes go along with each of the standard C types.

The Xcode compiler assigns 4 bytes to each int. Later in the book, in Chapter 8, we'll write a program that explores the size of a variety of C data types.

> **NOTE:** It's important to understand that the size of a type can change depending on factors such as your computer's processor type, operating system (OS X, Windows, or Linux, for example), and your development environment. Remember to read the documentation that comes with your compiler.

The variable declaration

```
int    myInt;
```

reserves 4 bytes of memory for the exclusive use of the variable `myInt`. If you later assign a value to `myInt`, that value is stored in the 4 bytes allocated for `myInt`. If you ever refer to `myInt`'s value, you'll be referring to the value stored in `myInt`'s 4 bytes.

If your compiler used 2-byte ints, the preceding declaration would allocate 2 bytes of memory for the exclusive use of `myInt`. As you'll see, it is important to know the size of the types you are dealing with.

Why is the size of a type important? The size of a type determines the range of values that type can handle. As you might expect, a type that's 4 bytes in size can hold a wider range of values than a type that's only 1 byte in size. Let's discuss how all this works.

Bytes and Bits

Each byte of computer memory is made up of 8 bits. Each bit has a value of either 1 or 0. Figure 4-3 shows a byte holding the value `00101011`. The value `00101011` is said to be the binary representation of the value of the byte. Look closer at Figure 4-3. Notice that each bit is numbered (the bit numbers are above each bit in the figure), with bit 0 on the extreme right side to bit 7 on the extreme left. This is a standard bit-numbering scheme used in most computers.

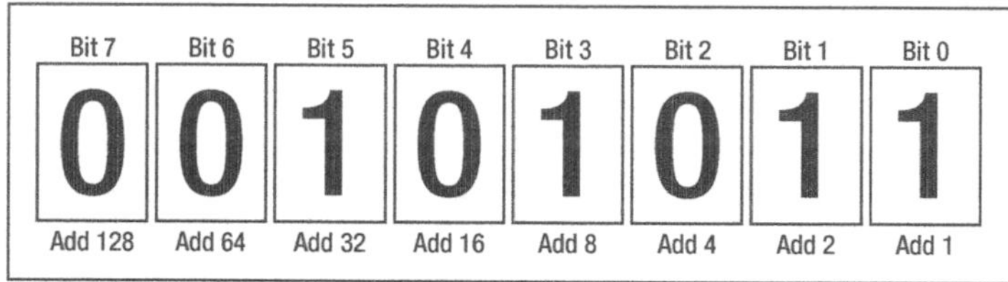

Figure 4-3. *A byte holding the binary value 00101011. Note that the rightmost bit is bit 0, and the leftmost bit is bit 7. Each bit contributes to the total value of the byte, if the bit is set to 1.*

Notice also the labels that appear beneath each bit in the figure ("Add 1," "Add 2," and so on). These labels are the key to binary numbers. Memorize them (it's easy: each bit is worth twice the value of its right neighbor). These labels are used to calculate the value of the entire byte. Here's how it works:

1. Start with a value of 0.
2. For each bit with a value of 1, add the label value below the bit.

That's all there is to it! In the byte pictured in Figure 4-3, you'd calculate the byte's value by adding 1 + 2 + 8 + 32 = 43. Where did we get the 1, 2, 8, and 32? They're the bottom labels of the only bits with a value of 1. Try another one. What's the value of the byte pictured in Figure 4-4?

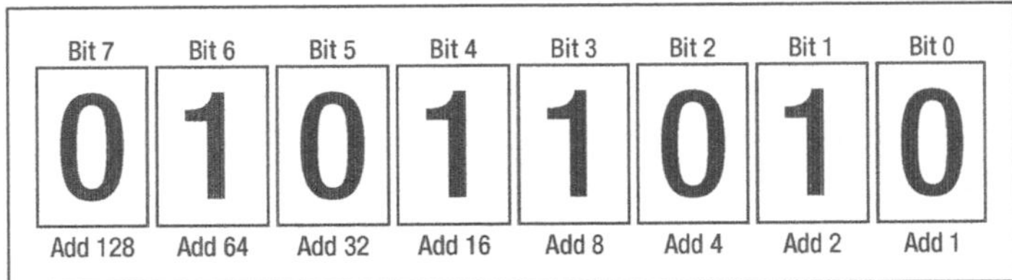

Figure 4-4. *What's the value of this byte? Remember, only the bits set to 1 contribute to the value of the byte.*

Easy, right? 2 + 8 + 16 + 64 = 90. Right! How about the byte in Figure 4-5?

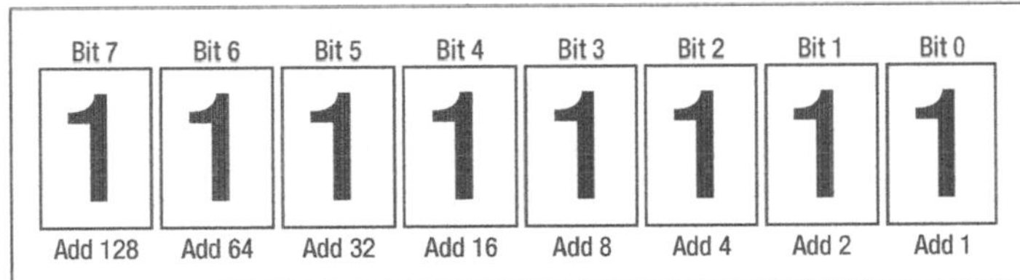

Figure 4-5. *What's the value of this byte? Note that this byte holds the largest value a byte can hold.*

This is an interesting one: 1 + 2 + 4 + 8 + 16 + 32 + 64 + 128 = 255. This example demonstrates the largest value that can fit in a single byte. Why? Because every bit is turned on. We've added everything we can add to the value of the byte.

The smallest value a byte can have is 0 (00000000). Since a byte can range in value from 0 to 255, a byte can have 256 possible values.

TWO'S COMPLEMENT NOTATION

Actually, the byte calculation approach in the "Bytes and Bits" section is just one of several ways to represent a number using binary. This approach is fine if you want to represent integers that are always greater than or equal to zero (known as *unsigned integers*). Computers use a different technique, known as *two's complement notation*, when they want to represent integers that might be either negative or positive.

To represent a negative number using two's complement notation:

1. Start with the binary representation of the positive version of the number.
2. Complement all the bits (turn the ones into zeros and the zeros into ones).

3. Add one to the result.

For example, the binary notation for the number 9 is `00001001`. To represent –9 in two's complement notation, flip the bits (`11110110`) and then add 1. The two's complement for –9 is `11110110 + 1 = 11110111`.

The binary notation for the number 2 is `00000010`. The two's complement for –2 would be `11111101 + 1 = 11111110`. Note that in binary addition, when you add `01 + 01`, you get `10`. Just as in regular addition, you carry the 1 to the next column.

One side effect of this scheme is that the most-significant bit (the bit on the far left, so called because it always has the largest value) is 1 whenever the number is negative and is 0 when the number is zero or positive. Consequently, it's often referred to as the *sign bit*.

Don't worry about the details of binary representation and arithmetic. What's important to remember is that the computer uses one notation for positive-only numbers and a different notation for numbers that can be positive or negative. Both notations allow a byte to take on one of 256 different values. The positives-only scheme allows values ranging from 0 to 255. The two's complement scheme (see the "Two's Complement Notation" sidebar) allows a byte to take on values ranging from –128 to 127. Note that both of these ranges contain exactly 256 values.

Going from 1 Byte to 2 Bytes

So far, you've discovered that 1 byte (8 bits) of memory can hold one of 2^8 or 256 possible values. By extension, 2 bytes (16 bits) of memory can hold one of 2^{16} or 65,536 possible values. If the 2 bytes are unsigned (never allowed to hold a negative value), they can hold values ranging from 0 to 65,535. If the 2 bytes are signed (allowed to hold both positive and negative values), they can hold values ranging from -32,768 to 32,767.

A 4-byte int can hold 2^{32} or 4,294,967,296 possible values. Wow! A signed 4-byte int can hold values ranging from –2,147,483,648 to 2,147,483,647, while an unsigned 4-byte int can hold values from 0 to 4,294,967,295. Not enough? Modern C compilers support 64-bit, or 8-byte, ints that can hold 2^{64} or 18,446,744,073,709,551,616 possible values. Now that's a lot of values.

To declare a variable as unsigned, precede its declaration with the unsigned qualifier. Here's an example:

```
unsigned int    myInt;
```

Now that you've defined the type of variable your program will use (in this case, unsigned int), you can assign a value to your variable.

Operators

Operators are a special character, or group of characters, that tell the computer that you want it to do something with your variables. The add operator symbol (+), for example, tells the compiler you want to add two numbers together. The meaning of most operators is fairly obvious; you'll pick up the others as you go along.

One way to assign a value to a variable is with the *assignment operator* (=). The assignment operator tells the computer to compute the value on the right side of the = and assign that value to the variable on the left side of the =. Take a look at this line of source code:

```
myInt = 237;
```

This statement causes the value 237 to be placed in the memory allocated for `myInt`. The one important rule for the assignment operator is that the thing on the left side of the = must be a variable that can hold the value of whatever is on the right side of the =. In this line of code

```
237 = myInt;
```

you are asking the compiler to copy the value in `myInt` to the number 237. Since you can't change the value of a number, the compiler will report an error when it encounters this line of code (most likely, the error message will say something about "expression is not assignable"). Go ahead; try this yourself.

> **NOTE:** As we just illustrated, you can use numerical constants (such as 237) directly in your code. In the programming world, these are called *literals*.

Look at this example:

```
#include <stdio.h>

int main( int argc, const char * argv[] )
{
    int         myInt, anotherInt;

    myInt = 503;
    anotherInt = myInt;
```

```
    return 0;
}
```

Note that we've declared two variables in this program. One way to declare multiple variables is the way we did here, separating the variables by a comma (,). There's no limit to the number of variables you can declare using this method.

We could have declared these variables using two separate declaration lines:

```
int    myInt;
int    anotherInt;
```

Either way is fine. As you'll see, C is an extremely flexible language. Let's look at some other operators.

The +, -, ++, and -- Operators

The addition (+) and subtraction (-) operators each take two values and reduce them to a single value. An operator that operates on two values is said to be a *binary operator*. An operator that operates on one value is said to be a *unary operator*. A value operated on by an operator is said to be an *operand*.

For example, the statement

```
myInt = 5 + 3;
```

will first resolve the right side of the = operator by adding the numbers 5 and 3 together. Once that's done, the resulting value (8) is assigned to the variable on the left side of the = operator. This statement assigns the value 8 to the variable `myInt`. Assigning a value to a variable means copying the value into the memory allocated to that variable.

Here's another example:

```
myInt = 10;
anotherInt = 12 - myInt;
```

The first statement assigns the value 10 to `myInt`. The second statement subtracts 10 from 12 to get 2, and then assigns the value 2 to `anotherInt`.

The increment (++) and decrement (--) operators operate on a single value only. ++ increments (raises) the value by 1, and -- decrements (lowers) the value by 1. Take a look:

```
myInt = 10;
myInt++;
```

The first statement assigns myInt a value of 10. The second statement changes myInt's value from 10 to 11. Here's another example:

```
myInt = 10;
--myInt;
```

This time the second line of code left myInt with a value of 9. You may have noticed that the first example showed the ++ operator following myInt, while the second example showed the -- operator preceding myInt.

The position of the ++ and -- operators determines when their operation is performed in relation to the rest of the statement. Placing the operator on the right side of a variable or expression (*postfix notation*) tells the compiler to resolve all values before performing the increment (or decrement) operation. Placing the operator on the left side of the variable (*prefix notation*) tells the compiler to increment (or decrement) first, and then continue evaluation. Confused? The following examples should make this point clear:

```
myInt = 10;
anotherInt = myInt--;
```

The first statement assigns myInt a value of 10. In the second statement, the -- operator is on myInt's right side. This use of postfix notation tells the compiler to assign myInt's value to anotherInt before decrementing myInt. This example leaves myInt with a value of 9 and anotherInt with a value of 10.

Here's the same example, written using prefix notation:

```
myInt = 10;
anotherInt = --myInt;
```

This time, the -- operator is on the left side of myInt. In this case, the value of myInt is decremented before being assigned to anotherInt. The result? myInt and anotherInt are both left with a value of 9.

NOTE: The uses of prefix and postfix notation shows both a strength and a weakness of the C language. On the plus side, C allows you to accomplish a lot in a small amount of code. In our examples, we changed the value of two different variables in a single statement. C is powerful.

On the downside, C code written in this fashion can be extremely cryptic and difficult to read for even the most seasoned C programmer. Write your code carefully.

The += and -= Operators

In C, you can place the same variable on both the left and right sides of an assignment statement. For example, the following statement increases the value of myInt by 10:

```
myInt = myInt + 10;
```

The same results can be achieved using the += operator. In other words,

```
myInt += 10;
```

is the same as

```
myInt = myInt + 10;
```

In the same way, the -= operator can be used to decrement the value of a variable.

The statement

```
myInt -= 10;
```

decrements the value of myInt by 10.

The *, /, %, *=, /=, and %= Operators

The multiplication (*) and division (/) operators each take two values and reduce them to a single value, much the same as the + and - operators do. The statement

```
myInt = 3 * 5;
```

multiplies 3 and 5, leaving myInt with a value of 15. The statement

```
myInt = 5 / 2;
```

divides 5 by 2, and assuming myInt is declared as an int (or any other type designed to hold whole numbers), assigns the integral (truncated) result to myInt. The number 5 divided by 2 is 2.5. Since myInt can only hold whole numbers, the value 2.5 is truncated and the value 2 is assigned to myInt.

> **NOTE:** Math alert! Numbers like –37, 0, and 22 are known as *whole numbers* or *integers*. Numbers like 3.14159, 2.5, and .0001 are known as *real* or *floating point numbers*.

The modulo (%) operator makes up for the fact that integer division truncates the quotient. Like the division operator (/) it divides the left number by the right number, but the result is the *remainder* of the division instead of the quotient. In the statements

```
quo = 16 / 5;
remain = 16 % 5;
```

the value of 16 is divided by 5 (3.2) and the truncated result (3) is assigned to the variable quo. In the second statement, the number 16 is again divided by 5 and the remainder of that division (1) is assigned to `remain`.

The `*=`, `/=`, and `%=` operators work much the same as their += and -= counterparts. The statement

```
myInt *= 10;
```

is identical to the statement

```
myInt = myInt * 10;
```

Similarly, this statement

```
myInt /= 10;
```

is identical to the statement

```
myInt = myInt / 10;
```

> **NOTE:** The / operator doesn't always perform truncation. The accuracy of the result is limited by the data type(s) of the operands. As an example, if the division is performed using ints, the result will be an int and is truncated to an integer value.
>
> Several data types (such as float) support floating point division using the / operator. We'll get to them later in this book.

To wrap up this discussion, it is worth mentioning that most C programmers prefer the shortcut version of each of the operators just covered. For example, most C programmers would use

```
myInt++;
myInt /= 2;
```

instead of

```
myInt = myInt + 1;
myInt = myInt / 2;
```

Both chunks of code will accomplish the same result. Use what you think will be easiest for you to read late at night with lots of caffeine coursing through your system and a steady stream of e-mails coming in from a client or boss demanding that you finish this project immediately—because that's when your coding choices will matter most.

Using Parentheses

Sometimes the expressions you create can be evaluated in several ways. Here's an example:

```
myInt = 5 + 3 * 2;
```

You can add 5 + 3 and then multiply the result by 2 (giving you 16). Alternatively, you can multiply 3 by 2 and add 5 to the result (giving you 11). Which is correct?

> **TIP:** In math class, you may have learned the *PEMDAS* mnemonic: do things in Parentheses first, then Exponents, then Multiplication and Division, and finally Addition and Subtraction. C also follows this rule, although the actual rules are a little more complex.

C has a set of built-in rules for resolving the order of operators. As it turns out, the * operator has a higher *precedence* than the + operator, so the multiplication will be performed first, yielding a result of 11.

Though it helps to understand the relative precedence of the C operators, keeping track of them all is hard. That's why the C gods gave us parentheses! Use parentheses in pairs to define the order in which you want your operators performed. The statement

```
myInt = ( 5 + 3 ) * 2;
```

will leave `myInt` with a value of 16. The statement

```
myInt = 5 + ( 3 * 2 );
```

will leave `myInt` with a value of 11. You can use more than one set of parentheses in a statement, as long as they occur in pairs—one left parenthesis associated with each right parenthesis. The statement

```
myInt = ( ( 5 + 3 ) * 2 );
```

will leave `myInt` with a value of 16.

Operator Precedence

The previous section referred to C's built-in rules for resolving operator precedence. If you have a question about which operator has a higher precedence, look it up in the chart in Table 4-1. Here's how the table works.

Table 4-1. *The Relative Precedence of C's Built-In Operators*

<table>
<tr><th>Operators by Precedence</th><th>Order</th></tr>
<tr><td>->, ., ++ postfix, -- postfix</td><td>Left to right</td></tr>
<tr><td>* pointer, & address of, + unary, - unary, !, ~, ++ prefix, -- prefix, sizeof</td><td>Right to left</td></tr>
<tr><td>Typecast</td><td>Right to left</td></tr>
<tr><td>* multiply, /, %</td><td>Left to right</td></tr>
<tr><td>+ binary, - binary</td><td>Left to right</td></tr>
<tr><td><< left-shift, >> right-shift</td><td>Left to right</td></tr>
<tr><td>>, >=, <, <=</td><td>Left to right</td></tr>
<tr><td>==, !=</td><td>Left to right</td></tr>
<tr><td>& bitwise-and</td><td>Left to right</td></tr>
<tr><td>^</td><td>Left to right</td></tr>
<tr><td>|</td><td>Left to right</td></tr>
<tr><td>&&</td><td>Left to right</td></tr>
<tr><td>||</td><td>Left to right</td></tr>
<tr><td>?:</td><td>Right to left</td></tr>
<tr><td>=, +=, -=, *=, /=, %=, >>=, <<=, &=, |=, ^=</td><td>Right to left</td></tr>
<tr><td>,</td><td>Left to right</td></tr>
</table>

The higher an operator is in the chart, the higher its precedence. For example, suppose you are trying to predict the result of this line of code:

```
myInt = 5 * 3 + 7;
```

First, look up the operator * in Table 4-1. Hmm, this one seems to be in the chart twice, once with label "pointer" and once with the label "multiply." You can tell just by looking at this line of code that we want the multiply version. The compiler is pretty smart. Just like you, it can tell that this is the multiply version of *.

OK, now look up +. Yup, it's in there twice also, once as unary and once as binary. A unary + or - is the sign that appears before a number, like +147 or –32768. In this line of code, the + operator has two operands, so clearly binary + is the one to pick.

Now that you've figured out which operator is which, you can see that the multiply * is higher up on the chart than the binary +, and thus has a higher precedence. This means that the * will get evaluated before the +, as if the expression were written as

```
myInt = (5 * 3) + 7;
```

So far so good. Now, what about the following line of code?

```
myInt = 27 * 6 % 5;
```

Both of these operators are on the fourth line in the chart. Which one gets evaluated first? If both operators under consideration are on the same line in the chart, the order of evaluation is determined by the entry in the chart's rightmost column. In this case, the operators are evaluated from left to right. In the current example, * will get evaluated before %, as if the line of code were written

```
myInt = (27 * 6) % 5;
```

What about this line of code?

```
myInt = 27 % 6 * 5;
```

In this case, the % will get evaluated before the *, as if the line of code were written

```
myInt = (27 % 6) * 5;
```

TIP: When in doubt, use parentheses! If the order of operations is important and isn't obvious—or you just can't remember what the operator precedence is—*use parentheses to force the order you want.* There's no cost to using parentheses,

> except readability should you use too many of them. It's much better that your program does what you meant, instead of what you wrote.

As you look through the chart, you'll definitely notice some operators that you haven't learned about yet. As you read through this book and encounter new operators, check back with Table 4-1 to see where they fit in.

Sample Programs

So far in this chapter we've discussed variables (mostly of type int) and operators (mostly mathematical). The program examples on the following pages combine variables and operators into useful C statements. You'll also learn a bit more about our friend from the Standard Library, the `printf()` function.

Opening Operator.xcodeproj

The next program, *Operator*, provides a testing ground for some of the operators covered in the previous sections. *main.c* declares a variable (`myInt`) and uses a series of statements to change the value of the variable. By including a `printf()` after each of these statements, *main.c* makes it easy to follow the variable, step by step, as its value changes.

In Xcode, close any project windows that may be open. In the Finder, locate the *Learn C Projects* folder and the *04.01 - Operator* subfolder, and double-click the file *Operator.xcodeproj*. The operator project window should appear (see Figure 4-6).

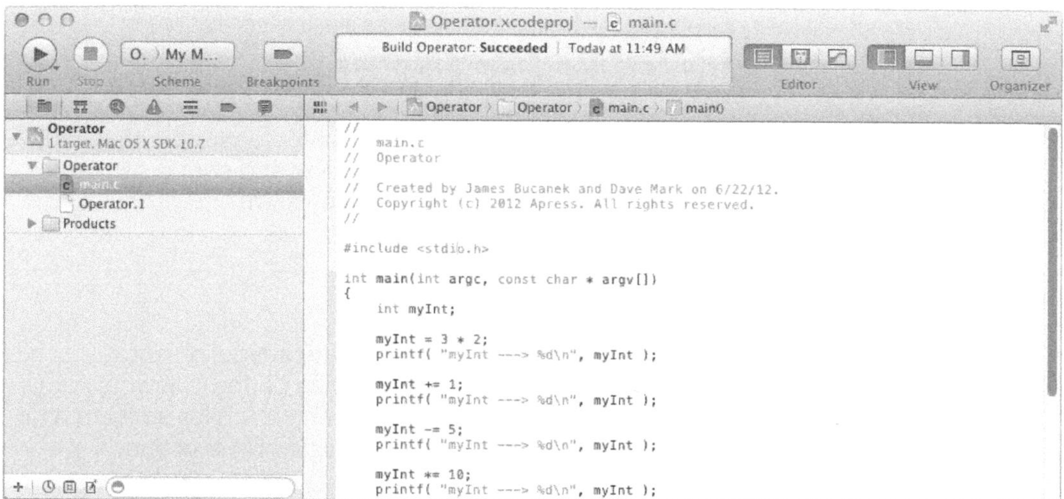

Figure 4-6. *The Operator project window*

Run *Operator* by selecting ***Run*** from the ***Product*** menu. Xcode will compile *main.c*, and then link and run the program. Compare your output to that shown in Figure 4-7. They should be about the same.

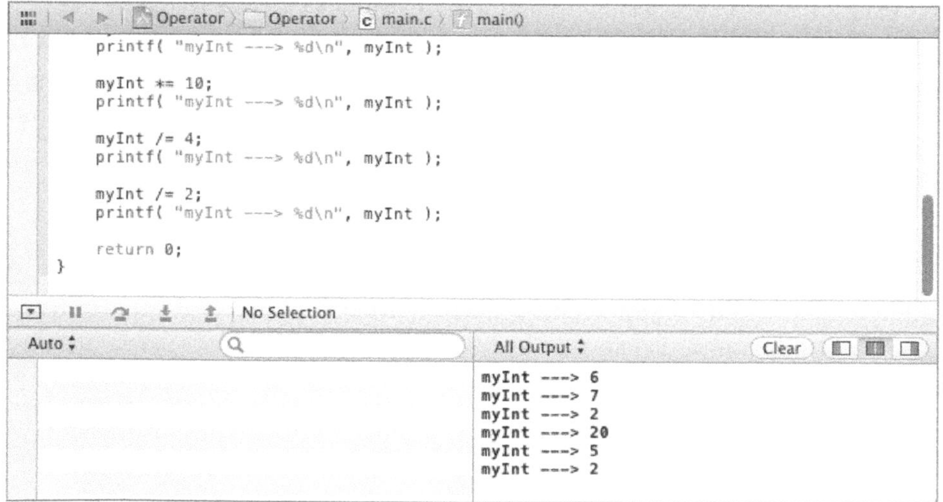

Figure 4-7. *The output from running the Operator project*

Stepping Through the Operator Source Code

Let's take a look at the *Operator* project's source code. In Xcode, bring up *main.c* in an editing window. *main.c* starts off with the usual #include of stdio.h. This provides access to printf().

```
#include <stdio.h>
```

main() starts out by defining an int named myInt:

```
int main(int argc, const char * argv[]) {
    int    myInt;
```

> **NOTE:** Earlier we used the phrase "declaring a variable" and now we're using the term "defining." What's the difference? A *variable declaration* is any statement that specifies a variable's name and type. The line int myInt; certainly does that. A *variable definition* is a declaration that causes memory to be allocated for the variable. Since the previous statement does cause memory to be allocated for myInt, it does qualify as a definition. Later in the book, you'll see some declarations that don't qualify as definitions. For now, just remember that a variable definition causes memory to be allocated.

At this point in the program (after myInt has been declared but before any value has been assigned to it), myInt is said to be uninitialized. In computerese, initialization refers to the process of establishing a variable's value for the first time. A variable that has been declared, but that has not had a value assigned to it, is said to be uninitialized. You initialize a variable the first time you assign a value to it.

Since myInt was declared to be of type int, and since Xcode is currently set to use 4-byte ints, 4 bytes of memory were reserved for myInt. Since we haven't placed a value in those 4 bytes yet, they could contain any value at all. If you want a variable to contain a specific value, assign the value to the variable yourself!

> **NOTE:** In Chapter 7, you'll learn about *global variables*. Global variables are always set to 0 when your program starts. Note that all of the variables used in this chapter are local variables, not global variables. Local variables are not initialized, unless you do so yourself.

The next line of code uses the * operator to assign a value of 6 to myInt. Following that, we use printf() to display the value of myInt in the console window.

```
myInt = 3 * 2;
printf( "myInt ---> %d\n", myInt );
```

The code between printf()'s left and right parentheses is known as an *argument list*. The arguments in an argument list are automatically provided to the function you are calling (in this case, printf()). The receiving function can use the arguments passed to it to determine its next course of action.

Interestingly, when you define or declare a function, the elements between the parentheses that correspond to the argument list are known as *parameters*. You'll learn more about parameters in Chapter 7. For the moment, let's talk about printf() and the arguments used by this Standard Library function.

The first argument passed to printf() defines what will be drawn in the console window. The simplest call to printf() uses a quoted text string as its only argument. A quoted text string consists of a pair of double-quote characters (") with zero or more characters between them. For example, this call of printf()

```
printf( "Hello!" );
```

will draw the characters Hello! in the console window. Notice that the double quote characters are not part of the text string.

In a slightly more complex scenario, you can request that printf() draw a variable's value in the midst of the quoted string. In the case of an int, do this by embedding the two characters %d within the first argument and by passing the int as a second argument. printf() will replace the %d with the value of the int.

In these two lines of code, we first set myInt to 6, use printf() to print the value of myInt in the console window.

```
myInt = 3 * 2;
printf( "myInt ---> %d\n", myInt );
```

This code produces this line of output in the console window:

```
myInt ---> 6
```

The two characters \n in the first argument represent a carriage return and tell printf() to move the cursor to the beginning of the next line before it prints any more characters. If we deleted all of the \n characters from the program, all the output would appear on a single line in the console window. Give it a try. Just remember to put them back in when you are done playing.

NOTE: The %d in the first argument is known as a *format specifier*. It specifies the type of the argument to be included in the string to be printed. The d in the format specifier tells `printf()` that you are printing an signed integer variable. The "d" stands for "decimal." You can also use `%i` ("i" for "integer") if that's easier to remember. The two are interchangeable.

You can place any number of % specifications in the first argument, as long as you follow the first argument by the appropriate number of values. Here's another example:

```
int    var1, var2;

var1 = 5;
var2 = 10;
printf( "var1 = %d\n\nvar2 = %d\n", var1, var2 );
```

This chunk of code will draw this text in the console window:

```
var1 = 5

var2 = 10
```

Notice the blank line between the two lines of output. It was caused by the `\n\n` in the first `printf()` argument. The first carriage return placed the cursor at the beginning of the next console line (directly under the v in `var1`). The second carriage return moved the cursor down one more line, leaving a blank line in its path.

Let's get back to the source code. The next line of `main.c` increments `myInt` from 6 to 7, and prints the new value in the console window.

```
myInt += 1;
printf( "myInt ---> %d\n", myInt );
```

The next line decrements `myInt` by 5 and prints its new value of 2 in the console window.

```
myInt -= 5;
printf( "myInt ---> %d\n", myInt );
```

Next, `myInt` is multiplied by 10, and its new value of 20 is printed in the console window.

```
myInt *= 10;
printf( "myInt ---> %d\n", myInt );
```

After that, `myInt` is divided by 4, resulting in a new value of 5.

```
    myInt /= 4;
    printf( "myInt ---> %d\n", myInt );
```

Finally, myInt is divided by 2. Since 5 divided by 2 is 2.5 (not a whole number), a truncation is performed, and myInt is left with a value of 2.

```
    myInt /= 2;
    printf( "myInt ---> %d\n", myInt );

    return 0;
}
```

Opening Postfix.xcode

The next program demonstrates the difference between postfix and prefix notation (recall the ++ and -- operators defined earlier in the chapter?) If you have a project open in Xcode, close it. In the Finder, go into the *Learn C Projects* folder and then into the *04.02 - Postfix* subfolder, and double-click the project file *Postfix.xcodeproj*.

Take a look at the source code in the file *main.c* and try to predict the result of the two printf() calls before you run the program. There's extra ice cream for everyone if you get this right. Careful, this one's tricky.

Once your guesses are locked in, select ***Run*** from the ***Product*** menu. How'd you do? Compare your two guesses with the output in Figure 4-8. Let's look at the source code.

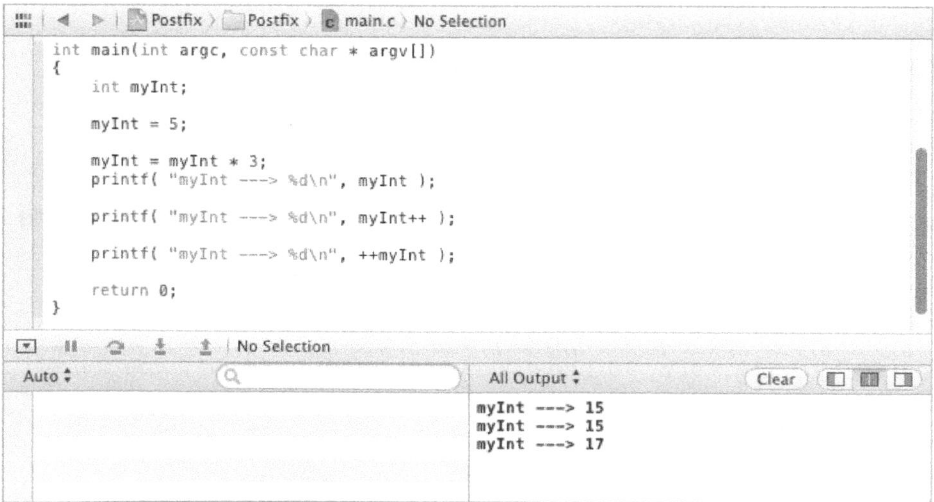

Figure 4-8. ***The output generated by Postfix***

Stepping Through the Postfix Source Code

The first half of *main.c* is pretty straightforward. The variable myInt is defined to be of type int. Then, myInt is assigned a value of 5. Next comes the tricky part.

```
#include <stdio.h>

int main(int argc, const char * argv[]) {
    int    myInt;

    myInt = 5;
```

The first call to printf() actually has a statement embedded in it. This is another great feature of the C language. Where there's room for a variable, there's room for an entire statement. Sometimes, performing two actions within the same line of code is convenient. For example, this line of code

```
printf( "myInt ---> %d\n", myInt = myInt * 3 );
```

first triples the value of myInt, and then passes the result (the tripled value of myInt) on to printf(). The same could have been accomplished using two lines of code.

```
myInt = myInt * 3;
printf( "myInt ---> %d\n", myInt );
```

In general, when the compiler encounters an assignment statement where it expects a variable, it first completes the assignment, and then passes on the result of the assignment as if it were a variable. Let's see this technique in action.

In *main.c*, our friend the postfix operator emerges again. Just prior to the two calls of printf(), myInt has a value of 15. The first of the two printf()'s increments the value of myInt using postfix notation:

```
    printf( "myInt ---> %d\n", myInt++ );
```

The use of postfix notation means that the value of myInt will be passed on to printf() before myInt is incremented. Therefore, the first printf() will accord myInt a value of 15. However, when the statement is finished, myInt will have a value of 16.

The second printf() acts in a more rational (and preferable) manner. The prefix notation guarantees that myInt will be incremented (from 6 to 7) before its value is passed on to printf().

```
    printf( "myInt ---> %d", ++myInt );

    return 0;
}
```

BREAKING THE PRINTF() INTO TWO STATEMENTS

Can you break each of these `printf()`s into two separate statements? Give it a try; then, read on.

The first `printf()` looks like this:

```
printf( "myInt ---> %d\n", myInt++ );
```

Here's the two-statement version:

```
printf( "myInt ---> %d\n", myInt );
myInt++;
```

Notice that the statement incrementing `myInt` was placed after the `printf()`. Do you see why? The postfix notation makes this necessary. Run through both versions, and verify this for yourself.

The second `printf()` looks like this:

```
printf( "myInt ---> %d\n", ++myInt );
```

Here's the two-statement version:

```
++myInt;
printf( "myInt ---> %d\n", myInt );
```

In this latter version, the statement incrementing `myInt` came before the `printf()`. This time, it's the prefix notation that makes this necessary. Again, go through both versions, and verify this for yourself.

Our purpose for demonstrating the complexity of the postfix and prefix operators is twofold. On one hand, it's extremely important that you understand exactly how these operators work from all angles. This will allow you to write code that works and will aid you in making sense of other programmers' code.

On the other hand, embedding prefix and postfix operators within function arguments may save you lines of code but, as you can see, may prove a bit confusing. So what's a coder to do? Put clarity before brevity. Make sure your code is readable. After all, you will likely have to go back and edit it at some point. Readable code is much easier to maintain. As long as your code is correct, the compiler will do the same thing with it. So write for the programmer, not the machine.

Sprucing Up Your Code

You are now in the middle of your C learning curve. You've learned about variables, types, functions, and bytes. You've learned about an important part of the Standard Library, the function `printf()`. At this point in the learning process, programmers start developing their coding habits.

Coding habits are the little things programmers do that make their code a little bit different (and hopefully better!) than anyone else's. Before you get too set in your ways, here are a few coding habits you can, and should, add to your arsenal.

Source Code Spacing

You may have noticed the tabs, spaces, and blank lines scattered throughout the sample programs. These are known in C as *white space*. With a few exceptions, white space is ignored by C compilers. Believe it or not, as far as the C compiler goes, the program:

```
#include <stdio.h>
int main (int argc,
const char * argv[])
                                                  {
    int myInt;myInt
=
        5
;    printf( "myInt = %d",
myInt);;}
```

is equivalent to the program

```
#include <stdio.h>

int main(int argc, const char * argv[]) {
    int myInt;

    myInt = 5;
    printf( "myInt = %d",  myInt  );
}
```

NOTE: A computer language that doesn't care about the positioning or white space in your code is called a *free-form* language. C is a free-form language. This is in contrast to languages like COBOL and Ruby that require statements to be on separate lines, or may even require statements to be at a particular column of a line to be correct.

While the C language is free-form, the C compiler isn't. The statements that begin with # (as in `#include <stdio.h>`) are called *pre-processor directives*. Pre-processor directives are, as the name implies, commands that give instructions to the compiler itself—before your C code is compiled (or processed). Pre-processor directives must begin with a # and must be the only statement on that line.

The C compiler doesn't care if you put five statements per line or if you put 20 carriage returns between your statements and your semicolons. One thing the compiler won't let you do is place white space in the middle of a word, such as a variable or function name. For example, this line of code won't compile:

```
my  Int = 5;
```

Instead of a single variable named `myInt`, the compiler sees two items, one named `my` and the other named `Int`. Indiscriminate white space can confuse the compiler.

Too little white space can also confuse the compiler. For example, this line of code won't compile:

```
intmyInt;
```

The compiler needs at least one piece of white space to tell it where the type (int) ends and where the variable (`myInt`) begins. On the other hand, as you've already seen, this line compiles just fine:

```
myInt=5;
```

Since a variable name can't contain the character =, the compiler has no problem telling where the variable ends and where the operator begins.

As long as your code compiles properly, you're free to develop your own white-space style. Here are a few hints:

- Place a blank line between your variable declarations and the rest of your function's code. Also, use blank lines to group related lines of code.
- Sprinkle single spaces throughout a statement. Compare

```
printf("myInt=",myInt);
```

with:

```
printf( "myInt =", myInt );
```

The spaces make the second line easier to read.

- When in doubt, use parentheses. Compare

```
myInt=var1+2*var2+4;
```

with

```
myInt = var1 + (2*var2) + 4;
```

What a difference parentheses and spaces make!

- Always start variable names with a lowercase letter, using an uppercase letter at the start of each subsequent word in the name. This yields variable names such as `myVar`, `areWeDone`, and `employeeName`.
- Always start function names with an uppercase letter, using an uppercase letter at the start of each subsequent word in the name. This yields function names such as `DoSomeWork()`, `HoldThese()`, and `DealTheCards()`.

These hints are merely suggestions. Use a set of standards that make sense for you and the people with whom you work. The object here is to make your code as readable as possible.

Comment Your Code

One of the most critical elements in the creation of a computer program is clear and comprehensive documentation. When you deliver your award-winning graphics package to your customers, you'll want to have two sets of documentation. One set is for your customers, who'll need a clear set of instructions that guide them through your wonderful new creation. The other set of documentation consists of the comments you'll weave throughout your code. Source code comments act as a sort of narrative, guiding a reader through your code. You'll include comments that describe how your code works, what makes it special, and what to look out for when changing it.

Well-commented code includes a comment at the beginning of each function that describes the function, the function arguments, and the function's variables. Sprinkling individual comments among your source code statements to explain the role each line plays in your program's algorithm is also a good idea. In addition, you should include a block of comments that describe your program's overall approach, solutions used, key concepts, and any other information that will help someone maintaining your code in the future to wrap their head around your project.

How do you add a comment to your source code? Let's take a look.

All C compilers recognize the sequence /* as the start of a comment and will ignore all characters until they hit the sequence */ (the end-of-comment characters). In addition, all C99-compliant compilers support the use of // to mark a single-line comment. All characters from // onward on the end of that line will be ignored.

Here's some commented code:

```
int main(int argc, const char * argv[]) {
    int    numPieces; // Number of pieces of pie left
    numPieces = 8;    // We started with 8 pieces
    numPieces--;      // Peter had a piece
    numPieces--;      // Quagmire had a piece
    numPieces -= 2;   // Cleveland had two pieces!!
    numPieces -= 4;   // Joe had the rest!!!

    printf( "Slices left = %d", numPieces );
                     /* How about
                        some cake
                        instead?  */
    return 0;
}
```

Notice that, although most of the comments fit on the same line, the last comment was split between three lines. The preceding code will compile just fine.

"COMMENTING OUT" CODE

A common use of comments is to save bits and pieces of code that you don't want to compile. As you experiment with code, you may write something and find you don't want it anymore—maybe you're going to try something different. Rather than simply deleting your hard work, turn it into a comment like this:

```
//SomeFunctionThatDoesNotWork();
ThisFunctionBetterWork();
```

The compiler ignores comments, no mater what they contain. There are three techniques to quickly "comment out" statements in your source.

- Insert a // at the beginning of each line. This one is so commonly used that Xcode has an editor command that will do it for you. Select one or more lines of source code and press ⌘/ (**Command+/**), or choose the **Editor ➤ Structure ➤ Comment Selection** command.
- Insert a /* before your code and */ at the end. This works because the /*...*/ style comment can extend beyond one line. It doesn't work on code that already contains /*...*/-style comments, because the first */ ends the comment. But it does work to comment out code within a single line.
- Insert a new line that reads `#if 0` before the first line of your code, and a new line that reads `#endif` after the last line. These are more pre-processor directives. They tell the compiler to only compile the code between the `#if` and the `#endif` if the value of the `#if` statement is non-zero. If it's zero, all of the lines are ignored (as if they were comments).

To "uncomment" your code so that it compiles again, simply reverse these steps. One advantage to the last technique is that you can turn them all on again simply by changing the 0 to a 1.

Since each of the programs in this book is examined in detail, line by line, the comments were left out. This was done to make the examples as simple as possible. In this instance, do as I say, not as I do. Comment your code. No excuses!

The Curly Brace Controversy

There are two generally accepted styles for placing curly braces in your code. The first style is the one we've been using:

```
int main(int argc, const char * argv[]) {
    printf( "Hello, world!");
    return 0;
}
```

The second style places the opening curly brace on its own line:

```
int main(int argc, const char * argv[])
{
    printf( "Hello, world!");
    return 0;
}
```

We prefer the second form. Here are the advantages to this approach: we think it makes your code look a bit cleaner, and that your eye can more easily find the matching closing brace that matches an opening brace.

The downside to this approach is that it adds an extra line of code to every block of code in which it is used. This means you see less code per screenful of code listing.

Experiment with both bracing styles to see which one works best for you. In this book, we've adopted the first style (left curly at the end of the line of code) because it's the default bracing style used by Xcode and most of Apple's sample code.

> **TIP:** Xcode makes typing and finding matching braces and parentheses magically simple. First, there's an Xcode preference that will automatically insert a closing brace whenever you type an opening brace. You just have to fill in the stuff that goes between them.
>
> When you type, or use the right arrow key to move the cursor over, a closing curly brace or parenthesis, Xcode will highlight and blink the matching opening brace or parenthesis. This is hugely helpful and fun to watch, too. Give it a try. There's also the code folding ribbon, just the left of your editing pane. Hover your cursor here and Xcode will highlight the entire block. Finally, double-click a parenthesis, curly bracket, or quote character and Xcode will select it, its matching sibling, and everything in between.

What's Next?

This chapter introduced the concepts of variables and operators, tied together in C statements, and separated by semicolons. You learned a lot of mathematical operators, how C decides what order they get evaluated, and how to use parentheses to change that order. You also learned how the Standard Library function `printf()` uses format specifiers (%d) to replace bits of the output with values you supply as parameters.

In Chapter 5 you'll take a little side trip from learning more C and spend a little time learning some Xcode magic instead. Trust us, it will be a fun excursion.

CHAPTER 4 EXERCISES

1. Find the error in each of the following code fragments:

   a. `printf( Hello, world );`

   b. `int    myInt  myOtherInt;`

   c. `myInt =+ 3;`

   d. `printf( "myInt = %d" );`

   e. `printf( "myInt = ", myInt );`

   f. `printf( "myInt = %d\", myInt );`

   g. `myInt + 3 = myInt;`

   h.
   ```
   int main(int argc, const char * argv[]) {
     int   myInt;
     myInt = 3;
     anotherInt = myInt;

     return 0;
   }
   ```

2. Compute the value of `myInt` after each code fragment is executed:

   a.
   ```
   myInt = 5;
   myInt *= (3+4) * 2;
   ```

   b.
   ```
   myInt = 2;
   myInt *= ( (3*4) / 2 ) - 9;
   ```

   c.
   ```
   myInt = 2;
   myInt /= 5;
   myInt--;
   ```

   d.
   ```
   myInt = 25;
   myInt /= 3 * 2;
   ```

   e.
   ```
   myInt = (3*4*5) / 9;
   myInt -= (3+4) * 2;
   ```

   f.
   ```
   myInt = 5;
   printf("myInt = %d", myInt = 2 );
   ```

   g.
   ```
   myInt = 5;
   myInt = (3+4) * 2;
   ```

h.
```
myInt = 1;
myInt /= (3+4) / 6;
```

Chapter 5

Debugging

So far you've learned a lot about how to work with Xcode to create, edit, and run your very own programming projects. You've learned about functions, variables, operators, and the process of using those items to manipulate your program's data. Hopefully, as you've been reading and making changes to your source code, you've been trying to anticipate the results of those changes. Learning how to "think like a computer" will be immensely useful as you develop your programming talent.

Sometimes it's really convenient to know what the computer is *actually* doing. You did this in the *Operators* and *Postfix* projects by using the `printf()` statement, like this:

```
myInt = 3 * 2;
printf( "myInt ---> %d\n", myInt );
```

The first statement stores the value for 6 in the memory assigned to the `myInt` variable. The second statement uses the `printf()` function to output the value of `myInt` to the console log so you could see, with your own eyes, that the value was, in fact, 6.

```
myInt ---> 6
```

While this is great—it confirms that what you thought the computer was doing and what the computer was actually doing were one in the same—using `printf()` statements between every step of your program is a little awkward.

Look at the source for the entire *Operators* project. Much of the code exists solely to help you track the value of the variables. As it turns out, there's a tool built right into Xcode that greatly simplifies the process of following along as the computer runs your program. This tool is called a *debugger*, so called because it helps you track down and eliminate bugs in your programs.

What's a Debugger?

If you've read or watched enough science fiction, you've undoubtedly encountered this scene: a physician places a patient on a table and produces some kind of portable scanner. A whirring noise ensues and suddenly every detail of the patient appears before the physician. The physician can see the patient's bones, organs, circulatory and nervous system. Vital statistics flash by. After a brief pause, the physician announces that the victim is suffering from a mimetic alien organism that is rewriting the telomeres of their intragenic DNA and he will need immediate synthetic reverse transcriptase therapy in a hyperbaric chamber … and quickly before he turn into a big lizard! Or something like that.

Modern doctors don't quite have medical scanners like those in science fiction (yet), but as programmers we have something that's pretty close to it. The *debugger* is a powerful tool built into Xcode that can peer into the inner workings of your program with an astonishing acuity. The debugger can stop your program in its tracks, examine the values of its variables, and let you observe and control every step of its execution.

The debugger is probably the single most powerful tool in the programmer's arsenal. Usually, you use it to find and correct mistakes ("bugs") in your program, but it can be just as useful in confirming that your program is doing what you were expecting it to do.

THE ORIGINS OF DEBUGGING

The modern use of the terms "bug" (meaning a flaw or mistake in a computer program) and "debug" (the act of correcting said flaw) are attributed to Rear Admiral Grace "Amazing Grace" Hopper. In 1947, then midshipman Hopper was working on the Harvard Mark I computer. And when we say "computer," we mean a mechanical device that filled an entire room, weighed 10,000 pounds, and consisted of relays, switches, wires, rotating shafts, motors, and clutches. A laptop it was not.

The program that the team was working on one day simply would not function property. After some investigation, they found that a moth had expired in one of the relays. The hapless moth was carefully extracted and taped into a notebook (there's a picture of it on the Grace Hopper Wikipedia page). From that day on, correcting a mistake in a program was referred to as "debugging" the program.

Rear Admiral Grace Hopper was a pretty amazing person. She had ground-breaking careers both in academics and the military. She was a pioneer of computer science and one of a handful of visionaries that conceived of the very *idea* of a computer language—describing what you want the computer to do and have that description translated into machine codes that the computer would execute. Before that, most people thought computers could only add numbers.

Controlling Execution

So how do you use the Xcode debugger to control your program? Guess what? You've been using the debugger since the first chapter!

Xcode's debugger takes over the execution of your program every time you run it from within Xcode. But unless you tell the debugger that you want it to do something specific, it just stands to the side and lets your program run. Let's revisit Chapter 3's *Hello3* project and get the debugger to do a little bit more.

Find the `03.02 - Hello3` project folder and open `Hello3.xcodeproj`. You can do that from the Finder or from within Xcode using the ***Open*** or ***Open Recent*** commands in the ***File*** menu.

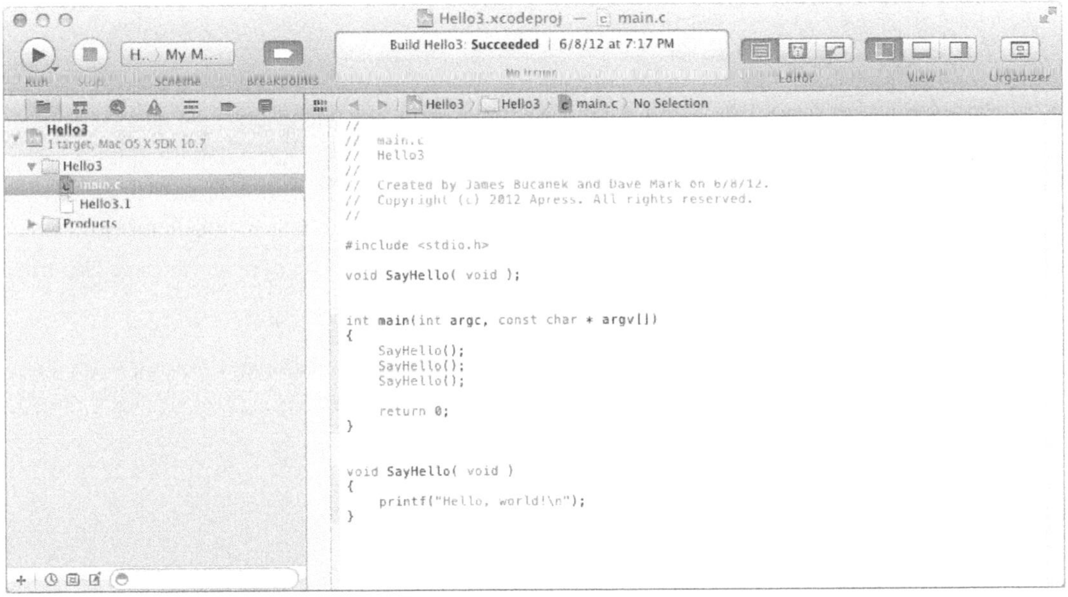

Figure 5-1. *The Hello3 project*

The project should still look like the one in Figure 5-1. If you run it, as you did in Chapter 3, it will output "Hello, World!" to the console three times.

Setting Breakpoints

Although you *can* use the debugger before your program starts or even after it finishes running, many of the really interesting things happen while your program is running. The debugger features a mechanism called a *breakpoint* that stops the program in its tracks and lets you examine and even change your program's variables. When you think breakpoint, think "coffee break" (as opposed to "break the Ming vase"). You're pausing, not being destructive!

Set a breakpoint by clicking in the margin to the left of any statement, as shown in Figure 5-2. A light blue arrow will appear, indicating an active breakpoint.

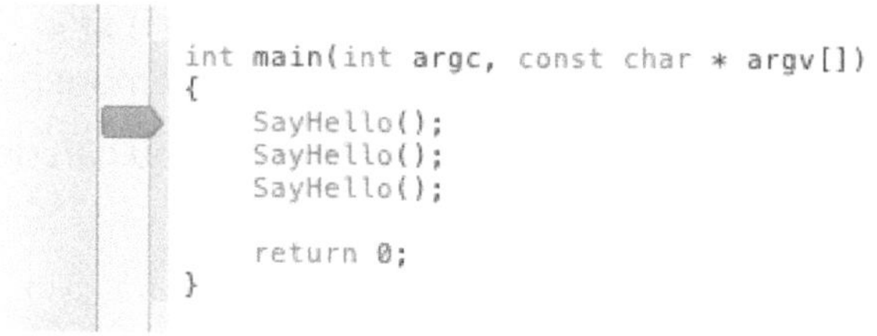

```
int main(int argc, const char * argv[])
{
    SayHello();
    SayHello();
    SayHello();

    return 0;
}
```

Figure 5-2. *Setting a breakpoint*

When you run your program in Xcode, your program will chug right along, right up to the point where it encounters the breakpoint; then it will freeze in its tracks, *before* it executes the line at which the breakpoint points.

Give it a try. Set a breakpoint, then run your program; click on the **Run** button in the toolbar, choose ***Project* ➤ *Run*** or press ⌘R. You should see something like the window in Figure 5-3.

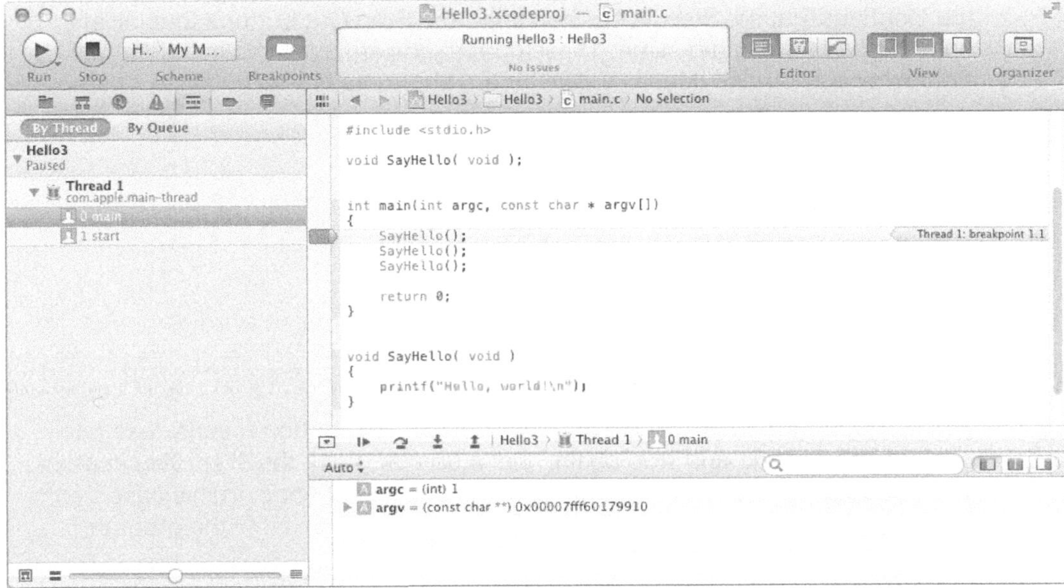

Figure 5-3. *Stopped at a breakpoint*

The short green arrow indicates the line of code that is about to be executed. In this example, the program is about to execute the first of the three calls to `SayHello()`.

> **NOTE:** The brains behind your computer, the *central processing unit* (CPU), keeps track of the currently running program, storing the location of the next line to be executed in a special memory pointer called the *program counter* (PC). The short green arrow corresponds to the program counter. When we say program counter, we are referring to that green arrow. Just thought you'd like to know!

Some interesting details have also appeared at the bottom of the workspace window. This is called the *debug area*. The ribbon at the top of the debug area has a number of important features. The icon on the immediate left edge of the ribbon allows you to hide the debug area. It looks like a rectangle with a small triangle inside. Go ahead and click on it—you know you want to. The debug area disappears and the ribbon moves to the bottom of the window. Cool. To make it reappear, click the icon again and the debug area will reappear.

Next up on the debug ribbon is a series of four buttons that you will use quite frequently as you debug your programs (Figure 5-4). From left to right, these are the Continue/Pause, Step Over, Step Into, and Step Out buttons that initiate commands of the same name. These commands are available in the ***Product* ➤ *Debug*** menu and have convenient keyboard shortcuts.

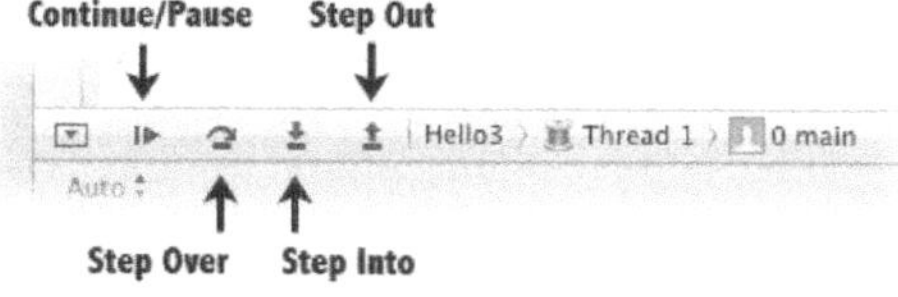

Figure 5-4. *Debugger controls*

Stepping Over a Statement

The first button to learn is the `Step Over` button. This button means "execute one line of my code and stop again." Let's do that. Click the `Step Over` button. The debugger will let your program execute one line of code, in this case the `SayHello()` function call, and stop again (see Figure 5-5). Now the program counter points to the second `SayHello()` statement.

```
int main(int argc, const char * argv[])
{
    SayHello();
    SayHello();
    SayHello();

    return 0;
}

void SayHello( void )
{
    printf("Hello, world!\n");
}
```

Figure 5-5. *Hello3 stopped after executing* `SayHello()` *once*

> **TIP:** The debugger lets you show and hide both the variables view (the left pane) and the console (right pane) in the debug area. As the name implies, the variables view lets you examine and work with your program's variables. You can show and hide both panes by clicking the appropriate icon on the right side of the debug area, just below the ribbon (see the mouse cursor in Figure 5-5).

The debugger let your program run one line of source code and stopped again. In this case, it was a call to the `SayHello()` function that in turn called the `printf()` function to output the first "Hello, World!" message to the console.

Notice that all of the statements in the `SayHello()` function executed before the program stopped again. In fact, it doesn't matter how many statements are in `SayHello()` or what other functions it calls; the Step Over button will let them all run and won't stop the program again until they have finished and execution returns to the `main()` function.

But what if you wanted to watch the details of the `SayHello()` function execute? You could set another breakpoint inside the `SayHello()` function. Remember that the debugger will stop whenever the program encounters an active breakpoint. Another way is to use the Step Into button.

Stepping Into a Function

With the program counter before the second call to `SayHello()`, use the Step Into button. The workspace window will now look something like Figure 5-6.

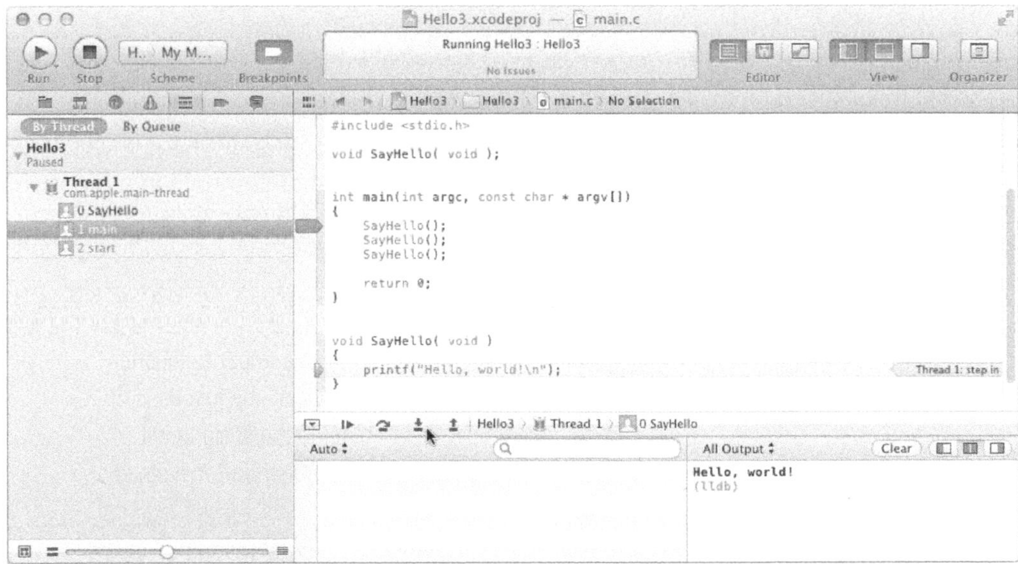

Figure 5-6. *Stepping into the `SayHello()` function*

Instead of letting the entire `SayHello()` function run, the debugger has advanced to the first statement in the `SayHello()` function and stopped again. Now you can step over the individual statements of the `SayHello()` function. Use the Step

Over button to execute the `printf()` statement. At this point, your workspace should look like Figure 5-7.

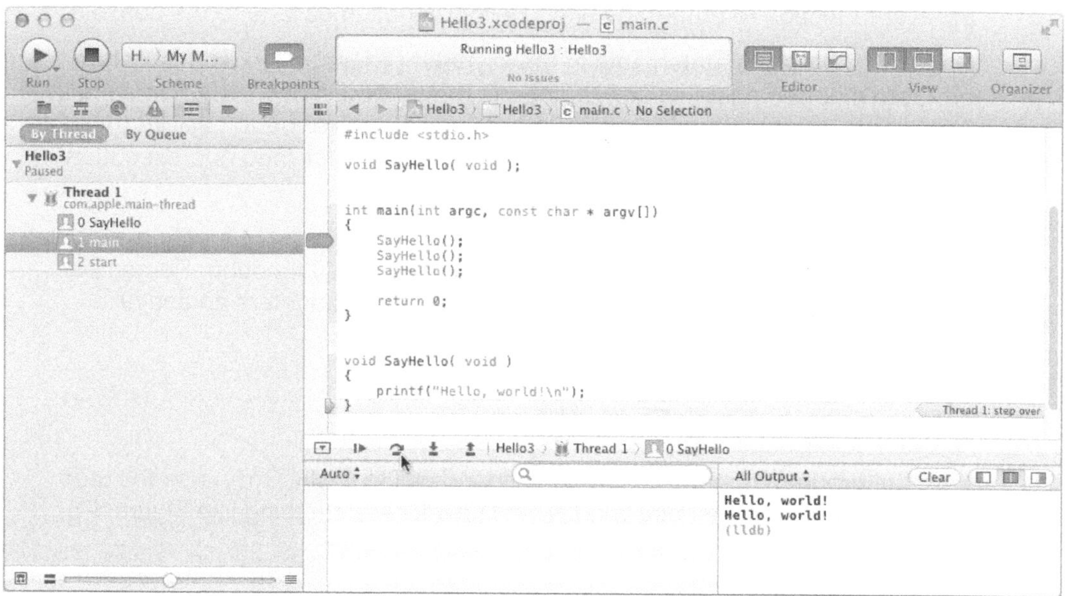

Figure 5-7. *Stepping over the `printf()` statement*

Although there's only one statement in `SayHello()`, this same technique will work with more complex functions. If you want all of the statements in a function to execute without interruption, use the Step Over button. If you want to dig into the details of a function and step through each of its statements individually, use the Step Into button.

> **NOTE:** The Step Into button only applies to statements that call another function. A simple assignment statement, such as `myInt = 3`, does not call any functions. If you try to "step into" this statement, the debugger will execute the assignment statement and stop again, just as if you had pressed the Step Over button instead.

Take a look at the left side of the workspace window, also shown in Figure 5-7. When the debugger took control of your program, it also conveniently switched your project navigator view to show the *debug navigator*. The debug navigator displays the thread(s) and stack(s) in your program. (Every thread has its own stack.) This is a really simple program, so you only have one thread and stack.

The stack, so called because it works like a stack of plates or cards, records the history of the functions that lead it to this point in your program. Each time a function is called, it gets placed on top of the stack. When the called function calls another function, that new function is added to the top of the stack. As functions exit, they are removed from the stack. Think of this as a trail of breadcrumbs that helps the CPU keep track of the sequence of function calls.

Take a look at the debug navigator on the left side of Figure 5-7. Reading the stack from the bottom up, you see there are three functions: `start`, `main`, and `SayHello`. `start()` is the function that started your program. Its job is to call `main()`, where the code you wrote begins. Your `main()` function called `SayHello()`, and that's where you are now. If `SayHello()` called another function, that function would be "pushed" onto the top of the stack and would appear above `SayHello`.

When `SayHello()` finishes, it "pops" off of the stack and control is returned to the calling function—in this case, back to `main()`.

If you continue to press the Step Over button, the `SayHello()` function will finish and you'll end up back in `main()`. When this happens, `SayHello` disappears from the stack.

> **TIP:** The stack records not only which functions called the function you are in now, but also the exact location where it was called from. It can also contain variables, and we'll talk about that later in the book.
>
> In the *Hello3* project, the stack shows that `start()` called `main()`, which called `SayHello()`. But which of the three calls to `SayHello()` are you in? You can determine this by clicking on the name of the calling function in the debug navigator pane. When you click on a function name in the stack, the debugger will move the PC indicator to show you the exact location where the call was made. In this case, if you click on `main` in the stack, the source code for `main()` will display in the editing pane and the green program counter arrow will point to the second `SayHello()` call.
>
> Changing the PC indicator doesn't change where the program is executing, only the debugger's display. Click back on the topmost function in the stack to return to where the program is currently stopped.

Imagine that `SayHello()` contained more than one statement. Imagine that it contained hundreds of statements! Having to click the Step Over button a hundred times to get back to `main()` makes our mouse finger hurt just to think about it. This brings us to the third debugger button, Step Out.

Stepping Out of a Function

The Step Out button is the complement to the Step Into button. The Step Out button tells the debugger to "let the program execute the rest of the statements in this function, return to the statement that called this function, and stop."

In this project, if you step into `SayHello()` and then press the Step Out button, the rest of `SayHello()` will execute and you'll find yourself back in `main()` again, immediately after the call to `SayHello()`. This is fun, isn't it?

STEPPING OUT OF C

So what will happen if you keep stepping, right past the end of `main()`? An advanced question, young Padawan! Here's the scoop.

If you keep pressing the Step Over button or click the Step Out button while in `main()`, you'll eventually see a screen similar to that shown in Figure 5-8.

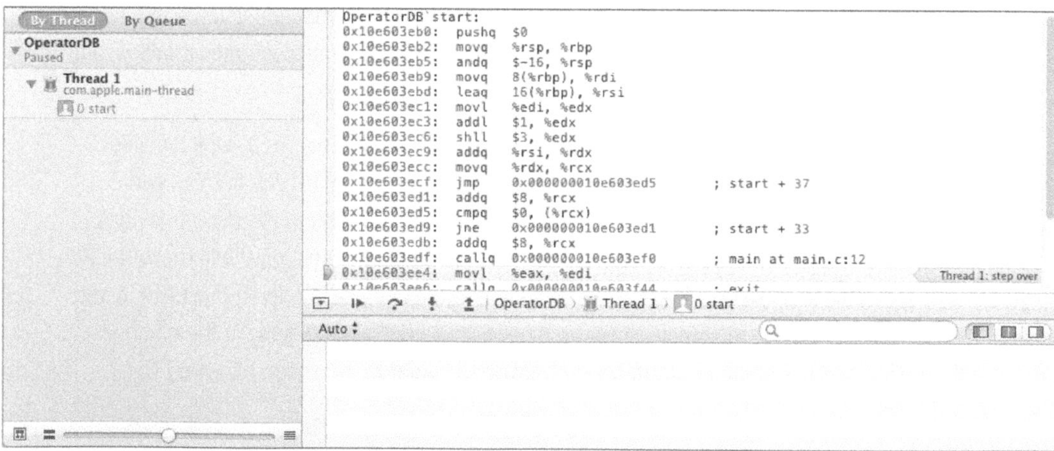

Figure 5-8. *Stepping into machine code*

Whoa! What happened? This doesn't look like C source code!

What you are looking at is disassembled machine code. As mentioned earlier in the book, C is a computer language that gets translated into machine code by a compiler. The machine code is what the CPU actually executes. Machine code is a string of numbers that makes sense to a CPU but is unreadable to most humans.

When you stepped out of `main()` you stepped into machine code that was compiled by Apple, the BSD Unix engineers, or possibly the compiler. Neither you nor Xcode has the source code for this machine code, so Xcode shows you the raw machine code instead. Xcode takes that machine code and *disassembles* it into a form that is a bit more readable than simple numbers, though clearly not as readable as C source code. Believe it or not, there are computer engineers who can read that disassembly.

Interestingly, since your source code does get translated into this same machine code, you can see your pretty C in this form if you like. Stop at a breakpoint in your program and check the **Product ➤ Debug Workflow ➤ Show Disassembly While Debugging** menu item. When you are done admiring the view, uncheck the same item to go back to C.

Full Speed Ahead

There are a couple more debugging commands of interest. The Continue button (see Figure 5-4) starts your program running again. It won't stop again until it encounters another breakpoint. It's useful for when you only want to stop at breakpoints that you've set, instead of stepping through code one line at a time. In this style of debugging, you set whatever breakpoints you want and click the Continue button, letting the program run at full speed until it hits another breakpoint.

Take the example shown in Figure 5-9, where a breakpoint has been set inside the `SayHello()` function. In this situation, the program will begin running `main()` and then stop when it encounters the `printf()` statement. If you press the Continue button, it might not appear that anything happens at all (except that a "Hello, World!" message will have appeared in the console) because the program counter didn't move. What happened was this: the rest of the `SayHello()` function executed; control returned to `main()`, which made a second call to `SayHello();` the program entered `SayHello()` for the second time; and the debugger ran into the same breakpoint again and stopped.

> **TIP:** Whenever you're running a program under Xcode's control the Stop button in the toolbar becomes active. Clicking the Stop button will completely stop (also called "abort," "terminate," "force quit" or "kill") your program. Try to run your program again while it's still running, and Xcode will politely ask if it can stop the one that's running before starting it again.

Now, let's say that you've set some breakpoints, made changes to your program, and just want to let the code run freely. But when you press the *Run* button in Xcode, the debugger dutifully stops your program at the first breakpoint.

You could remove all of the breakpoints in your program, but that seems tedious. You have two choices, one surgical and one sweeping.

First, you can disable any individual breakpoint by clicking on the breakpoint once, as shown in Figure 5-9.

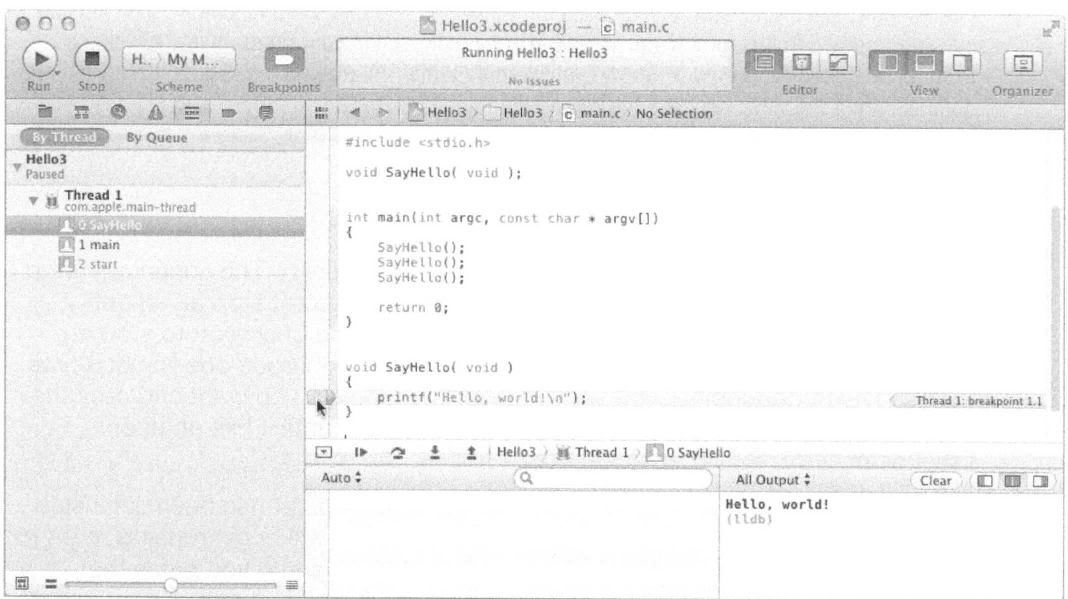

Figure 5-9. *A disabled breakpoint*

A disabled breakpoint appears lighter in color. Xcode remembers that you have a breakpoint here, but the debugger will ignore it.

Your second choice is to deactivate all breakpoints using the ***Product* ➤ *Debug* ➤ *Deactivate Breakpoints*** command. All of your breakpoints will turn grey. This command tells the debugger to "ignore all breakpoints, whether they are disabled or not." It's an obtuse way of telling the debugger to just step aside and let your program run on its own. To go back to debugging, choose the **Activate Breakpoints** command.

Take a breath. You've learned a lot about the debugger, how to control the execution of your program, step over statements, and step into and out of functions. But it doesn't do much good to step through each statement in your program if you can't see what's happening internally, does it? That's what you're going to learn next.

Examining Variables

The debugger can also examine the values in variables, which (as you'll see) is incredibly useful. Close up any open projects, find the *05.01 - OperatorsDB* project folder, and open up `OperatorsDB.xcodeproj`. It should look like the workspace window in Figure 5-10.

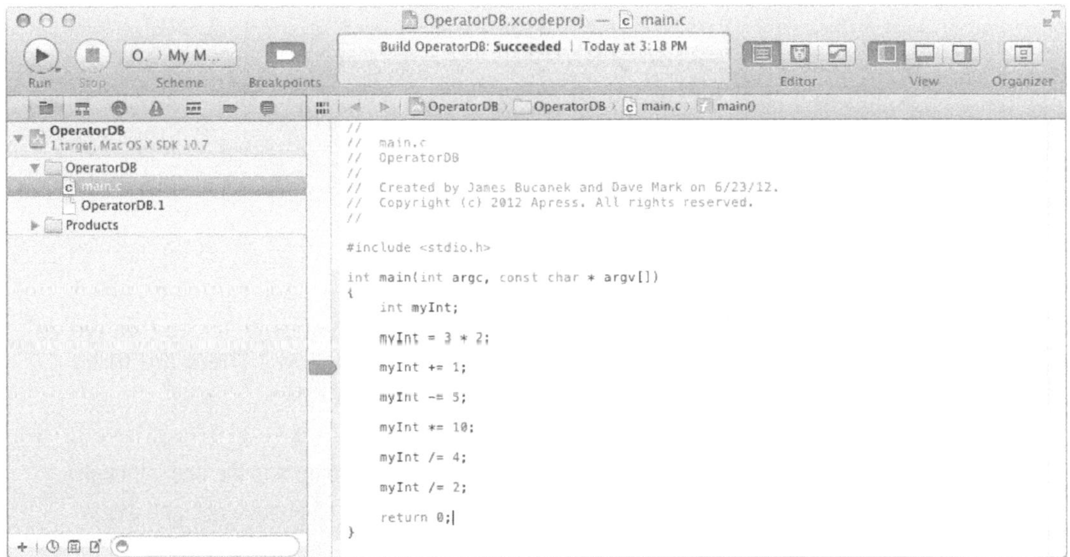

Figure 5-10. OperatorsDB *project workspace*

You'll notice that this is identical to the *Operators* project you worked on in the last chapter, but all of the `printf()` statements have been removed. Armed with the debugger, you don't need them anymore.

Set a breakpoint at the second assignment statement, as shown in Figure 5-10, and run the program. Xcode will compile and run your program, and the debugger will stop it at the breakpoint, as shown in Figure 5-11.

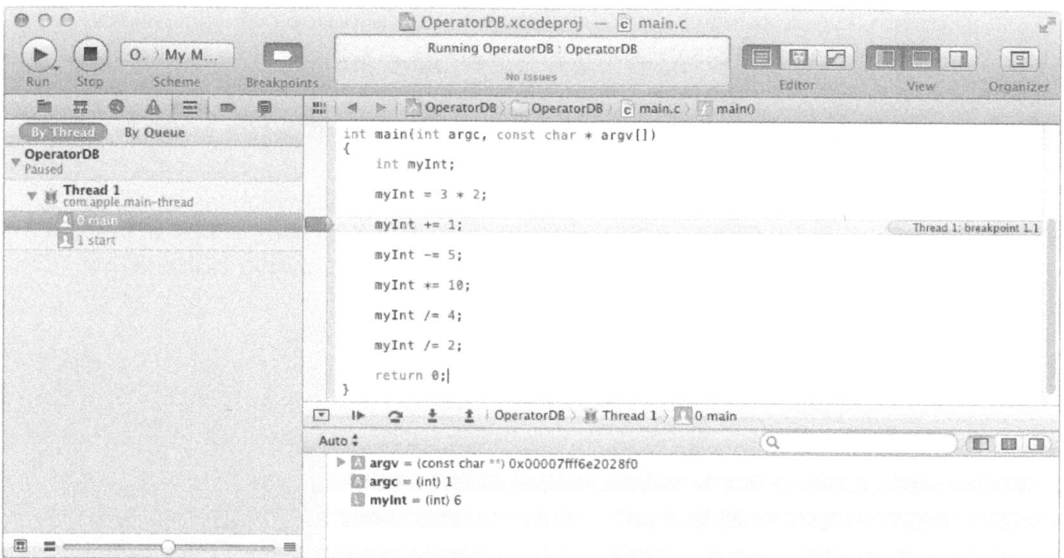

Figure 5-11. *OperatorsDB stopped at breakpoint*

Look at the debug area the bottom of the workspace window. (Note that we've closed the console and are just showing the variables view.) There are three variables listed in the variable view, `argv`, `argc`, and `myInt`.

> **NOTE:** The variables `argv` and `argc` are part of every C program in the book, though not something you need to worry about here. We'll tell you all about `argc` and `argv` in Chapter 9.

The listing for `myInt` says `myInt = (int)6`, telling you that the `myInt` variable holds an integer value of 6. This is correct because you stopped the program *after* the first assignment statement executed (the one setting its value to `2 * 3`) and just *before* the second assignment statement was to execute (the one that would add 1 to it). Remember that the PC indicator (the green arrow) always points to the line of code that is about to execute, not the one that has finished executing.

You can also discover the value of a variable simply by pointing to it with the mouse. Hover the cursor over any `myInt` symbol in this function and its value will pop up, as shown in Figure 5-12.

Figure 5-12. *Variable inspector pop-up*

From the last section, you know all about controlling the execution of your program. It's time to put that knowledge to use. Click the Step Over button to execute the next line of source code (see Figure 5-13).

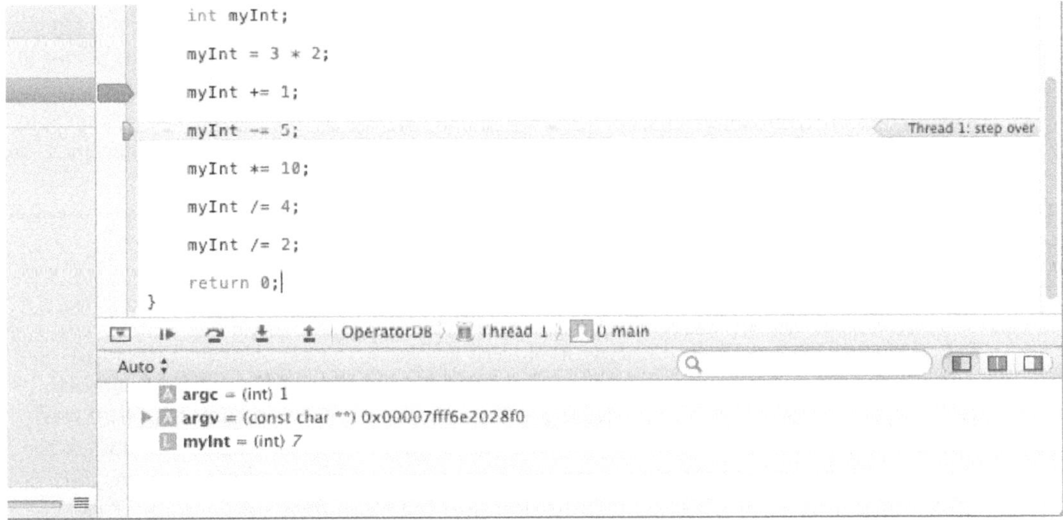

Figure 5-13. `myInt` *after executing second assignment statement*

The line of code executes, the value of 1 was added to the `myInt` variable, and the new value of `myInt` appears in the debug area.

We're sure you have the basic idea by now. Continue to press the Step Over button and watch how the `myInt` variable changes after each statement. Pretty nifty, isn't it?

> **TIP:** Don't forget that each of the debugger control buttons has a menu command with a keyboard shortcut that does the same thing. If you find yourself stepping over a lot of code, check out the commands in the ***Product* ➤ *Debug*** menu and learn the keyboard shortcuts.

IN DEFENSE OF PRINTF()

You might be thinking that, now that you know about this amazing debugger thing, you'll never have to write another `printf()` statement again—at least not for the purposes of finding out what your program is doing. That's probably not true. While it's possible to use the debugger for almost all of your debugging needs, sometimes a simple `printf()` statement is just what the doctor ordered, and we'll continue to use them in this book.

One of the downsides to being able stop your program and examine it in detail is that, well, your program stops. Let's say you're developing a game where you try to save innocent zombies from being skewered by evil pink unicorns. But something goes wrong when you try to rescue a zombie with your Apache attack helicopter. You could set a breakpoint at that point in the code, but it will be really awkward—even impossible—to duplicate the problem if your game comes to a screeching halt just as begin your maneuver. Using `printf()` (or any number of similar logging functions, and there are a few), you can output the state of your zombie and helicopter to the console and the program will keep running. You can make a few attempts at saving your zombie and then stop to examine the console log.

How is a Debugger like an Iceberg?

We hope you appreciate the power of setting breakpoints, stepping through your code, and examining variable, but don't for an instant think that's all the debugger can do. The Xcode debugger is a really, really, complex tool that has hundreds of functions, commands, and features. In addition, Xcode includes a suite of additional programming analysis tools called Instruments. Taken altogether, there's probably no programming problem they can't track down.

Don't feel bad if you haven't learned everything about the debugger in one day, or a week, or several years. Seriously, you'll probably be learning debugger tricks for the rest of your programming life.

What's Next?

You can now hang "debugger" on you programming utility belt. And it's going to be handy because in the next chapter you're going to learn how to control your program's flow.

CHAPTER 5 EXERCISE

Open the *Hello3* project. Set a breakpoint before the second call to `SayHello()` function in `main()`. Set a second breakpoint before the `printf()` statement in the `SayHello()` function. Run the program. Repeatedly press the Continue button until the program ends.

1. What was the total number of times the debugger stopped the program?
2. How many times did the debugger stop before the `printf()` statement?
3. Can you explain why?

Chapter 6

Controlling Your Program's Flow

So far, you've learned quite a bit about the C language. You know about functions (especially one named `main()`), which are made up of statements, each of which is terminated by a semicolon. You know about variables, which have a name and a type. Up to this point, you've dealt with variables of type `int`.

You also know about operators, such as =, +, and +=. You've learned about postfix and prefix notation and the importance of writing clear, easy-to-understand code. You've learned about the Standard Library, a set of functions that comes as standard equipment with every C programming environment. You've also learned about `printf()`, an invaluable component of the Standard Library, and how to use the debugger to control execution and examine variables.

Finally, you've learned a few housekeeping techniques to keep your code fresh, sparkling, and readable. Comment your code, because your memory isn't perfect, and insert some white space to keep your code from getting too cramped.

Next up on the panel? Learning how to control your program's flow.

Flow Control

The programs you've written so far have all consisted of a straightforward series of statements, one right after the other. Every statement is executed in the order it occurred. Flow control is the ability to control the order in which your program's statements are executed. The C language provides several keywords you can use in your program to control your program's flow. One of these is the `if` keyword.

The if Statement

The `if` keyword allows your program to make a decision, choosing from one of two courses of action. In English, you might say something like this:

If it's raining outside, I'll bring my umbrella; otherwise I won't.

In this sentence, you're using `if` to choose between two options. Depending on the weather, you'll do one of two things: you'll bring your umbrella, or you won't bring your umbrella. C's `if` statement gives you this same flexibility. Here's an example:

```
#include <stdio.h>
int main (int argc, const char * argv[])
{
    int myInt;
    myInt = 5;
    if ( myInt == 0 )
        printf( "myInt is equal to zero" );
    else
        printf( "myInt is not equal to zero" );
    return 0;
}
```

This program declares `myInt` to be of type `int` and sets the value of `myInt` to 5. Next, the `if` statement tests whether `myInt` is equal to 0. If `myInt` is equal to 0 (which you know is not true), it'll print one string. Otherwise, it'll print a different string. As expected, this program prints the string "myInt is not equal to zero."

`if` statements come in two flavors. The first, known as plain old `if`, fits this pattern:

```
if ( expression )
    statement
```

An `if` statement will always consist of the word "if," a left parenthesis, an expression, a right parenthesis, and a statement (we'll define both "expression" and "statement" in a minute). This first form of `if` executes the statement if the expression in parentheses is true. An English example of the plain if might be

If it's raining outside, I'll bring my umbrella.

Notice that this statement only tells you what will happen if it's raining outside. No particular action will be taken if it is not raining.

The second form of `if`, known as `if-else`, fits this pattern:

```
if ( expression )
    statement
else
    statement
```

An `if-else` statement will always consist of the word "if," a left parenthesis, an expression, a right parenthesis, a statement, the word "else," and a second statement. This form of `if` executes the first statement if the expression is true and executes the second statement if the expression is false. An English example of an `if-else` statement might be

> *If it's raining outside, I'll bring my umbrella, otherwise I'll wear a hat.*

Notice that this example tells you what will happen if it is raining outside (I'll bring my umbrella) and if it isn't raining outside (I'll wear a hat). The example programs presented later in the chapter demonstrate the proper use of both `if` and `if-else`.

The next step is to define the terms "expression" and "statement."

Expressions

In C, an *expression* is anything that has a value. For example, a variable is a type of expression, since variables always have a value. Even uninitialized variables have a value—you just don't know what the value is! The following are all examples of expressions:

```
myInt
myInt + 3
( myInt + anotherInt ) * 4
myInt++
```

An assignment statement is also an expression. Can you guess the value of an assignment statement? Think back to Chapter 4. Remember when you included an assignment statement as a parameter to `printf()`? The value of an assignment statement is the value that gets assigned to the left side. Check out the following code fragment:

```
myInt = 5
myInt += 3
```

Both of these statements qualify as expressions. The value of the first expression is 5. The value of the second expression is 8 (because you added three to `myInt`'s previous value).

Here's similar code, stitched together into a single statement:

```
myOtherInt = ( myInt = 5 ) + 3;
```

The first expression (`myInt = 5`) is performed, which assigns the value of 5. The computer then evaluates the rest of the express (`(5)+3`), calculates the number 8, and assigns it to the `myOtherInt` variable.

> **TIP:** It's usually considered poor programming form to include assignment statements inside expressions because it's so easy to misread the intent of the code. This feature of C is really handy in those rare cases where you need it, but if there's a more obvious way to write your code, try to avoid this construct.

Literals can also be used as expressions. The number "8" has a value. Guess what? Its value is 8. All expressions, no matter what their type, have a numerical value.

> **NOTE:** Technically, there is an exception to the rule that all expressions have a numerical value. The C language has a special variable type, `void`, that literally means "nothing." Any value, variable, or function that is (or is cast to) the `void` type has no value. It can't be used in, or as, an expression. Now if you're asking, "what's a cast?" or "what is type `void`?" we'll get to both of these topics later in this book. For the moment, when you see `void`, think "no value."

True Expressions

Earlier, we defined the `if` statement as follows:

```
if ( expression )
    statement
```

We then said the statement gets executed if the expression is true. Let's look at C's concept of truth.

Everyone has an intuitive understanding of the difference between true and false. We can all agree that the statement

5 equals 3

is false. We can also agree that the following statement is true:

5 and 3 are both greater than 0

This intuitive grasp of true and false carries over into the C language. In the case of C, however, both true and false have numerical values. Here's how it works.

In C, any expression that has a value of 0 is said to be false. Any expression with a value other than 0 is said to be true. As stated earlier, an `if` statement's statement gets executed if its expression is true. To put this more accurately, an `if` statement's statement gets executed if (and only if) its expression has a value other than 0.

Here's an example:

```
myInt = 27;
if ( myInt )
    printf( "myInt is not equal to 0" );
```

The `if` statement in this piece of code first tests the value of `myInt`. Since `myInt` is not equal to 0, the `printf()` gets executed.

Comparative Operators

C's comparative operators let your program compare two numbers. Comparative operators compare their left side with their right side and produce a value of either 1 (true) or 0 (false), depending on the relationship of the two sides.

For example, the operator `==` determines whether the expression on the left is equal in value to the expression on the right. The expression

```
myInt == 5
```

evaluates to 1 if `myInt` is equal to 5 and to 0 if `myInt` is not equal to 5.

Here's an example of the == operator at work:

```
if ( myInt == 5 )
    printf( "myInt is equal to 5" );
```

If `myInt` is equal to 5, the expression `myInt == 5` evaluates to 1, and `printf()` gets called. If `myInt` isn't equal to 5, the expression evaluates to 0, and the `printf()` is skipped. Just remember, the key to triggering an `if` statement is an expression that resolves to a value other than 0.

Table 6-1 shows some of the other comparative operators. You'll see some of these operators in the example programs later in the chapter.

Table 6-1. *Comparative Operators*

Operator	Resolves to 1 if . . .
==	Left side is equal to right
!=	Left side is not equal to right
<	Left side is less than right
>	Left side is greater than right
<=	Left side is less than or equal to right
>=	Left side is greater than or equal to right

Logical Operators

The C standard provides a pair of constants that really come in handy when dealing with the next set of operators. The constant `true` has a value of 1, while the constant `false` has a value of 0. Both of these constants are defined in the include file *<stdbool.h>*. You can use these constants in your programs to make them a little easier to read. Read on, and you'll see why.

> **NOTE:** In addition to `true` and `false`, most C environments also provide the constants `TRUE` and `FALSE` (with values of 1 and 0 respectively). Before the C99 standard, the C language didn't have a Boolean variable type, so programmers created these ad hoc constants. If you're writing modern C code, use `bool`, `true`, and `false`. If you see `TRUE` and `FALSE` in other people's code, just know it means the same thing.

The members of the next set of operators are known, collectively, as logical operators. The set of logical operators is modeled on the mathematical concept of truth tables. If you don't know much about truth tables (or are just frightened by mathematics in general), don't panic. Everything you need to know is outlined in the next few paragraphs.

NOTE: Truth tables are part of a branch of mathematics known as *Boolean algebra*, named for George Boole, the man who developed it in the late 1830s. The term "Boolean" has come to mean a variable that can take one of two values. Bits are Boolean; they can take on the value 0 or 1.

The Not Operator

The first of the set of logical operators is the ! operator, which is commonly referred to as the *not* operator. For example, `!A` is pronounced "not A."

The ! operator turns true into false and false into true. Table 6-2 shows the truth table for the ! operator. In this table, T stands for true, which has the value 1, and F stands for false, which has the value 0. The letter "A" in the table represents an expression. If the expression A is true, applying the ! operator to A yields the value false. If the expression A is false, applying the ! operator to A yields the value true.

Table 6-2. *Truth Table for the ! Operator*

A	!A
T	F
F	T

Here's a piece of code that demonstrates the ! operator:

```
bool myFirstBool, mySecondBool;
myFirstBool = false;
mySecondBool = ! myFirstBool;
```

The first thing you'll notice about this chunk of code is the new data type, `bool`. A `bool` can hold either a 0 or a 1. That's it. Note that `bool`s are perfect for working with logical operators. This example starts by declaring two `bool`s. You assign the value false to the first `bool`, and then use the ! operator to turn the `false` into a `true` and assign it to the second `bool`.

Take another look at Table 6-2. The ! operator converts `true` into `false` and `false` into `true`. What this really means is that ! converts 0 to 1 and any non-zero value to 0, which comes in handy when you are working with an `if` statement's expression, like this one:

```
if ( mySecondBool )
    printf( "mySecondBool must be true" );
```

The previous chunk of code translated `mySecondBool` from `false` to `true`, which is the same thing as saying that `mySecondBool` has a value of 1. Either way, `mySecondBool` will cause the `if` to fire, and the `printf()` will get executed.

Take a look at this piece of code:

```
if ( ! mySecondBool )
    printf( "mySecondBool must be false" );
```

This `printf()` will get executed if `mySecondInt` is `false`. Do you see why? If `mySecondBool` is `false`, then `!mySecondInt` must be `true`.

The And and Or Operators

The ! operator is a unary operator. Unary operators operate on a single expression. The other two logical operators, && and ||, are binary operators. Binary operators, such as the == operator presented earlier, operate on two expressions, one on the left side and one on the right side of the operator.

The && operator is commonly referred to as the logical *and* operator. The result of an && operation is true if, and only if, both the left side and the right side are true. Here's an example:

```
bool hasCar, hasTimeToGiveRide;
hasCar = true;
hasTimeToGiveRide = true;
if ( hasCar && hasTimeToGiveRide )
    printf( "Hop in - I'll give you a ride!\n" );
else
    printf( "I have no car, no time, or no car and no time!\n" );
```

This example uses two variables. One indicates whether the program has a car, the other whether the program has time to give you a ride to the mall. All philosophical issues aside (can a program have a car?), the question of the moment is, which of the two `printf()`'s will fire? Since both sides of the && are true, the first `printf()` will be called. If either one (or both) of the expressions were false, the second `printf()` would be called. Another way to think of this is that you'll only get a ride to the mall if your friendly program has a car *and* has time to give you a ride. If either of these is not true, you're not getting a ride. By the way, notice the use here of the second form of `if`, the `if-else` statement.

The || operator is commonly referred to as the logical *or* operator. The result of an || operation is true if the left side, the right side, or both sides of the || are true. Put another way, the result of an || is false if, and only if, both the left side and the right side of the || are false. Here's an example:

```
bool nothingElseOn, newEpisode;
nothingElseOn = true;
newEpisode = true;
if ( newEpisode || nothingElseOn )
    printf( "Let's watch Family Guy!\n" );
else
    printf( "Something else is on or I've seen this one.\n" );
```

This example uses two variables to decide whether or not you should watch Family Guy. One variable indicates whether anything else is on right now, and the other tells you whether this episode is a rerun. If this is a brand-new episode or if nothing else is on, you'll watch Family Guy.

Here's a slight twist on the previous example:

```
int nothingElseOn, itsARerun;
nothingElseOn = true;
itsARerun = false;
if ( (! itsARerun) || nothingElseOn )
    printf( "Let's watch Family Guy!\n" );
else
    printf( "Something else is on or I've seen this one.\n" );
```

This time, the variable `newEpisode` has been replaced with its exact opposite, `itsARerun`. Look at the logic that drives the `if` statement. Now you're combining `itsARerun` with the ! operator. Before, you cared whether the episode was a `newEpisode`. This time, you are concerned that the episode is not a rerun. See the difference?

Both the && and the || operators are summarized in the table in Table 6-3. Note that `A&&B` is only true if A and B are both true. `A||B` is true if A, B, or both are true.

Table 6-3. *Truth Table for the && and || Operators*

A	B	A && B	A || B
T	T	T	T
T	F	F	T
F	T	F	T
F	F	F	F

> **NOTE:** On most keyboards, you type an & (ampersand) character by holding down the Shift key and typing a 7. You type a | character by holding down the Shift key and typing a \ (backslash). Don't confuse the | with the letters L or I, or with the ! character.

TruthTester.xcodeproj

If you look in the folder *Learn C Projects*, you'll find a subfolder named *06.01 - TruthTester* that contains a project that implements the three examples just mentioned. Open the project *TruthTester.xcodeproj*. Take a look at the source code in *main.c*. Play with the code. Take turns changing the variables from true to false and back again. Use this code to get a good feel for the !, &&, and || operators.

You might also try commenting out the line `#include <stdbool.h>` toward the top of the file. To do this, just insert the characters // at the very beginning of the line. You'll quickly see a number of errors complaining that `bool`, `true`, and `false` are undeclared. Remember this! As you write your own programs, be sure to `#include <stdbool.h>` if you want to use `bool`, `true`, and `false`.

Compound Expressions

All of the examples presented so far have consisted of relatively simple expressions. Here's an example that combines several different operators:

```
int myInt;
myInt = 7;
if ( (myInt >= 1) && (myInt <= 10) )
    printf ( "myInt is between 1 and 10" );
else
    printf ("myInt is not between 1 and 10" );
```

This example tests whether a variable is in the range between 1 and 10. The key here is the expression that lies between the `if` statement's parentheses:

```
(myInt >= 1) && (myInt <= 10)
```

This expression uses the && operator to combine two smaller expressions. Notice that the two smaller expressions were each surrounded by parentheses to avoid any ambiguity. If you leave out the parentheses, like

```
myInt >= 1 && myInt <= 10
```

the expression is exactly the same; refer to the Operator Precedence section in Chapter 3. Once again, you use parentheses just to clarify exactly what you mean.

Statements

At the beginning of the chapter, we defined the if statement as follows:

```
if ( expression )
    statement
```

We've covered expressions pretty thoroughly. Now, let's look at the statement. At this point in this book, you probably have a pretty intuitive model of the statement. You'd probably agree that

```
myInt = 7;
```

is a statement. But is the following one statement or two?

```
if ( isCold )
    printf( "Put on your sweater!" );
```

Actually, this code fragment is a statement within another statement: printf() is one statement residing within a larger statement, the if statement.

The ability to break your code out into individual statements is not a critical skill. Getting your code to compile, however, is critical. As new types of statements are introduced (like the if and if-else introduced in this chapter), pay attention to the statement syntax. And pay special attention to the examples. Where do the semicolons go? What distinguishes this type of statement from all other types?

As you build up your repertoire of statement types, you'll find yourself using one type of statement within another. That's perfectly acceptable in C. In fact, every time you create an if statement, you'll use at least two statements, one within the other. Take a look at this example:

```
if ( myVar >= 1 )
    if ( myVar <= 10 )
        printf( "myVar is between 1 and 10" );
```

This example used an if statement as the statement for another if statement. This example calls the printf() if both if expressions are true; that is, if myVar is greater than or equal to 1 and less than or equal to 10.

You could have accomplished the same result with this piece of code:

```
if ( ( myVar >= 1 ) && ( myVar <= 10 ) )
    printf( "myVar is between 1 and 10" );
```

This piece of code is a little easier to read.

There are times, however, when the method demonstrated in the first piece of code is preferred. Take a look at this example:

```
if ( myVar != 0 )
    if ( ( 1 / myVar ) < 1 )
        printf( "myVar is in range" );
```

One thing you don't want to do in C is divide a number by zero. Any number divided by zero is infinity, which can't be represented as an integer, no matter how many bits your integer has. Consequently, most computers will simply terminate a program that attempts to divide an integer by 0. It will typically report an "arithmetic exception" and your program will simply stop. The first expression in this example tests to make sure `myVar` is not equal to zero. If `myVar` is equal to zero, the second expression won't even be evaluated! The sole purpose of the first `if` is to make sure the second `if` never tries to divide by zero. Make sure you understand this point.

What would happen if you wrote the code this way:

```
if ( (myVar != 0) && ((1 / myVar) < 1) )
    printf( "myVar is in range" );
```

As it turns out, exactly the same thing. (Don't feel bad if you guessed some other result.) If the left half of the && operator evaluates to false, the right half of the expression will *never be evaluated* and the entire expression will evaluate to false. Why? Because if the left operand is false, it doesn't matter what the right operand is—true or false—the expression will evaluate to false. Be aware of this as you construct your expressions.

> **NOTE:** The approach of not evaluating the remainder of an expression if the evaluation of the first portion of the expression determines the value of the expression is known as *short circuit evaluation* or *minimal evaluation*.

The Curly Braces

Earlier in this book, you learned about the curly braces ({}) that surround the body of every function. These braces also play an important role in statement construction. Just as parentheses can be used to group terms of an expression together, curly braces can be used to group multiple statements together. Here's an example:

```
onYourBack = true;
if ( onYourBack ) {
    printf( "Flipping over" );
    onYourBack = false;
}
```

In this example, if `onYourBack` is true, both of the statements in curly braces will be executed. A pair of curly braces can be used to combine any number of statements into a single super-statement, also known as a *block*. You can use this technique anywhere a statement is called for. In other words, anywhere C will allow a single statement, you can replace that with a block containing any number of statements.

Curly braces can be used to organize your code, much as you'd use parentheses to ensure that an expression is evaluated properly. This concept is especially appropriate when dealing with nested statements. Consider this code:

```
if ( myInt >= 0 )
    if ( myInt <= 10 )
        printf("myInt is between 0 and 10.\n" );
else
    printf("myInt is negative.\n" ); // <-- Error!!!
```

Do you see the problem with this code? Again, don't feel bad if you don't. The mistake is pretty subtle. The problem is this: which `if` does the `else` belong to? As written (and as formatted), the `else` looks like it belongs to the first `if`. That is, if `myInt` is greater than or equal to 0, the second `if` is executed; otherwise, the second `printf()` is executed. Is this right?

Nope. As it turns out, an `else` belongs to the `if` closest to it (the second `if`, in this case). Here's a slight rewrite to show you how the compiler interprets the code:

```
if ( myInt >= 0 )
    if ( myInt <= 10 )
        printf("myInt is between 0 and 10.\n" );
    else
        printf("myInt is not between 0 and 10.\n" );
```

One point here is that formatting is nice, but it won't fool the compiler. More importantly, this example shows how easy it is to make a mistake. Check out this version of the code:

```
if ( myInt >= 0 ) {
    if ( myInt <= 10 )
        printf( "myInt is between 0 and 10.\n" );
} else {
    printf( "myInt is negative.\n" );
```

```
}
```

Do you see how the curly braces help? In a sense, they act to hide the second `if` inside the first `if` statement. There is no chance for the `else` to connect to the hidden `if`.

No one we know ever got fired for using too many parentheses or too many curly braces.

Where to Place the Semicolon

So far, the statements you've seen fall into two categories: *simple statements* and *compound statements*. Function calls, such as calls to `printf()`, and assignment statements are called simple statements. Always place a semicolon at the end of a simple statement, even if it is broken over several lines, like this:

```
printf( "%d%d%d%d",
        var1, var2, var3, var4 );
```

Statements made up of several parts, including (possibly) other statements, are called compound statements. Compound statements obey some pretty strict rules of syntax. The `if` statement, for example, always looks like this:

```
if ( expression )
    statement
```

Notice that there are no semicolons in this definition. The statement part of the `if` can be a simple statement, a block, or another compound statement. If the statement is simple, follow the semicolon rule for simple statements and place a semicolon at the end of the statement. If the statement is a block, it will be two braces ({}) with other statements between them. If the statement is compound, repeat these rules.

Remember that using curly braces, or curlies, to build a block out of smaller statements does not require the addition of a semicolon; a simple statement ends with a semicolon, while a block begins and ends with curly braces.

Two Common Pitfalls

While we're on the subjects of where to place semicolons and using assignment operators as values, here are a couple of common C programming mistakes and how to avoid them.

The Loneliest Statement

We've talked about how much you can cram into a statement, but how little can you put in a statement? Guess what? A single semicolon qualifies as a statement, albeit a somewhat lonely one. For example, this code fragment

```
if ( isDark )
    ;
```

is a legitimate (and thoroughly useless) `if` statement. If `isDark` is true, the semicolon statement gets executed. The semicolon by itself doesn't do anything but fill the bill where a statement is needed.

Now look at this code:

```
if ( isDark );
```

This looks like a perfectly respectable C statement. (Hey, it ends in a semicolon!) Remember that C is a free-form language and doesn't care about indenting or whitespace. The problem is that this statement also does absolutely nothing, and this really becomes a problem when you then write this classic gem:

```
if ( isDark );
    TurnOnLights();
```

The problem, as you might have guessed, is that the statement `TurnOnLights()` gets performed whether the `isDark` variable is true or false. Now there are times where the semicolon by itself is exactly what you need, but after an `if` statement isn't one of them.

Unintentional Assignment

Earlier we talked about using the value of an assignment operator (=) as an expression. Sometime these appear when we don't intend them to, as in this bit of foolishness:

```
i = 3;
if ( i = 5 )
    printf( "Never print this statement" );
```

So what do you think happens when this code executes? If you guessed "the text 'Never print this statement' appears on the console," give yourself a gold star. What happens is this:

1. The value 3 is assigned to the variable `i`.
2. The value 5 is assigned to the variable `i`.

3. The `if` statement evaluates its expression (5) and determined that it is true (not zero).
4. The `printf()` function is executed.

Do you see the mistake now? Instead of using the equals operator (==) in the expression, we used the assignment operator (=) instead. So instead of comparing `i` to 5, the value of `i` was inadvertently set to 5.

Avoiding Common Pitfalls

These are a few more common mistakes that C programmers make—even seasoned ones. So how do you avoid them? Clever programmers have used various tricks over the years. For example, one trick that you'll see often is to place the constant on the left in `if` statements, like this:

```
if ( 5 == i )
    printf( "Never print this statement" );
```

If you accidentally substitute = for ==, the expression will not compile. Remember back in Chapter 4 where you flipped the assignment around so that you were assigning a variable to a constant? You can't do that, and the compiler will tell you that you can't. But this only helps in some circumstances. What if you're comparing two variables?

The folks who develop compilers are a pretty talented bunch, and they haven't been sitting on their hands. A modern C compiler will issue a variety of warnings when it sees something suspicious. Look what happens in Xcode when we try to write an `if` statement with an assignment (see Figure 6-1).

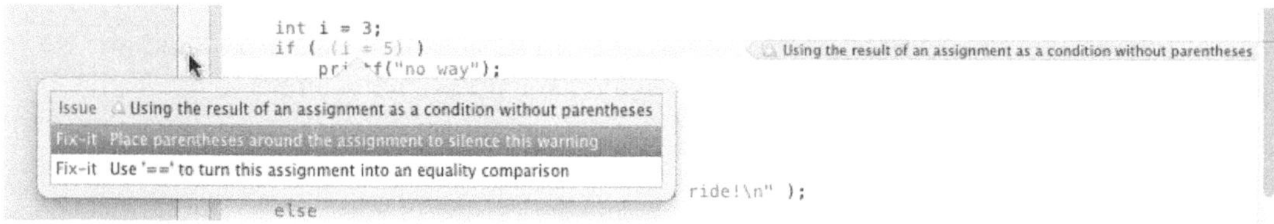

Figure 6-1. *An `if` statement with assignment warning*

The compiler thinks that it's pretty unusual to find an assignment operator as the expression of an `if` statement. It kindly offers to change the assignment (=) into a comparison (==), which is actually what we meant to write. It also offers to wrap the assignment in a gratuitous set of parentheses. This unneeded set of parentheses doesn't change the meaning of the statement, but it is a nod to the compiler that says, "I know this is an assignment expression; please don't complain about it." This is one of those rare situations where using unnecessary parentheses can trip you up.

Let's look at what the compiler has to say about our second faux pas (see Figure 6-2).

```
if ( hasCar && hasTimeToGiveRide );                    If statement has empty body
    printf( "Hop in - I'll give you a ride!\n" );
```

Figure 6-2. *An `if` statement with empty body*

Again, the compiler caught the mistake. The warning in Figure 6-2 says that there's no actionable statement associated with this `if` statement, so the entire `if` statement is useless. It's not a compiler error because, technically, it's valid C syntax. It just doesn't make any sense. You can't brush the compiler off on this one; it knows this is a useless statement. You either need to remove the errant semicolon or remove the `if` statement altogether to make the warning go away.

TURNING ON COMPILER WARNINGS

There are actually scores of suspicious patterns that the compiler will look out for. If you want to enlist the compilers help in pointing them out, you can turn more of these warnings on in the Xcode build settings. Start by selecting the top-level project in the project navigator as shown in Figure 6-3.

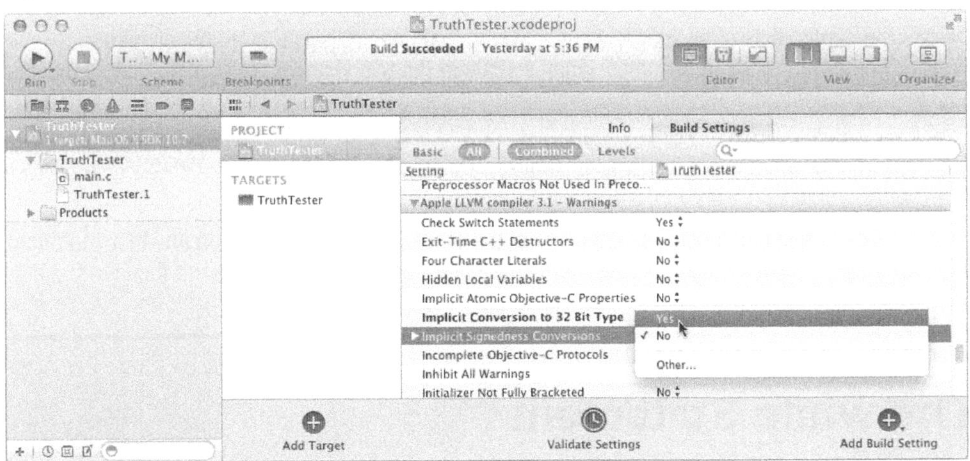

Figure 6-3. *Enabling additional warnings*

The project's settings will appear in the editor pane, also shown in Figure 6-3. Select the project's name under the *Project* heading (on the left side of the editor pane); this will edit the setting for the entire project. Choose the **Build Settings** tab, then choose *All* and *Combined*. Scroll down until you find the compiler warnings section.

In Figure 6-3, we're turning on the ***Implicit Signedness Conversion***. "The what?" you say? OK, some of the warnings can be a bit confusing. To get a better explanation choose ***View ➤ Utilities ➤ Show Quick Help Inspector***, as shown in Figure 6-4.

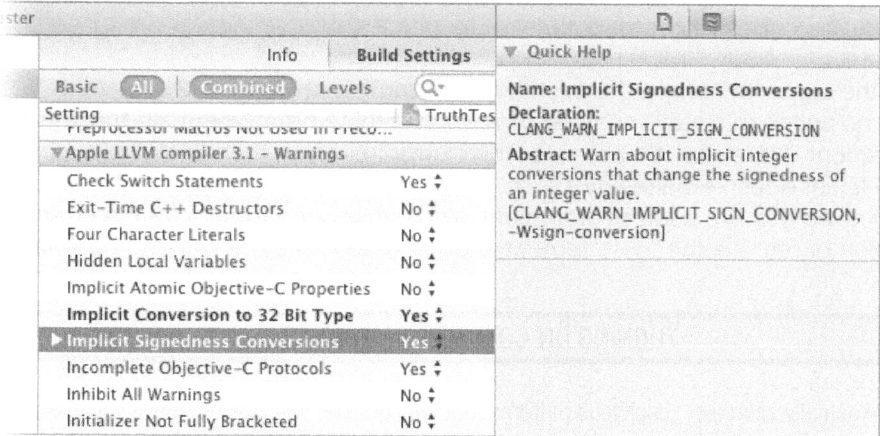

Figure 6-4. *Quick help for compiler warnings*

The help explains that this compiler setting warns "about implicit integer conversions that change the signedness of an integer value." Maybe that doesn't help that much, so let us explain. Remember back in Chapter 3 when we talked the two ways of representing integers, unsigned (simple) and signed (two's compliment)? If you turn on this setting, it will warn you whenever you assign an unsigned integer to a variable that's interpreted as a signed integer, and vice versa. If the value of the number is negative, the assignment will change the interpretation of the value—and that's probably something you don't want.

With the *Quick Help* panel open, select some of the other warnings and turn on any that you think might be helpful. Experienced programmers tend to turn on lots of warnings, and then write their code so it doesn't trip any of those warnings. It's a good habit to adopt.

The while Statement

The `if` statement uses the value of an expression to decide whether to execute or skip over a statement. If the statement is executed, it is executed just once. Another type of statement, the `while` statement, repeatedly executes a statement as long as a specified expression is true. The while statement follows this pattern:

```
while ( expression )
    statement
```

The `while` statement is also known as the `while` loop, because once the statement is executed, the `while` loops back to reevaluate the expression. Here's an example of the `while` loop in action:

```
int     i;
i=0;
while ( ++i < 3 )
    printf( "Looping: %d\n", i );
printf( "We are past the while loop." );
```

This example starts by declaring a variable, `i`, of type int. `i` is then initialized to 0. Next comes the `while` loop. The first thing the `while` loop does is evaluate its expression. The `while` loop's expression is

```
++i < 3
```

Before this expression is evaluated, `i` has a value of 0. The prefix notation used in the expression (++1) increments the value of `i` to 1 before the remainder of the expression is evaluated. The evaluation of the expression results in true, since 1 is less than 3. Since the expression is true, the `while` loop's statement, a single `printf()`, is executed.

Here's the output after the first pass through the loop:

```
Looping: 1
```

Next, the `while` loops back and reevaluates its expression. Once again, the prefix notation increments `i`, this time to a value of 2. Since 2 is less than 3, the expression evaluates to true, and the `printf()` is executed again.

Here's the output after the second pass through the loop:

```
Looping: 1
Looping: 2
```

Once the second `printf()` completes, it's back to the top of the loop to reevaluate the expression. Will this never end? Once again, `i` is incremented, this time to a value of 3. Aha! This time, the expression evaluates to false, since 3 is not less than 3. Once the expression evaluates to false, the `while` loop ends, and control passes to the next statement, the second `printf()` in the example:

```
printf( "We are past the while loop." );
```

The `while` loop was driven by three factors: initialization, modification, and termination. *Initialization* is any code that affects the loop but occurs before the loop is entered. In this example, the critical initialization occurred when the variable `i` was set to 0.

COUNTER VARIABLE NAMING

Frequently, you'll use a variable in a loop that changes value each time through the loop. In this example, the variable `i` was incremented by 1 each time through the loop. The first time through the loop, `i` had a value of 1. The second time, `i` had a value of 2. Variables that maintain a value based on the number of times through a loop are known as counters.

In the interest of clarity, some programmers use names like `counter` or `loopCounter`. The nice thing about names like `i`, `j`, and k is that they don't get in the way, as they don't take up a lot of space on the line. On the other hand, your goal should be to make your code as readable as possible, so it would seem that a name like `counter` would be better than the uninformative `i`, `j`, or k.

One popular compromise holds that the closer a variable's use is to its declaration, the shorter its name can be. Once again, pick a style you are comfortable with, and stick with it!

Modification is any code within the loop that changes the value of the loop's expression. In this example, the modification occurred within the expression itself when the counter, `i`, was incremented.

Termination is any condition that causes the loop to terminate. In this example, termination occurs when the expression has a value of false. This occurs when the counter, `i`, has a value that is not less than 3.

Take a look at this example:

```
int i;
i = 1;
while ( i < 3 ) {
    printf( "Looping: %d\n", i );
    i++;
}
printf( "We are past the while loop." );
```

This example produces the same results as the previous example. This time, however, the initialization and modification conditions have changed slightly. In this example, `i` starts with a value of 1 instead of 0. In the previous example, the

++ operator was used to increment i at the very top of the loop. This example modifies i at the bottom of the loop.

Both of these examples show different ways to accomplish the same end. The phrase "there's more than one way to eat an Oreo" sums up the situation perfectly. There will always be more than one solution to any programming problem. Don't be afraid to do things your own way. Just make sure your code works properly and is easy to read.

The for Statement

Nestled inside the C language, right next to the while statement, is the for statement. The for statement is similar to the while statement, following the basic model of initialization, modification, and termination. Here's the pattern for a for statement:

```
for ( expression1 ; expression2 ; expression3 )
    statement
```

The first expression represents the for statement's initialization. Typically, this expression consists of an assignment statement, setting the initial value of a counter variable. This first expression is evaluated once, before the loop begins.

The second expression is identical in function to the expression in a while statement, providing the termination condition for the loop. This expression is evaluated each time through the loop, before the statement is executed.

Finally, the third expression provides the modification portion of the for statement. This expression is performed at the bottom of the loop, immediately following execution of the statement.

Note that all three of these expressions are optional and may be left out entirely. For example, here's a for loop that leaves out all three expressions:

```
for ( ; ; )
    DoSomethingForever();
```

Since this loop has no terminating expression, it is known as an infinite loop. Infinite loops are generally considered bad form and should be avoided like the plague! The for loop can also be described in terms of a while loop:

```
expression1;
while ( expression2 ) {
    statement
    expression3;
}
```

TIP: Since you can always rewrite a `for` loop as a `while` loop, why does C have a `for` loop at all? The `for` loop represents a particular programming concept: stepping through a range of numbers or elements, performing some action at each step. A `while` loop represents a slightly different concept: perform some action repeatedly until a condition is met. Technically, you can write any `for` loop using a `while` statement, and any `while` loop using a `for` statement. But one of the goals of programming is transparency; your code should look like what it does. So choose the keyword that most closely matches your intent. As you gain experience programming, you'll get a sense for when a `for` statement or a `while` statement makes the intent of your code clearer—even if they're doing exactly the same thing.

Here's an example of a very typical `for` loop:

```
int i;
for ( i = 1; i < 3; i++ )
    printf( "Looping: %d\n", i );
printf( "We are past the for loop." );
```

This example is identical in functionality to the `while` loops presented earlier. Note the three expressions on the first line of the `for` loop. Before the loop is entered, the first expression is performed.

```
i = 1
```

Once the expression is executed, `i` has a value of 1. You're now ready to enter the loop. At the top of each pass through the loop, the second expression is evaluated.

```
i < 3
```

If the expression evaluates to true, the loop continues. Since `i` is less than 3, you can proceed. Next, the statement is executed.

```
printf( "Looping: %d\n", i );
```

Here's the first line of output:

```
Looping: 1
```

Having reached the bottom of the loop, the `for` loop performs its third expression.

```
i++
```

This changes the value of `i` to 2. You go back to the top of the loop and evaluate the termination expression.

```
i < 3
```

Since `i` is still less than 3, the loop continues. Once again, `printf()` does its thing. The console window looks like this:

```
Looping: 1
Looping: 2
```

Next, the `for` statement performs expression3, incrementing the value of `i` to 3.

```
i++
```

Again, you go back to the top of the loop and evaluate the termination expression.

```
i < 3
```

Lo and behold! Since `i` is no longer less than 3, the loop ends and the second `printf()` in the example is executed.

```
printf( "We are past the for loop." );
```

As was the case with `while`, `for` can take full advantage of a pair of curly braces, like so:

```
for ( i = 0; i < 10; i++ ) {
    DoThis();
    DoThat();
    DanceALittleJig();
}
```

In addition, both `while` and `for` can take advantage of the loneliest statement, the lone semicolon:

```
for ( i = 0; i < 1000; i++ )
    ;
```

This example does nothing 1,000 times. Actually, the example does take some time to execute. The initialization expression is evaluated once, and the modification and termination expressions are each evaluated 1,000 times. Here's a `while` version of the loneliest loop:

```
i = 0;
while ( i++ < 1000 )
      ;
```

> **NOTE:** Some compilers will eliminate a loop containing only the semicolon and just set `i` to its terminating value (the value it would have if the loop executed normally). This is an example of code optimization. The nice thing about code optimization is

that it can make your code run faster and more efficiently. The downside is that an optimization pass on your code can sometimes cause unwanted side effects, like eliminating the `while` loop just discussed. Optimization is controlled in your project's build settings, the same place you were setting the compiler warnings (see Figure 6-3). Xcode projects, by default, do not perform optimization while you're editing and testing, but will perform optimization when you're ready to compile your program and give it to someone else (called a *deployment* build). Search the Xcode help for "build settings" and "Xcode scheme" for more information.

LoopTester.xcodeproj

Interestingly, there is an important difference between the `for` and `while` loops you just saw. Take a minute to look back and try to predict the value of `i` the first time through each loop and after each loop terminates. Were the results the same for the `while` and `for` loops? Hmm … you might want to take another look.

Here's a sample program that should clarify the difference between these two loops. Look in the folder *Learn C Projects*, inside the subfolder named 06.02 - LoopTester, and open the project *LoopTester.xcodeproj*. *LoopTester* implements a `while` loop and two slightly different `for` loops. Run the project. Your output should look like that shown in Figure 6-5.

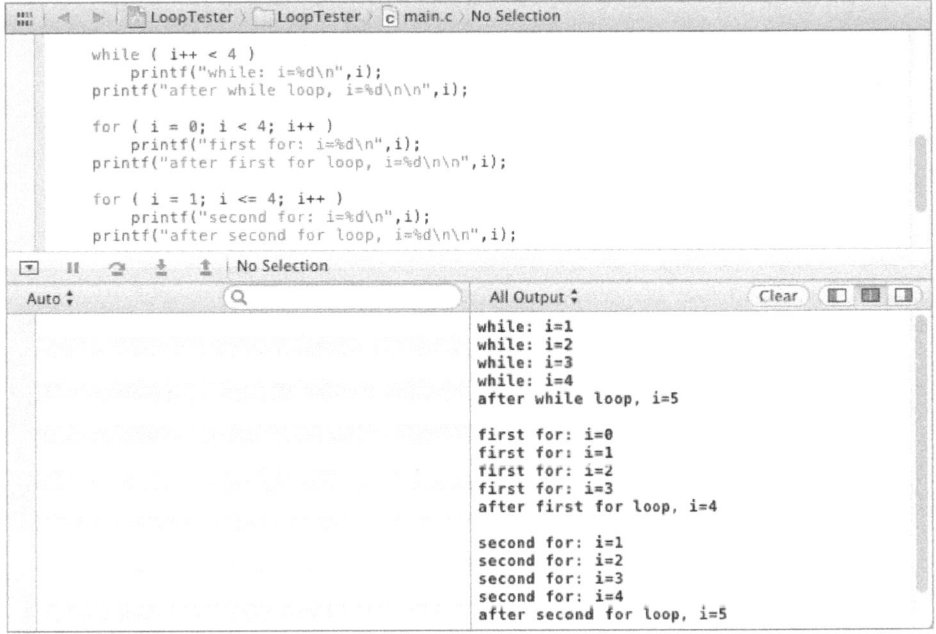

LoopTester › LoopTester › main.c › No Selection
while (i++ < 4)
printf("while: i=%d\n",i);
printf("after while loop, i=%d\n\n",i);
for (i = 0; i < 4; i++)
printf("first for: i=%d\n",i);
printf("after first for loop, i=%d\n\n",i);
for (i = 1; i <= 4; i++)
printf("second for: i=%d\n",i);
printf("after second for loop, i=%d\n\n",i);
No Selection
Auto
All Output
Clear
while: i=1
while: i=2
while: i=3
while: i=4
after while loop, i=5
first for: i=0
first for: i=1
first for: i=2
first for: i=3
after first for loop, i=4
second for: i=1
second for: i=2
second for: i=3
second for: i=4
after second for loop, i=5

Figure 6-5. *The output from* LoopTester, *showing the results from a* `while` *loop and two slightly different* `for` *loops*

LoopTester starts off with the standard `#include`. `main()` defines a counter variable `i` and sets `i` to 0.

```
#include <stdio.h>
int main (int argc, const char * argv[]) {
    int i;
    i = 0;
```

`main()` then enters a `while` loop.

```
while ( i++ < 4 )
    printf( "while: i=%d\n", i );
```

The loop executes four times, resulting in this output:

```
while: i=1
while: i=2
while: i=3
while: i=4
```

Do you see why? If not, set a breakpoint and step over each statement using the debugger. Watch the value for `i` change as the loop progresses, as shown in Figure 6-6. Remember, since you are using postfix notation (i++), `i` gets incremented after the test is made to see if it is less than 4. The test and the increment happen at the top of the loop, before the loop is entered.

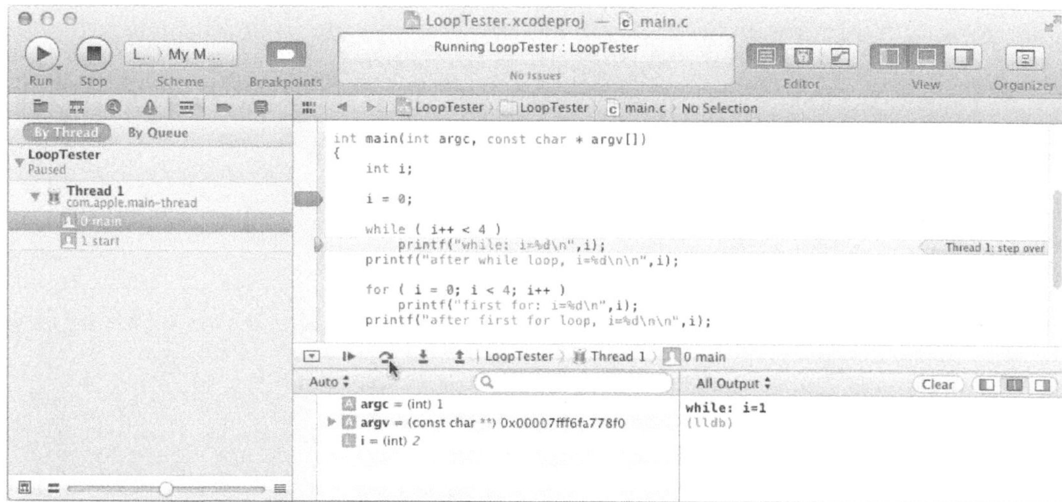

Figure 6-6. *Watching `i` change in a `while` loop*

Once the loop completes, it prints the value of `i` again.

```
printf( "after while loop, i=%d.\n\n", i );
```

Here's the result:

```
after while loop, i=5
```

Here's how you got that value. The last time through the loop (with `i` equal to 4), you go back to the top of the `while` loop, test to see if `i` is less than 4 (it no longer is), and then do the increment of `i`, bumping it from 4 to 5.

OK, one loop down, two to go. This next loop looks like it should accomplish the same thing. The difference is that you don't do the increment of `i` until the bottom of the loop, after you've been through the loop once already.

```
for ( i = 0; i < 4; i++ )
    printf( "first for: i=%d\n", i );
```

As you can see by the output, `i` ranges from 0 to 3 instead of from 1 to 4.

```
first for: i=0
first for: i=1
first for: i=2
first for: i=3
```

Once you drop out of the `for` loop, you again print the value of `i`.

```
printf( "After first for loop, i=%d.\n\n", i );
Here's the result:
```

```
after first for loop, i=4
```

This time, the while loop ranged i from 1 to 4, leaving i with a value of 5 at the end of the loop. The for loop ranged i from 0 to 3, leaving i with a value of 4 at the end of the loop.

So how do you make the for loop so it works the same way as the while loop? Take a look:

```
for ( i = 1; i <= 4; i++ )
    printf( "second for: i=%d\n", i );
```

This for loop started i at 1 instead of 0. It tests to see if i is less than or equal to 4 instead of just less than 4. You could also have used the terminating expression i < 5 instead. Either one will work. As proof, here's the output from this loop:

```
second for: i=1
second for: i=2
second for: i=3
second for: i=4
```

Once again, you print the value of i at the end of the loop.

```
        printf( "After second for loop, i=%d.\n", i );
    return 0;
}
```

Here's the last piece of output:

```
after second for loop, i=5
```

This second for loop is the functional equivalent of the while loop. Take some time to play with this code. You might try to modify the while loop to match the first for loop. Step through the code with the debugger and see what effect your changes have.

By far, the while and for statements are the most common types of C loops. For completeness, however, we'll cover the remaining loop, a little-used gem called the do statement.

The do Statement

The do statement is a while statement that evaluates its expression at the bottom of its loop, instead of at the top. Here's the pattern a do statement must match:

```
do
    statement
while ( expression );
```

Here's a sample:

```
i = 1;
do {
    printf( "%d\n", i );
    i++;
} while ( i < 3 );
printf( "We are past the do loop." );
```

The first time through the loop, `i` has a value of 1. The `printf()` prints a 1 in the console window, and the value of `i` is bumped to 2. It's not until this point that the expression `( i < 3 )` is evaluated. Since 2 is less than 3, a second pass through the loop occurs.

During this second pass, the `printf()` prints a 2 in the console window, and the value of `i` is bumped to 3. Once again, the expression `( i < 3 )` is evaluated. Since 3 is not less than 3, you drop out of the loop to the second `printf()`.

The simple thing to remember about `do` loops is this: since the expression is not evaluated until the bottom of the loop, the body of the loop (the statement) is *always* executed at least once. Since `for` and `while` loops both check their expressions at the top of the loop, either can drop out of the loop before the body of the loop is executed.

Let's move on to a completely different type of statement, known as `switch`.

The switch Statement

The `switch` statement uses the value of an expression to determine which of a series of statements to execute. The basic form of a `switch` statement looks likes this:

```
switch ( expression ) {
    case constant1:
        statement1
    case constant2:
        statement2
    …
    default:
        statement
}
```

The `switch` statement consists of an expression and a series of cases, each identified by a *case label*—the keyword `case`, followed by a numeric constant and a colon. The value of the expression is evaluated (once) and execution jumps directly to the label that matches the value. If no case label matches the value, execution skips to the special `default` label. If there's no default label, none of the statements are executed.

Here's an example that should make this concept a little clearer:

```
switch ( theYear ) {
    case 1066:
        printf( "Battle of Hastings" );
        break;
    case 1492:
        printf( "Columbus sailed the ocean blue" );
        break;
    case 1776:
        printf( "Declaration of Independence\n" );
        printf( "A very important document!!!" );
        break;
    default:
        printf( "Don't know what happened during this year" );
}
```

> **NOTE:** The `switch` statement and the `if` statement are both known as *selection statements*.

If `theYear` has a value of 1066, execution continues with the statement following the label `case 1066:`, which in this case (no pun intended) refers to the following line:

```
printf( "Battle of Hastings" );
```

Execution continues, line after line, until either the bottom of the switch (the right curly brace) or a break statement is reached. In this example, the next line is a `break` statement, so no further statements in the switch statement are executed.

The `break` statement comes in handy when you are working with `switch` statements. The `break` tells the compiler to "jump out of the switch statement." Execution continues with the next statement after the end of the `switch`.

Continuing with the example, if `theYear` has a value of 1492, the switch jumps to these lines:

```
printf( "Columbus sailed the ocean blue" );
break;
```

A value of 1776 jumps to these lines:

```
printf( "Declaration of Independence\n" );
printf( "A very important document!!!" );
break;
```

Notice that this case has two statements before the break. There is no limit to the number of statements a case can have. Having one is OK; having 653 is OK. You can even have a case with no statements at all.

This example also contains a `default` case. If the `switch` can't find a case that matches the value of its expression, the switch looks for a case labeled `default`. So if the value of `theYear` is not 1066, 1492, or 1776, this statement is executed:

```
printf( "Don't know what happened during this year" );
```

Remember that the `default` label is optional and lets you write a `switch` statement that does nothing if none of case labels match the expression.

> **NOTE:** Almost all parts of a switch statement are optional. You can have as many case labels as you want, but you don't have to have any. The case labels don't have to be in any particular order, so case 1 can be followed by 99, followed by 4, followed by -23. A case label can be followed by as many statements as you like or none at all. You can include a default label or not. You can include break statements or leave them out. Many of these combinations might not make any sense, but technically they're all valid C code.

A case with No Statements

Why would you want a case with no statements? Here's an example:

```
switch ( numberOfEggs ) {
    case 1:
    case 2:
        HardBoilThem();
        break;
    case 3:
        MakeAnOmelet();
}
```

In this example, if `numberOfEggs` has a value of 1 or 2, the function `HardBoilThem()` is called. If `numberOfEggs` has a value of 3, the function `MakeAnOmelet()` is called. If `NumberOfEggs` has any other value, nothing happens. Use a `case` with no statements when you want two different cases to execute the same statements.

But what happens if you have 4 eggs? You get no breakfast? Not cool. Here's a better plan.

```
switch ( numberOfEggs ) {
    case 1:
    case 2:
        HardBoilThem();
        break;
    case 3:
        MakeAnOmelet();
        break;
    default:
        FrenchToastForEveryone();
}
```

This example adds a default case. Now, if you have 4 eggs or more, everyone will get French toast. Yay!

Well, almost. Do you see the flaw here? What happens if `numberOfEggs` is zero? It's a little tricky making French toast with no eggs. Add the following code to the `switch` statement, and you're rescued from that embarrassing situation:

```
case 0:
    if ( hasMilk )
        MakeCereal();
    else
        GoOutForBreakfast();
    break;
```

This also illustrates that the code in a switch statement can consist of any valid C code, not just simple statements. A `switch` case can include `if` statements, loops, even other `switch` statements.

> **TIP:** Unusual, unexpected, or atypical values are called *edge conditions* in engineering. Good programmers worry about edge conditions. You want your program to behave itself no matter what values it has to deal with. We'll talk more about this in Chapter 12.

The Mixed Blessing of Fall-Through

Think about what happens with this example:

```
switch ( myVar ) {
    case 1:
        DoSometimes();
    case 2:
```

```
        DoFrequently();
    default:
        DoAlways();
}
```

Notice anything unusual? This code contains no `break` statements. If `myVar` is 1, all three functions will get called. This is called *fall-through*, because you execute `DoSometimes()`, "fall through" the case label and execute `DoFrequently()`, and then "fall through" and execute `DoAlways()`.

If `myVar` is 2, `DoFrequently()` and `DoAlways()` will get called. If `myVar` has any other value, `DoAlways()` gets called by itself.

As this example showed, fall-through allows you to layer your switch cases, adding more functionality as you fall through the cases. With careful planning, fall-through is a nice tool to have.

That said, fall-through does have its downside. Imagine that you needed to modify the code. You realized that when `myVar` is 2, you need to call the function `OnlyWhenMyVarIs2()`. So you modify the code to look like this:

```
switch ( myVar ) {
    case 1:
        DoSometimes();
    case 2:
        DoFrequently();
        OnlyWhenMyVarIs2();
    default:
        DoAlways();
}
```

Do you see the problem here? In this version, `OnlyWhenMyVarIs2()` will get executed when `myVar` is 1 or 2. The lack of a `break` at the end of case 1 means that anything you add to case 2 will also affect case 1. Not a big deal—you can rewrite the code using breaks. The real problem is that if you have not looked at this code for a while, you might miss the fact that the `break` is not there and just assume each case is its own separate entity. One way to solve this problem is to heavily comment your code, making it clear for the future that you are using fall-through. Another way to solve this problem is to avoid fall-through. As always, code carefully; plan for the future.

switch Wrap-Up

At the heart of each `switch` is its expression. Most `switch` statements are based on single variables, but any calculation makes a perfectly acceptable expression.

Each case is based on a constant. Numbers (like 47 or -12932) are valid constants. Variables, such as `myVar`, are not. As you'll see later, single-byte characters (like `'a'` or `'\n'`) are also valid constants. Multiple-byte character strings (like "Gummy-bear") are not.

If your `switch` uses a default case, make sure you use it as shown in the preceding pattern. Don't include the word "case" before the word "default."

Breaks in Loops

The break statement has other uses besides the `switch` statement. Just as it "breaks out of" a switch statement, it can also be used to "break out of" a loop.

Here's an example of a break used in a `while` loop:

```
i = 1;
while ( i <= 9 ) {
    PlayAnInning( i );
    if ( IsItRaining() )
        break;
    i++;
}
```

This example tries to play nine innings of baseball. As long as the function `IsItRaining()` returns with a value of false, the game continues uninterrupted. If `IsItRaining()` returns a value of true, the break statement is executed, and the program drops out of the loop, interrupting the game.

The break statement allows you to construct loops that depend on multiple factors. The termination of the loop depends on the value of the expression found at the top of the loop, as well as on any outside factors that might trigger an unexpected break.

The continue Statement

A close cousin of the `break` statement, the `continue` statement causes a loop to jump ahead, instead of stopping altogether. A `continue` statement skips the rest of the statements in a loop, but doesn't stop the loop from continuing (thus the name). It's useful for when you want to skip some action in a loop but don't want the entire loop to end. A `continue` statement can only appear in the body of a `while`, `for`, or `do` loop.

Here's a fanciful example for a motel room-cleaning algorithm:

```
int room;
```

```
for ( room = 101; room <= 139; room++ ) {
    if ( IsRoomOccupied( room ) && DoNoDisturbSignOnRoom( room ) )
        continue;
    CleanRoom( room );
    RestockSnacksInRoom( room );
}
```

In this example, the loop wants to clean motel rooms 101 through 139. (Hey, if a loop can play baseball, it can clean motel rooms!) The loop first considers if guests occupy the room. If so, it checks to see if the guests have hung a "do not disturb" sign on the door. If true, the `continue` statement is executed.

The `continue` statement causes all of the rest of the code in the body of the loop to be skipped. The loop performs its normal end-of-loop statement (`room++`) and then reevaluates its termination expression (`room <= 139`).

In a nutshell, the loop is going to try to clean and restock each room in the motel. If a room is unoccupied or does not have a "do not disturb" sign, the room will be cleaned and the loop moves on to the next room. If the room is occupied and is showing a "do not disturb" sign, then the room is skipped. But the loop doesn't stop. It moves right on to the next room and repeats the process.

IsOdd.xcodeproj

This next program combines `for` and `if` statements to tell you whether the numbers 1 through 20 are odd or even and if they are an even multiple of 3. Go into the *Learn C Projects* folder, into the 06.03 - IsOdd subfolder, and open the project *IsOdd.xcodeproj*.

Run the `IsOdd` program. You should see something like the workspace window shown in Figure 6-7, which shows a line for each number from 1 through 20. Each of the numbers will be described as either odd or even. Each of the multiples of 3 will have additional text describing them as such. Let's do a walkthrough of the code.

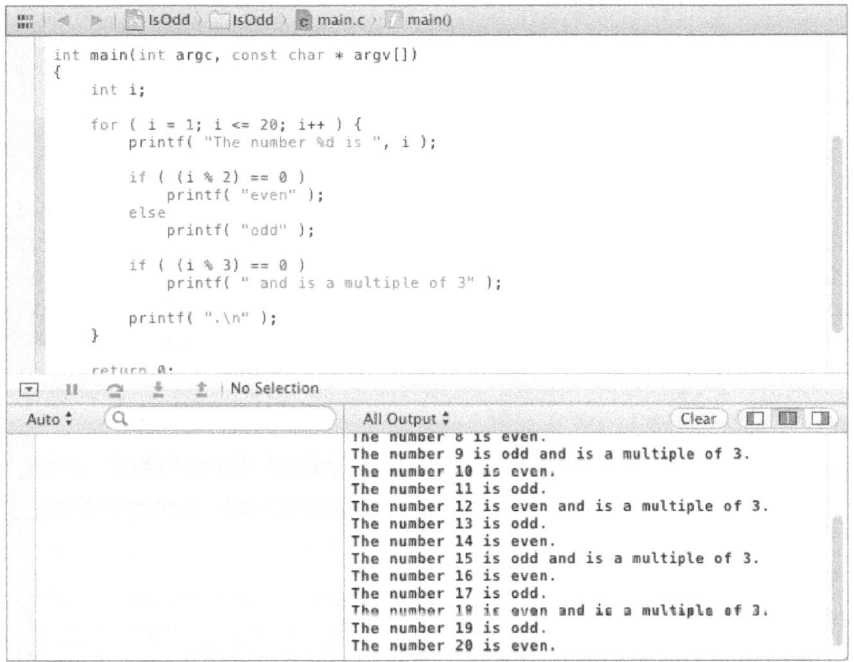

Figure 6-7. *The* IsOdd *program steps through each number from 1 to 20*

Stepping Through the IsOdd Source Code

IsOdd starts off with the usual `#include` and the beginning of `main()`. `main()` starts off by declaring a counter variable named `i`.

```
#include <stdio.h>
int main (int argc, const char * argv[])
{
    int i;
```

The goal here is to step through each of the numbers from 1 to 20. For each number, you want to check to see if the number is odd or even. You also want to check whether the number is evenly divisible by 3. Once you've analyzed a number, you'll use `printf()` to print a description of the number in the console window.

> **TIP:** As mentioned in Chapter 4, the scheme that defines the way a program works is called the program's algorithm. It's a good idea to try to work out the details of your program's algorithm before writing even one line of source code.

As you might expect, the next step is to set up a `for` loop using `i` as a counter. `i` is initialized to 1. The loop will keep running as long as the value of `i` is less than or equal to 20. This is the same as saying the loop will exit as soon as the value of `i` is found to be greater than 20. Every time the loop reaches the bottom, the third expression, `i++`, will be evaluated, incrementing the value of `i` by 1. This is a classic `for` loop:

```
for ( i = 1; i <= 20; i++ ) {
```

Now you're inside the `for` loop. Your goal is to print a single line for each number (i.e., one line each time through the `for` loop). If you check back to Figure 6-7, you'll notice that each line starts with the phrase

`The number x is`

where x is the number being described. That's the purpose of this first `printf()`:

```
printf( "The number %d is ", i );
```

Notice that this `printf()` wasn't part of an `if` statement. You want this `printf()` to print its message every time through the loop. The next sequence of `printf()`s are a different story altogether.

The next chunk of code determines whether `i` is even or odd and uses `printf()` to print the appropriate word in the console window. Because the last `printf()` didn't end with a new-line character (`'\n'`), the word "even" or "odd" will appear immediately following

`The number x is`

on the same line in the console window.

Remember from Chapter 3 that the modulo (`%`) is a binary operator that returns the remainder when the left operand is divided by the right operand. For example, `i % 2` divides 2 into `i` and returns the remainder. If `i` is even, this remainder will be 0. If `i` is odd, this remainder will be 1.

```
if ( (i % 2) == 0 )
    printf( "even" );
else
    printf( "odd" );
```

In the expression `i % 3`, the remainder will be 0 if `i` is evenly divisible by 3, and either 1 or 2 otherwise.

```
if ( (i % 3) == 0 )
    printf( " and is a multiple of 3" );
```

If `i` is evenly divisible by 3, you'll add the phrase " and is a multiple of 3"

to the end of the current line. Finally, you add a period and a newline (`".\n"`) to the end of the current line, placing you at the beginning of the next line of the console window.

```
printf( ".\n" );
```

The loop ends with a curly brace. `main()` ends with the normal `return` and curly brace.

```
    }
    return 0;
}
```

Set a breakpoint and step through this entire program, one line at a time, to see each decision as it is made. Then you'll be ready to move on to an even more ambitious program.

NextPrime.xcodeproj

The next program focuses on the mathematical concept of prime numbers. A prime number is any number whose only factors are 1 and itself. For example, 6 is not a prime number because its factors are 1, 2, 3, and 6. The number 5 is prime because its factors are limited to 1 and 5. The number 12 isn't prime—its factors are 1, 2, 3, 4, 6, and 12.

The program *NextPrime* will find the next prime number greater than a specified number. For example, if you set your starting point to 14, the program would find the next prime, 17. You have the program set up to check for the next prime after 235. Lock in your guess, and give it a try.

Go into the folder *Learn C Projects*, into the subfolder *06.04 - NextPrime*, and open the project *NextPrime.xcodeproj*. Run the project. You should see something like the console window shown in Figure 6-8. As you can see, the next prime number after 235 is (drum roll, please…) 239. Let's look at how the program works.

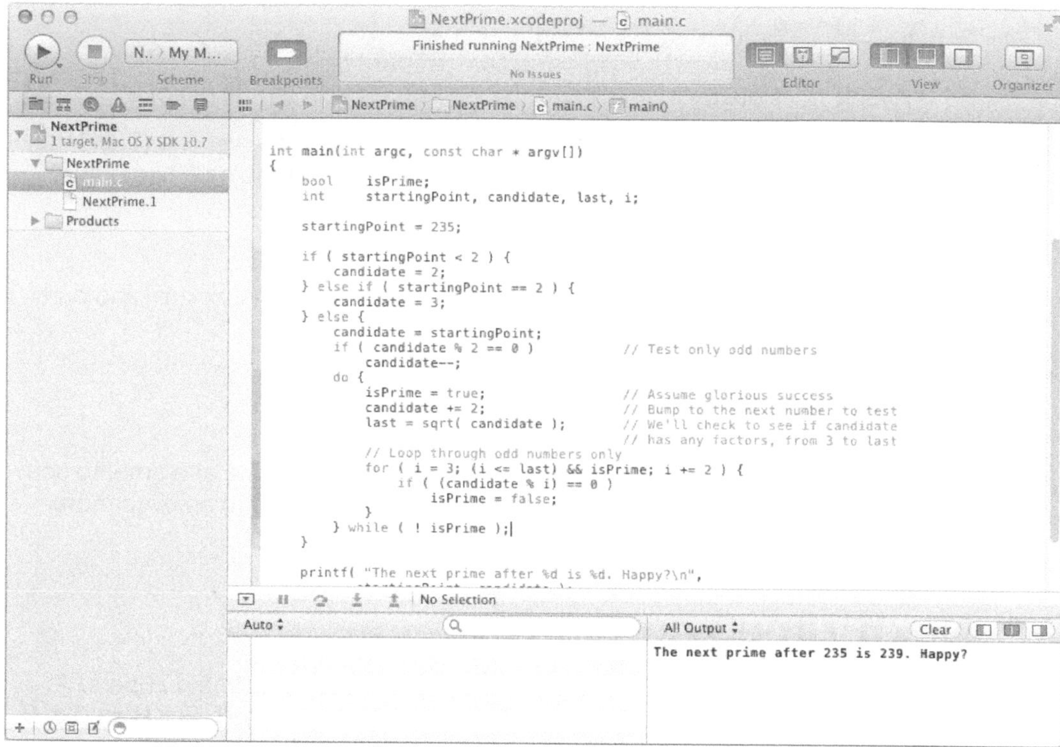

Figure 6-8. NextPrime *reports that the next prime after 235 is 239*

Stepping Through the NextPrime Source Code

In addition to #include of <stdio.h>, you added in a #include of <stdbool.h> to include the definition of true and false, as well as a #include of <math.h>. <math.h> provides access to a series of math functions, most notably the function sqrt(). sqrt() takes a single parameter and returns the square root of that parameter. You'll see how this works in a minute.

```
#include <stdio.h>
#include <stdbool.h>
#include <math.h>
int main(int argc, const char * argv[]) {
```

You're going to need a boatload of variables. isPrime is defined as a bool. The rest are defined as ints.

```
bool    isPrime;
int     startingPoint, candidate, last, i;
```

startingPoint is the number you want to start off with. You'll find the next prime after startingPoint. candidate is the current candidate you are considering. Is candidate the lowest prime number greater than startingPoint? By the time you're done, it will be!

```
startingPoint = 235;
```

Since 2 is the lowest prime number, if startingPoint is less than 2, you know that the next prime is 2. By setting candidate to 2, your work is done.

```
if ( startingPoint < 2 ) {
    candidate = 2;
}
```

If startingPoint is 2, the next prime is 3, and you'll set candidate accordingly.

```
else if ( startingPoint == 2 ) {
    candidate = 3;
}
```

If you got this far, you know that startingPoint is greater than 2. Since 2 is the only even prime number, and since you've already checked for startingPoint being equal to 2, you can now limit your search to odd numbers only. You'll start candidate at startingPoint, then make sure that candidate is odd. If not, you'll decrement candidate.

Why decrement instead of increment? If you peek ahead a few lines, you'll see you're about to enter a do loop, and that you bump candidate to the next odd number at the top of the loop. By decrementing candidate now, you're preparing for the bump at the top of the loop, which will take candidate to the next odd number greater than startingPoint.

```
else {
    candidate = startingPoint;
    if (candidate % 2 == 0)
        candidate--;
```

This loop will continue stepping through consecutive odd numbers until you find a prime number. You'll start isPrime off as true, and check the current candidate to see if you can find a factor. If you do find a factor, you'll set isPrime to false, forcing you to repeat the loop.

```
do {
    isPrime = true;
    candidate += 2;
```

Now you'll check to see if candidate is prime. This means verifying that candidate has no factors other than 1 and candidate. To do this, you'll check the numbers from 3 to the square root of `candidate` to see if any of them divide evenly into `candidate`. If not, you know you've got yourself a prime!

```
last = sqrt( candidate );
```

> **NOTE:** Why don't you check from 2 up to candidate-1? Why start with 3? Since candidate will never be even, you know that 2 will never be a factor. For the same reason, you know that no even number will ever be a factor.
>
> Why stop at the square root of candidate? Good question! To help understand this approach, consider the factors of 12, other than 1 and 12. They are 2, 3, 4, and 6. The square root of 12 is approximately 3.46. Notice how this fits nicely in the middle of the list of factors. Each of the factors less than the square root will pair up with a factor greater than the square root. In this case, 2 pairs with 6 (that is, 2 * 6 = 12) and 3 pairs with 4 (that is, 3 * 4 = 12). This will always be true. If you don't find a factor by the time you hit the square root, there won't be a factor, and the candidate is prime.

Take a look at the top of the `for` loop. You start `i` at 3. Each time you hit the top of the loop (including the first time through the loop), check to make sure you haven't passed the square root of candidate and that `isPrime` is still true. If `isPrime` is false, you can stop searching for a factor, since you've just found one! Finally, each time you complete the loop, you bump `i` to the next odd number.

```
for ( i = 3; (i <= last) && isPrime; i += 2 ) {
```

Each time through the loop, check to see if `i` divides evenly into candidate. If so, you know it is a factor, and you can set `isPrime` to false.

```
            if ( (candidate % i) == 0 )
                isPrime = false;
        }
    } while ( ! isPrime );
}
```

Are you lost? Don't worry; you always have your friend the debugger. Set a breakpoint and step over each line of code, watching as the variables change, as shown in Figure 6-9. Try different starting numbers and watch how the path the code takes is altered.

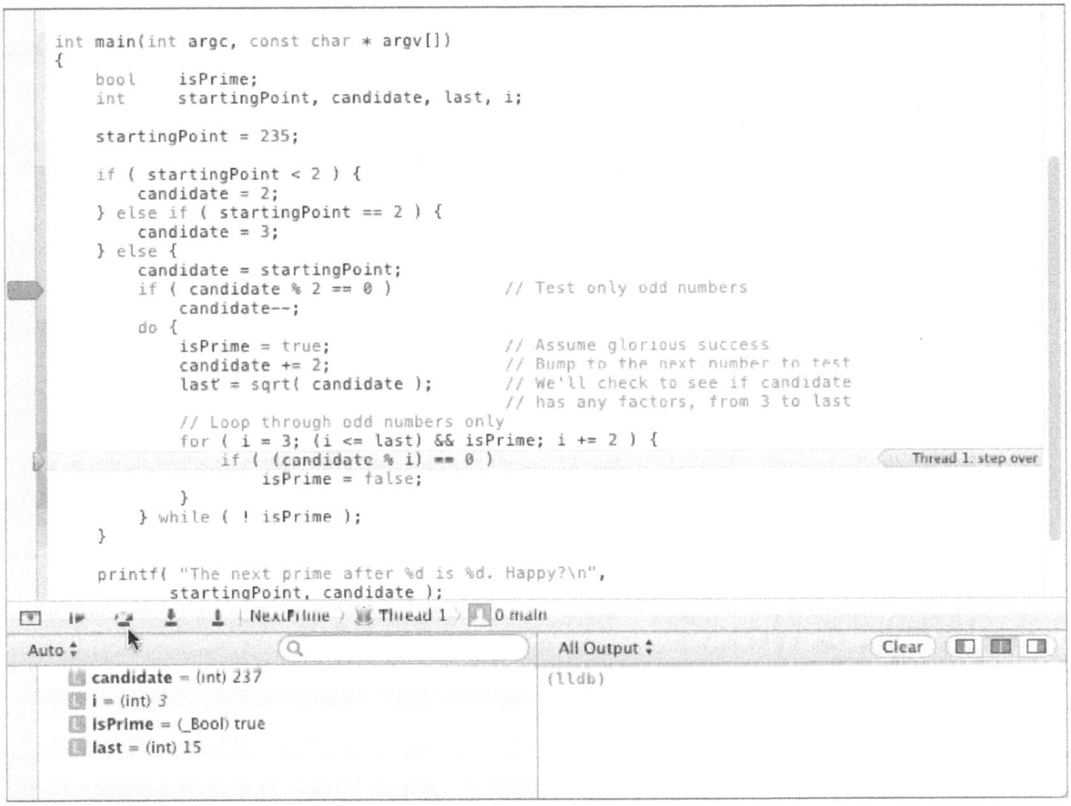

```
int main(int argc, const char * argv[])
{
    bool    isPrime;
    int     startingPoint, candidate, last, i;

    startingPoint = 235;

    if ( startingPoint < 2 ) {
        candidate = 2;
    } else if ( startingPoint == 2 ) {
        candidate = 3;
    } else {
        candidate = startingPoint;
        if ( candidate % 2 == 0 )              // Test only odd numbers
            candidate--;
        do {
            isPrime = true;                    // Assume glorious success
            candidate += 2;                    // Bump to the next number to test
            last = sqrt( candidate );          // We'll check to see if candidate
                                               // has any factors, from 3 to last
            // Loop through odd numbers only
            for ( i = 3; (i <= last) && isPrime; i += 2 ) {
                if ( (candidate % i) == 0 )
                    isPrime = false;
            }
        } while ( ! isPrime );
    }

    printf( "The next prime after %d is %d. Happy?\n",
           startingPoint, candidate );
```

```
candidate = (int) 237
i = (int) 3
isPrime = (_Bool) true
last = (int) 15
```

Figure 6-9. *NextPrime variables in the debugger*

Once you drop out of the do loop, you use `printf()` to print both the starting point and the first prime number greater than the starting point.

```
    printf( "The next prime after %d is %d. Happy?\n",
           startingPoint, candidate );
    return 0;
}
```

If you are interested in prime numbers, play around with this program. Take a look at the exercises following this chapter for ideas.

TAKING OFF THE TRAINING WHEELS

Can you think of another way of writing this program? We bet you can. There are hundreds of different ways you could write the *NextPrime* program, all of them producing the same result. The way we wrote it isn't the smallest, the most obvious, or the fastest. It's kind of a compromise between all of those traits.

If you want to really spread your programming wings, close your eyes and think about what you want your code to accomplish and how it's going to do that. Now open your eyes, create a new project, and write this same program your own way.

It doesn't hurt to try. You won't hurt the computer.

If you want to get an idea of just how different the *NextPrime* program could be, get on the Web and look up "Sieve of Eratosthenes" (`http://en.wikipedia.org/wiki/Sieve_of_Eratosthenes`) for a radically different way of searching for prime numbers.

What's Next?

Congratulations! You made it through some tough concepts. You learned about the C statements that allow you to control your program's flow. You learned about C expressions and the concepts of true and false. You also learned about the logical operators based on the values `true` and `false`. You learned about the `if`, `if-else`, `for`, `while`, `do`, `switch`, `break`, and `continue` statements. In short, you learned a lot!

The next chapter introduces the concept of pointers. Pointers are a big deal and a big concept. Learning how to use pointers will seriously up your game. In addition, Chapter 7 will discuss function parameters. You've been passing values to functions as parameter this whole time, and now you'll learn how to use them yourself. As usual, plenty of code and sample applications will be included to keep you busy. See you there.

CHAPTER 6 EXERCISES

1. Each of the following examples contains a syntax or logical error. What is it?

   a.
   ```
   if i
       i++;
   ```
   b.
   ```
   for ( i=0; i<20; i++ )
       i--;
   ```
   c.
   ```
   while ( )
       i++;
   ```
   d.
   ```
   do ( i++ )
       until ( i == 20 );
   ```
   e.
   ```
   switch ( i ) {
       case "hello":
       case "goodbye":
           printf( "Greetings." );
           break;
       case default:
           printf( "Boring." )
       }
   ```
   f.
   ```
   if ( i < 20 )
       if ( i == 20 )
           printf( "Lonely..." );
   ```
   g.
   ```
   while ( done = true )
       done = ! done;
   ```
   h.
   ```
   for ( i=0; i<20; i*20 )
       printf( "Modification..." );
   ```

2. Modify *NextPrime* to compute the prime numbers from 1 to 100.

3. Modify *NextPrime* to compute the first 100 prime numbers.

Chapter 7

Pointers and Parameters

You've come a long way. You've mastered variable basics, operators, and statements. You're about to add some powerful new concepts to your programming toolbox.

For starters, we'll introduce the concept of *pointers*, also known as *references*. From now on, you'll use pointers in almost every C program you write. (You've actually been using them already, it just wasn't obvious.)

We can't overstate this: pointers are a really important concept, and one that's traditionally difficult to grasp at first. It's not an exaggeration to say that pointers are what make all modern software possible. Without them, the programs you use every day would be impossible to write. Learning pointers is like going from 2D to 3D. It's like trading in your wheels for a set of wings. If you were a World of Warcraft Mage, it'd be like acquiring a Rune of Portal spell. Seriously, it's a big deal.

We're going to walk you through pointers, from basic concept to the ins and outs of using them in a program. Along the way, you're also going to learn about function parameters and return values. These will allow you to exchange values between your functions.

What Is a Pointer?

In programming, pointers are *references* to other things. When someone calls your name to get your attention, they're using your name as a pointer. Your name is one way people refer to you.

Your home address can also serve as a pointer, telling your mail carrier where to deliver your shiny new Death Star tea infuser (yes, that's a real thing!) Your home address is unique and distinguishes your house from all the other houses in the world.

When you declare a variable in C, memory is allocated to hold its value. This memory has a specific, numeric address. C pointers are special variables, specifically designed to hold one of these addresses.

Later in the chapter, you'll learn how to create a pointer, how to make it point to a specific variable, and how to use the pointer to change the variable's value.

Why Use Pointers?

Pointers can be extremely useful, allowing you to access your data in ways that ordinary variables just don't allow. Here's a real-world example of pointer flexibility.

When you go to the library in search of a specific title, chances are you start your search in an online catalog of some sort. Library catalogs contain thousands of entries, one for every book in the library or, in some cases, in a group of libraries. Each entry contains information about a specific book, including the author's name, the book's title, and the copyright date.

Most library catalogs allow you to search using a variety of methods. For example, you might search for a book using the author's name, the book title, the subject, or some combination of all these. Figure 7-1 shows a search of the Laramie County, Wyoming library catalog. This search specifies an author named Einstein and a book entitled *The Meaning of Relativity*. (What can we say? Einstein fascinates us.)

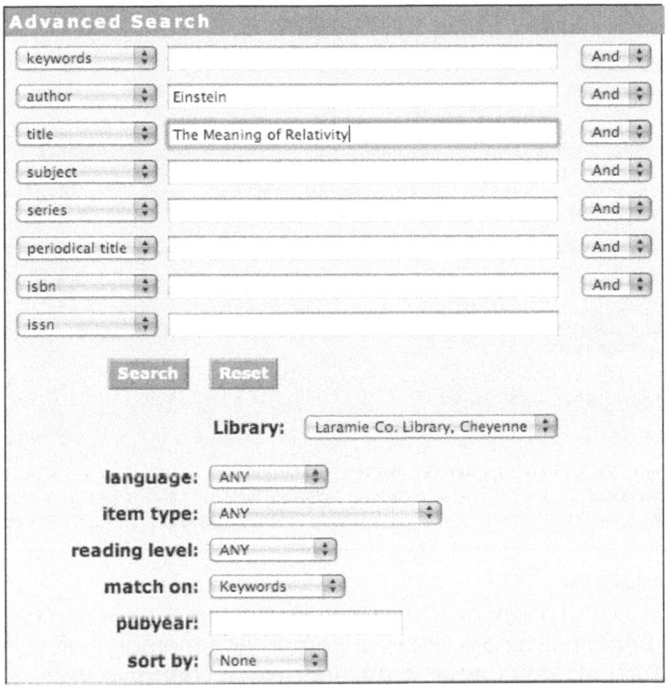

Figure 7-1. *Search window from the Laramie County library in Cheyenne*

Figure 7-2 shows the results of this search, a catalog entry for Albert Einstein's famous book on relativity, called *The Meaning of Relativity*. Take a minute to look over the figure. Pay special attention to the catalog number located just above the book title. The catalog number for this book is 530.1. This number tells you exactly where to find the book among all the other books on the shelves. The books are ordered numerically, so you'll find this book in the 500 shelves, between 530 and 531.

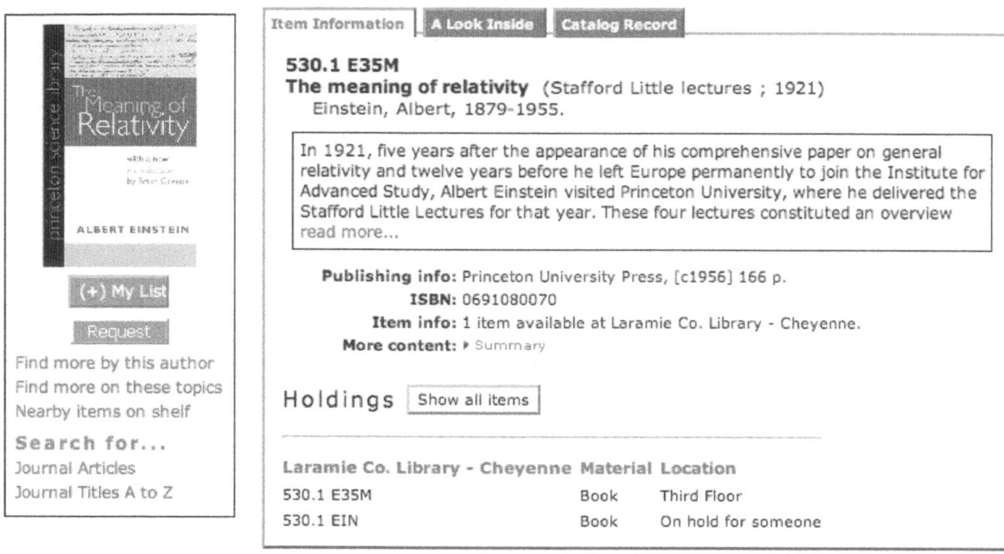

Figure 7-2. *Catalog entry for a famous book*

In this example, the library bookshelves are like your computer's memory, with the books acting as data. The catalog number is the address of your data (a book) in memory (on the shelf).

As you might have guessed, the catalog number acts as a pointer. The library catalogs use these pointers to rearrange all the books in the library, without moving a single book. Think about it. If you search the catalog by subject, it's just as if all the books in the library are arranged by subject. Physically, the book arrangements have nothing to do with subject; the books are arranged numerically by catalog number. By adding a layer of pointers between you and the books, the librarians achieve an extra layer of flexibility.

In the same way, if you search the catalog by title, it's just as if all the books in the library are arranged alphabetically by title. Again, physically, the book arrangements have nothing to do with title. By using pointers, all the books in the library are arranged in different ways without ever leaving the shelves. The books are arranged physically (sorted by catalog number) and logically (sorted in by author, subject, title, and so on). Without the support of a layer of pointers, these logical book arrangements would be impossible.

NOTE: Adding a layer of pointers is also known as adding a *level of indirection*. The number of levels of indirection is the number of pointers you have to use to get to your library book (or to your data).

Checking Out of the Library

So far, we've talked about pointers in terms of house addresses and library catalog numbers. The use of pointers in your C programs is not much different from those models. Each catalog number points to the location of a book on the library shelf, just as each street address identifies a specific house. In the same way, each pointer in your program will point to the location of a piece of data in computer memory.

If you wrote a program to keep track of your DVD collection, you might maintain a list of pointers, each one of which might point to a block of data that describes a single DVD. Each block of data might contain such information as the name of the movie, the name of the director, the year of release, and a category (such as drama, comedy, documentary). If you got more ambitious, you could create several pointer lists. One list might sort your DVDs alphabetically by movie title. Another might sort them chronologically by year of release. Yet another list might sort your DVDs by category. You get the picture.

There's a lot you can do with pointers. By mastering the techniques presented in these next few chapters, you'll be able to create programs that take full advantage of pointers.

The goal for this chapter is to help you master pointer basics. We'll talk about C pointers and C pointer operations. You'll learn how to create a pointer and how to make the pointer point to a variable. You'll also learn how to use a pointer to change the value of the variable the pointer points to.

Pointer Basics

Pointers are address variables. Instead of an address such as 1313 Mockingbird Lane, Raven Heights, California 90263, a variable's address refers to a memory location within your computer. As we discussed in Chapter 2, your computer's memory—also known as random access memory (RAM)—consists of a sequence of bytes. One megabyte of RAM has exactly 2^{20} (or 1,048,576) bytes of memory, while 8 megabytes of RAM has exactly $8 * 2^{20} = 2^{23}$ = 8,388,608 bytes of memory. One gigabyte of RAM has exactly 2^{30} bytes = 1,024 megabytes = 1,073,741,824 bytes of memory, and so on.

Every one of those bytes has a unique *address*. Computer addresses typically start with zero and continue up, one at a time, until they reach the highest address. The first byte has an address of 0, the next byte has an address of 1, and so on. Figure 7-3 shows the addressing scheme for a computer with a gigabyte of RAM. Notice that the addresses run from 0 (the lowest address) all the way up to 1,073,741,823 (the highest address). The same scheme would hold true for 10 gigabytes, or even a terabyte (1,024 gigabytes).

1,073,741,823	00000000
1,073,741,822	00000000
1,073,741,821	00000000
1,073,741,820	00000000
	⋮
3	00000000
2	00000000
1	00000000
0	00000000

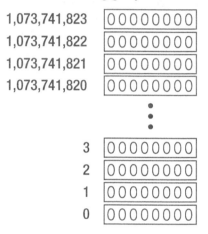

Figure 7-3. *The memory addresses of a computer with 1GB of RAM*

The Address of a Variable

When you run a program, one of the first things the computer does is allocate memory for your program's variables. When you declare an int in your code, like this

```
int myVar;
```

the compiler reserves memory for the exclusive use of `myVar`.

> **NOTE:** As mentioned earlier in this book, the amount of memory allocated for an int depends on your development environment. Xcode currently defaults to using 4-byte ints.

Each of myVar's bytes has a specific address. Figure 7-4 shows the computer's 1 gigabyte of memory with 4 bytes allocated to the variable myVar. In this picture, the 4 bytes allocated to myVar have the addresses 836, 837, 838, and 839.

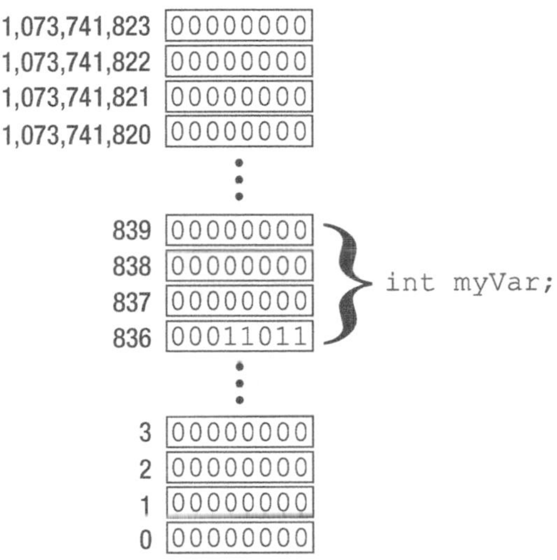

Figure 7-4. *Memory allocated for the variable* myInt

By convention, a variable's address is said to be the address of its first byte (the first byte is the byte with the lowest numbered address). If a variable uses memory locations 836 through 839 (as myVar does), its address is 836 and its length is 4 bytes.

> **NOTE:** When a variable occupies more than 1 byte of memory, the bytes are always consecutive (next to each other in memory). You will never see an int whose byte addresses are 508, 509, 510, and 695. A variable's bytes are like family—they stick together.

As we showed earlier, a variable's address is a lot like the library catalog number in a library book's catalog entry. Both act as pointers, one to a book on the library shelf and the other to a variable. From now on, when we use the term "pointer" with respect to a variable, we are referring to the variable's address.

Now that you understand what a pointer is, your next goal is to learn how to use pointers in your programs. The next few sections will teach you some valuable pointer programming skills. You'll learn how to create a pointer to a variable. You'll also learn how to use that pointer to access the variable to which it points.

The C language provides you with a few key tools to help you. These tools come in the form of two special operators: & and *.

The & Operator

The & operator, called the *address-of* operator, is a unary operator that pairs with a variable name to produce the variable's address. The expression

```
myVar
```

retrieves the value stored in the myVar variable, while the expression

```
&myVar
```

refers to myVar's address in memory. If myVar occupied memory locations 836 through 839 (as in Figure 7-4), the expression &myVar would have a value of 836. The expression &myVar is a pointer to the variable myVar.

An expression like &myVar is a common way to obtain the address of a variable. But what can you do with that address? Store it into a pointer variable, of course! A *pointer variable* is a variable specifically designed to hold the address of another variable.

Declaring a Pointer Variable

C supports a special notation for declaring pointer variables. The following line declares a pointer variable named myPointer:

```
int *myPointer:
```

The * is not part of the variable's name. Instead, it tells the compiler that the associated variable is a pointer, specifically designed to hold the address of an int variable. Technically, when * appears in a declaration it is a *type modifier*, not an operator. It modifies the int variable declaration and turns it into an int pointer variable declaration. Simply stated, int myInt means "allocate a variable that will hold an integer," while int *myInt means "allocate a variable that will hold the memory address of a variable that holds an integer." If there was a data type called bluto, you could declare a variable designed to point to a bluto like this:

```
bluto *blutoPointer;
```

NOTE: This declaration is perfectly legal: `int* myPointer;`

This line also declares a variable named `myPointer` designed to hold the address of an int. The fact that the white space comes after the * does not matter to the compiler. We'll be using the former format, simply because it's the most common. Both are acceptable.

For the moment, we'll limit ourselves to pointers that point to ints. Look at this code:

```
int *myPointer, myVar;

myPointer = &myVar;
```

The variable declaration allocates two variables: a pointer to an int, and an int. The assignment statement puts `myVar`'s address in the variable `myPointer`. If `myVar`'s address is 836, this code will leave `myPointer` with a value of 836. Note that this code has absolutely no effect on the value of `myVar`.

We're sure you've got the concept of memory addresses, and you understand that every value stored in memory has an address associated with it. You now know how to obtain that address of a variable with the address-of (&) operator and store that address in a pointer variable (a variable for storing memory addresses).

So now what? This is where pointers start to get interesting.

The * Operator

The complement to the address-of (&) operator is the unary * or *indirection* operator. It does just the opposite of the & operator: it takes a pointer variable and turns it into the variable the pointer variable points to. Confusing, isn't it? Here's a simple example.

NOTE: The * operator's official name in the C standard is the "indirection operator," but it's also commonly referred to as the "star," "pointer," or "dereference" operator.

```
int *myPointer;
int myVar;

myVar = 3;
myPointer = &myVar;
```

```
*myPointer = 27;
```

The first assignment statement (`myVar = 3`) makes perfect sense. You've been using that form since Chapter 2. The second assignment statement is only a slight variation of the first. It's still storing a value into the variable named on the left side of the assignment operator (=), but this time the value is a memory address. At this point, `myPointer` holds the address of `myVar`. So far, so good.

The third assignment statement is the game changer. It copies the value 27 into the memory address pointed to by `myPointer`.

The indirection operator (*) takes the value stored in `myPointer` and treats it like the address of a variable. In other words, the computer will take the memory address stored in the variable `myPointer` and use it to locate the `int` variable somewhere else in memory, and then store the value 27 there. The value of the `myPointer` variable does not change. After the assignment, it still contains the address of `myVar`.

If `myPointer` contains the address of `myVar`, as is the case in our example, referring to `*myPointer` is equivalent to referring to `myVar`. For example, this line

```
*myPointer = 27;
```

is the same as this one

```
myVar = 27;
```

Still confused? Don't worry; we're going to walk through this again with illustrations. Figure 7-5 joins our program in progress, just after the variables `myVar` and `myPointer` were declared:

```
int *myPointer, myVar;
```

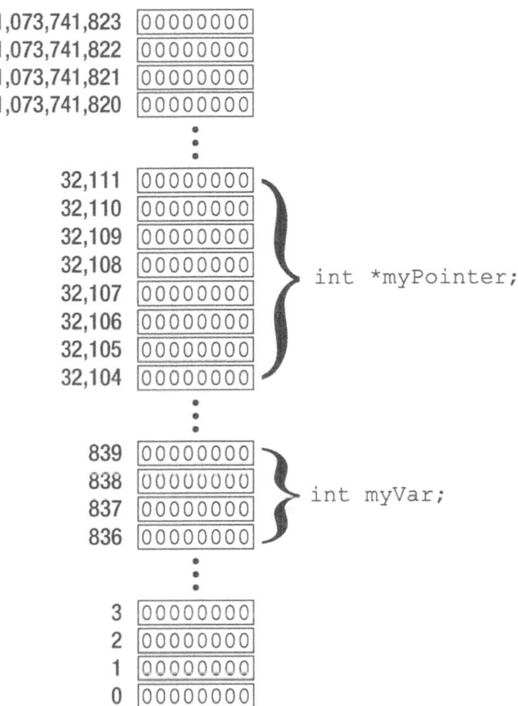

Figure 7-5. *Memory allocated for* `myVar` *and* `myPointer`

COMPUTER ARCHITECTURE AND POINTER SIZES

If you're curious to know why an int variable takes up 4 bytes of memory and a pointer variable takes up 8 bytes of memory, read on.

As of this writing, the default size for an int variable is 4 bytes, or 32 bits. 32 bits is enough to represent any whole number between 0 and 4,294,967,295. If this isn't perfectly clear, review the section "Size of a Type" in Chapter 4.

A pointer variable is, essentially, an integer variable that stores the address of a byte in memory. Logically, it has to be big enough to represent all of the possible memory addresses your computer has. That means that every pointer variable in a program has to be capable of storing a number between 0 and the last address, since a variable can (theoretically) be allocated at any memory address.

If you've shopped for a shiny new Mac recently, you know that (with some spare cash) it's not difficult to load it up with more than 4GB of RAM. A 32-bit (4 byte) integer can only represent numbers between 0 and 4,294,967,295 (4GB). Clearly, that's inadequate for today's computers.

Modern CPUs use 64-bit (8 byte) pointers. This allows a pointer to store the address of any memory location between 0 and 18,446,744,073,709,551,615—yikes, that's big number! It works out to 16 exabytes, or 16 billion gigabytes—a really, really, big number, and way more RAM than you can afford.

The size of pointers is intimately tied to the computer's hardware. Back in the days of the original Apple II, micro-computers used 16-bit pointers. Simply stated, it means the CPU could directly address 65,536 memory locations (64K). Hey, it seemed like a lot at the time.

Not surprisingly, it wasn't very long before this wasn't enough. By the time the original Mac was introduced, CPUs were starting to use 32-bit pointers. The Motorola 68000 processor in the original Mac could, theoretically, address up to 4GB of RAM. Of course, no one made memory modules that big and you couldn't install that much RAM on the motherboard even if you could get your hands on it. But for programmers, it meant that pointer variables were now 4 bytes long.

Fast-forward 30 years and the 4GB of addresses that seemed almost inexhaustible in the 1980s looks puny now. CPU design has, naturally, been trying to keep up and desktop computers have now largely transitioned to using 64-bit (8 byte) pointers. Again, that doesn't mean you can actually install 16 exabytes of RAM in your Mac, but a program that uses 64-bit pointers will run on such a system.

64-bit pointers should hold us for some time to come. To put it in perspective, if the surface of a Popsicle stick represents all of the memory that a 32-bit pointer can address, a 64-bit pointer can address the surface area of the Golden Gate Bridge. Given the exponential rate that memory density keeps increasing, and computer programs keep using more memory, the transition from 32- to 64-bit pointers should hold us for about 90 years. Of course, we won't be surprised if our great grandchildren are one day shaking their heads wondering how we ever got by with "only" 16 exabytes of addressable memory.

Once memory is allocated for `myVar` and `myPointer`, you move on to the statement:

```
myPointer = &myVar;
```

The address of the variable `myVar` is stored in the 8 bytes allocated to `myPointer`. In this example, `myVar`'s address is 836. Now, `myPointer` is said to *point to* `myVar`. See Figure 7-6.

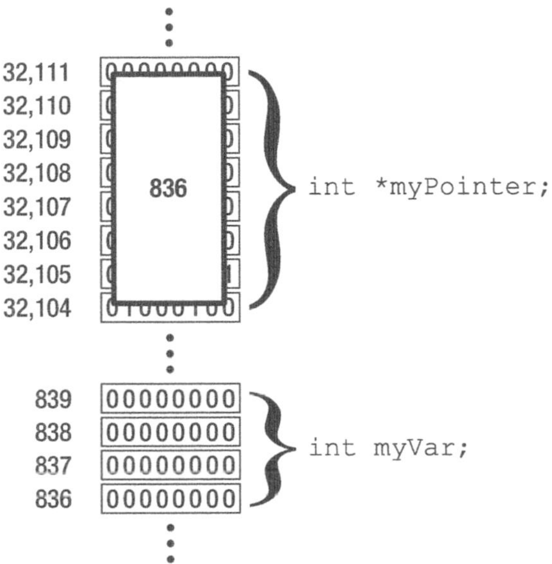

Figure 7-6. *The address of* `myVar` *assigned to* `myPointer`

OK, you're almost there. The next line of the example writes the value 27 to the location pointed to by `myPointer`:

```
*myPointer = 27;
```

Without the * operator, the computer would place the value 27 in the memory allocated to `myPointer`. The * operator *dereferences* `myPointer`. Dereferencing a pointer turns the pointer into the variable it points to. Figure 7-7 shows the end results.

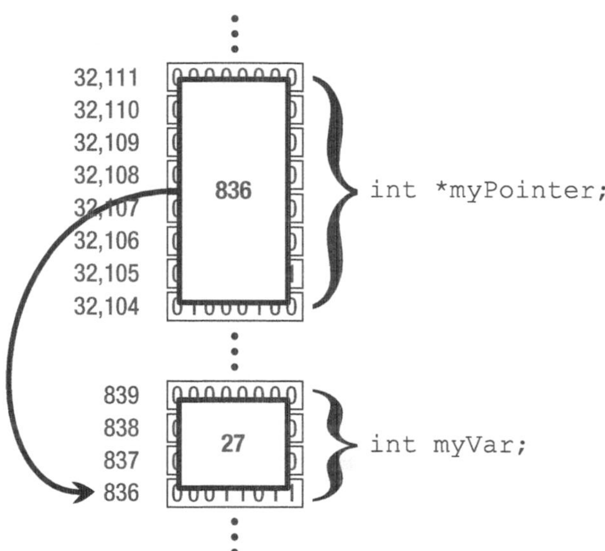

Figure 7-7. *Finally, the value 27 is assigned to *myPointer.*

If you step through the 07.01 – Pointer project with the debugger, you can watch each of these steps happen. Of course, the address of `myVar` won't be 836, but other than that everything else should be consistent with the illustrations.

The workspace window, shown in Figure 7-8, shows the values of `myPointer` and `myVar`. The Xcode debugger conveniently adds an expansion triangle next to pointer values, which let you easily see the value that they point to. This will become really useful as you continue to explore pointers.

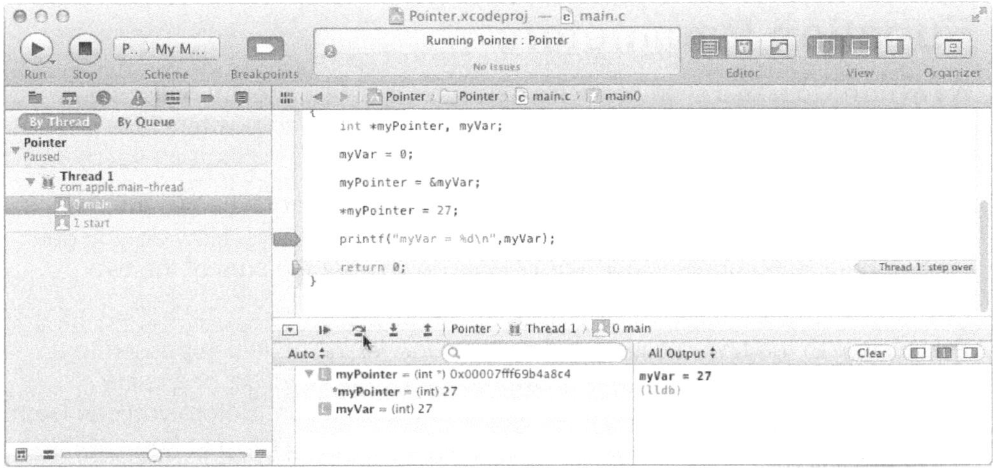

Figure 7-8. *Stepping through the* Pointer *project*

The * operator works equally well at retrieving a value. The expression

```
*myPointer + 4
```

evaluates to 31. Why? Let's walk through this together.

Earlier, we saw that `myPointer` contained the address of the variable `myVar`. Since `myVar` contains the value 27, `*myPointer` also evaluates to 27 and, therefore, `*myPointer + 4` evaluates to 31.

> **TIP:** Interestingly enough, the * (pointer type modifier), the * (unary indirection operator), and the * (binary multiplication operator) are almost never confused for one another, thanks to context. For example, `2 * * myPointer` means "Two times the value stored at pointer myPointer." In the rare instances where they might get mixed up, throw in some parentheses to make it clear to the compiler which one you mean, like this: `2*(*myPointer)`

If the concept of pointers seems alien to you, don't worry. You are not alone. Programming with pointers is one of the most difficult topics you'll ever take on. Just keep reading, and make sure you follow each of the examples line by line. By the end of the chapter, you'll be a pointer expert!

Function Parameters

We're going to take a short break from pointers and talk about functions and how to exchange values with them. How does this relate to pointers? Be patient, as we'll come back around to that soon enough.

Suppose you want to write a function called `AddTwo()` that takes two numbers, adds them together, and returns the sum of the two numbers. How do you get the two original numbers to `AddTwo()`? How do you get the sum of the two numbers back to the function that called `AddTwo()`?

The answer to the first question is *function parameters*, or values passed to a function. The second question is answered with a *return value*, or a value passed from the function back to the caller of that function. Before you can learn how to pass values around, or even why you need to, you need to know a little about the concept of scope.

Variable Scope

In C, every variable is said to have a *scope*. A variable's scope defines where in the program you have access to that variable. In other words, if a variable is declared inside one function, can another function refer to that same variable?

Simply stated, the scope of a variable is defined by where it's declared. The scope of a variable declared inside a function is limited to the code inside that function.

> **NOTE:** Technically, the scope of a variable declared inside any block ({...}) of code ends at the closing brace of that block.

This definition is important. It means you can't declare a variable inside one function, and then refer to that same variable inside another function. Here's an example that will never compile:

```
#include <stdio.h>

int main (int argc, const char * argv[])
{
    int numDots;
    numDots = 500;
    DrawDots();
    return 0;
}
```

```
void DrawDots( void )
{
    int i;
    for ( i = 1; i <= numDots; i++ )
        printf( "." );
}
```

The error in this code occurs when the function `DrawDots()` tries to reference the variable `numDots`. According to the rules of scope, `DrawDots()` doesn't even know about the variable `numDots`. If you tried to compile this program, the compiler would complain that `DrawDots()` tried to use the variable `numDots` without declaring it.

The problem you are faced with is getting the value of `numDots` to the function `DrawDots()` so `DrawDots()` knows how many dots to draw. The answer to this problem is function parameters.

> **TIP:** `DrawDots()` is another example of the value of writing functions. We've taken the code needed to perform a specific function (in this case, draw some dots) and embedded it in a function. Now, instead of having to duplicate the code inside `DrawDots()` every time we want to draw some dots in our program, all we need is a single line of code: a call to the function `DrawDots()`.

How Function Parameters Work

Function *parameters* are variables, but instead of being declared at the beginning of a function, parameters are listed between the parentheses of the function's declaration, like this:

```
void DrawDots( int numDots )
{
    /* function's body goes here */
}
```

When you call a function you simply provide a value for each parameter, making sure you pass the function what it expects. To call the version of `DrawDots()` just defined, make sure you place an `int` between the parentheses. The call to `DrawDots()` inside `main()` passes the value 30 into the function `DrawDots()`:

```
int main (int argc, const char * argv[])
{
    DrawDots( 30 );
    return 0;
}
```

When DrawDots() starts executing, it sets its parameter to the passed-in value. In this case, DrawDots() has one parameter, an int named numDots. When this call executes

```
DrawDots( 30 );
```

the function DrawDots() sets its parameter, numDots, to a value of 30.

To make things a little clearer, here's a revised version of the example:

```
#include <stdio.h>

void DrawDots( int numDots );

int main (int argc, const char * argv[])
{
    DrawDots( 30 );
    return 0;
}

void DrawDots( int numDots )
{
    int i;
    for ( i = 1; i <= numDots; i++ )
        printf( "." );
}
```

This version of drawDots will compile and run properly. It starts with the #include of <stdio.h> and follows with the function prototype for DrawDots(). Recall the concept of function prototypes that we introduced in Chapter 3. Imagine the compiler making its way down the file, processing one chunk of code at a time. Without the prototype, it would hit the call of DrawDots(30) inside main() and not have anything to verify it against. The prototype assures the compiler that you intend to provide a function named DrawDots(), that it will not return a value (that's why it is declared as void), and that it will take an int as an argument. As the compiler continues to process the file and comes across the actual call of DrawDots(), it can make an intelligent assessment of the call to decide if it was made properly.

After the DrawDots() prototype, you enter main(). main() calls DrawDots(), passing as a parameter the constant 30. DrawDots() receives the value 30 in its int parameter, numDots. This means that the function DrawDots() starts execution with a variable named numDots having a value of 30.

Inside DrawDots(), the for loop behaves as you might expect, drawing 30 periods in the console window. Figure 7-9 shows a picture of this program in action. You can run this example yourself. The project file, DrawDots.xcodeproj, is located in the *Learn C Projects* folder in a subfolder named 07.02 - DrawDots.

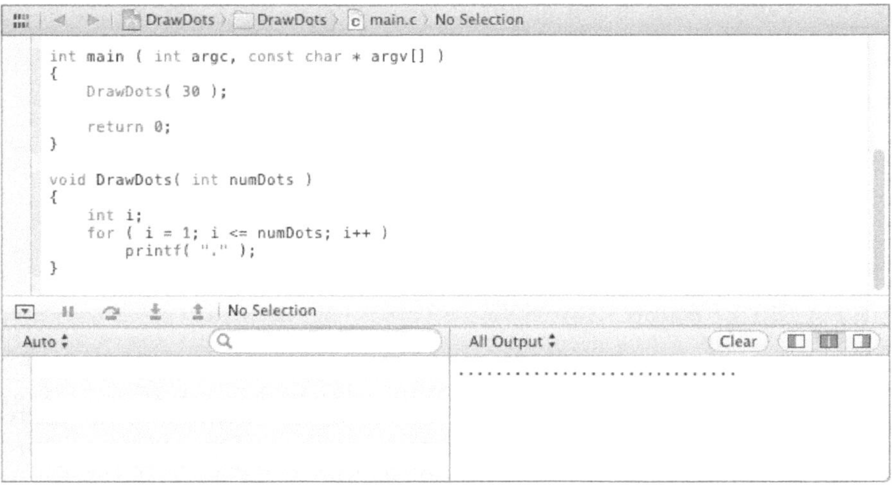
DrawDots
DrawDots
main.c
No Selection
int main (int argc, const char * argv[])
{
DrawDots(30);
return 0;
}
void DrawDots(int numDots)
{
int i;
for (i = 1; i <= numDots; i++)
printf(".");
}
No Selection
Auto
All Output
Clear
....

Figure 7-9. *The function* `DrawDots()` *drawing 30 dots*

Parameters Are Temporary

When a function gets called, a temporary variable is created for each of its parameters. When the function exits (returns to the calling function), that variable goes away.

In the example, you passed a value of 30 into `DrawDots()` as a parameter. The value came to rest in the temporary variable named `numDots`. Once `DrawDots()` exited, this version of `numDots` ceased to exist.

> **NOTE:** Remember, a variable declared inside a function can only be used inside that function. For this reason, they are often called *local* variables.

It is perfectly acceptable for two functions to use the same variable names for completely different purposes. For example, using a variable name like `i` as a counter in a `for` loop is fairly standard. What happens when, in the middle of just such a `for` loop, you call a function that also uses a variable named `i`? Here's an example:

```
#include <stdio.h>

void DrawDots( int numDots );

int main (int argc, const char * argv[])
{
```

```
    int i;
    for ( i=1; i<=10; i++ ) {
        DrawDots( 30 );
        printf( "\n" );
    }
    return 0;
}

void DrawDots( int numDots )
{
    int i;
    for ( i = 1; i <= numDots; i++ )
        printf( "." );
}
```

This code prints a series of 10 rows of dots, with 30 dots in each row. After each call to `DrawDots()`, a carriage return (\n) is printed, moving the cursor in position to begin the next row of dots.

Notice that `main()` and `DrawDots()` each feature a variable named `i`. `main()` uses the variable `i` as a counter, tracking the number of rows of dots printed. `DrawDots()` also uses `i` as a counter, tracking the number of dots in the row it is printing. Won't `DrawDots()`'s copy of `i` mess up `main()`'s copy of `i`? No!

When `main()` starts executing, memory gets allocated for its copy of `i`. When `main()` calls `DrawDots()`, additional memory gets allocated for the `DrawDots()` copy of `i`. When `DrawDots()` exits, the memory for its copy of `i` is deallocated—freed up so it can be used again for some other variable.

> **NOTE:** A parameter or variable declared within a function is known as an *automatic variable*, so called because they are automatically allocated when the function begins, and then automatically deallocated when the function ends. `DrawDots()` has a two automatic variables: the variable `i` and the `numDots` parameter.

The Difference Between Arguments and Parameters

Here's one final point: the value passed into a function is known as an *argument*. The variable declared to receive that argument is known as a *parameter*. In this line of code

```
DrawDots( 30 );
```

the constant 30 is an argument being passed to DrawDots(); it's not a parameter.

Many programmers use the terms "argument" and "parameter" interchangeably. For example, someone might talk about passing a parameter to a function. Strictly speaking, you pass an argument to a function to be received as a parameter. As long as you understand that point, the term "parameter passing" will do just fine.

Function Return Value

Parameters let you copy values to functions, but what about getting values from functions? That's where a function's return value comes into play. A *return value* passes a single value from the function back to the function that called it.

You declare the type of value a function will return right at the beginning of the function's definition. This permits the function to be used in an expression, just as if the function was a variable of that type. The return statement at the end of the function's body determines what that value will be.

Now we can finally explain the mysterious `return 0;` statement that's been in every example in this book. The function `main` is declared to return an int value:

```
int main( int argc, const char *argv[] )
```

When the `main()` function ends, it returns a value of 0 to whoever called it using this statement:

```
return 0;
```

The function that called `main()`—`start()`, if you must know—receives the value when `main()` ends. The meaning of the value must be agreed upon in advance. In the case of `main()`, the value returned is the program's so-called "status" value. A zero indicates that the program ran successfully. Any other value indicates that the program failed to run or encountered some problem.

To see function return values in action, let's create a function named `Average()`. You'll find this function in the *Average* project in the 07.03 - Average folder. `Average()` takes two `int`s and returns the average of those two values:

```
#include <stdio.h>

int Average( int a, int b );

int main (int argc, const char * argv[])
{
    int avg;
```

```
    avg = Average( 7, 23 );
    printf( "The average of 7 and 23 is %d.\n", avg );

    return 0;
}

int Average( int a, int b )
{
    return ( a + b ) / 2;
}
```

The function `Average()` is defined to take two `int` parameters (`a` and `b`) and return an `int` value. The call to `Average()` in `main()` copies two values (7 and 23) into the two parameters and executes the code in the function.

The `Average()` function has a single `return` statement. The expression in the `return` statement calculates a new value using the values of the two parameters and returns the result to the caller.

Back in `main()`, the value calculated by `Average()`'s return statement becomes the value of the `Average( 7, 23 )` statement in the expression. You can use that returned value any way you like. You can use it as an expression in an `if` statement (`if ( Average(i,j) > 100 )`), assign it another variable (as we've done here), make it part of a more complex expression (`1+Average(i,j)*2`)—the choices are all yours. The key thing to remember is that the value of a function call in an expression will be the value returned by the function.

printf() Returns a Value

You are also within your rights to completely ignore the value returned by a function, like this:

```
Average( 2, 108 );
```

If you write a function call, but ignore its return value, nothing bad happens. The function executes and the value it returns simply disappears into the mist. For a function like `Average()` that would be silly, because the whole purpose of the function is to calculate a value. If you weren't interested in the value, you wouldn't have called the function.

But a lot of functions perform useful tasks while also returning a value, which may or may not be of interest to the caller. It is worth noting that `printf()` is actually declared to return an int. The value returned is the number of characters generated, or a negative value if an error occurred. The vast majority of programmers ignore this return value because all they're interested in is getting a message sent to the console. That's all we've cared about so far. But if you ever find yourself in a situation where you want to know exactly how many characters the `printf()` function sent to the console, all you have to do is observe the value returned by the `printf()` function call, like this:

```
int lineLength;
lineLength = printf( "The average of 7 and 23 is %d.\n", Average(7, 23) );
printf( "The previous line is %d characters long.\n", lineLength-1 );
```

Multiple Return Statements

Let's create a slightly more complex example that also highlights a feature of `return` statements. In the folder 07.04 - Minimum, open the *Minimum* project. It contains a function named `Minimum()` that takes two `int` parameters and returns the smaller of the two.

```
#include <stdio.h>

int Minimum( int a, int b );

int main (int argc, const char * argv[])
{
    printf( "%d is the smaller of 7 and 23\n", Minimum(7,23) );
    printf( "%d is the smaller of 23 and 7\n", Minimum(23,7) );
    return 0;
}

int Minimum( int a, int b )
{
    if ( a < b )
        return a;
    return b;
}
```

For a function that returns a value—we'll get to functions that don't shortly—the `return` statement expresses what value is to be returned. But the `return` statement has another important attribute: it ends the function.

Just as the `break` statement you used in Chapter 6 will jump out of any remaining code in a loop, the `return` statement jumps out of any remaining code in that function. Typically, you'll find a single `return` statement at the very end of the function, as you've seen in `main()`, where its purpose is to state the value to be returned. But you can have additional `return` statements elsewhere in the function. If a `return` isn't the last statement, it causes the function to exit immediately and return the stated value to the caller. No further code in the function is performed.

In the `Minimum()` function, the `if` statement determines if the value of `a` is less than the value of `b`. If it is, the `return a;` statement is performed. This causes the value of `a` to be returned as the value for this function and no further statements in `Minimum()` are performed.

If `a` is not less than `b`, the statement following the `if` statement is executed instead. The `return b;` statement causes the value of `b` to be returned. The end result is that the value of the `Minimum()` function call will be the smaller of its two argument values.

Returning Nothing at All

Earlier in the book we alluded to the `void` type. The `void` type is a special type that means "nothing" or "no value." You use it in places to indicate that something doesn't have any value at all, and `void` has two very important roles in functions.

Both of these roles are illustrated in this function definition from the *Hello3* project you ran in Chapter 3:

```
void SayHello( void );
```

A return type of `void` indicates that the function does not return a value. That's it. The function does not pass a value of any kind back to the caller. You can call a function with a `void` return type—called a *void function*—like this:

```
SayHello();
```

But you can't use it in an expression, because it has no value:

```
myVar = SayHello();     // <-- error, SayHello() does not return a value
```

The other use of `void` is in the parameter list of a function that does not have any parameters. The definition `SayHello( void )` means that there are no values passed to `SayHello()`. When you call `SayHello()`, you don't put any arguments between the two parentheses.

> **NOTE:** You can still use a `return` statement in a `void` function; you just omit the expression. This is sometimes called an *empty return* statement. It will still stop the function and return execution to the function that called it, but no value is passed.

A function can have a return value and no parameters, parameters but no return value, or any other combination that makes sense.

TIP: The compiler will help you use the `return` statement correctly. If you try to use a `return` with an expression in a `void` function, or forget the expression in a function that returns a value, or just forget the `return` statement altogether, the compiler will issue a warning. Check for those warnings to make sure you are using the appropriate `return` statement.

Putting it All Together

Brace yourself. You are about to use almost everything you've learned about C so far. You've learned about variables, expressions, functions, `if` statements, loops, pointers, and parameter passing. Now we're going to show a program that uses them all together. Open the *Factor* project in Xcode, which you'll find in the 07.05 - Factor folder, fasten your seatbelt, and please keep your arms and legs inside the vehicle at all times.

Using Pointers as Parameters

Combining the individual pieces of C definitely creates a whole that is more than a sum of its parts. The first bit of alchemy we'll perform is to combine pointers with function parameters.

You've seen how function parameters can be used to pass any number of values to a function, and the function's return value can pass a single value back. But what if you need to pass more than one value back? Passing pointers as parameters neatly solves this problem.

The *Factor* project defines a function named `Factor()`. The purpose of the `Factor()` function is to examine a number, determine if the number is prime, and find two factors of that number. If you were sleeping that day in math class, the factors of a number are any two numbers that when multiplied together equal the original number. If the number is prime, its factors will be 1 and the number itself.

Define the function like this:

```
bool Factor( int number, int *firstFactorPtr, int *secondFactorPtr );
```

`Factor()` returns a Boolean value (true or false) to the caller and it takes three parameters: an `int` value, and two pointers to `int` values. Remember that a pointer is a memory address of another variable. Instead of passing a value, as you've done so far, you're going to pass the address of a value to the function via a parameter. Can you see where this is going?

Inside the `Factor()` function, the `*firstFactorPtr` and `*secondFactorPtr` expressions refer to whatever `int` values those two pointers point to. The `Factor()` function doesn't have to know the names of those variables, nor must they be in the same scope, but it can still use and modify those values using the indirection operator (*).

To make this work, the `main()` function first declares two `int` variables and then passes the addresses of those variables to `Factor()` as arguments.

```
int n;
int factor1, factor2;
bool isPrime;
n = 15;
isPrime = Factor( n, &factor1, &factor2 );
```

In the `Factor()` function, the pointers to the two factor variables appear as its parameters. The function calculates the values and uses the indirection operator to store the answer in `int` values that were defined back in `main()`.

```
bool Factor( int number, int *firstFactorPtr, int *secondFactorPtr )
{
    int factor;
    /* ... imagine code that calculates factor here ... */
    *firstFactorPtr = factor;
    *secondFactorPtr = number / factor;
    return false;
}
```

Back in `main()`, after `Factor()` returns, `main()` now has three values: the value returned directly by the `Factor()` function and the values that were set indirectly using pointers.

```
if ( isPrime )
    printf( "the number %d is prime\n", n );
else
    printf( "the number %d has %d and %d as factors\n", n, factor1, factor2 );
```

The end result is that `Factor()` used a combination of a return value and pointers to pass three values back to `main()`.

Factor.xcodeproj

Enough teasing, here's the entire program:

```
#include <stdio.h>
#include <stdbool.h>
#include <math.h>

bool Factor( int number, int *firstFactorPtr, int *secondFactorPtr );

int main(int argc, const char * argv[])
{
    int n;
    for ( n = 2; n <= 20; n++ ) {
        bool isPrime;
        int factor1, factor2;

        isPrime = Factor( n, &factor1, &factor2 );
        if ( isPrime )
            printf( "the number %d is prime\n", n );
        else
            printf( "the number %d has %d and %d as factors\n", n, factor1, factor2 );
        }

    return 0;
}


bool Factor( int number, int *firstFactorPtr, int *secondFactorPtr )
{
    int factor;
    for ( factor = sqrt(number); factor > 1; factor-- ) {
        if ( (number % factor) == 0 ) {
            break;
        }
    }

    *firstFactorPtr = factor;
    *secondFactorPtr = number / factor;
    return ( factor == 1 );
}
```

Figure 7-10 shows the output of the program when run.

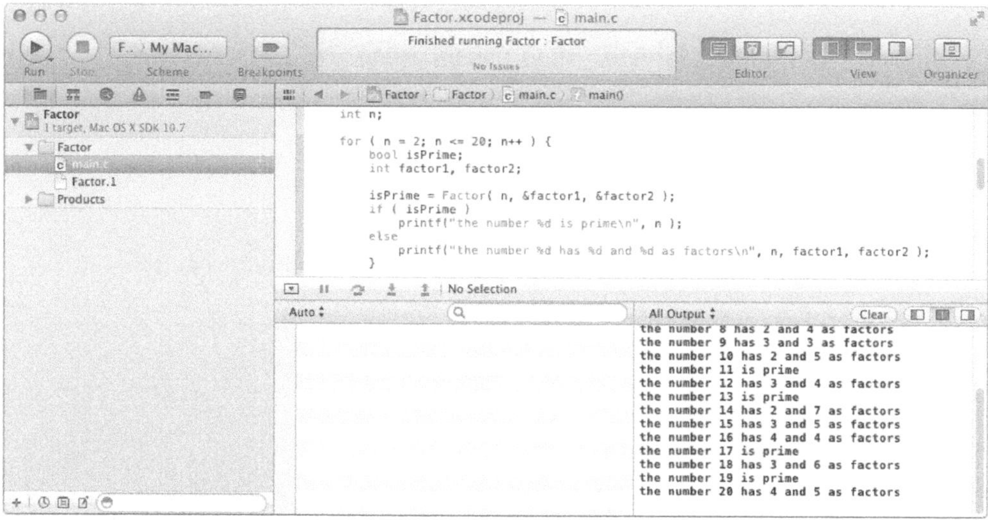

Figure 7-10. *The output of Factor*

By this point in your journey to master C, you should understand practically every aspect of this program.

- You know how to #include the needed header files to get the types and functions your program will use.
- You know how function prototypes are defined.
- You know that the main() function is where your program starts.
- You know how to declare a variable.
- You understand the for loop that sets n = 2 and then tests each number up to, and including, 20.
- You know how a function is called.
  - You know how to pass values to a function that becomes its parameters.
  - You know how the value returned by a function can be used in an expression.
  - You know how to use the `return` statement to decide what value is returned.
- You know how to use an if statement to test a condition and choose between alternate statements.

- You know how to get the address of a variable, and how to store it in a pointer or pass it as a parameter.
- You know how to use the indirection operator (*) to act on the variable that a pointer variable points to.

Go through each line of this code. If anything looks unfamiliar, go back and find that section of the book to review—but we bet you won't have to. Step through it line by line in the debugger and watch how it works.

Some Pointers on Pointers

There are some finer points (no pun intended) about pointers and parameters that you should know about. These will help you understand the best ways to use, and maybe when not to use, pointers in your program.

Pass-By-Value vs. Pass-By-Reference

In the program *Average*, you passed simple (`int`) values to the `Average()` function. The values of the argument expressions were copied into the function's parameters before the function executed. The function could change its parameter variables, but that has no effect on the original values. (We know you know all of this; we're just restating it so it's clear.)

In programming lingo this is called *pass-by-value*. A copy of the value is passed to the function and the function can do anything it wants to with its copy; it will never affect another variable in the program.

In the *Factor* program you passed the addresses of two variables. The `Factor()` function was able to use those pointers to affect variables outside its scope. This method of passing values is called *pass-by-reference*. Instead of copying the value, a reference to the value is passed to the function. The function can use this reference to access and/or modify the original value at will.

Whether to use pass-by-value or pass-by-reference is a perennial topic of debate among programmers, In general, our approach is to use pass-by-value unless there's a compelling reason to use pass-by-reference.

Compelling reasons to use pass-by-reference might be

- The value is a group or collection of values. (This will make sense after you read about arrays in the next chapter.)

- A function must return more than one value. (There are also other solutions to this particular problem that you'll learn about in Chapter 9.)
- The amount of data you need to pass to, or from, a function is cumbersome to copy. Remember the library example at the start of the chapter? Even if you could make a copy of an entire book, it's still much easier to give someone the catalog number of the book instead.
- The information that needs to be passed is a complex collection of values, and the function needs to examine some values and modify others. (Again, this will make more sense after Chapter 9.) It's easier to pass a single reference to the whole mess rather than copying every value the function will need.

The NULL Pointer Value

The C language defines a special pointer value named `NULL` that means "no address." You can assign the `NULL` value to any pointer (`myPointer = NULL`) and you can compare pointer values with `NULL`, as in `if ( myPointer==NULL )`. `NULL` gives you a value that means the pointer doesn't point to any variable at all.

Earlier we stated that memory addresses start at zero and go up, and a variable can be allocated at any address. In practice, that's not entirely true. Addresses do start at 0, but OS X and BSD Unix never allocate variables at address 0, or anywhere near address 0. The reasons why are many, but one important one is so that programmers can be guaranteed that no valid variable address will ever be zero.

The `NULL` constant is address 0. Assigning `NULL` to a pointer is the same as setting its integer value to 0. One side effect is that a lot of C programmers use a short-hand for testing to see if a pointer variable points to a value or not:

```
if ( myPointer ) {
```

Remember that an `if` statement performs its action if the expression is non-zero. Since `NULL` is always zero and any valid variable address will not be zero, this statement is equivalent to `if ( myPointer != NULL )`. We suggest you write out the long form, simply because it makes your intentions clearer; both are common.

The Dark Side of Pointers

> *With great power comes great responsibility.*
>
> – Uncle Ben, from *The Amazing Spider-Man*

(Cue sinister music.) Pointers are very powerful, but they have a dark side. They occupy a dangerous land full of hazards just waiting to snare an unsuspecting programmer. The correct, and safe, use of pointers requires careful planning and attention to detail.

The principle peril of pointers is that they can point anywhere. There are no safeguards to ensure that a pointer points to the kind of value you expect it to. It can just as easily point to another kind of value, or unused memory, or the part of memory where the code for your program is stored, or an address that doesn't even exist.

The effects of using pointers that point to the wrong thing range from the perplexing to the disastrous. If a pointer points to some other variable, changing it will have a bizarre effect on your program—the value you expected to change won't, and some other unrelated variable will spontaneously change. If the pointer points to memory that doesn't exist, the hardware will catch it and terminate your program with a "segment fault" signal, colloquially known as a "crash."

PHYSICAL AND LOGICAL MEMORY ADDRESSES

If you're reading this book carefully, you might have detected an inconsistency.

We said that memory addresses start at zero and go up. We said C reserves address 0 (`NULL`) to mean "no address." We said that if you try to access a memory address that doesn't exist, your program will crash. And we said that if you try to access address 0 (via a pointer set to `NULL`), your application will crash. But why? Doesn't address 0 always exist? Isn't address 0 the one address in every computer that exists?

Yes and no. The answer lies in the difference between physical memory addresses and logical memory addresses.

In *physical* memory—the RAM that's soldered to your motherboard—address 0 is the first byte of memory. But your program never addresses physical memory directly. It works with what are called *logical* addresses.

Modern computers use a system called *virtual memory* that maps (translates) the logical addresses that your program uses into the physical addresses of your RAM. This is done through (surprise!) a bunch of pointers called a *page map*. When your program is started it is allocated a range of logical memory addresses to use. These addresses might start at, say, one million (1,000,000) and go up from there. You'll notice that address 0 is intentionally left out. If your program allocates an integer at address 1,000,000 and stores a value in it, the CPU uses its page map to translate that logical address into the actual physical address of your RAM. Don't worry about the complexity of this; it's all handled by hardware and it's mind-numbingly fast.

This arrangement benefits your program in two ways. The first is security. If you accidently use an uninitialized pointer, your program could end up accessing a memory address that's not even part of your program. Imagine if your program could change values in another running program! Well, relax; you can't. Your program can only access the logical addresses that have been assigned to it. Try to access anything outside that range and your program will crash.

The second benefit is simplicity. Every program can allocate its first variable at address 1,000,000. Each program has the same logical addresses, but the page map translates them into different physical addresses. One program doesn't have to worry about using addresses of another program. Each program lives in its own separate universe, and they never collide.

The short and long of it is that you don't need to worry about it. You'll never see the actual (physical) address that your data is stored in. When programming and debugging, everything will be in the logical addresses allotted to your program.

Here are some tips for staying safe with pointers:

- Make sure your pointer variables are initialized. An uninitialized integer variable simply contains a goofy number, but an uninitialized pointer variable will point to some random, likely invalid, memory location.
- If you don't have a value to put in a pointer, set it to NULL. Test the pointer to make sure it isn't equal to NULL before you use it. Dereferencing a NULL pointer is the fastest, and most common, way to crash your program. If a pointer is no longer valid, set it to NULL again.

- Make sure you don't use pointers to variables that no longer exist. In the Factor program, main() allocated a variable and passed its address to Factor(), which used that pointer. The variable existed before, and after, the call to Factor() so that was safe. But what happens if you reverse it? What if Factor() allocates a variable and passes its address back to main()? It's unsafe for main() to use that pointer. Why? Because the variable created by Factor() disappeared as soon as the function returned to main(), so the pointer that main() has now points to a variable that no longer exists. That is a recipe for disaster.

Don't feel bad if you make a mistake with pointers, because *you will make a mistake with pointers*. We doubt there's a C programmer alive that hasn't crashed their application using a `NULL` or uninitialized pointer. Professional programmers with decades of experience do it. In fact, it's the number one reason applications crash.

Global and Static Variables

So far we've used function parameters, return values, and pointers to pass values to and from other functions. We did this because the scope of an automatic variable is confined to the function (or block) it was declared in. This is, by far, the most common way that values are passed around inside a program. There is, however, an alternative.

Global Variables

A *global variable* is a variable that is accessible from every function in your program. Said another way, the scope of a global variable is the entire program. The variable is created before the program begins and exists until it ends.

Global variables provide an alternative to passing values via parameters. Global variables are just like regular variables, with the exception that they can be referenced inside any of your program's functions. One function might initialize the global variable; another might change its value; and another function might print the value of the global variable in the console window.

As you design your programs, you'll have to make some basic decisions about data sharing between functions. If you'll be sharing a variable among a number of functions, you might want to consider making the variable a global. Globals are especially useful when you want to share a variable between two functions that are several calls apart.

Several calls apart? At times, you'll find yourself passing a parameter to a function, not because that function needs the parameter, but because the function calls another function that needs the parameter.

Look at this code:

```
#include <stdio.h>
void PassAlong( int myVar );
void PrintMyVar( int myVar );

int main( void )
{
    int myVar;
    myVar = 10;
    PassAlong( myVar );
    return 0;
}

void PassAlong( int myVar )
{
    PrintMyVar( myVar );
}

void PrintMyVar( int myVar )
{
    printf( "myVar = %d\n", myVar );
}
```

Notice that `main()` passes `myVar` to the function `PassAlong()`. `PassAlong()` doesn't actually make use of `myVar`. Instead, it just passes `myVar` along to the function `PrintMyVar()`. `PrintMyVar()` prints `myVar` and then returns. If `myVar` were a global, you could have avoided some parameter passing. `main()` and `PrintMyVar()` could have shared `myVar` without the use of parameters.

WHEN TO USE GLOBALS

When should you use parameters? When should you use globals?

In a nutshell, you should generally avoid using globals unless there's a compelling reason to do so. Global variables offer a shortcut that saves you from having to pass information up and down your chain of function calls and gives disparate functions access to the same information. They do save time, but sometimes at the cost of proper program design. As you move on to object programming languages like Objective-C, you'll find that you rarely (if ever) need globals.

So why learn about them? There are times when a global is absolutely the correct solution. On the other hand, a telltale sign of an inexperienced programmer is overuse of globals.

None of these decisions are cut and dried. There's a very influential book titled *Design Patterns: Elements of Reusable Object-Oriented Design* written by the so-called "Gang of Four," Erich Gamma, Richard Helm, Ralph Jonson, and John Vlissides. The book describes common programming problems and elegant solutions to those problems. These "design patterns," as they have become known as, are universal and can be applied to just about any computer language. If you're serious about programming, you should become familiar with design patterns.

At the same time, people have observed "anti-patterns," bad programming practices used by poor programmers. Using too many global variables is an anti-pattern, and here's why. One philosophy of variable scope is that it should match the scope of its purpose. In other words, a variable should be available (in scope) to that code that makes use of that variable, and not much else. Functions shouldn't have access to unrelated variables. A global variable is accessible everywhere, but it's rare to find a variable whose purpose is applicable to every function in your program. As your programs get larger, they become even more rare.

Let's take a look at the proper way to add globals to your programs.

Adding Globals to Your Programs

Adding globals to your programs is easy. Just declare a variable outside of any function. Here's the example we showed you earlier, using globals in place of parameters:

```
#include <stdio.h>

void PassAlong( void );
void PrintMyVar( void );

int gMyVar;

int main (int argc, const char * argv[])
{
    gMyVar = 10;
    PassAlong();
    return 0;
}

void PassAlong( void )
{
    PrintMyVar();
}

void PrintMyVar( void )
{
    printf( "gMyVar = %d\n", gMyVar );
}
```

This example starts with a variable declaration, right at the top of the program. Because gMyVar was declared outside of a function, gMyVar becomes a global variable, accessible to each of the program's functions. Notice that none of the functions in this version use parameters. As a reminder, when a function is declared without parameters, use the keyword void in place of a parameter list.

> **NOTE:** Did you notice that letter g at the beginning of the global's name? Many C programmers start each of their global variables with the letter g (for global). Doing this will distinguish your local variables from your global variables.

Static Variables

So far all of the variables you've defined have a lifespan equal to their scope. Parameter and automatic variables defined in a function are created when the function starts and disappear again when it ends; this is also the same span of code that has access to that variable. Likewise, a global variable exists as long as the program does, and it's accessible anywhere in the program.

A static variable is a hybrid that has the scope of an automatic variable and the longevity of a global variable. It's created when the program starts, but its scope (the code that can "see" that variable) is limited to one function or block of code. Here's an example:

```
#include <stdio.h>
void Countdown( void );

int main (int argc, const char * argv[])
{
    Countdown();
    Countdown();
    Countdown();
    Countdown();

    return 0;
}

void Countdown( void )
{
    static int count = 3;

    if ( count != 0 )
        printf( "%d ...\n", count-- );
    else
        printf( "Lift-off!\n" );
}
```

The variable count is defined as `static` and includes an *initializer*. The variable is created when the program starts and is immediately assigned the value after the equals sign. This happens only once. Even though it looks like it would be set to 3 every time the function runs, it doesn't. And that's good, because you want it to remember its value over time.

> **NOTE:** Both globals and statics can have initializer values. If you don't specify an initializer value, the variable is set to 0 before your program starts. Automatic variables can be uninitialized, but global and static variables are always initialized. The value of your initializer must be a constant; it can't be an expression that uses variables or function calls.

Run the program and you'll see this output:

```
3 ...
2 ...
1 ...
Lift-off!
```

Each time the `Countdown()` function runs it looks at the value in count. If it's not 0, it outputs that number and then subtracts one from it. If it is 0, it outputs the message "Lift-off!"

This works because the value of count is set to 3 before the program starts. Every time `Countdown()` is called, it decrements the count variable by 1 until it gets to 0.

The scope of count is still limited to the `Countdown()` function. You can't refer to the count variable in `main()` or any other function. `Countdown()` can, however, safely get the address of `count` (`&count`) and pass that pointer to another function or return it. It's safe because count doesn't go away when `Countdown()` returns, so that address will always point to a valid variable.

OTHER SCOPES

Variables can have scopes besides local and global. The `static` keyword can be added to a global variable or function to limit its scope to a single source file (like `main.c`), which is called a module; technically it's a *translation unit*, but only hard-core compiler geeks ever call it that. Also note that variables and functions defined in other modules aren't automatically available everywhere. You must use the `extern` keyword to define the functions and global variables you plan to use from other modules. Poke around some of the header (.h) files that you've been #includeing and you'll see this a lot.

The extern and static keywords are particularly useful when organizing your program into multiple modules. We'll show you how to do that in Chapter 11.

What's Next?

Wow! You really are becoming a C programmer. In this chapter alone you covered pointers, function parameters (both by-value and by-reference), global and static variables, and function return values.

You're starting to develop a sense of the power and sophistication of the C language. You've built an excellent foundation. Now you're ready to take off.

The second half of this book starts with an introduction of the concept of data types. Throughout this book, you've been working with a single data type, the int. The next chapter will introduce the concept of arrays, strings, pointer arithmetic, and other kinds of numbers. Let's go.

CHAPTER 7 EXERCISES

1. Predict the result of each of the following code fragments:

   a.
```
void AddOne( int *myVar );
int main (int argc, const char * argv[])
{
    int num, i;
    num = 5;
    for ( i = 0; i < 20; i++ )
        AddOne( &num );
    printf( "Final value is %d.\n", num );
    return 0;
}

void AddOne( int *myVar )
{
     (*myVar) ++;
}
```

b.
```
int gNumber;
int MultiplyIt( int myVar );
int main (int argc, const char * argv[])
{
    int i; gNumber = 2;
    for ( i = 1; i <= 2; i++ )
        gNumber *= MultiplyIt( gNumber );
    printf( "Final value is %d.\n", gNumber );
    return 0;
}

int MultiplyIt( int myVar )
{
    return( myVar * gNumber );
}
```

c.
```
int gNumber;
int DoubleIt( int myVar );
int main (int argc, const char * argv[])
{
    int i;
    gNumber = 1;
    for ( i = 1; i <= 10; i++ )
        gNumber = DoubleIt( gNumber );
    printf( "Final value is %d.\n", gNumber );
    return 0;
}

int DoubleIt( int myVar )
{
    return 2 * myVar;
}
```

2. In the *Factor* project, add the following code just before the return statement in `main()`:

```
if ( isPrime )
    printf( "The last number tested was prime.\n" );
```

Explain why this code will not compile.

3. In the *Factor* project, a combination of a return value and pointers were used to return three distinct values from the `Factor()` function. We also said that use of pointers should be considered only when they are "compelling." Are pointers really needed for the `Factor()` function to work? Think about the problem a moment. All three numbers returned by `Factor()` are related to each other, or can be derived from one of the other values; either factor

can be calculated using the original number and the other factor, and the value of the factors will tell you if the number is prime. Rewrite the *Factor* project so that the `Factor()` function doesn't use any pointers.

Chapter 8

More Data Types

You may now consider yourself a C Programmer, First Class. At this point, you've mastered all the basic elements of C programming. You know that C programs are made up of functions, one (and only one!) of which is named `main()`. Each of these functions uses keywords (such as `if`, `for`, and `while`), operators (such as =, ++, and *=), and variables to manipulate data and make decisions.

Sometimes you'll use a parameter to pass values between a calling and a called function. Sometimes these parameters are passed by value; other times pointers are used to pass a parameter by address. Some functions return values. Others, declared with the `void` keyword, don't return a value.

So far, all of the variables you've declared are `int`s. In this chapter, you'll focus on other types of variables. As you'll soon see, there are many other data types are out there.

Data Types Beyond Int

So far, the focus has been on `int`s, which are extremely useful when it comes to working with integer numbers. You can add two `int`s together. You can check if an `int` is even, odd, or prime. There are a lot of things you can do with `int`s, as long as you limit yourself to integer numbers.

> **NOTE:** Just as a reminder that 1, 2, 3, 527, 33, and –2 are all *integer* numbers, while 35.7, 0.1, and -1.2345 are not.

What do you do if you want to work with numbers such as 3.14159 and –98.6? Check out this slice of code:

```
int myNum;

myNum = 3.5;
printf( "myNum = %d", myNum );
```

Since `myNum` is an `int`, the number 3.5 will be truncated before it is assigned to `myNum`. When this code ends, `myNum` will be left with a value of 3 and not 3.5 as intended. Do not despair. C provides *floating point* data types, specifically designed to deal with non-integer numbers.

> **NOTE:** Floating point numbers are extremely flexible. They can store very large numbers (47,951,200,000,000,000,000,000,000,000,000.0) and very small numbers (0.0000000017346). The name "floating point" refers to the fact that the *radix point* (also called the "decimal point") can be placed anywhere relative to the significant digits, which is what allows floating point values to represent such a wide range of numbers.

The three floating point data types are `float`, `double`, and `long double`. The types differ in the number of bytes allocated to each and, therefore, the range of values each can hold. The relative sizes of these three types will vary depending on what kind of CPU you are using and other variables. Let's look at a program you can run to tell you the size of these three types in your development environment and to show you various ways to use `printf()` to print floating point numbers.

FloatSizer

Look inside the *Learn C Projects* folder, inside the subfolder named *08.01 - FloatSizer*, and open the project named *FloatSizer.xcodeproj*. Figure 8-1 shows the results of running `FloatSizer` on a 64-bit Intel Mac Pro using Xcode. The first three lines of output tell you the size, in bytes, of the types `float`, `double`, and `long double`, respectively.

Never assume the size of a type. As you'll see when you go through the source code, C gives you everything you need to check the size of a specific type in your development environment. If you need to be sure of a type's size, write a program to check the size for yourself.

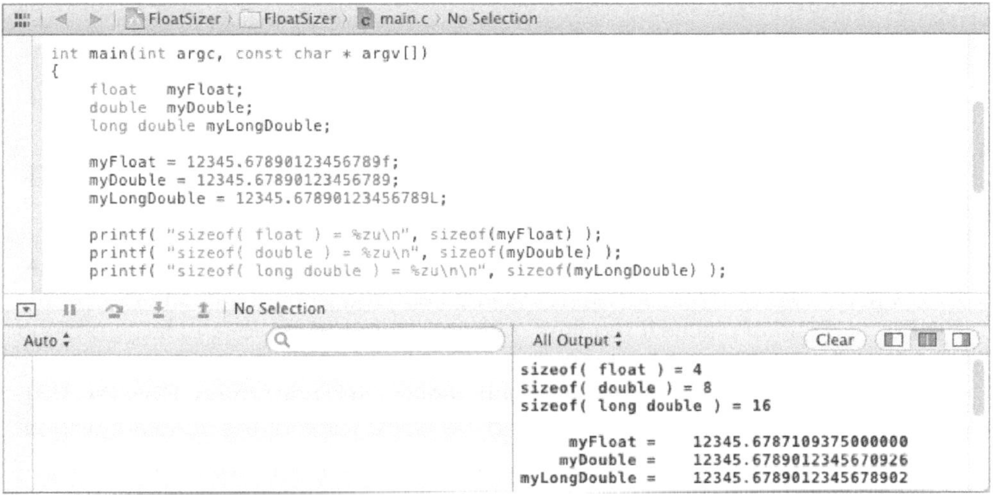

Figure 8-1. *The output of FloatSizer*

Walking Through the FloatSizer Source Code

FloatSizer starts with the standard #include:

```
#include <stdio.h>
```

main() defines three variables, a float, a double, and a long double.

```
int main (int argc, const char * argv[])
{
    float           myFloat;
    double          myDouble;
    long double     myLongDouble;
```

Next, you assign a value to each of the three variables. Notice that you've assigned the same number to each. The "f" at the end of the number assigned to myFloat tells the compiler that this constant is of type float. You could also have used an "F" at the end of the constant to say the same thing. The "L" at the end of the constant assigned to myLongDouble signifies a long double. An "l" would have accomplished the same thing. Floating point constants (that is, any number with a decimal place) with no letter at the end are assumed to be of type double.

```
    myFloat = 12345.67890123456789f;
    myDouble = 12345.67890123456789;
    myLongDouble = 12345.67890123456789L;
```

> **TIP:** Programmers tend to use the capital "L" at the end of long constants, because the lower case "l" can be easily confused with the number "1".

Why should you care about this? Assigning the right type to a constant ensures that the appropriate amount of memory is allocated for each constant. A numeric constant in a C program has a type (and size) just like a variable, and in this case it's important that they match. As you'll see as you get further into the program, a `float` (4 bytes) is not nearly large enough to hold this constant at the number of decimal places it requires. A `double` (8 bytes) is close to large enough but not quite. Declaring the constant as a `float` or `double` means that some rounding will occur before the first assignment is even performed. Only the `long double` (16 bytes) is large enough to hold the entire value of the constant without rounding.

Let's continue walking through the source code. `main()` uses C's `sizeof` operator to print the size of each of your three floating point types. Even though `sizeof` doesn't look like the other operators you've seen (+, *, /, and so on), it is indeed an operator. Stranger still, `sizeof` is typically followed by a pair of parentheses surrounding a single operand and looks much like a function call. The operand is either a type (like `long double`) or a variable (like `myLongDouble`). `sizeof` returns the size, in bytes, of its operand.

```
printf( "sizeof( float ) = %zu\n", sizeof( float ) );
printf( "sizeof( double ) = %zu\n", sizeof( double ) );
printf( "sizeof( long double ) = %zu\n\n", sizeof( long double ) );
```

The rest of this program is dedicated to various and sundry ways you can print your floating point numbers. So far, all of your programs have printed ints using the `%d` format specifier. The Standard Library has a set of format specifiers for all of C's built-in data types, including several for printing floating point numbers.

THE RIGHT SPECIFIER

Did you notice that we changed from using the `%d` conversion specifier in the `printf()` function to using `%zu`?

The type of the `sizeof` operator is an obscure, but important, type called `size_t`. The `size_t` (for "size type") type is an unsigned integer type that is guaranteed to be large enough to count all of the bytes your computer can address. See the sidebar "Computer Architecture and Pointer Sizes" in Chapter 7 for a refresher. The size of the `size_t` type will be different depending on the CPU architecture, but will generally be an integer that's the size of a pointer. The purpose of `size_t` is so that you don't have to care. When you're dealing with values that represent the size of things in memory, use a `size_t` variable or expression and it will always work. (We'll talk more about this in the next section.)

The `printf()` function has a special format specifier (%zu) just for `size_t` values. The "u" means it's an unsigned integer (you can't have a negative number of bytes), and the "z" means it's a "size" value.

The format specifier `%f` will print `float` and `double` variables and `%Lf` will print `long double` variables, all in their natural, decimal format.

```
printf( "myFloat = %f\n", myFloat );
printf( "myDouble = %f\n", myDouble );
printf( "myLongDouble = %Lf\n\n", myLongDouble );
```

Here's the result of these three `printf()`s:

```
myFloat = 12345.678711
myDouble = 12345.678901
myLongDouble = 12345.678901
```

NOTE: The number you see on your computer might be different. Different CPUs use subtly different methods for representing floating point numbers. This results in slightly different accuracy and rounding.

As a reminder, all three of these numbers were assigned the value

```
12345.67890123456789
```

Notice that each of the printed numbers was cut off six digits after the decimal place. That is the default for the `%f` format specifier. The fact that `myDouble` and `myLongDouble` are a bit more accurate than `myFloat` makes sense, since `myFloat` is only 4 bytes long, so less memory means less accuracy. If you were dealing with a number like 3.275, a `float` would be plenty big, and six digits after the decimal place would be plenty wide enough to accommodate the number. As is, the 4-byte limit of the `float` is causing the original number to be rounded, and the six digits past the decimal limit is causing your `double` and `long double` to be clipped. Let's keep going.

Format Specifier Modifiers

Your next `printf()`s will use format specifier modifiers (that's a mouthful, isn't it?) to more closely control the output produced by `printf()`. Like C types, `printf()` format specifiers have a basic type that can be augmented by combining it with various modifiers.

A specifier begins with a % and ends with the basic specifier. So far we've shown you the signed integer (%d or %i), unsigned integer (%u), and floating point (%f) specifiers. Between the % and the specifier are where the modifiers go. The long (L) and size (z) modifiers alter the size of the value the printf() is expecting in its argument list. We're now going to show you some other formatting modifiers.

By using %25.16f instead of %f, you tell printf() to print the floating point number with an accuracy of 16 places past the decimal and to add spaces, if necessary, in front of the number so it takes up at least 25 character positions.

```
printf( "myFloat = %25.16f\n", myFloat );
printf( "myDouble = %25.16f\n", myDouble );
printf( "myLongDouble = %25.16lf\n\n", myLongDouble );
```

Here's the result of these three printf()s:

```
myFloat =     12345.6787109375000000
myDouble =     12345.6789012345670926
myLongDouble =     12345.6789012345678902
```

The number (25) before the decimal point is called the *minimum field width* modifier. The decimal point and the number (.16) after it are, together, called the *precision* modifier.

printf() printed each of these numbers using a "precision" of 16 places past the decimal point. Go on, count them; we'll wait. If the digits stop before 16 places are reached, zeros are added. This is called *padding*. The 16 digits to the right of the decimal, plus one for the decimal, plus the five digits to the left of the decimal total 22 (16 + 1 + 5 = 22) characters. You asked printf() to use at least 25 characters, so printf() added three spaces to the left of each number (padding with spaces).()

THE ACCURACY OF NUMBERS IN C

You originally asked printf() to print a float with the following value:

```
12345.67890123456789
```

The best approximation of this number you were able to represent using a float is this:

12345.6787109375000000

Where did this approximation come from? It has to do with the way your computer stores floating point numbers.

Chapter 4 described, at length, how integer numbers are represented (computer science majors call this *encoded*) using a sequence of binary bits. Floating point numbers are also represented by a sequence of bits, but it's a little more complicated than integers. (Who are we kidding?

Everything in a computer is a sequence of binary bits! Your bank account balance is a sequence of binary bits. Your copy of the movie *Finding Nemo* is a sequence of binary bits. We promise to stop reminding you of this in the future.)

A single floating point number is basically two numbers that combine to form its value: an integer that represents the significant digits of the number (with the funny name *significand*, also known as the *mantissa* or *coefficient*) and a second integer that is an exponent. If you've ever studied any science or engineering, you've run across scientific notation, like the following:

$2.738 \cdot 10^9$

It's a two-part number that consists of the significant digits of the number plus a power of ten that tells you where the decimal place goes. In the example given, the number is 2,738,000,000. If the exponent was 10^2, the number would be 273.8. If the exponent was 10^{-4}, the number would be 0.0002738. Both the significand and the exponent can be negative.

Floating point numbers use, essentially, the same scheme. The biggest difference is that the exponent is a power of 2 instead of 10 because computers have bits, not fingers.

So why is all this important? Just as ints can't represent integer values beyond the range of bits it has, a floating point number can't represent more *significant digits* than the range of bits it uses for its significand. This is the critical difference to understand. An integer variable has a *fixed range* based on its size. A floating point variable has a *fixed accuracy* based on its size.

Assign any number to a floating point variable and—no matter how big or small the value is—the first handful digits will be accurately represented. But as the number of digits gets longer and longer, it requires more bits of the significand. At some point the number will be too complex to store. But unlike an integer (that simply can't store a number that's too big), a floating point number will store a number that's as close as it can to the original number.

The take-away message is this: the bigger the floating point type, the greater its accuracy. If a float can't store the exact value, it will store the number that's as close to the real number as it can represent.

The next four printf()s show you the result of using different modifier values to print the same float:

```
printf( "myFloat = %10.1f\n",myFloat );
printf( "myFloat = %.2f\n", myFloat );
printf( "myFloat = %.12f\n", myFloat );
printf( "myFloat = %.9f\n\n", myFloat );
```

Here's the output produced by each of the printf()s:

```
myFloat =    12345.7
myFloat = 12345.68
myFloat = 12345.678710937500
myFloat = 12345.678710938
```

The specifier %10.1f told printf() to print one digit past the decimal and to use ten character positions for the entire number. The specifier %.2f told printf() to print two digits past the decimal and to use as many character positions as necessary to print the entire number. Notice that printf() rounds off the result for you and doesn't simply cut off the number after the specified number of places.

The specifier %.12f told printf() to print 12 digits past the decimal, and the specifier %.9f told printf() to print 9 digits past the decimal. Again, notice the rounding that takes place.

Your format specifier can include a minimum field width, a precision, both, or neither. Unless you need to exactly control the total number of characters used to print a number, you'll probably leave off the first (minimum field width) modifier and just specify the number of digits past the decimal you want printed, using specifiers like %.2f and %.9f.

If you do use a minimum field width, like %4.2f, remember that it's a *minimum* width. printf() will never cut off numbers to make it fit in that many characters; it will only add padding if the number is too short.

Scientific and General Specifiers

The next printf() uses the specifier %e, asking printf() to print the float using scientific or exponential notation.

```
printf( "myFloat = %e\n", myFloat );
```

Here's the corresponding output:

```
myFloat = 1.234568e+04
```

1.234568e+04 is equal to 1.234568 times 10 to the fourth power (1.234568 o 10^4 or 1.234568 o 10,000), which is equal to 12,345.68.

> **TIP:** You can write floating point constants in your C source using exponential notation, too. The compiler understands a number, followed by the letter "e", followed by a power-of-10 exponent. For example, the three statements myDouble = 123456000000.0, myDouble = 1.23456e11, and myDouble = 123456e6 all mean the same thing.

The next two printf()s use the %g specifier. The %g specifier is bit of a chameleon and is more interested in the number of significant digits than the number of digits to the right of the decimal point. If the number can be comfortably formatted using %f, it uses the %f style format. If not, it automatically switches to %e style formatting. For example, the code

```
myFloat = 12345.6789;
printf( "myFloat = %g\n", myFloat );
myFloat = 123456789.0;
printf( "myFloat = %g\n", myFloat );
```

produces the following output:

```
myFloat = 12345.7
myFloat = 1.23457e+08
```

> **TIP:** If you want a mnemonic to help you remember the three floating point specifiers, try this: f=fixed point, e=exponential, g=general.

All three floating point specifiers (%f, %e, and %g) can have a precision modifier. While %f and %e use their precision to determine the number of digits to the right of the decimal point, %g uses it to mean the number of significant digits to display, regardless of where the decimal point goes. If the number can be shown with the desired number of significant digits using the %f format, it is; otherwise, it switches to %e.

To see how this works, return to the FloatSizer project and add these statements:

```
printf( "myFloat = %.20g", myFloat );
printf( "myFloat = %.20g", myDouble );
printf( "myFloat = %.20Lg", myDoubleFloat );
```

You're asking printf() to display each number with up to 20 significant digits. The output will look something like this:

```
myFloat = 12345.6787109375
myDouble = 12345.678901234567093
myLongDouble = 12345.678901234546789
```

Notice that %g doesn't pad the number with zeros. If the number stops after five significant digits, that's as long as it will be.

This %g specifier really highlights the difference in precision between the three floating point variable sizes: float, double, and long double. Notice that while the float value is close, it drifts away from the original value by the 9th digit. The double hangs in there for a whopping 17 digits, but is still slightly off the mark. The long double, however, is spot on, storing exactly the number you wrote in the source.

The Integer Types

At this point you've learned about five different variable types: three floating point types (`float`, `double`, and `long double`) and two integer types (`int` and `unsigned int`). In this section, we'll introduce you to the remaining 10 different types, but hopefully in a way that will make things seem simpler, not more complex.

There are actually only two kinds of numbers in C: integer and floating point. All of the numeric types are just variations on those two themes. The integer types, `int` and `char`, form the first family. You're very familiar with `int`. The `char` (character) type is just another integer type, but one more suited for working with text, which we'll get to later in this chapter. But for now, just know that `char` is just another integer variable type. And you've recently met the floating point family of `float` and `double`.

All of the remaining types in C are variations created by using one the four base types combined with several *type modifiers*. You've already used one modifier (long) to create a `long double`. Here are some of the type modifiers that you'll be working with:

- The long modifier creates a type that uses even more bits for increased range/precision. Note that long can be used with int and double to create a bigger int or a more precise double.
- The short modifier is the opposite of the long modifier and makes a smaller version of the base type for a number that has less range/precision. Note that short can only modify an int.
- The long long modifier (yes, that's "long" twice) uses even more bits than the long type for even greater range. Note that long long can only be used with int.
- The unsigned modifier means the integer can only represent zero and positive numbers. Note that unsigned can modify an int or char.
- The signed modifier is the opposite of unsigned, which means the integer is stored using the twos-compliment format and can represent both positive and negative numbers. (See Chapter 4 again if that didn't make sense.) Note that signed can modify an int or char.

The first three modifiers (`short`, `long`, and `long long`) are size modifiers and you can only use one. That is, you can't create a `short long int`.

The `signed` and `unsigned` modifiers are also mutually exclusive, meaning that you can use one or the other, but never both. You'll rarely see the signed modifier in C source code, because all variable types are `signed` unless you specify otherwise. Thus, the type `signed int` is redundant, so almost no one ever writes that (although it's perfectly legal). Floating point variables are always `signed`; you don't get a choice there.

Programmers are traditionally a lazy lot and very soon tired of writing "long int" and "unsigned int." We're sure they calculated that if they could save themselves 200 keystrokes a day, it would mean they could retire to a desert island that much sooner. Whatever.

Regardless, programmers often exploit a quirk of the integer type modifiers to write less code. If you use any of the `short`, `long`, `long long`, `signed`, or `unsigned` keywords, the compiler *assumes* you are declaring an `int` type—unless you specify otherwise. This means you can leave the actual "int" out of the declaration without changing its meaning. Here are three verbose `int` declarations:

```
unsigned int noSign;
short int kindaSmall;
unsigned long int kindaBig;
```

The following code means exactly the same thing, and you'll find this second form used often:

```
unsigned noSign;
short kindaSmall;
unsigned long kindaBig;
```

We don't care which you use. The compiler doesn't care which you use. Just don't fall into the trap of thinking that `short`, `long`, and `unsigned` are distinct data types. They're not. They're all variations of `int`.

Now that you understand the secret formula for declaring numeric types in C, we'll now list every type of numeric variable in the C99 standard:

```
(signed) char
unsigned char
(signed) short int
unsigned short int
(signed) int
unsigned int
(signed) long int
unsigned long int
(signed) long long int
unsigned long long int
float
double
```

```
long double
```

As you can see, it's not all that complicated. Every C numeric type is a descendant of either a base integer or floating point type. You can make them longer, shorter, or change their sign. The `IntSizer` project will show you how this all works in a real program.

IntSizer.xcodeproj

Open the `IntSizer` project. You'll find it in the *08.02 - IntSizer* folder. `IntSizer` uses some simple `printf()` statements to explore these new types, like this:

```
printf( "sizeof( char ) = %zu\n", sizeof( char ) );
printf( "sizeof( unsigned char ) = %zu\n", sizeof( unsigned char ) );
printf( "sizeof( short int ) = %zu\n", sizeof( short int ) );
...
```

Run the project and you'll see output like that in Figure 8-2.

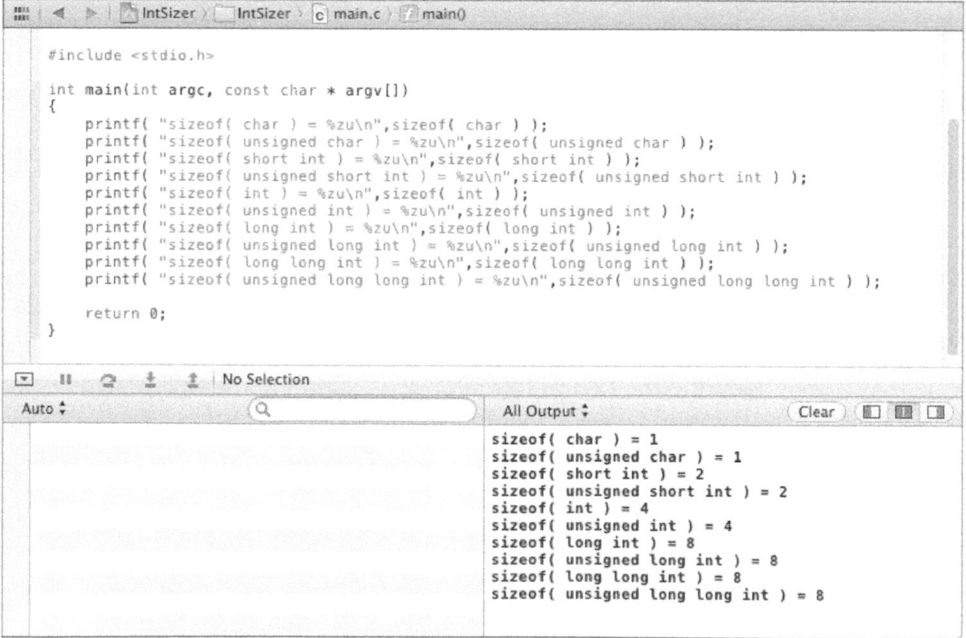

Figure 8-2. *Output of IntSizer*

The first thing you'll notice is that all of the `signed` variables have the same size as their `unsigned` counterparts. That makes sense because the `unsigned` modifier doesn't change the size of the variable, just how the bits in the variable represent numbers.

The other thing you'll notice is that `long int` and `long long int` are the same size. Or, maybe not. Maybe on your system, the `int` and the `long int` values are the same size.

What's up with that? Isn't "long" supposed to mean "use more bits" and "long long" mean "use even more bits?" As it turns out, it's entirely up to the compiler to decide the size of the various integer and floating value sizes. The sizes can overlap, change over time, and be different for different CPUs.

Not long ago, all C `ints` were 2 bytes (16-bits). Then the default size of `ints` became 32 bits; tomorrow it might be 64. In the example shown in 8-1, `ints` are 4 bytes (32-bits). A `long int` may be longer than an `int`, or it might be the same size. A `long long int` might be the same size as a `long int`, or it might be longer. The only guarantee that the compiler will give you is that a `long int` will never be shorter than an `int`.

The reasons for this are many. Factors include the history of the C language and compatibility with software that's already been written, but mostly it has to do with your CPU. It may seem counterintuitive, but modern CPUs can work with 32- and 64-bit numbers *faster* than they can work with 16- and 8-bit numbers. A C compiler designed to produce the fastest software for a given CPU will choose the size of `int` that balances the needs of the programmer with the best performance aspects of that particular CPU.

The bottom line is that there are no guarantees. Choose the kind of integer that best fits your needs and let the compiler worry about how many bits it will have.

Which brings us to the questions that you have probably been forming in your head for the past three or four pages: "Why are we talking about all of this?" "What are my needs?" "Can't I just use `int` for everything?"

These are astute observations, Padawan. Let's explore the answers together.

The Long and Short of ints

Table 8-1 shows a summary of what you've learned about `int` value sizes and the range of numbers each can represent.

Table 8-1. *Ranges of Various int Variables*

sizeof(type)	Bits	Signed Range	Unsigned Range
1	8	-128 – 127	0 – 255
2	16	-32,768 – 32,767	0 – 65,535
4	32	-2,147,483,648 – 2,147,483,647	0 – 4,294,967,295
8	64	-9,223,372,036,854,775,808 – 9,223,372,036,854,775,807	0 – 18,446,744,073,709,551,615

Programming problems will arise when you choose a variable size that is too small, and there can be other kinds of problems if you choose a type that is too large. The easiest way to explain this is to simply demonstrate three common problems with `ints`. Then we'll give you some advice on how to pick the type you need.

Inadequate Range

Suppose a customer asked you to write a program designed to print the numbers 1 through 100, one number per line. Sounds pretty straightforward— just create a `for` loop and embed a `printf()` in the loop. Use an `unsigned char` to act as the loop's counter. Remember that `char` is just another integer type. Refer to Table 8-1 and see that if you declare your counter as an `unsigned char`, it can hold values ranging from 0 to 255. That should be plenty, right?

```
unsigned char    counter;
for ( counter=1; counter<=100; counter++ )
    printf( "%d\n", counter );
```

This program works just fine. But suppose your customer comes back asking you to extend the program to count from 1 to 1,000 instead of just to 100. You happily change the 100 to 1,000, like so, and take it for a spin:

```
unsigned char    counter;
for ( counter=1; counter<=1000; counter++ )
    printf( "%d\n", counter );
```

What do you think will happen when you run it? To find out, open the *Learn C Projects* folder, the *08.03 - TypeOverflow* subfolder, and the project *TypeOverflow.xcodeproj*. Change the loop constant from 100 to 1000, select **Run** from the **Product** menu, and then bring up the console window. This output in the console pane keeps repeating, on and on, ad infinitum. Congratulations on your first infinite loop!

> **CAUTION:** You'll want to stop this program by pressing the big Stop button in the toolbar. If you let it run unabated, it will eat up all of Xcode's available memory as an infinite number of messages fill up the console window. This will cause Xcode some grief.

If you scroll through the console window, you'll see that the program generates the numbers 1 through 255, one number per line, and then goes to 0 and starts climbing again (see Figure 8-3).

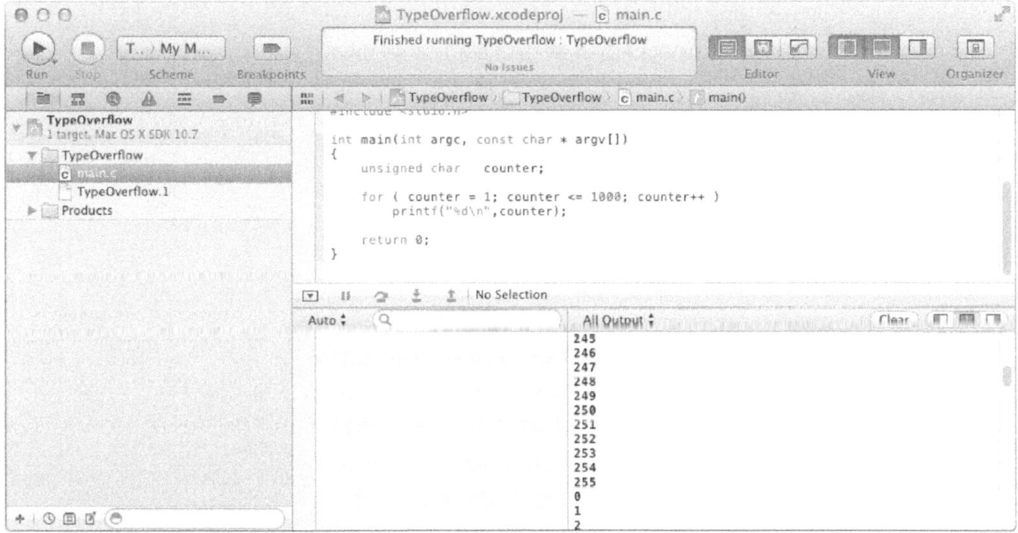

Figure 8-3. *TypeOverflow running in an infinite loop*

The problem with this program occurs when the `for` loop increments the counter when it has a value of 255. Since an `unsigned char` can hold a maximum value of 255, incrementing it gives it a value of 0 again. Since counter can never get higher than 255, the `for` loop never exits.

Just for kicks, edit the code, and change the `unsigned char` to a `signed char`. What do you think will happen? Try it!

The real solution here is to use the right type for your situation and to test, test, test your code. Change the `char` to `int` and everything will work exactly as you planned. As your programming skills mature, start reading up on the process of testing your code. Testing your code is a vital part of delivering a successful product.

Implicit Conversion

Here's probably the simplest program that doesn't work:

```
int au;
au = 149597870700;
```

Set a breakpoint after the assignment statement, as shown in Figure 8-4, in the AstronomicalUnit program that you'll find in the 08.04 - AstronomicalUnit folder. Run the program and examine the value of the au variable using the debugger.

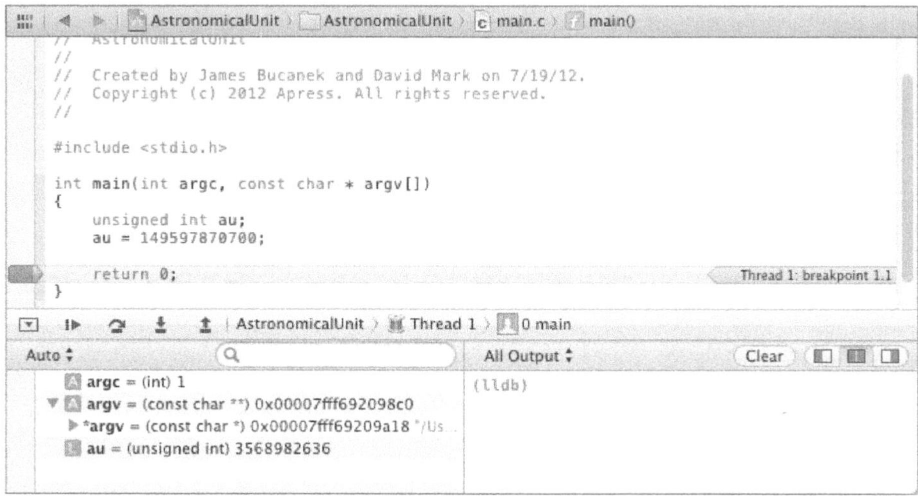

Figure 8-4. *Examining the value of au*

The code assigns the value 149,597,870,700 (one astronomical unit, or the mean radius of the earth's orbit in meters—just in case you were wondering) to the `int` variable `au`. But, as you know from experimenting and from Table 8-1, an `unsigned int` can't represent a number that large. So only some of the bits were stored, and the result was the number 3,568,982,636, which is well inside the orbit of Mercury—and way off the mark.

You can probably fix this problem in your sleep, right? Change the `unsigned int` into an `unsigned long int` and try again. See, you're getting the hang of this now.

The compiler will help you find these kinds of mistakes. As you did in the section "Avoiding Common Pitfalls" in Chapter 6, go into your project's build settings and turn on the "Suspicious Implicit Conversions" warning. This warning will tell you when the compiler thinks a statement might lose information because what you're assigning it to is too small, as shown in Figure 8-5.

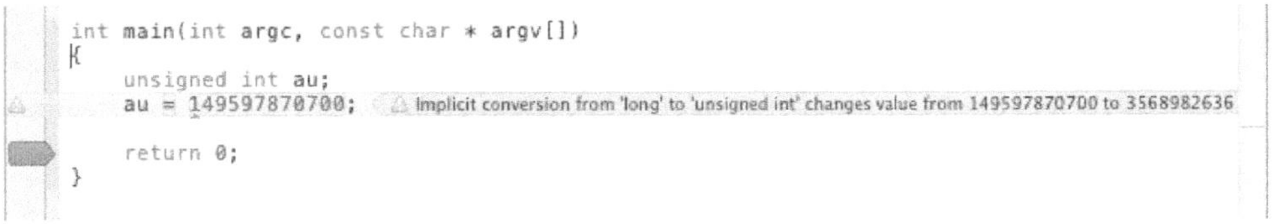

```
int main(int argc, const char * argv[])
{
    unsigned int au;
    au = 149597870700;   Implicit conversion from 'long' to 'unsigned int' changes value from 149597870700 to 3568982636

    return 0;
}
```

Figure 8-5. *Suspicious conversion warning*

Sign Conversion

Another hazard is inadvertently changing the representation of a number by assigning a `signed` value to an `unsigned` variable, and vice versa. The following code won't work the way it's written:

```
unsigned int neverNegNum;
neverNegNum = -2;
```

Instead of assigning the value of -2 to `neverNegNum`, its value gets set to 4,294,967,294. That's because `neverNegNum` is an `unsigned` integer. Unsigned variables can't represent a negative number, so the value is some number with the same bits as the twos-complement representation of -2. The bits weren't changed or lost; it just changed how they are interpreted. To demonstrate this, add some more code:

```
int anyNum;
anyNum = neverNegNum;
```

Open the `SignedUnsigned` project that you'll find in the *`08.05 - SignedUnsigned`* folder and step through this code with the debugger, as shown in Figure 8-6.

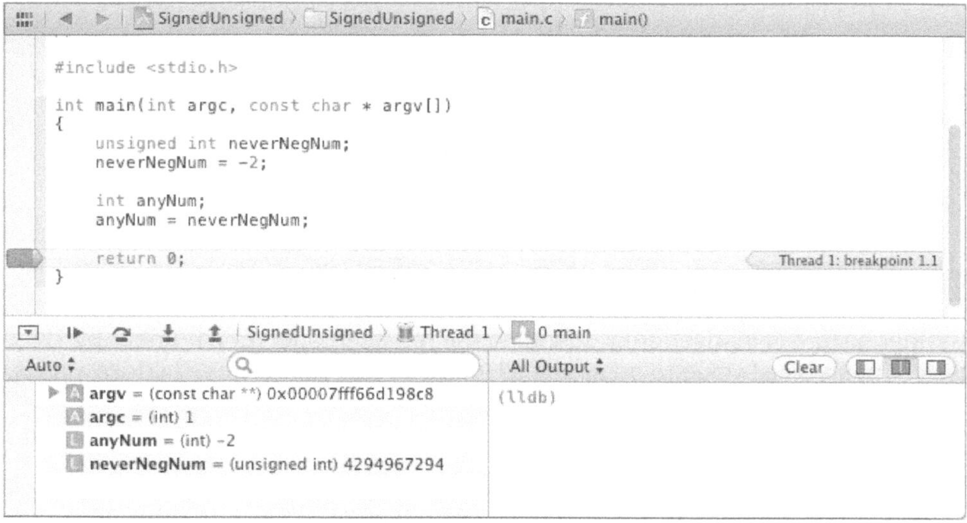

Figure 8-6. *Conversion of signed to unsigned and back to signed int*

Did you see what happened? The bits in `neverNegNum` were copied into `anyNum` and the number became -2 again. It's all in the interpretation.

The Best int for the Job

As promised, here's a short course in choosing the right kind of `int` to use.

1. Choose an int type that agrees with the other ones you're using. If a function returns a long int, store that in a long int variable. Read the section about semantic types.
2. If you encounter a mixture of types, choose a size that's equal to or larger than the largest size.
3. If you don't have a good reason to choose an unsigned type, use a signed type.
4. If you know the numbers you are going to be using are particularly large, make sure you choose a size that can adequately represent all of the numbers you'll ever need to store.
5. If none of the above rules apply, use an int.

When you need to choose an int type, read these guidelines one at a time and stop at the first one that applies to your situation. Pretty soon you'll be doing it in your sleep. The next few sections explain the reasoning behind these guidelines, along with a few refinements.

Semantic Types

The C language, the Standard Library, most other libraries, and more than a few programmers, create *semantic types*. This isn't part of the C language; it's just a programming convention. We'll show you how to create your own types in Chapter 13. For now, just know that a custom type (like size_t) is just a synonym for one of the int types the compiler understands.

Semantics is the study of the meaning of things. A *semantic type* is a custom data type that describes the purpose or meaning of the values it can store. You've already seen the size_t type returned by the sizeof operator. You can declare a size_t variable just like you declare any other kind of variable.

```
size_t mySize;
```

So what kind of int is mySize? The beauty is that you don't have to care. The purpose of the size_t type is to define a variable that will store any count of bytes that this CPU can address. The size_t type will be different kinds of ints for different kinds of computers. The point is that by choosing a data type that has meaning, it will always work. If a new CPU comes out and size_t needs to change, that's something for the authors of the Standard Library to worry about, not you.

Other examples are the uid_t type that defines a variable that can identify a user's account on a system (called the "user ID"). An off_t type variable is guaranteed to be big enough to describe the position ("offset") within any file. The list goes on and on; there are literally hundreds of these kinds of types.

The corollary to rule #1 is this: if you're working with values that have a semantic type (like size_t), use that type. You know that it will always work for that purpose.

Exact-Width Types

There's another set of custom data types defined in the Standard Library that define integers of exactly the size you want. Declaring an int doesn't guarantee you a particular size of int, just one that's well suited for your particular CPU. So what if you need an int that's always exactly 16 bits long? You could run a program like *IntSizer* to find an `int` type that's 2 bytes long and use that. But that only works as long as your compiler never changes and you never compile your program for a different CPU.

The standard library header `<stdint.h>` defines a family of custom types that define integers of specific sizes. The `int16_t` defines a signed integer variable that will always be exactly 2 bytes (16 bits) long no matter where your program is compiled. The rest of the types (`int8_t`, `int32_t`, `int64_t`) do the same and there's a matching set for the unsigned integer types (`uint8_t`, `uint16_t`, `uint32_t`, and `uint64_t`). There are types that guarantee a minimum size (`int_least16_t`, `int_least32_t`, and so on) but might be bigger. For performance hounds, there are types that guarantee a minimum size but might be bigger if the bigger version is faster on this particular CPU (`int_fast16_t`, `uint_fast8_t`). Want the biggest integer your CPU can handle? Use `intmax_t`.

When considering rule #4, include this advice: if you need an integer that's a specific size, use one of the exact-width types.

Integer vs. Floating Point

The last bit of advice we're going to impart before we move on to the `char` type is when to use an integer type and when to use a floating point type. Our advice is simple: use integer for all discrete values and general variables. Use floating point only for "continuous" values.

The vast majority of your variables will be integers. Integer variables are small, efficient, and really fast. But most importantly, they're discrete. They will never store a fractional value, which makes them well suited to making decisions, controlling loops, addressing elements in an array (later in this chapter), and so on. You can't run a `for` loop 2.3 times.

Floating point variable are best suited for values that are not discrete. The `au` variable used in the earlier example should have been a floating point value. A spaceship can just as easily be 2,000 km above the earth as it can be 2,000.6 km. Time, distance, color, transparency, field strength, amplitude, speed, and angles should be floating point numbers.

In the past, programmers avoided floating point numbers like the plague, mostly because they were so incredibly slow. But modern computers have dedicated floating point processing units that are so fast that the difference in performance is now rarely a consideration.

> **NOTE:** How fast are floating point numbers on modern computers? To put it into perspective, in 1990 the most powerful supercomputer in the world was the Cray-2. It stood 9 feet tall and was capable of performing 1.9 GFLOPs (1.9 billion floating point calculations per second). Today, you can walk into your neighborhood electronics mega-mart and pick up any number of computers, even laptops, that can perform 70 GFLOPs, which is more floating point operations per second than all of the Cray-2 supercomputers ever made combined.

Now let's take a look at that "other" integer type, the `char`.

Working with Characters

With its minimal range, you might think that a `char` isn't good for much. Actually, the C deities created the `char` for a good reason. It is the perfect size to hold a single alphabetic character. In C, an alphabetic character is a single character placed between a pair of single quotes (as in `'a'`). Here's a test to see if a `char` variable contains the letter `'a'`:

```
char    c;

c = 'a';
if ( c == 'a' )
    printf( "The variable c holds the character 'a'." );
```

As you can see, the character `'a'` is used in both an assignment statement and an `if` statement, just as if it were a number. A value written this way is called a *character constant*.

The ASCII Character Set

In C, a `signed char` takes up a single byte and can hold a value from –128 to 127. Now, how can a `char` hold a numerical value, as well as a character value, such as `'a'`or `'+'`? The answer lies with the ASCII character set.

> **NOTE:** ASCII stands for the American Standard Code for Information Interchange.

The ASCII character set is a set of 128 standard characters, featuring the 26 lowercase letters, the 26 uppercase letters, the 10 numerical digits, and an assortment of other exciting characters, such as } and =. Each of these characters corresponds to a value between 0 and 127. The ASCII character set ignores the values between –128 and –1.

For example, the character `'a'` has an ASCII value of 97. When a C compiler sees the character `'a'` in a piece of source code, it substitutes the value 97. Each of the values from 0 to 127 is interchangeable with a character from the ASCII character set.

WIDE CHARACTER DATA TYPES

Though you'll make use of the ASCII character set throughout this book, you should know that there are other character sets out there. Most non-Roman alphabets have more characters than can be represented by a single byte. To accommodate these multi-byte characters, ISO C features wide character and wide string data types.

Though you won't get into multi-byte character sets in this book, you should keep these things in mind as you write your own code. Read up on the multi-byte extensions introduced as part of the ISO C standard. There's an excellent writeup in Samuel Harbison and Guy Steele's *C: A Reference Manual*; the fifth edition was released in 2002 (Prentice Hall) and is a terrific C reference well worth the purchase price.

For an article with a title that tells it all, read "The Absolute Minimum Every Software Developer Absolutely, Positively Must Know About Unicode and Character Sets (No Excuses!)" by Joel Spolsky at `http://joelonsoftware.com/articles/Unicode.html`. Rock on, Joel!

ASCII.xcodeproj

Here's a program that will make the ASCII character set easier to understand. Go into the *Learn C Projects* folder and then into the *08.06 - ASCII* subfolder, and open the project *ASCII.xcodeproj*.

Before you step through the project source code, take it for a spin. Select **Run** from the **Product** menu or click the run button in the toolbar. A console pane similar to the one shown in Figure 8-7 should appear. The first line of output shows the characters corresponding to the ASCII values from 32 to 47. Why start with 32? The ASCII characters between 0 and 31 are nonprintable characters like the backspace (ASCII 8) or the carriage return (ASCII 13); see Table 8-2 later in this section for a rundown of these characters.

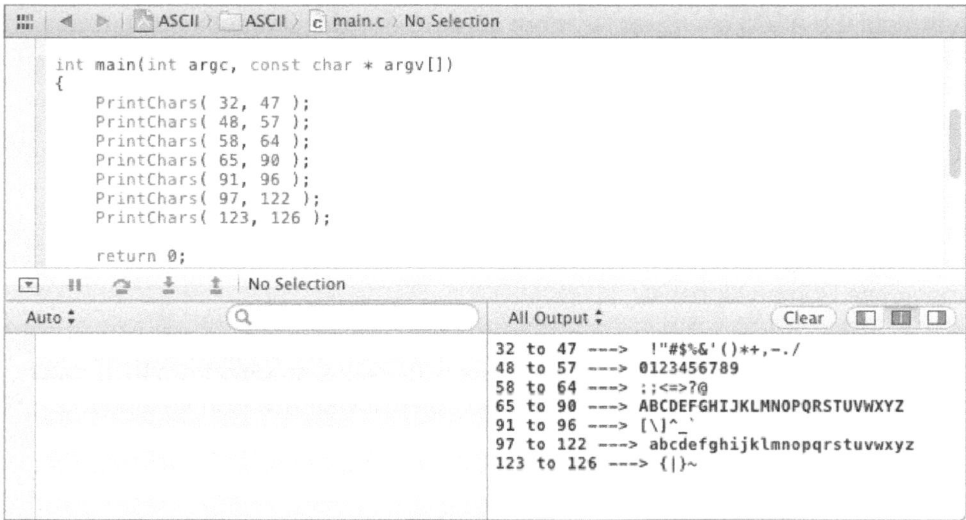

Figure 8-7. *The ASCII program generating a list of printable ASCII characters.*

Notice that ASCII character 32 is a space, also known as ' '. ASCII character 33 is '!'. ASCII character 47 is '/'. This presents some interesting coding possibilities. For example, this code is perfectly legitimate:

```
int sumOfChars;
sumOfChars = '!' + '/';
```

What a strange piece of code! Though you will probably never do anything like this, try to predict the value of the variable `sumOfChars` after the assignment statement. And the answer is that the character '!' has a value of 33 and the character '/' has a value of 47. Therefore, `sumOfChars` will be left with a value of 80 following the assignment statement. C allows you to represent most numbers between 0 and 127 in two different ways: as an ASCII character or as a number. Let's get back to the console window in Figure 8-7.

The second line of output shows the ASCII characters from 48 through 57. As you can see, these 10 characters represent the digits 0 through 9. Here's a little piece of code that converts an ASCII digit to its numerical counterpart:

```
char   digit;
int    convertedDigit;

digit = '3';
convertedDigit = digit -'0'; // That is a zero and not the letter "Oh"
```

This code starts with a `char` named `digit` initialized to hold the ASCII character '3'. The character '3' has a numerical value of 51. The next line of code subtracts the ASCII character `'0'` from `digit`. Since the character `'0'` has a numerical value of 48, and `digit` started with a numerical value of 51, `convertedDigit` ends up with a value of 51 – 48, also known as 3. Isn't that interesting?

The next line of the console window (shown in Figure 8-7) shows the ASCII characters with values ranging from 58 to 64. The following line is pretty interesting. It shows the range of ASCII characters from 65 to 90. Notice anything familiar about these characters? They represent the complete uppercase Roman alphabet.

The next line in Figure 8-7 lists ASCII characters with values from 91 through 96. The following line lists the ASCII characters with values ranging from 97 through 122. These 26 characters represent the complete lowercase Roman alphabet.

> **NOTE:** Adding 32 to an uppercase ASCII character yields its lowercase equivalent. Likewise, subtracting 32 from a lowercase ASCII character yields its uppercase equivalent.
>
> Guess what? You never want to take advantage of this information! Instead, use the Standard Library routines `tolower()` and `toupper()` to do the conversions for you.
>
> As a general rule, try not to make assumptions about the order of characters in the current character set. Use Standard Library functions rather than working directly with character values. Though it is tempting to do these kinds of conversions yourself, by going through the Standard Library, you know your program will work across single-byte character sets.

The final line in Figure 8-7 lists the ASCII characters from 123 to 126. As it turns out, the ASCII character with a value of 127 is another non-printable character. Table 8-2 shows a table of these unprintable characters. The left column shows the integer value of each code. Next is the character constant (if there is one), followed by the official name of the character in the ASCII standard. The right-most column describes the keyboard equivalent or common name. We've included comments about the more interesting ones.

> **NOTE:** The low ASCII codes are called *control characters* because, in the past, they were all intended as instructions (so-called "control codes") to terminals, modems, card readers, and other devices. There are codes that mean "here's the next piece of data," "move to the next line," "this is where the data stops," "cancel the program,"

"that last message wasn't received," and so on. Over time, these codes have fallen into disuse. The only control codes you're likely to use are 0 (NUL) and 10 (line feed), and possibly 9 (horizontal tab) and 13 (carriage return).

Table 8-2. *The ASCII Unprintables*

Code	C Constant	ASCII Name	Common Name
0	'\0'	NUL	Null (used to terminate text strings, explained in the "Text Strings" section)
1		SOH	Control-A
2		STX	Control-B
3		ETX	Control-C
4		EOT	Control-D (the end-of-file mark)
5		ENQ	Control-E
6		ACK	Control-F
7	'\a'	BEL	Control-G (beep; works in Terminal but not in Xcode)
8	'\b'	BS	Control-H (backspace)
9	'\t'	HT	Control-I (tab)
10	'\n'	LF	Control-J (line feed)
11	'\v'	VT	Control-K (vertical feed)
12	'\f'	FF	Control-L (form feed)
13	'\r'	CR	Control-M (carriage return, no line feed)
14		SO	Control-N
15		SI	Control-O

16		DLE	Control-P
17		DC1	Control-Q
18		DC2	Control-R
19		DC3	Control-S
20		DC4	Control-T
21		NAK	Control-U
22		SYN	Control-V
23		ETB	Control-W
24		CAN	Control-X
25		EM	Control-Y
26		SUB	Control-Z
27		ESC	Control-[(escape character)
28		FS	Control-|
29		GS	Control-]
30		RS	Control-^
31		US	Control-_
127		DEL	Delete

Stepping Through the ASCII Source Code

Before you move on to the next topic, take a look at the source code that generated the ASCII character listing in Figure 8-7. The ASCII program starts off with the usual `#include` and follows it by a function prototype of the function `PrintChars()`. `PrintChars()` takes two parameters that define a range of `chars` to print.

```
#include <stdio.h>
void    PrintChars( char low, char high );
```

main() calls PrintChars() seven times in an attempt to functionally organize the ASCII characters.

```
int main (int argc, const char * argv[])
{
    PrintChars( 32, 47 );
    PrintChars( 48, 57 );
    PrintChars( 58, 64 );
    PrintChars( 65, 90 );
    PrintChars( 91, 96 );
    PrintChars( 97, 122 );
    PrintChars( 123, 126 );

    return 0;
}
```

PrintChars() declares a local variable, c, to act as a counter as you step through a range of chars.

```
void PrintChars( char low, char high )
{
    char    c;
```

You use low and high to print a label for the current line, showing the range of ASCII characters to follow. Notice that you use %d to print the integer version of these chars. %d can handle any integer types no bigger than an int.

```
    printf( "%d to %d --->", low, high );
```

Next, a for loop is used to step through each of the ASCII characters, from low to high, using printf() to print each of the characters next to each other on the same line. The printf() bears closer inspection. Notice the use of %c (instead of your usual %d) to tell printf() to print a single ASCII character.

```
    for ( c = low; c <= high; c++ )
        printf( "%c", c );
```

Once the line is printed, a single newline is printed, moving the cursor to the beginning of the next line in the console window. Instead of using printf() again, you use a new function named putchar(). putchar() outputs a single character to the console. That's all it does. Unlike printf(), it doesn't output multiple characters or perform any formatting of values. Its single parameter is the numeric value of the character to output, so you pass it the character constant of the line feed character (note the use of single quotes instead of double quotes):

```
    putchar( '\n' );
}
```

The char data type is extremely useful to C programmers (such as yourself). The next two topics, arrays and text strings, will show you why. As you read through these two sections, keep the concept of ASCII characters in the back of your mind. As you reach the end of the section on text strings, you'll see an important relationship develop among all three topics.

Arrays

The next topic for discussion is arrays. An array is a list of variables. For example, this declaration

```
int  myNumber[ 3 ];
```

creates three separate int variables, referred to in your program as myNumber[0], myNumber[1], and myNumber[2]. Each of these variables is known as an *array element*. The number between the brackets ([and] are known as brackets or square brackets) is called an *index*. In this declaration

```
char myChar[ 20 ];
```

the name of the array is myChar. This declaration will create an array of type char with a dimension of 20. The *dimension* of an array is its number of elements. The array elements will have index values that run from 0 through 19.

> **NOTE:** In C, array indexes always run from 0 to one less than the array's dimension. It's called *zero-based indexing*. Some other computer languages use *ordinal-based indexing* (where the first element has an index of 1).

This slice of code first declares an array of 100 ints and then assigns each int a value of 0:

```
int    myNumber[ 100 ], i;

for ( i=0; i<100; i++ )
    myNumber[ i ] = 0;
```

You could have accomplished the same thing by declaring 100 individual ints and initializing each individual int. Here's what that code might look like:

```
int    myNumber0, myNumber1, ..., myNumber99;

myNumber0 = 0;
myNumber1 = 0;
```

```
      .
      .
      .
myNumber99 = 0;
```

Note that the dots in this last chunk of code are not valid C syntax. They are there to save our fingers from typing out the other 97 statements. It would take 100 lines of code just to initialize these variables! Using an array accomplishes the same thing in just a few lines of code. Look at this code fragment:

```
int sum = 0;
for ( i=0; i<100; i++ )
    sum += myNumber[ i ];

printf( "The sum of the 100 numbers is %d.\n", sum );
```

This code adds together the value of all 100 elements of the array `myNumber`.

> **NOTE:** In the preceding example, the `for` loop is used to step through an array, performing some operation on each of the array's elements. You'll use this technique frequently in your own C programs.

Why Use Arrays?

Programmers would be lost without arrays. Arrays allow you to keep lists of things. For example, if you need to maintain a list of 50 employee numbers, you could declare an array of 50 `ints`. You can declare an array using any C type. For example, this code

```
float salaries[ 50 ];
```

declares an array of 50 floating point numbers. This might be useful for maintaining a list of employee salaries.

Use an array when you want to maintain a list of related data, or if you want to get at the different variables using an expression (index). The next sections show an example.

Dice.xcode

Look in the *Learn C Projects* folder, inside the *08.07 - Dice* subfolder, and open the project *Dice.xcodeproj*. Dice simulates the rolling of a pair of dice. After each roll, the program adds the two dice together, keeping track of the total. It rolls the dice 1,000 times and then reports on the results. Give it a try!

Run `Dice` by selecting **Run** from the **Product** menu or toolbar. A console pane should appear, similar to the one shown in Figure 8-8. Take a look at the output—it's pretty interesting. The first column lists all the possible totals of two dice. Since the lowest possible roll of a pair of six-sided dice is a one and a one, the first entry in the column is 2. The column counts all the way up to 12, the highest possible roll (achieved by a roll of a six and a six).

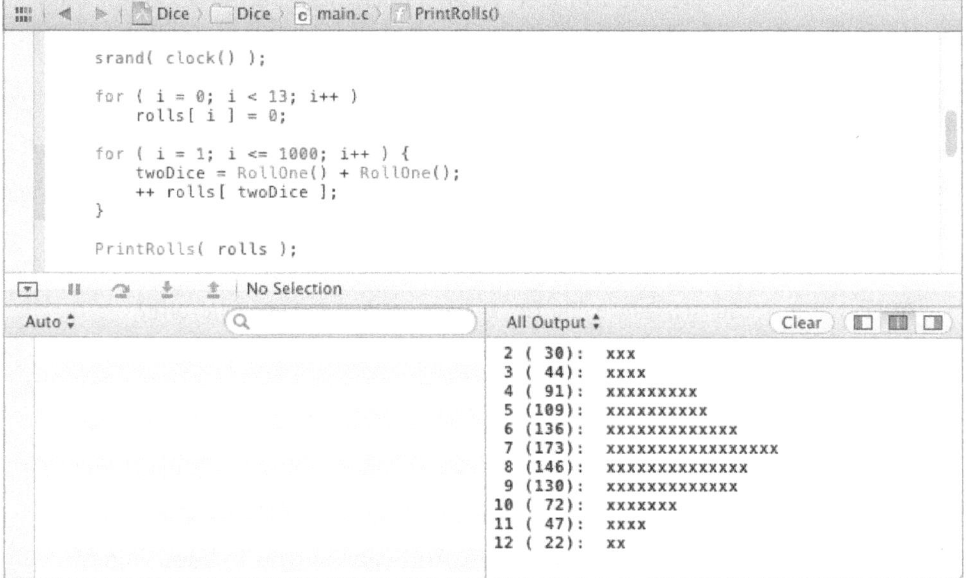

Figure 8-8. *Output of the Dice program, simulating 1,000 rolls of a pair of dice*

The number in parentheses is the total number of rolls (out of 1,000) that matched that row's number. For example, the first row describes the dice rolls that total 2. In this run, the program rolled 30 twos. Finally, the program prints an x for every ten of these rolls. Since 30 twos were rolled, three xs were printed at the end of the twos' row. Since 173 sevens were rolled, 17 xs were printed at the end of the sevens' row.

> **NOTE:** Recognize the curve depicted by the xs in Figure 8-8? The curve represents a "normal" probability distribution, also known as a bell curve. According to the curve, you are about 6.1 times more likely to roll a 7 as you are to roll a 12. Want to know why? Check out a book on probability and statistics.

Let's take a look at the source code that makes this possible.

Stepping Through the Dice Source Code

Dice starts off with three #includes. <stdlib.h> gives you access to the routines rand() and srand(), <time.h> gives you access to clock(), and <stdio.h> gives you access to printf().

```
#include <stdlib.h>
#include <time.h>
#include <stdio.h>
```

Here are the function prototypes for RollOne(), PrintRolls(), and PrintX(). You'll see how these routines work as you walk through the code.

```
int RollOne( void );
void PrintRolls( int rolls[] );
void PrintX( int howMany );
```

main() declares an array of 13 ints named rolls. rolls will keep track of the 11 possible types of dice rolls. rolls[2] will keep track of the total number of twos, rolls[3] will keep track of the total number of threes, and so on, up until rolls[12], which will keep track of the total number of twelves rolled. Since there is no way to roll a zero or a one with a pair of dice, rolls[0] and rolls[1] will go unused.

```
int main (int argc, const char * argv[])
{
    int rolls[ 13 ], twoDice, i;
```

NOTE: You could have rewritten the program using an array of 11 ints, thereby saving two ints worth of memory. If you did that, rolls[0] would track the number of twos rolled, rolls[1] would track the number of threes rolled, and so on. This would have made the program a little harder to read, since rolls[i] would be referring to the number of (i+2) values rolled.

In general, it is OK to sacrifice memory to make your program easier to read, as long as program performance isn't compromised.

The function srand() is part of the Standard Library. It initializes a random number generator, using a seed provided by another Standard Library function, clock(), which returns the current date and time. The value of clock() is always changing and never repeats—such is the nature of time. Using clock() to initialize the random number generator means it will produce a different random sequence of numbers every time you run your program.

```
    srand( clock() );
```

Once the random number generator is initialized, another function, `rand()`, can be called to obtain `int`s with a random values.

Why random numbers? Sometimes you want to add an element of unpredictability to your program. For example, in this program, you want to roll a pair of dice again and again. The program would be pretty boring if it rolled the same numbers over and over. By using a random number generator, you can generate a random number between 1 and 6, thus simulating the roll of a single die!

`main()`'s next step is to initialize each of the elements of the array rolls to 0. This is appropriate since no rolls of any kind have taken place yet.

```
    for ( i = 0; i< 13; i++ )
        rolls[ i ] = 0;
```

Let's roll some dice! This `for` loop rolls the dice 1,000 times. As you'll see, the function `RollOne()` returns a random number between 1 and 6, simulating the roll of a single die. By calling it twice and storing the sum of the two rolls in the variable `twoDice`, you've simulated the roll of two dice.

```
    for ( i = 1; i <= 1000; i++ ) {
        twoDice = RollOne() + RollOne();
```

The next line is pretty tricky, so hang on. At this point, the variable `twoDice` holds a value between 2 and 12, the total of two individual dice rolls. You'll use that value to specify which of the rolls' `int`s to increment. If `twoDice` is 12 (if you rolled a pair of sixes) you'll increment `rolls[12]`. Get it? If not, go back and read through this again. If you still feel stymied (and it's OK if you are), find a C buddy to help you through this. It is important that you get this concept. Be patient.

```
        ++ rolls[ twoDice ];
    }
```

Once you're finished with your 1,000 rolls, you pass `rolls` as a parameter to `PrintRolls()`.

```
    PrintRolls( rolls );

    return 0;
}
```

Notice that you used the array name without the brackets (`rolls` instead of `rolls[]`). The name of an array is a pointer to the first element of the array. If you have access to this pointer, you have access to the entire array. You'll see how this works when you look at `PrintRolls()`.

`RollOne()` first calls `rand()` to generate a random number ranging from 0 to 32,767 (actually, the upper bound is defined by the constant `RAND_MAX`, which is guaranteed to be at least 32,767). Next, the % operator is used to return the remainder when the random number is divided by 6. This yields a random number ranging from 0 to 5. Finally, 1 is added to this number, converting it to a number between 1 and 6, and that number is returned.

```
int RollOne( void )
{
    return ( rand() % 6 ) + 1;
}
```

PrintRolls() starts off by declaring a single parameter, an array pointer named rolls. Notice that rolls was declared using square brackets, telling the compiler that rolls is a pointer to the first element of an array (in this case, to an array of ints).

```
void PrintRolls( int rolls[] )
{
    int i;
```

The for loop steps through the rolls array, one int at a time, starting with rolls[2] and making its way to rolls[12]. For each element, PrintRolls() first prints the roll number and then, in parentheses, the number of times (out of 1,000) that roll occurred. Next, PrintX() is called to print a single x for every ten rolls that occurred. Finally, a carriage return is printed, preparing the console window for the next roll.

```
    for ( i = 2; i<= 12; i++ ) {
        printf( "%2d (%3d):  ", i, rolls[ i ] );
        PrintX( rolls[ i ] / 10 );
        putchar( '\n' );
    }
}
```

PrintX() is pretty straightforward. It uses a for loop to print the number of xs—using putchar() again—specified by the parameter howMany.

```
void PrintX( int howMany )
{
    int i;

    for ( i = 1; i <= howMany; i++ )
        putchar( 'x' );
}
```

Danger, Will Robinson!

Before you move on to the next topic, there is one danger worth discussing at this point. See if you can spot the potential hazard in this piece of code:

```
int myInts[ 3 ], i;
for ( i=0; i<20; i++ )
    myInts[ i ] = 0;
```

Yikes! The array `myInts` consists of exactly 3 array elements, yet the `for` loop tries to initialize 20 elements. This is called *exceeding the bounds of your array*. C will let you get away with this kind of source code. To you, that means Xcode will compile this code without complaint. Your problems will start as soon as the program tries to initialize the fourth array element, which was never allocated.

What will happen? The safest thing to say is that the results will be unpredictable. The problem is that the program is trying to assign a value of 0 to a block of memory that it doesn't necessarily own. Anything could happen. The program could crash or stop behaving in a rational manner. We've seen cases where the computer actually leaps off the desk, hops across the floor, and jumps face first into the trashcan.

Well, OK, not really. Remember the section about how pointers are dangerous? Arrays are pointers. Pointers are arrays. Think about it. The same kind of caution you must exercise to make sure your pointers point to the right thing must be used with arrays to make sure you don't try to access something outside that array.

The #define Directive

When you send your *.c* file to the compiler, the compiler first invokes a preprocessor, asking it to go through the source code file and perform a series of tasks to prepare the source code for the actual compilation. Here's a link to an excellent Wikipedia article that describes the C preprocessor:

`http://en.wikipedia.org/wiki/C_preprocessor`

The preprocessor responds to *preprocessor directives* it finds in your source file. One preprocessor directive you've already used is the `#include` directive. Another preprocessor directive, the `#define` (pronounced "pound-define" or just "define"), tells the compiler to substitute one piece of text for another throughout your source code. This statement

```
#define kDiceSides    6
```

tells the compiler to substitute the character `6` every time it finds the text `kDiceSides` in the source code. `kDiceSides` is known as a *macro*. As the preprocessor goes through your code, it replaces every macro that's been define as it goes.

> **NOTE:** It's important to know that the compiler never actually modifies your source code. Macro substitution is performed "on the fly" as the source code is translated into machine code.

Here's an example of a #define in action:

```
#define kMaxArraySize    100

int main (int argc, const char * argv[])
{
    char    myArray[ kMaxArraySize ];
    int     i;

    for ( i=0; i <kMaxArraySize; i++ )
        myArray[ i ] = 0;

    return 0;
}
```

The #define at the beginning of this example substitutes 100 for kMaxArraySize everywhere it appears in the source code file. In this example, the substitution will be done twice. Though your source code is not actually modified, here's the effect of this #define:

```
int main (int argc, const char * argv[])
{
    char    myArray[ 100 ];
    int        i;

    for ( i=0; i<100; i++ )
        myArray[ i ] = 0;

    return 0;
}
```

Note that a #define must appear in the source code file before it is used. In other words, this code won't compile:

```
int main (int argc, const char * argv[]) {
    char   myArray[ kMaxArraySize ];
    int    i;
#define kMaxArraySize   100
    for ( i = 0; I <kMaxArraySize; i++ )
        myArray[ i ] = 0;
    return 0;
}
```

Having a #define in the middle of your code is just fine. The problem here is that the first use of kMaxArraySize appears before the #define!

> **CAUTION:** We mentioned this awhile back, but it bears repeating. While C is a free-form language, the preprocessor is not. A preprocessor directive *must* be on its own line, with no C code or other directives on the same line. Preprocessor directives are not C statements and don't end in a semicolon.

If you use #defines effectively, you'll write more flexible and readable code. In the previous example, you can change the size of the array by modifying a single line of code, the #define. If your program is designed well, you can change the line to

```
#define kMaxArraySize    200
```

Recompile your code and your program will still work properly. A good sign that you are using #defines properly is an absence of constants in your code. In the preceding examples, the constant 100 was replaced by kMaxArraySize.

> **NOTE:** Many programmers use a naming convention for #defines that's similar to the one they use for global variables. Instead of starting the name with a g (as in gMyGlobal), a #define that's used as a constant starts with a k (as in kMyConstant).
>
> Unix programmers tend to name their #define constants using all uppercase letters, sprinkled with underscores (_) to act as word dividers (as in MAX_ARRAY_SIZE). Neither is wrong; just be consistent.

Using #defines in Your Code

Let's revisit the Dice program. You'll notice that there were a lot of constants scattered about.

```
int rolls[ 13 ], twoDice, i;
for ( i = 0; i < 13; i++ )
for ( i = 1; i <= 1000; i++ ) {
return ( rand() % 6 ) + 1;
for ( i = 2; i <= 12; i++ ) {
```

The program works fine now, but what if you want a program that will calculate rolls of 8-sided dice or 20-sided dice. Or maybe you want to roll the dice 2,000 times or 1,000,000 times. You'd have to go through and recalculate new constants and change every one in the source. This is both tedious and error prone. As your programs get bigger, it becomes even more tedious and error prone.

Using preprocessor macros, you can let the computer do the work of updating all of the constants, and even do some of the math for you! Start by adding some #define directives to the beginning of the Dice program, or go open the Dice2 project inside the *08.08 - Dice2* folder and follow along.

```
#define kDiceSides      6
#define kLowestRoll     (1*2)
#define kHighestRoll    (kDiceSides*2)
#define kRollArraySize  (kHighestRoll+1)
#define kRolls          1000
```

The next step is to replace the constant values in the code with their new names.

```
    int rolls[ kRollArraySize ], twoDice, i;
    for ( i = 0; i < kRollArraySize; i++ )
    for ( i = 1; i <= kRolls; i++ ) {
    return ( rand() % kDiceSides ) + 1;
    for ( i = kLowestRoll; i <= kHighestRoll; i++ ) {
```

Not only is your program now easier to update, it's easier to read. The expression

```
( rand() % kDiceSides ) + 1
```

is a lot more descriptive than

```
( rand() % 6 ) + 1
```

If you came back to this program six months from now, you might have no idea what "6" is. But kDiceSides is something you would understand.

Stepping Through the Preprocessor

So let's see how this works by walking through the steps the preprocessor takes. First, the preprocessor encounters the #define directives.

```
#define kDiceSides      6
#define kLowestRoll     (1*2)
#define kHighestRoll    (kDiceSides*2)
#define kRollArraySize  (kHighestRoll+1)
```

It creates macros for kDiceSides, kLowestRoll, kHighestRoll, and kRollArraySize. It then moves on to the source code. When it encounters this line of code

```
int rolls[ kRollArraySize ], twoDice, i;
```

it discovers a macro name that it knows (`kRollArraySize`). It replaces that symbol with its definition. Inside the compiler, the line now looks like this:

```
int rolls[ (kHighestRoll+1) ], twoDice, i;
```

That doesn't look like it helped much, but bear with us a little longer. The preprocessor doesn't just make one substitution and move on. It performs what are known as *recursive substitutions*. In other words, if the definition of one macro contains another macro, the processor keeps replacing them. After replacing `kHighestRoll`, the line now looks like this:

```
int rolls[ ((kDiceSides*2)+1) ], twoDice, i;
```

The second replacement substituted `kHighestRoll` with `(kDiceSides*2)`. But it's still not done. After one more substitution, the line looks like this:

```
int rolls[ ((6*2)+1) ], twoDice, i;
```

The macro `kDiceSides` is replaced with its definition (6) and the preprocessor has now run out of things to replace. The final declaration—`int rolls[ ((6*2)+1) ]`—is what gets compiled by the C compiler.

> **TIP:** Don't worry about the math involved in a statement like `int rolls[ ((6*2)+1) ]`. This formula won't be calculated when your program runs. C compilers have a *constant recognizer*; it's an optimization that replaces any expression, or part of an expression, that only contains constants with a single constant value. If you write the statement `y = ( x * ( 4 * 7 - 1 ) ) + ( ( 100 / 4 ) * ( 9 - 3 ) ) - ( 4 + 2 )`, the compiler will reduce all of the constants in the expression. The code that gets compiled will be `y = x * 27 + 144`.

The Advantages of Using #define Directives

An obvious benefit of using `#define` directives in our previous example is that the preprocessor determined how big your array needed to be based on the number of sides on the dice being rolled! The rest of the code is easier to read, too. It's now obvious that the statement

```
for ( i = 0; i < kRollArraySize; i++ )
```

is looping through the elements of the `rolls` array. Similarly, the loop

```
for ( i = kLowestRoll; i <= kHighestRoll; i++ ) {
```

is going to work through each possible roll of the dice.

> **CAUTION:** When defining macros that are going to be used in expressions, use parentheses generously. When the macro is replaced with its definition, you don't want there to be any confusion over what the expression means.

But the real beauty—and the real power—of the preprocessor shows up when you need to update your program. Change the 6 in the `#define kDiceSides` directive to `12` and rerun the program, as shown in Figure 8-9.

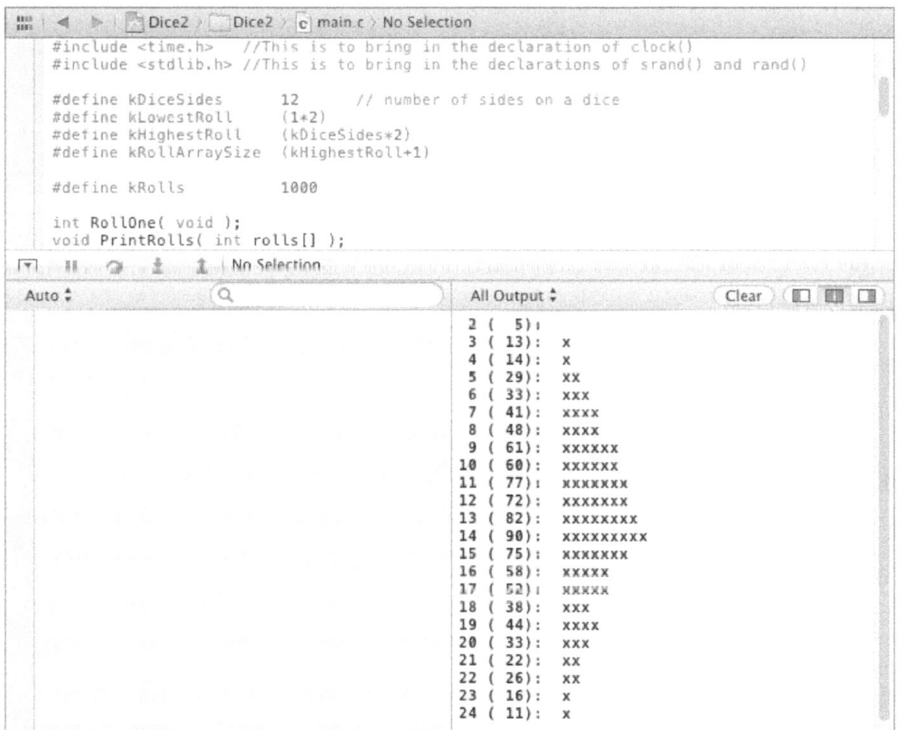

```
#include <time.h>   //This is to bring in the declaration of clock()
#include <stdlib.h> //This is to bring in the declarations of srand() and rand()

#define kDiceSides      12      // number of sides on a dice
#define kLowestRoll     (1*2)
#define kHighestRoll    (kDiceSides*2)
#define kRollArraySize  (kHighestRoll+1)

#define kRolls          1000

int RollOne( void );
void PrintRolls( int rolls[] );
```

```
 2 (  5):
 3 ( 13):  x
 4 ( 14):  x
 5 ( 29):  xx
 6 ( 33):  xxx
 7 ( 41):  xxxx
 8 ( 48):  xxxx
 9 ( 61):  xxxxxx
10 ( 60):  xxxxxx
11 ( 77):  xxxxxxx
12 ( 72):  xxxxxxx
13 ( 82):  xxxxxxxx
14 ( 90):  xxxxxxxxx
15 ( 75):  xxxxxxx
16 ( 58):  xxxxx
17 ( 52):  xxxxx
18 ( 38):  xxx
19 ( 44):  xxxx
20 ( 33):  xxx
21 ( 22):  xx
22 ( 26):  xx
23 ( 16):  x
24 ( 11):  x
```

Figure 8-9. *Dice2 after changing the #define kDiceSides macro definition to 12*

By changing one (one!) number, the `rolls[]` array was sized correctly so it could hold all of the results (it's now 23 elements long), the `for` loop initialized the correct number of array elements, the `RollOne()` function now returns a value between 1 and 12, and the `PrintRolls()` function outputs 21 results.

Try playing around with *Dice2* a little. Change kDiceSides to 20. Change kRolls to 2000.

> **NOTE:** Interestingly, you could have reversed the order of these #defines and your code would still have compiled. As long as all macros are defined at the point they are needed, the order they occur in the source is not important. What is important is that every #define appears in the source code *before* any source code that refers to it.

Function-like #define Macros

But wait! Macros don't stop there. You can create a #define macro that takes one or more arguments. Here's an example:

```
#define SQUARE( A )    ((A) * (A))
```

This macro takes a single argument. The argument can be anything. If you use this macro

```
myInt = SQUARE( myInt + 1 );
```

the compiler would use its first pass to turn the line into this:

```
myInt = (( myInt + 1 ) * ( myInt + 1 ));
```

Notice the usefulness of the parentheses in the macro. If the macro were defined like this

```
#define SQUARE( A )    A * A
```

the compiler would have produced

```
myInt = myInt + 1 * myInt + 1;
```

which is not what you wanted. The multiplication that gets performed by this statement is `1 * myInt` because the * operator has a higher precedence than the + operator.

Be sure you pay strict attention to your use of white space in your #define macros. For example, there's a world of difference between this macro

```
#define SQUARE( A )    ((A) * (A))
```

and this macro

```
#define SQUARE ( A )   ((A) * (A))
```

Note the space between SQUARE and (A). This second form creates a #define constant named SQUARE, which is defined as (A) ((A) * (A)). A call to this macro won't even compile because the compiler doesn't know what A is.

Here's another interesting macro side effect. Imagine calling this macro

```
#define SQUARE( A )    ((A) * (A))
```

like this

```
mySquare = SQUARE( myInt++ );
```

The preprocessor pass expands this macro call to this:

```
mySquare = ((myInt++) * (myInt++));
```

Do you see the problems here? First off, myInt will get incremented twice by this macro call (probably not what was intended). Second, the first myInt++ will get executed before the multiplication happens, yielding a final result of myInt*(myInt+1), which is definitely not what you wanted! The point here is to be careful when you pass an expression as a parameter to a macro that it doesn't have what are called unwanted side effects.

Here's one final point. Keeping all your #define statements together toward the top of the file is good form. People generally expect to find a #define at the top of the file, not in the middle.

Text Strings

The first C program in this book made use of a text string:

```
printf( "Hello, world!" );
```

This section will teach you how to use text strings like "Hello, world!" in your own programs. It will teach you how these strings are stored in memory and how to create your own strings from scratch.

A Text String in Memory

Take a look at Figure 8-10. This figure represents the text string "Hello, world!" as it exists in memory. The string is stored as a sequence of 14 consecutive bytes. The first 13 bytes consist of the 13 ASCII characters in “Hello, world!” Note that the seventh byte contains a space (ASCII value 32).

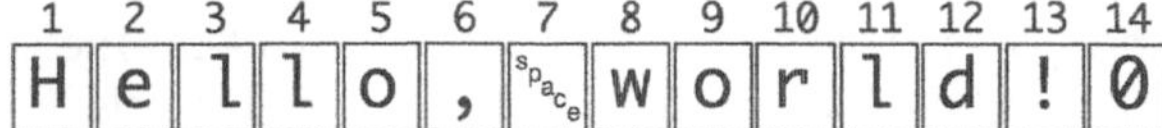

Figure 8-10. *The "Hello, world!" text string*

The final byte has an integer value of 0 (ASCII character NUL), not to be confused with the ASCII character '0' (the digit) or 'O' (the 15th letter of the Roman alphabet). The NUL is what makes this string a *C string*. Every C string ends with a `'\0'` character, and is called a *NUL-terminated string*.

Notice that the bytes in the string are numbered from 0 up to 13, instead of from 1 to 14. In effect, a string is an array of `chars`, and in C, arrays are zero-based.

When you use a quoted string like `"Hello, world!"` in your code, the compiler creates the string for you. This type of string is called a *string constant*. When you use a string constant in your code, the detail work is done for you automatically. In this example

```
printf( "Hello, world!" );
```

the 14 bytes needed to represent the string in memory are allocated. The value of each character is stored in the correct element. The `'\0'` character is placed in the 14th element automatically. The string constant in an expression evaluates to a pointer to the first character in the array. It's this address that gets passed to `printf()` as its first argument.

String constants are great, but they can't be used for everything. The biggest disadvantage is that they are, well, constants; you can't change them. Computers are generally useful because they deal with data that changes, so clearly string constants won't work everywhere.

What you need is a variable that can hold a series of characters that can be used to store a NUL-terminated string.

Hmmmm, what that would look like?

(Jump in anytime.)

If you guessed "an array of `chars`," give yourself a big pat on the back!

Character arrays are exactly how you manipulate strings in C. Let's look at a simple example of how to use `char` arrays to alter strings.

FullName.xcodeproj

Open the `FullName` project in the *`08.09 - FullName`* folder. By now, the first part of this program should be perfectly understandable.

```
#include <stdio.h>
#include <strings.h>

void PrintFullName( char *firstName, char *lastName );

int main(int argc, const char * argv[])
{
    PrintFullName( "David", "Mark" );
    PrintFullName( "James", "Bucanek" );

    return 0;
}
```

The `<strings.h>` header file is included so that you have access to the many string functions supplied by the Standard Library. You declare a `PrintFullName()` function that takes two `char` pointers.

In C, there is *no difference* between a pointer to a single variable and a pointer to the first element of an array of variables. Whether the pointer points to one variable or a thousand is determined entirely by how the pointer is used. To make this distinction a little clearer, when talking about pointers we'll refer to a pointer to the first element of an array of characters as a "string pointer" and a pointer to a single char variable as a "`char` pointer."

The `main()` function calls the `PrintFullName()` function twice. Each time, it supplies two string pointers. The string pointers were automatically created using string constants. Now here's the part of the program that's interesting:

```
void PrintFullName( char *firstName, char *lastName )
{
    char fullName[ 20 ];

    strcpy( fullName, lastName );
    strcat( fullName, ", " );
    strcat( fullName, firstName );

    printf( "full name: %s\n", fullName );
}
```

The `PrintFullName()` function declares its two parameters, `firstName` and `lastName`. These will point to the first character of the two string constants allocated in `main()`.

The first statement declares an array, named `fullName`, which consists of 20 char elements.

```
char fullName[ 20 ];
```

Like any uninitialized automatic variable, the values of those 20 `chars` is a complete mystery.

The first function call is to the strcpy() Standard Library function.

```
strcpy( fullName, lastName );
```

The strcpy() (called "string copy") function takes two string pointers. The function copies the char values from the array of characters pointed to by the second argument into the character array pointed to by the first argument. It keeps copying characters until it has copied the '\0' character at the end of the second array (string). The first parameter is called the destination pointer (because that's where the chars get copied to) and the second parameter is called the source pointer (because those are the chars that get copied).

strcpy() is the string equivalent of an assignment statement. Its sole function is copy the bytes of one string to the destination array, duplicating the string in the process. Because it keeps copying characters until it copies the '\0' character at the end of the second string, it doesn't matter how long the string is. Your only job is to make sure the destination array has enough room to accommodate the copied chars.

Set a breakpoint and examine the contents of fullName following the strcpy() function call. The Xcode debugger is smart enough to know that an array of chars is probably a string and so displays the string to the right of the variable name, as shown in Figure 8-11. Note that when displaying strings, the debugger doesn't display the values for every element in the array. It only shows those characters up to the first '\0', which ends the string.

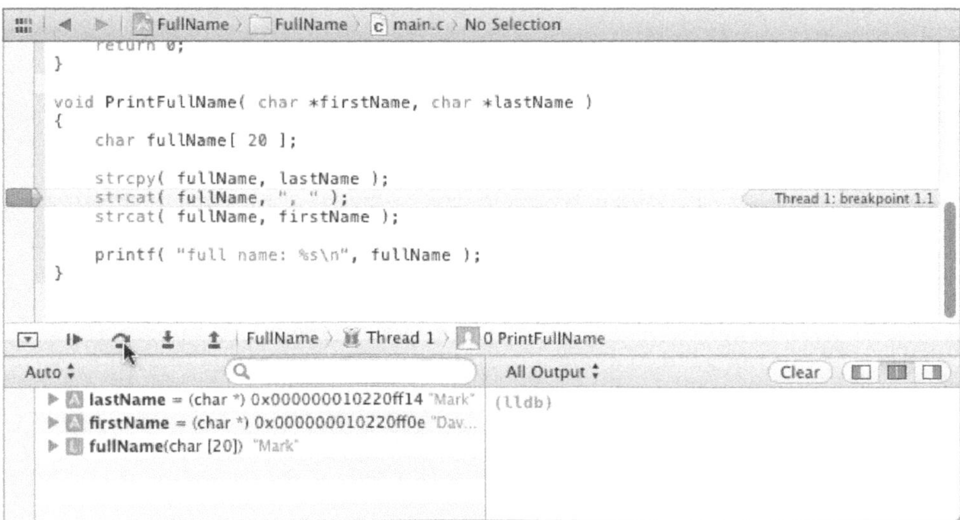
FullName › FullName › main.c › No Selection
}
void PrintFullName(char *firstName, char *lastName)
{
char fullName[20];
strcpy(fullName, lastName);
strcat(fullName, ", ");
strcat(fullName, firstName);
printf("full name: %s\n", fullName);
}
Thread 1: breakpoint 1.1
FullName › Thread 1 › 0 PrintFullName
Auto
All Output
Clear
lastName = (char *) 0x000000010220ff14 "Mark"
firstName = (char *) 0x000000010220ff0e "Dav...
fullName(char [20]) "Mark"
(lldb)

Figure 8-11. *The effect of copying as string using strcpy()*

Now the `fullName` array contains a copy of the characters from the `lastName` string constant. The next function you're going to use is `strcat()`.

```
strcat( fullName, ", " );
```

Similar to `strcpy()`, the `strcat()` (called "string concatenate," or just "string cat") function also copies the characters passed in the second argument to the character array passed in the first argument. But unlike `strcpy()`, it doesn't replace the characters at the beginning of the array. Instead, it steps through the characters that are already in the destination array looking for the `'\0'` that terminates the string. When it finds it, it then begins copying characters from the source string, one at a time, until it copies all of them and the terminating `'\0'`.

The effect of `strcat()` is to join together, or "concatenate," two strings by appending the characters pointed to by the second parameter to the end of the string pointed to by the first parameter. You can see this in the debugger by performing one `step over` command, as shown in Figure 8-12.

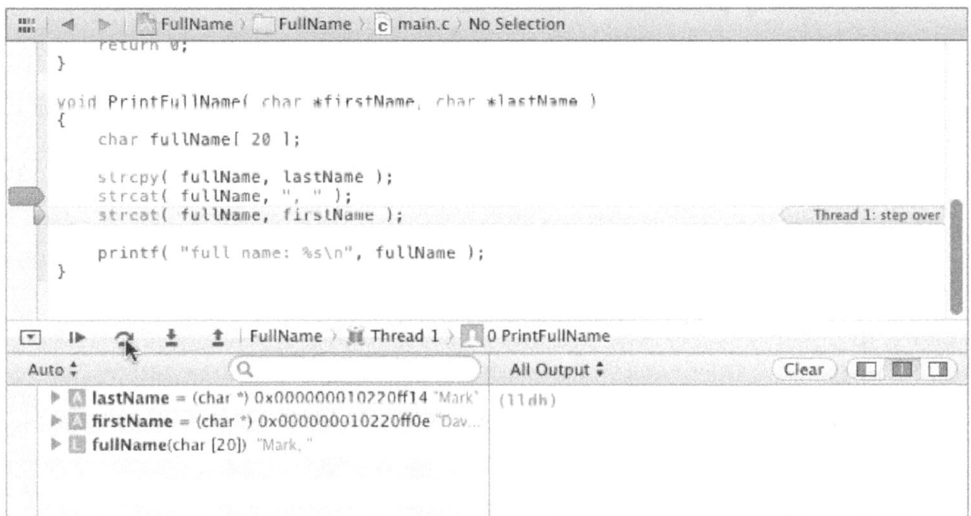
FullName
FullName
main.c
No Selection
}
void PrintFullName(char *firstName, char *lastName)
{
char fullName[20];
strcpy(fullName, lastName);
strcat(fullName, ", ");
strcat(fullName, firstName);
Thread 1: step over
printf("full name: %s\n", fullName);
}
FullName
Thread 1
0 PrintFullName
Auto
All Output
Clear
lastName = (char *) 0x000000010220ff14 "Mark"
firstName = (char *) 0x000000010220ff0e "Dav...
fullName(char [20]) "Mark, "
(lldb)

Figure 8-12. *The effect of appending a second string to the first using strcat()*

Now the `fullName` array contains the characters from `lastName` plus two more characters, a comma and a space. After the second call to `strcat()`, the array contains both names separated by a comma, as shown in Figure 8-13.

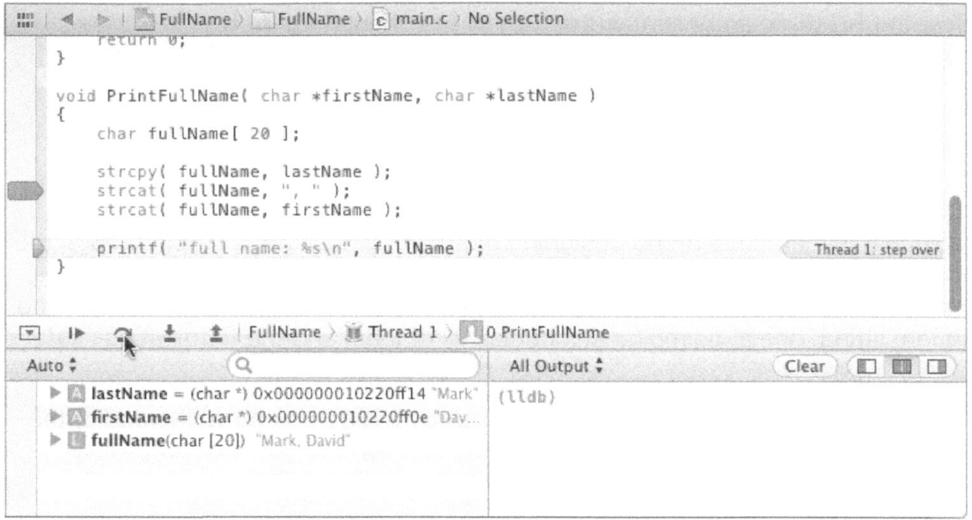

FullName › FullName › main.c › No Selection
}
void PrintFullName(char *firstName, char *lastName)
{
char fullName[20];
strcpy(fullName, lastName);
strcat(fullName, ", ");
strcat(fullName, firstName);
printf("full name: %s\n", fullName);
}
Thread 1: step over
FullName › Thread 1 › 0 PrintFullName
Auto
All Output
Clear
lastName = (char *) 0x000000010220ff14 "Mark"
firstName = (char *) 0x000000010220ff0e "Dav...
fullName(char [20]) "Mark, David"
(lldb)

Figure 8-13. *Final fullName string after the second call to strcat()*

The final step is to print out the results. This is done using the `printf()` function, but this time you use a format specifier of `%s`.

```
printf( "full name: %s\n", fullName );
```

The `%s` specifier outputs a C string. The argument must be a pointer to a NUL-terminated array of characters. `printf()` replaces the `%s` with every character in the string up to, but not including, the terminating `'\0'` character.

> **NOTE:** Clever readers (and we're sure that's you) would probably point out that `PrintFullName()` could have also been accomplished using a single `printf()` statement, like this:
>
> ```
> printf( "full name: %s, %s\n", lastName, firstName );
> ```
>
> But then you wouldn't have learned all this great stuff about `char` arrays and functions like `strcat()`.

We made one of those "it's your responsibility" comments a page or so back. Let's take a look at that now.

Overflow.xcodeproj

Open the `Overflow` project, which you'll find in the *08.10 - Overflow* folder. It's identical to the `FullName` project, except for one additional line of code:

```
PrintFullName( "Wilhelmina", "Romanowski" );
```

Run the project. On our machine, it doesn't get very far. Instead of running as expected, the program halts in the debugger with a fatal SIGABRT, as shown in Figure 8-14.

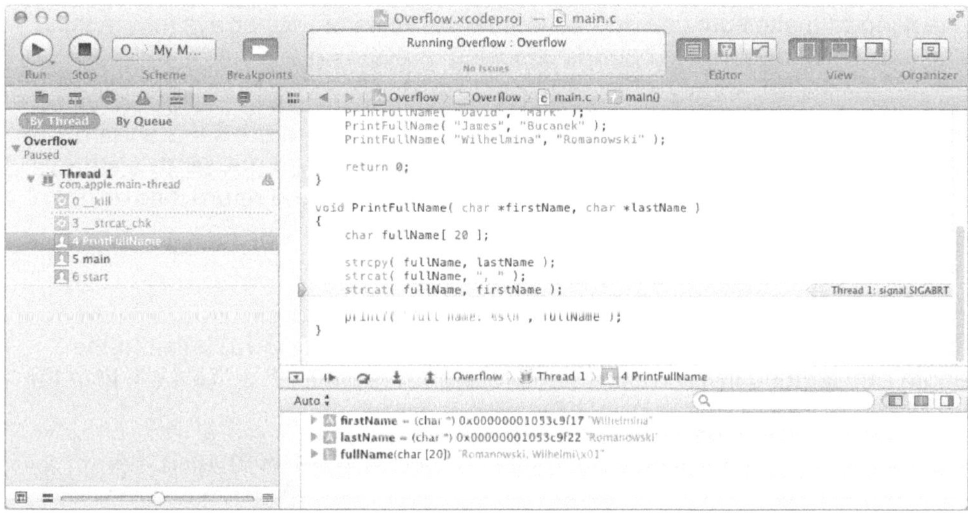

Figure 8-14. *The Overflow program crashing at the strcat() function call*

The SIGABRT message means the program died. Crashed. Dead in its tracks. Kicked the bucket. Bit the dust. Pushing up daisies. Why did this happen?

Earlier we talked about the danger of writing data outside of an array, and that's exactly what this program did. The `fullName` array only has 20 character elements. So the maximum size of a string that can be stored there is 19 characters long (you always need one more element to hold the `'\0'` character).

Poor Wilhelmina Romanowski's name is longer than that. The `strcat()` function just does what it's told: it copies characters from one place to another. It has no way of knowing if there's enough room in the `fullName` array. That's your job.

> **CAUTION:** This kind of programming bug is called a *buffer overflow*, and it's one of the most exploited weaknesses in software. Hackers will intentionally feed programs bizarre or ridiculously large amounts of data in an attempt to trick the program into writing values where it shouldn't, overwriting other variables in the program. Sometimes hackers can use this technique to take over a program and insert their own code. Seriously.

Checking to make sure you don't overflow the limits of your arrays (or anything else) can be done through bounds checking or planning.

To employ *bounds checking*, you include code that checks to make sure what you're about to do is safe before you do it. For example, there's a Standard Library function named `strlen()` ("string length"). Pass it a pointer to a string and it will count the number of characters in that string and return it as an `int`. Using that function, you could add the following code to *Overflow*:

```
if ( strlen(fullName) + strlen(firstName) + 1 <= 20 )
    strcat( fullName, firstName );
```

This new conditional adds the length of the string already in `fullName` to the length of the string in `firstName`. If the total (plus room for the `'\0'`) will fit in the `fullName` array, then the `strcat()` function is called.

It's important to do this kind of bounds checking, and the authors of the Standard Library know that. The Standard Library has evolved to include a raft of "safe" functions that perform the necessary bounds checking. Instead of adding a whole mess of extra `if` statements to your program, let's replace the `strcpy()` and `strcat()` functions with safer alternatives, like the following:

```
strlcpy( fullName, lastName, sizeof(fullName) );
strlcat( fullName, ", ", sizeof(fullName) );
strlcat( fullName, firstName, sizeof(fullName) );
```

The `strlcpy()` and `strlcat()` functions take three parameters instead of two. The third parameter is the total size of the `char` array pointed to by the first parameter. Note how convenient the `sizeof` operator is here. Now the functions have all of the information they need to make an intelligent decision about how many characters can be safely copied. Both of these functions will copy only the characters that will fit into the destination array. If the array fills up, they stop. Now your program runs safely, as shown in Figure 8-15—although Wilhelmina might want to change her name to "Cher."

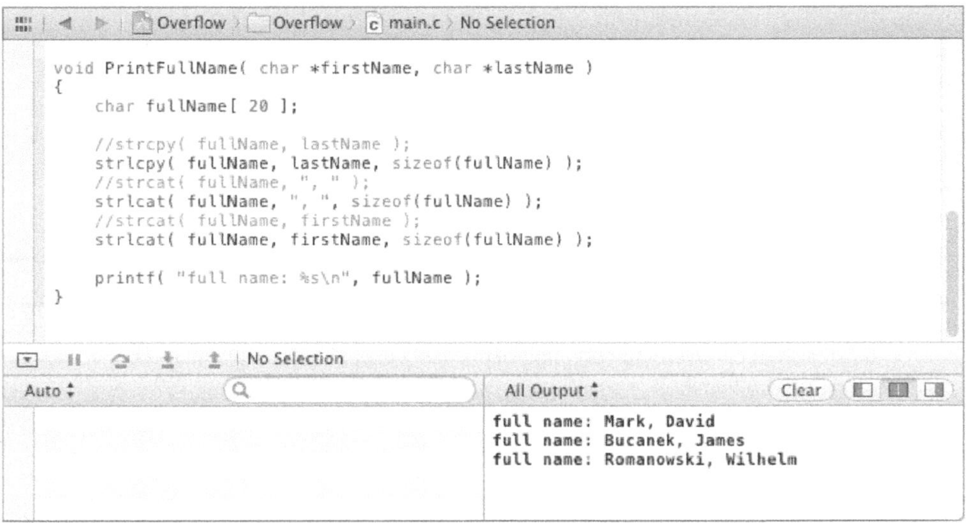
Overflow
Overflow
main.c
No Selection
void PrintFullName(char *firstName, char *lastName)
{
char fullName[20];
//strcpy(fullName, lastName);
strlcpy(fullName, lastName, sizeof(fullName));
//strcat(fullName, ", ");
strlcat(fullName, ", ", sizeof(fullName));
//strcat(fullName, firstName);
strlcat(fullName, firstName, sizeof(fullName));
printf("full name: %s\n", fullName);
}
No Selection
Auto
All Output
Clear
full name: Mark, David
full name: Bucanek, James
full name: Romanowski, Wilhelm

Figure 8-15. *Safely coded string copy routines*

Another way of solving this kind of problem is to use the planning approach; write your code so there's always enough room in the array, either by making sure the array is big enough or making sure the data going in won't overflow it.

For example, you could use a relatively new feature of the C language called *variable length arrays*. In English, it means that the size of an automatic array variable can be determined using an expression; it doesn't have to be a constant. Every time the `PrintFullName()` function runs, the array can be a different size. This would allow you to replace the array declaration

```
char fullName[ 20 ];
```

with this declaration

```
char fullName[ strlen( firstName ) + strlen( lastName ) + 2 + 1 ];
```

Now, no matter how long the first and last name strings are (within reason), the `fullName` array will always have exactly enough elements to store both names, a comma, a space, and the terminating `'\0'` character.

What's Next?

Congratulations! You made it through one of the longest chapters in this book. You mastered several new data types, including `float`s and `char`s. You learned how to use arrays, especially in conjunction with `char`s. You learned about C strings, how they're stored, and a few Standard Library functions for manipulating them. You also learned about C's text-substitution mechanism, the #define preprocessor directive.

In Chapter 9 you're going to create a real, honest-to-goodness, program. Along the way you're going to learn some important stuff about OS X and some really clever things you can do with pointers.

CHAPTER 8 EXERCISES

1. Each of the following code fragments has a logical flaw or syntax error. Can you find it?

a.
```
char c;
int i;
i=0;
for ( c=0; c<=255; c++ )
    i += c;
```

b.
```
float myFloat;
myFloat = 5.125;
printf( "The value of myFloat is %d.\n", f );
```

c.
```
charc;
c = "a";
printf( "c holds the character %c.\n", c );
```

d.
```
char c[ 5 ];
c = "Hello, world!";
```

e.
```
#define kMaxArraySize    200;
```

f.
```
char c[kMaxArraySize];
#define kMaxArraySize    20
int i;
for ( i=0; i<kMaxArraySize; i++ )
    c[ i ] = 0;
```

g.
```
#define kMaxArraySize 200
char c[ kMaxArraySize ];
c[ kMaxArraySize ] = 0;
```

2. Rewrite *Dice*, showing the possible rolls using three (or more) dice instead of two.

3. Rewrite *Overflow* to use a variable length array so the `fullName` array is never too small. Try passing `PrintFullName()` shorter, and even longer, names.

Chapter 9

The Command Line

Everything you've done up to this point has been inside the safe confines of the Xcode sandbox. There's nothing wrong with that; professional programmers spend most of their time inside Xcode. But ultimately, the goal is create a "real" program that runs on its own. A program you can copy to another computer and run there. Maybe one day, a program you upload to the App Store and sell to multitudes of people around the world.

All of the projects in this book build a single executable file. A *binary executable*, as they are known, is the simplest form of a program that the operating system understands: a single file that contains machine code. It doesn't get much simpler than that. When an executable is run, those machine codes are read from the file and copied into the computer's RAM, where the CPU executes them.

Xcode can create other kinds of programs, many quite complex. If you go on to learn Objective-C or iOS, you'll create some of those other kinds of applications. But for now, you'll stay with simple executables.

In this chapter, you're going to learn about the command line—the *other* computer interface. You're also going to learn how to build your program so you can run it on its own, give it to your friends to run, deliver it to your employer, or even sell it. This stage of software development is called *deployment*. You're going to use those deployment skills to create and install your own command-line tool. Along the way you're going to learn a little about OS X's underpinnings, especially paths, and some clever things you can do with pointers. Let's get started.

Command Line Basics

If you've spent some time using the command line, a lot of this section will be familiar to you. You might want to skim through it, or skip it entirely if you and the command line are old friends.

Before big LCD displays and wireless keyboards, before graphical user interfaces with overlapping windows, before the trackpad, before the mouse even, there was the command line. A *command-line interface* (CLI) is an incredibly simple way to control a computer, and almost self-explanatory. You type words (commands) on a line and press the Return key. The computer performs those commands and then waits for you to type another. For an era, the command-line interface was just about the only interface computers had. Apple's original computer, the Apple II, relied on a command-line interface.

In OS X, the command line lives on in the Terminal application. Launch the Terminal application—you'll find it in the Applications folder, then inside the *Utilities* subfolder—and you'll see a stark window, like the one shown in Figure 9-1.

> **NOTE:** If you're thinking that the command-line interface is still around just for nostalgia, think again. While we now use a graphical user interface (GUI) to do most of our work, the command-line interface remains a powerful tool. It can be used to automate your development, examine and control running processes, help you debug applications, set hidden preferences, administer and control remote computers, and so much more. On your journey to obtaining *OS X High Wizard* status, you'll come to appreciate the formidable capabilities of the command line.

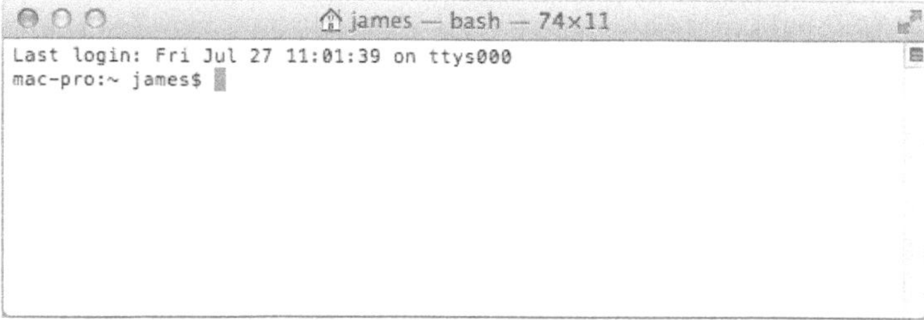

Figure 9-1. *Terminal window*

Each Terminal window runs a shell session. A *shell* is a program that implements a command-line interface. It's the program that waits for you to type something and then performs the actions you commanded.

> **NOTE:** The default shell program in OS X is bash (pronounced just like the word "bash"). It's an abbreviation for the Bourne-Again shell, a successor to the original Bourne shell (sh) written by Stephen Bourne.
>
> Other popular shells are the Korn shell (ksh), Z shell (zsh), C shell (csh), and TENEX C shell (tcsh). OS X includes all of these shells and others. The C and TENEX C shells are interesting because their syntax is intended to mimic the C programming language. There are specialty shells like the Remote shell (rsh) and Secure shell (ssh) for executing commands on another computer.

Traditionally, a shell will begin by outputting a salutation. That's the first line you see in the window in Figure 9-1:

```
Last login: Wed Jul 27 11:01:39 on ttys000
```

The salutation might alert you to unread mail that's waiting for you, a message of the day, or even a joke. After the salutation is the prompt:

```
mac-pro:~ james$
```

The prompt is just that—the shell is saying that it's waiting for you to type a command. The standard prompt includes the name of your computer (called its hostname), the current directory (we'll get to that later), your user account name, and a prompt character ($).

You enter your command after the prompt by typing on the keyboard and pressing the Return key. Try it. Type the letters "ls" and press Return. The shell performs the ls ("list directory contents") command and the output appears after your command in the window, as shown in Figure 9-2.

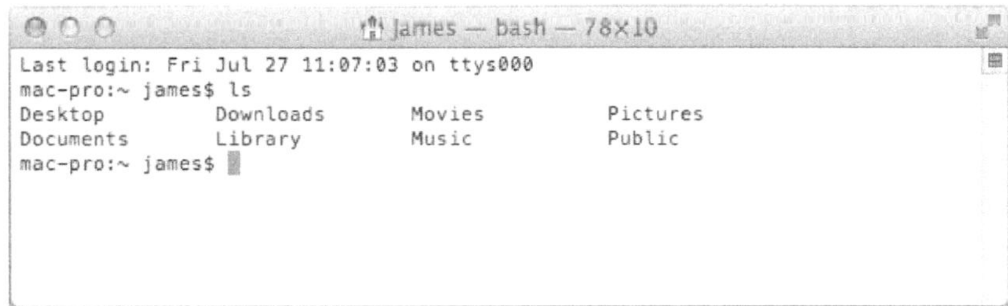

Figure 9-2. *Output of ls command*

The ls command lists the objects in the current directory. The shell outputs another prompt, telling you that it's finished and is ready for another command.

> **NOTE:** Command line tools use UNIX parlance. In UNIX-speak, a *directory* is a folder. A *file* is a document. A *file system object* is a generic term for any named entity on your file system (which includes files, directories, and other things).

Command Arguments

Commands, like C functions, can also have arguments. Arguments follow the command and are separated from the command, and other arguments, by spaces. An argument that alters the behavior of a command is called an *option* or *switch*, and it is traditionally prefixed by one or two hyphens (-), pronounced "dash." Try the `ls` command again, but this time add a `-l` (that's a lower case letter l) switch before pressing Return.

```
james — bash — 78×17
Last login: Fri Jul 27 11:07:03 on ttys000
mac-pro:~ james$ ls
Desktop         Downloads       Movies          Pictures
Documents       Library         Music           Public
mac-pro:~ james$ ls -l
total 0
drwx------+  6 james  staff   204 Jul 27 10:58 Desktop
drwx------+  5 james  staff   170 Jul 27 09:47 Documents
drwx------+  4 james  staff   136 Jul 25 22:28 Downloads
drwx------@ 38 james  staff  1292 Jul 26 22:16 Library
drwx------+  3 james  staff   102 Jul 25 22:28 Movies
drwx------+  3 james  staff   102 Jul 25 22:28 Music
drwx------+ 14 james  staff   476 Jul 27 11:20 Pictures
drwxr-xr-x+  4 james  staff   136 Jul 25 22:28 Public
mac-pro:~ james$
```

Figure 9-3. *Output of ls -l command*

The `ls` command's `-l` switch changes its output to the "long" format (see Figure 9-3), which shows the type, permissions, size, ownership, and last modified date of each item in your home folder. In most commands, multiple switches can be combined. The following three commands are identical:

```
ls -l -h -n
ls -lhn
ls -ln -h
```

Command arguments that are not switches are generally a path to something, which the command will act on. The command `ls -l Music` will list the items in your Music directory, rather than your home directory.

Learning More About Commands

What switches, options, and arguments a command understands or allows differs with each command. To learn about a command, use the `man` ("manual") command. Type the command `man ls` and press Return, as shown in Figure 9-4.

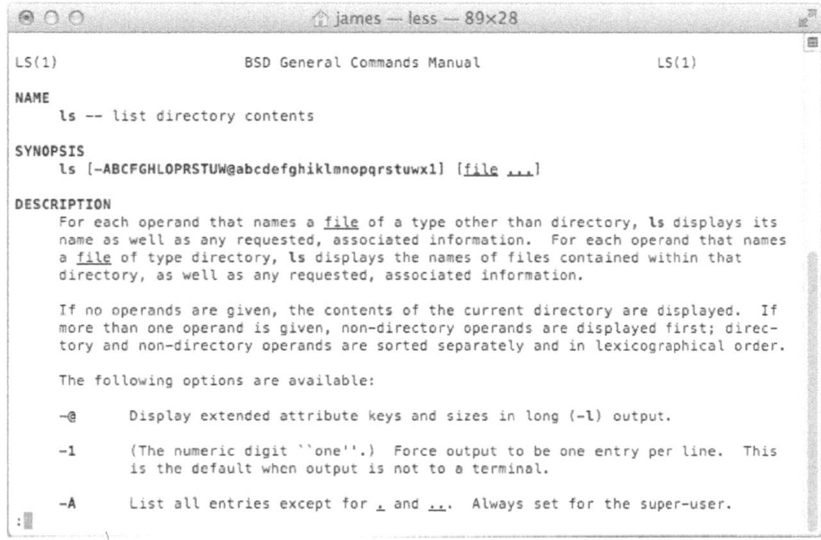

Figure 9-4. *The man page for the ls command*

The `man` command will present the "manual" page for the command named in the argument. Most commands have a man page. The `man` command uses another command, named `less`, to present the information to you. The `less` command is the UNIX equivalent of Apple's Preview application; it's the all-purpose text viewer. Press the space bar to advance one page at a time. Press the "u" and "d" keys to move up or down one half page. The "g" key will run you back up to the top, the "h" key will show you a help page, and the "q" key will quit less and return you to back to the shell.

> **NOTE:** Unfortunately, there are no hard rules when it comes to UNIX commands and switches. For every one hundred commands that use switches that start with a hyphen (-), there's one that doesn't. There are hundreds of commands that act on files, and hundreds that don't. Most commands will let you combine switches, but there are a few that won't. The advice to commit to memory is "read the man page."

Naturally, there's a man page about man (`man man`), and there's a man page for less (`man less`).

So how do you discover commands? One way is with another command. The `apropos` command will search the database of man pages for keywords. For example, this command

```
apropos time
```

lists all of the man pages that mention the word "time" in their name or summary. Here's the tail end of the output produced by the apropos time command:

```
…
tmutil(8)                - Time Machine utility
touch(1)                 - change file access and modification times
tzfile(5)                - timezone information
uevent_onidle(n), uevent::onidle(n) - Request merging and deferal to idle time
uptime(1)                - show how long system has been running
zdump(8)                 - timezone dumper
zic(8)                   - timezone compiler
```

Man pages are organized into sections. The pages with sections (1) or (8) after their name are generally the ones you're interested in. Section 1 documents regular shell commands. Section 8 documents utilities, some of which are useful commands. Other sections, like section 5, simply document the format of particular files. Section 2 documents programming functions, like `printf()`. This section has been moved into Xcode's help, so you won't find section 2 man pages in OS X anymore.

As you peruse the list of time-related man pages, you discover `uptime(1)`. Enter `uptime` in the Terminal window and press Return, and you'll see something like this:

```
marchhare:~ james$ uptime
14:30  up 13 days,  2:46, 2 users, load averages: 0.28 0.39 0.36
```

`uptime` is a simple command that outputs the current time, how long your computer has been running since it was last booted, how many users are logged in, and some statistics on how hard your CPU is working.

You now have enough information that you can spend hours looking up new commands using `apropos`, and reading all about them using the `man` command. Now let's move on to why any of this matters.

Where Shell Commands Come From

You might be wondering what all this has to do with C programming. After all, it would appear that the shell, although very talented, is just a program that understands a bunch of text commands. But that's not true at all. The shell doesn't understand *any* of the commands you've given it.

The shell is a remarkably simple, and subtly brilliant, concept. When you type in a command (like `ls`), the shell simply looks for an executable named `ls` and runs it. That's basically all it does. All of the commands you've used so far (`ls`, `man`, `less`, `apropos`, `uptime`), and hundreds of other commands you can give it, are all separate executable programs written in—drum roll, please—C.

Every project in this book could be used as a command in the shell. All you have to do to create a new command is follow these steps.

1. Write and build an executable command-line program (which you've already done).
2. Put it where the shell can find it.

That's it. As soon as you've done that, your computer's command-line interface magically has a new command—a command that you created!

We're now going to show you how to create and install your own command-line tools. But before we do that, let's talk just a little more about the shell. We've oversimplified the shell a bit. It does have other talents:

- The shell understands a small number of keywords that, like C language keywords, allows it to declare variables, compute values, makes decisions using if statements, perform for and while loops, and even define functions that can be reused. In this sense, a shell is a kind of programming language—but a decidedly limited one when compared to C.
- The shell can link commands together to accomplish complex jobs.
- A sequence of shell commands can be saved in a file, called a shell script, and used again later. This makes it possible to create complex sequences of shell commands (which might include if decisions and for loops) and easily reuse them.
- A shell script can, in turn, be used as a command.

If you want to learn more, you can spend an evening (or two!) reading the `bash` man page. Warning: it's over 200 screens of dense, often technical, descriptions. There are whole books just on shell scripting; check the `www.apress.com` web site. But you won't need to learn any of that to get through this book. We're not going to concentrate on the shell so much as what it takes to create a C program that can run as a shell command.

Creating a Command-Line Tool

A *command-line tool* is an executable file that's designed to be useful when used from a command-line interface. Remember that the shell can start just about any executable file that exists on your system, but not all of those are going to be useful as commands. What we refer to as a "command-line tool" is, therefore, not a technical description so much as a statement of its intent.

So while every executable you've created so far could be run from the command line, very few of them would be considered command-line tools. For example, the `AstronomicalUnit` project from Chapter 8 would make a terrible command. The program simply stores a number in memory and then exits. The program doesn't do any useful work. It doesn't output any interesting information. It doesn't accept any input. It basically starts, does nothing, and stops again. Boring.

Useful command-line tools tend to interact with the user or other tools. They do this through *input* and *output*. You're already familiar with the output half—all of those `printf()` calls output text to the shell (when you're not running your program from within Xcode).

Now you're going to explore the input side of the equation. Command-line tools get their input from two sources: *command-line arguments* and *standard input* or *stdin*.

Command-line arguments are strings passed from the shell to your program. When you execute a command with one or more arguments, like `ls -l`, those arguments are converted into C strings and passed along to the program. The program can examine the arguments—in this example, the `ls` program sees you used an `-l` switch—and uses them to alter its behavior. How a tool uses arguments is entirely up to it.

The other input option is standard input, referred to in code as `stdin`. Standard input is the complement to standard output (`stdout`). The functions `printf()` and `putchar()` send characters to standard output, where they end up in the Xcode console window, or the Terminal window, or possibly elsewhere. A command-line program's standard input is where it can receive characters sent to it by you or from another program. Let's start with command-line arguments.

Command Arguments and main()

Earlier we said that a command-line tool may accept arguments, like C functions, allowing you to pass values to the command. It's more than a similarity; it's exactly what happens.

When the shell runs a command, it uses a special mechanism to turn the text you typed on the command line into a series of C strings. These C strings are allocated and copied into your program before it begins execution, and you've been staring right at them since the first chapter. Let's revisit the definition of `main()`:

```
int main( int argc, char argv[] )
```

The two parameters to `main()` contain all of the arguments passed to your program from the shell (or any other program that knows how to pass arguments). The `argc` variable will be the number of strings that were passed. The `argv` parameter is an array of `char` pointers. Each element is a `char` pointer that points to one command-line argument string. The dimension of the `argv` array is always `argc` elements long, so the valid elements of `argv` are always `argv[0]` through `argv[argc-1]`.

If you create a command-line tool named `SeeArgs` and run it from the command line, you get this:

```
mac-pro:~ james$ SeeArgs see args run
```

When `SeeArg`'s `main()` function starts, the values of `argc` and `argv` will be those shown in Table 9-1.

Table 9-1. *Values of argc and argv[]*

Variable	Value
argc	4
argv[0]	"SeeArgs"
argv[1]	"see"
argv[2]	"args"
argv[3]	"run"

Notice that the path (or name) of the command-line tool is included in the list. There are situations where it's handy to know where your program is located or the name that was used to run it, so the shell passes this as the first string. This also means that your program should always have at least one string in the array. If your command was run with one or more arguments, the remaining strings will be those arguments.

> **CAUTION:** Never assume that the first `argv[]` string is the command's name, or that there even is a first string. This is a convention adhered to by all shell programs and other well behaved programs that might run your program—but it's not guaranteed. A poorly written program may run your program with an arbitrary first string, or no strings at all. Always check `argc` and code cautiously.

SeeArgs.xcodeproj

So let's get to it. Open the SeeArgs project in the *09.01 - SeeArgs* folder. The program looks likes this:

```
#include <stdio.h>

int main( int argc, const char * argv[] )
{
    int i;

    for ( i = 0; i < argc; i++ ) {
        printf( "argv[%d] = '%s'\n", i, argv[i] );
    }

    return 0;
}
```

You can probably figure this one out in your sleep by now. The `main()` function loops through the array of arguments that were passed to it and outputs each, one per line.

So how do you test this? To test your new command-line program, you must supply it with some arguments. That means you have to compile the program, copy it somewhere the shell can run it, and then run it from the command line. But that also means you can't use Xcode and all its great tools—especially the debugger! What if the program doesn't work? How will you find out what's wrong and fix it?

Don't worry, Xcode has you covered. To allow you to test command-line tools, or any other program that expects arguments, you can set up test arguments in Xcode. The test arguments will be passed to your program when you run it.

To set this up, edit the Run scheme for your project. From the **Project** menu, choose the **Edit Scheme…** command, or choose the same command from the left side of the *Scheme* button in the toolbar. You'll see an edit scheme dialog, as shown in Figure 9-5.

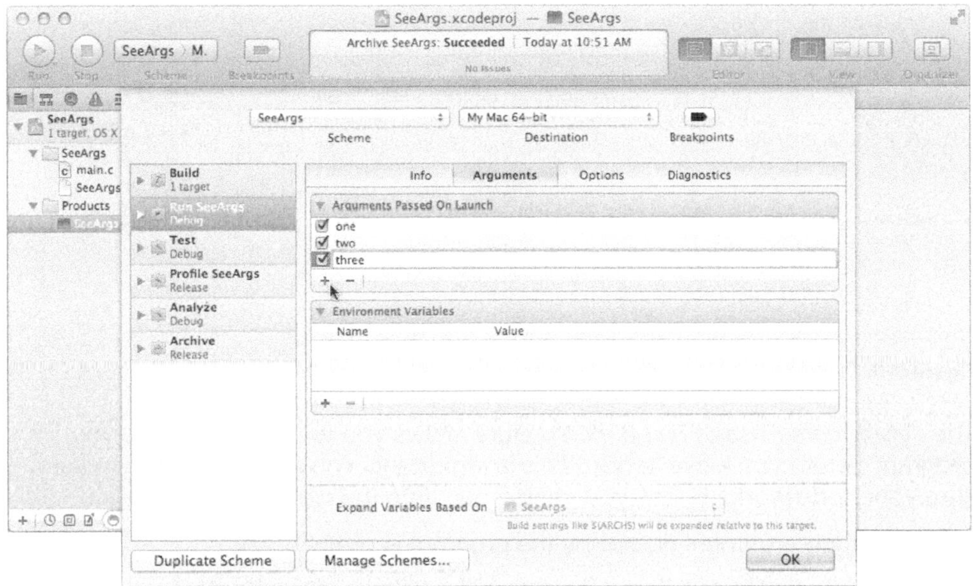

Figure 9-5. *Edit scheme dialog*

Select the *Run SeeArgs* scheme on the left. On the right, find the *Arguments Passed on Launch* area. Click the + button at the bottom to add a new argument. Enter "one" as the first argument. Repeat until you've added several arguments. Click the *OK* button.

> **TIP:** The check box next to each entry in the *Arguments Passed on Launch* area allows you choose just the arguments you want passed. You set up several combinations of arguments, and then select just the ones you want to test. Testing your program with a variety of test cases to make sure it behaves itself under all circumstances is a good practice.

Now when you run your program, Xcode will build and run it, passing it the arguments you set up in the Run scheme, just as if you had typed them in a shell. When the program runs, it prints out the arguments, as shown in Figure 9-6.

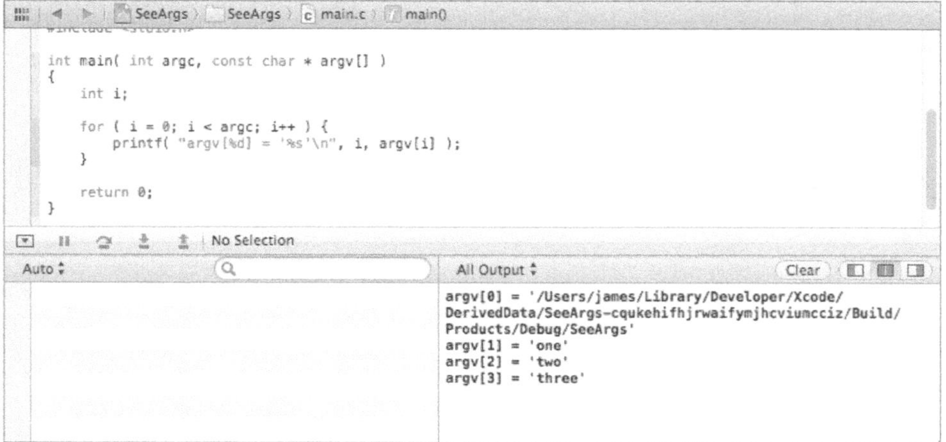

Figure 9-6. *Output of SeeArgs test*

The *Arguments Passed on Launch* feature allows you to test and debug your program before you leave Xcode. This is important. You always want to make sure your code works before you send it out "into the world," as it were.

The first string argument output by the program is pretty crazy:

```
argv[0] = '/Users/james/Library/Developer/Xcode/DerivedData/SeeArgs-
cqukehifhjrwaifymjhcviumcciz/Build/Products/Debug/SeeArgs'
argv[1] = 'one'
argv[2] = 'two'
argv[3] = 'three'
```

Remember that the first argument is the name, or path, to your program. In this case, it's the path to where Xcode stores your compiled program during development. The exact location isn't important. It's something you let Xcode worry about. Just know that Xcode is being a good shell citizen by passing the path of your program as its first argument.

The remaining strings are exactly the arguments you set up. It looks like your first command-line tool works!

Deploying the Program

The next step is to build your program so that it's suitable to be *deployed*. Deploying a program means to package it up so that it can be delivered to other developers, testers, or your end users. This might mean nothing more complicated that copying the finished program to a folder on your own computer. But you might copy it to a USB drive, put it in a disk image, upload it to a web server, or even submit it to Apple's App Store.

Use Xcode's Archive command to prepare your program for delivery. The Archive command compiles your program in a form suitable for distribution, and then packages up all of the parts that get delivered. These files are called, appropriately enough, the *deliverables*. For a command line tool, there's really only one file (the executable), but Xcode will produce two files. We'll explain why in a bit.

Prepare your archive by choosing the **Archive** command from the **Product** menu. Xcode will rebuild your project and convert the finished product into an Xcode archive. The archive will appear in the Organizer window, as shown in Figure 9-7.

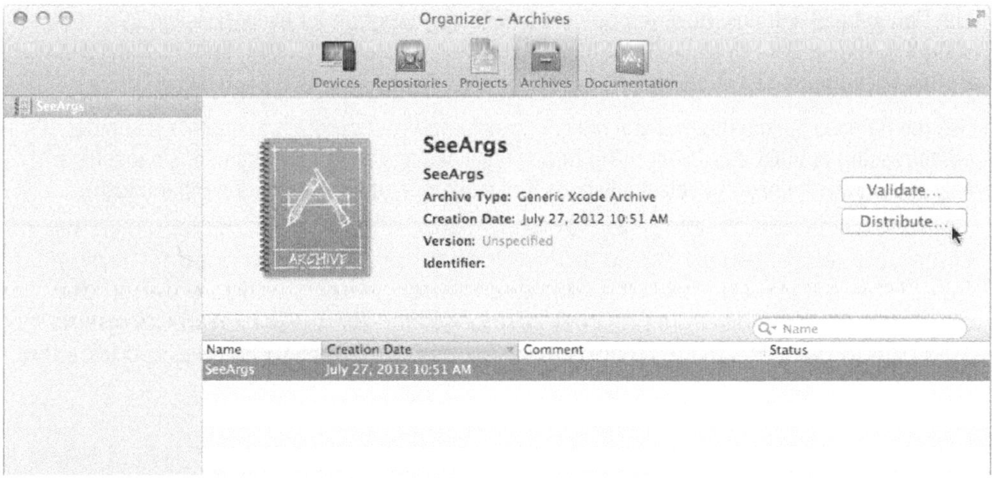

Figure 9-7. *Finished SeeArgs archive in Organizer window*

The Archive command behaves according to your project's Archive scheme. You saw how to edit schemes earlier. If you choose **Edit Schemes** and then the *Archive* scheme, you can edit its options. But you shouldn't have to. The default options should be perfect.

BUILD SETTINGS

Xcode compiles and links your program using a huge collection of options called the *build settings*. By default, your project will have two sets of build settings: Debug and Release. The Debug settings are used while you test and debug your code. The Release settings are used when you archive for deployment.

The differences between these settings are many, but two of them are pretty important. The Debug setting turns off most of the compiler optimizations and adds in a lot of data that allows the debugger to do its job. Without those settings, it would be difficult (sometimes impossible) to debug your application. On the other hand, you want your finished application to be as fast and lean as possible. So when deploying your program, use the Release settings, in which those optimizations are enabled.

The other important setting involves the CPU architecture. Different models of Macs have different CPUs, and a single executable isn't compatible with all of them. When using the Release build settings, Xcode compiles your program multiple times, one for each supported CPU architecture. Your finished program is actually a collection of several copies of your program, one for each family of CPU. When your program is run, the OS loads the version of the program that it understands.

The Debug build settings, however, do not compile your program for every possible CPU. It only compiles it for your CPU, since it assumes you're the only one that's going to run it. Why compile a bunch of code that's never going to be run?

Use the Release build settings if you plan on transferring your program to another computer. It's embarrassing to build a program using Debug build settings and copy it someone's machine, only to discover it doesn't contain any code that will run. And yes, we've done that (blush).

Once you've created an Xcode archive for your program, you need to deploy it. Select the archive and click the *Distribute* button, shown in Figure 9-7. In the distribute dialog, shown in Figure 9-8, choose the *Save Built Products* option. This option causes Xcode to copy your finished program to the desired location.

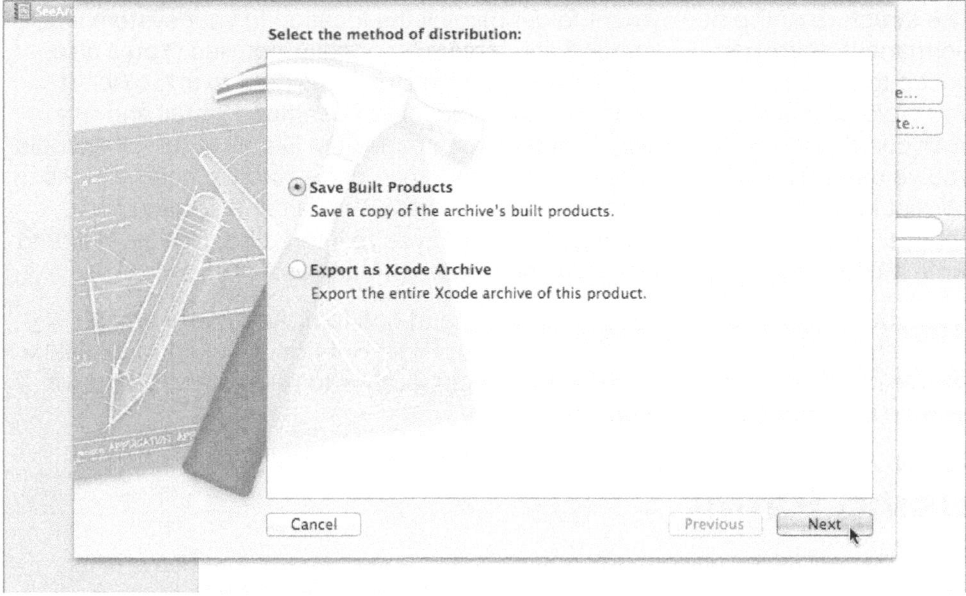

Figure 9-8. *Distribute archive options*

Click the *Next* button and choose a name and location to save your finished application. Navigate to your Desktop and change the deployment package name to *MyDeployment*. (You can choose a different name and location, but you'll have to adjust the instructions in the rest of this section accordingly.)

Open the *MyDeployment* folder on your desktop. You should see a file structure like that shown in Figure 9-9.

MyDeployment

Name	Date Modified	Size	Kind
usr	Today 10:51 AM	--	Folder
local	Today 10:51 AM	--	Folder
bin	Today 10:51 AM	--	Folder
SeeArgs	Today 10:51 AM	8 KB	Unix Executable File
share	Today 10:51 AM	--	Folder
man	Today 10:51 AM	--	Folder
man1	Today 10:51 AM	--	Folder
SeeArgs.1	Today 10:51 AM	3 KB	Document

Figure 9-9. *Contents of a deployment folder*

The structure of the deployment folder mimics the location in your system where permanent, third-party, command-line tools are normally installed. You'll also notice that the folder includes a *SeeArgs.1* file stored inside a *man1* folder. If you were producing a tool that you expected lots of people to install and use, your command-line tool would include a man page, just like all of the other tools you've used. The *SeeArgs.1* file contains that man page, and if placed it in the correct location, will join the other man pages that the `man` and `apropos` tools access. We'll ignore the man page for now. If you're interested, Google "How to write a UNIX man page" and you'll find dozens of tutorials.

Now you're ready to install your new command-line tool. And guess what? You're going to do it using just the command line! But first we need to explain a couple of concepts that will make this process easier to understand—and will also be important in later chapters.

Using Paths

Every file and folder on your volume has a name and a path. The name is its name. Its path is a string that describes exactly where that item is on your computer by listing every directory, in order, that contains that item. A path ends with the name of the item.

Think of it this way. Josephine is a person. Her name is Josephine. Her "path" is Milky Way Galaxy, Earth, United States of America, New Mexico, Sometown, Power Road, 1234, Josephine. Admittedly, the "Milky Way Galaxy" part might have been a bit excessive, but the idea is to write down an unambiguous description of Josephine that can't possibly be confused with any other Josephine *in the entire universe*.

A *path* in UNIX is sequence of directory and file names, each separated by a "/" ("slash") character, also referred to as the *path separator*. The complete path to an item in the file system is called an *absolute path*. An absolute path always starts with a "/" (called the "root" directory), followed by all of the directory names leading to the item, and ending with that item's name. Here's an example of an absolute path on James's hard drive:

```
/Users/james/Music/iTunes/iTunes Music/Moscow Symphony Orchestra/The
Egyptian/Valley of the Kings.mp3
```

This path describes the 17th track from the soundtrack *The Egyptian*, in the iTunes collection stored in James's account. Dave might also have the same track, from the same album, stored in his iTunes library. But since Dave has a different home folder, the absolute path to his file will be different:

```
/Users/davemark/Music/iTunes/iTunes Music/Moscow Symphony Orchestra/The
Egyptian/Valley of the Kings.mp3
```

So even if Dave has the same tastes in movie soundtracks that James exhibits, there's no ambiguity as to which file each path refers to. On the other hand, it's going to get really tedious typing out the absolute path of every file you want to work with. This brings us to relative paths.

Current Directory and Relative Paths

A *relative path* is a partial path that relies on the context of another path to complete it. Relative paths do not start with a "/"—that's how you tell that it's a relative path. That context is the *current directory*, also called the *working directory*.

The current directory is always an absolute path to a directory. A relative path starts where the current directory ends. The absolute path of an item is obtained by simply joining (concatenating) the current directory with the relative path. For example, if the current directory was `/Users/james`, the relative path of James's iTunes folder would be, simply, `Music/iTunes`.

```
Current directory: /Users/james
Relative path: Music/iTunes
Absolute path: /Users/james/Music/iTunes
```

Returning to the previous analogy, if you were in the United States of America, you could address Josephine as "New Mexico, Sometown, Power Road, 1234, Josephine." You don't have to specify the country or planet because those are assumed. Similarly, if you were in Sometown, New Mexico, the path "Power Road, 1234, Josephine" would do the trick. If you were standing in front of the house at 1234 Power Road, you could just say "Josephine" and there still wouldn't be any confusion about whom you were talking about.

Similarly, if the current directory was `/Users/james`, the path to track 17 would be `Music/iTunes/iTunes Music/Moscow Symphony Orchestra/The Egyptian/Valley of the Kings.mp3`. If the current directory was iTunes's music folder (`/Users/james/Music/iTunes/iTunes Music`), that same file could be addresses as `Moscow Symphony Orchestra/The Egyptian/Valley of the Kings.mp3`.

There are two big advantages to using relative paths. The first is brevity. If the current directory is Dave's home folder (`/Users/davemark`), Dave can refer to his *Download* folder simply by typing `Download` and not `/Users/davemark/Download` every time.

> **TIP:** Use the `cd` ("change directory") command to change the current directory path in the shell. The `cd` command takes a single argument, the new directory path (as in `cd Documents`). Notice that the path can be relative to the previous current directory. If you omit the path, your home directory becomes the current directory. To find out what the current directory is, issue the `pwd` ("print working directory") command. All paths you use in the shell are relative to the current directory.

The second advantage is that the same (relative) path can be reused at different locations simply by changing the current directory. You can write a program that uses the paths `Documents`, `Downloads`, `Music`, and `Pictures`. If the current directory is `/Users/james`, all of those paths refer to folders that belong to James. If the current directory is changed to `/Users/davemark`, now those same paths refers to the `Documents`, `Downloads`, `Music`, and `Pictures` folder that belong to Dave.

Table 9-2 shows the relative paths to the `Music` folder and the `Valley of the Kings.mp3` file given three different current directories. The paths for the *Music* directory might be unexpected. These are special directory names.

Table 9-2. *Examples of Relative Paths*

Current Directory	Path to Music	Path to Valley of the Kings
/Users/james	Music	Music/iTunes/iTunes Music/Moscow Symphony Orchestra/The Egyptian/Valley of the Kings.mp3
/Users/james/Music	.	iTunes/iTunes Music/Moscow Symphony Orchestra/The Egyptian/Valley of the Kings.mp3
/Users/james/Music/iTunes/iTunes Music	../..	Moscow Symphony Orchestra/The Egyptian/Valley of the Kings.mp3

Special Directory Names

There are two special directory names that can be used in a path: "`.`" and "`..`" (that's one and two periods, pronounced "dot" and "dot-dot").

The `.` directory name means "this directory." You can use it anywhere in a path, but it's most useful at the beginning of a relative path or by itself. If the current directory is `/Users/james/Music` and you want a relative path to the `Music` folder, the path would be empty, which is awkward in places like the command line where an argument needs to be "something." In this situation, the lone `.` path fits the bill perfectly. It's also used to emphasize that the path starts at the current directory; The paths `iTunes` and `./iTunes` mean exactly the same thing.

The `..` directory name is a bit more interesting. It means "the directory that contains this directory." This is known by various names, but *parent directory* and *enclosing folder* are the most common.

The file system organization uses a "tree" analogy: every path starts at the "root" (/), follows a number of "branches" (directories), until it gets to a "leaf" (file). Technically it's called a *directed graph*, but we'll ignore its official name because that doesn't help the squirrels.

Imagine that your computer is a squirrel. When the squirrel wants to find the item at a path like `/Users/james/Documents/Winter/Nuts.txt`, it starts at the root of the directory tree. It then scampers down the `Users` branch. There, it finds the `james` branch, then the `Documents` branch, then the `Winter` branch. Finally, on the `Winter` branch it finds the `Nuts.txt` leaf. In a sense, a path is a sequence of directions (turn right, go three blocks, turn left) that lead to a final destination.

The `..` name is a direction that says "go back to the branch this one's attached to." Can you guess what the following path leads to?

```
/Users/james/Music/iTunes/../../Documents/Winter/Nuts.txt
```

If you guessed `/Users/james/Documents/Winter/Nuts.txt`, you are correct. The squirrel started at the root, ran down the `Users`, `james`, `Music`, and `iTunes` branches. It then turned around and went back up one branch (now it's back at `Music`), went back up another branch (now it's back at `james`), then turned around and followed the `Documents` and `Winter` branches down to the `Nuts.txt` leaf.

> **TIP:** One peculiarity of the tree/branch/leaf analogy is that computer science engineers have always gotten the directions backwards from real trees. In computer terms, you "descend" the tree as you move towards the leaves. So when you move from the root, to a branch, to a leaf you are moving "down" the tree. In real trees, of course, you'd be going up. Likewise, moving from a directory to its parent directory is described as "ascending" or "going up" the directory tree. If it helps, think of your file system as an upside down tree, planted in the ceiling and growing towards the floor.

The `..` directory name is very useful in relative paths. If the current directory is `/Users/james/Documents`, the relative path to James's `Music` folder is `../Music`: the current directory is `Documents`, `..` means "go up to `james`," and `Music` means "from there, go down to `Music`." The relative path to Dave's `Music` folder is `../../davemark/Music`.

The Home Directory Name

There's one last special directory name; the ~ path is the *home directory*. The ~ is the tilde character, usually found in the upper left corner of your keyboard next to the 1 key. The ~ replaces the / at the beginning of an absolute path. The ~ directory translates into the "home directory of the current user." When James is logged into his computer, ~ is replaced with `/Users/james`. When Dave is logged in, ~ becomes `/Users/davemark`. The path `~/Music` translates to "the `Music` folder inside the home folder of the currently logged in user."

The ~ directory is particularly handy for specifying the path to the user's standard items (`Documents`, `Download`, `Music`, `Pictures`, `Library`, and so on). Since it's an absolute path, it doesn't depend on the current directory.

All of these features—absolute paths, current/working directory, the `.` and `..` directory names—are part of the UNIX file system, upon which OS X is built. The one exception is the ~ path. The home path is a convention that you can use in the shell, but most C file functions don't understand it. This will become important when you start accessing files in Chapter 11. But feel free to use ~ on the command line.

Now that you understand the home directory, current directory, absolute paths, relative paths, and special directory names, it's time to install your command-line tool.

Installing a Command-Line Tool

Earlier we said that to install a program so that it becomes a command in the shell, one must

> *2. Put it where the shell can find it.*

The easiest way to do this is to simply tell the shell exactly where your program is. If the command is an explicit pathname to an executable program, the shell runs that program, no questions asked. For example, you can run your new command line tool right now. Open a Terminal window and enter this command after the prompt:

```
~/Desktop/MyDeployment/usr/local/bin/SeeArgs Moe Larry Curly
argv[0] = '/Users/james/Desktop/MyDeployment/usr/local/bin/SeeArgs'
argv[1] = 'Moe'
argv[2] = 'Larry'
argv[3] = 'Curly'
```

> **TIP:** The shell has a feature called auto-completion (similar to Xcode's auto-completion). When typing a long path, type just enough letters to identify the directory and press the Tab key. If you typed enough letters, the shell will fill in the remainder of the name. If you didn't, it will beep. Keep typing and try again. You could type the path `~/Desktop/MyDeployment/usr/local/bin/SeeArgs` using the keystrokes "~", "/", "D", "e", Tab, "M", "y", Tab, Tab, "l", Tab, Tab, Tab. Notice that in a directory with only one choice you don't have to type anything except the Tab.
>
> Path auto-completion is found in a lot of places in OS X, so don't hesitate to try the Tab key.

Congratulations! You just ran your first command-line tool from the shell. Before you crank up the Karaoke machine to celebrate, it would be nice if you didn't have to enter the entire path to your tool every time you wanted to run it. What you really want is to be able to type the command

```
SeeArgs Moe Larry Curly
```

and have the shell find your program and run it, like it does with `ls`, `man`, and all those others.

So where does the shell look for command-line tools? If the command is just a name (like `ls`), it looks in a sequence of directories contained in a shell variable named `PATH`. As we said, a shell is kind of programming language that has variables. You can see the value of this variable using this command:

```
echo $PATH
/usr/bin:/bin:/usr/sbin:/sbin:/usr/local/bin
```

This value tells the shell to look for a command-line tool first in the `/usr/bin` directory. If it doesn't find one with the right name there, it looks in `/bin`. It keep working through the (colon-separated) list of directories until it finds the command or runs out of directories—in which case you'll get a "command not found" error.

To add your tool to the family of command-line tools that the shell will seamlessly find, you need to either copy it to one of the directories in that list or expand the list of directories where the shell looks for commands.

So you could simply copy your SeeArgs program to the /usr/local/bin directory. /usr/local/bin is the directory traditionally reserved for user-installed tools that are local to this computer. It's not a good idea to start adding tools to the system's tool folders, /bin, /sbin, and so on. Leave those alone, unless you really know what you're doing.

Instead, we're going to show you how to create your own private bin directory, install your tool there, and add it to the shell's list of tool directories. And you're going to accomplish this with just three commands!

Creating a Private bin Directory

Return to the Terminal window. This first command will create a new folder in your home directory named bin. Type it in and press the Return key.

```
mkdir ~/bin
```

The mkdir ("make directory") command is just like the **New Folder** command in the Finder, except that it creates the folder and names it all in one step. If you open up your home folder in the Finder, you'll now see a new subfolder named bin.

bin (short for "binaries") is the traditional name for folders that contain executable files, just as Applications is the name used for a folder of regular applications. Your bin folder will be the place to put all of the command-line tools that you want to use via the shell. Since it's your folder, it won't conflict with any of the tools already installed by the system or by anyone else.

Installing the Tool

Now you need to get your program into your bin folder. Do that using the mv command:

```
mv ~/Desktop/MyDeployment/usr/local/bin/SeeArgs ~/bin
```

The mv ("move") command moves one or more items to a directory. The items to move are listed first in the arguments, and the directory you want them all moved to is last. The mv command will also rename files and folders—in UNIX, there's no distinction between moving something and renaming it.

If you open up the bin folder in your home folder, you will see that your SeeArgs program is now there. Using the mv command is identical to switching to the Finder and dragging the SeeArgs file from its deployment folder into your new bin folder.

Configuring the PATH Variable

The final command is a bit tricky. You need to reconfigure the shell so it also looks in your new, private, `~/bin` folder in addition to the regular ones. You're going to do this by adding a new shell command to the `.bash_profile` file. Yes, that filename started with a period. Enter the following command in the shell, and be really careful with this one; the single quotes, double quotes, spaces, and punctuation have to be just so or it won't work. Be sure you get the double quote followed by a single quote after `~/bin`:

```
echo 'PATH="$PATH:~/bin"' >> ~/.bash_profile
```

The `echo` command is a tool that's not much more complicated than the one you just wrote. It does nothing more than output (echo) all of its arguments to standard output—just like yours, but without any embellishment. In this case, its single argument is the shell statement `PATH="$PATH:~/bin"`, surrounded by single quotes. This statement works something like a C assignment statement. It says that the `PATH` variable is to be set to the contents of the previous `PATH` variable plus a colon and one more path, `~/bin`.

This statement gets added to a special file named `.bash_profile`. The `>>` operator took care of redirecting the echo's output and appending it to the end of the `.bash_profile` file. We'll explain all about redirection later in this chapter.

Every time the bash shell starts up, it looks for a file named `.bash_profile` in your home folder. If it finds it, it executes all of the statements it finds there. By adding this statement, every new shell will be configured to look for commands in your private `bin` folder.

Oh, and don't bother looking for this file—you won't find it. Names that begin with a period (so-called "dot files") are invisible. They don't appear in the Finder or when you list a directory using the `ls` command (unless you add the `-a` or `-A` switch). If you want to see the contents of this file, use the command `cat ~/.bash_profile`. There's also a simple text editor you can use. The command `pico ~/.bash_profile` will let you interactively edit the file. Type Control+X to quit the `pico` editor and return the shell.

Close the Terminal window and open a new one. Remember, the `.bash_profile` only gets run when the shell starts, so to see your changes, you need a new shell.

If everything went according to plan, your updated `PATH` is all set up, as demonstrated in Figure 9-10.

```
mac-pro:~ james$ echo $PATH
/usr/bin:/bin:/usr/sbin:/sbin:/usr/local/bin:~/bin
mac-pro:~ james$ SeeArgs eins zwei drei
argv[0] = 'SeeArgs'
argv[1] = 'eins'
argv[2] = 'zwei'
argv[3] = 'drei'
mac-pro:~ james$
```

Figure 9-10. *Reconfigured shell PATH and user-installed command*

From here on, all you have to do to install new command tools is copy them into your `~/bin` folder. The setup stuff only needs to be done once.

Character Input

Let's take stock of what you've accomplished so far. You've learned a little about the command-line interface and shells. You know how to start a shell, execute commands, and pass arguments to those commands. More importantly, you learned how to create your own command-line programs, using the C language, that can use those arguments to do something useful. That's huge.

On this last leg of the "Grand Command Line Tour," you're going to learn the other way that command-line tools receive input from the shell, see how your program's input and output connect with other programs, and find out a little about pointers along the way.

Pipes

You already know that functions like `printf()` and `putchar()` write characters to standard output, and that somehow that makes those characters appear in the Xcode console (when your program is running in Xcode), or in the Terminal window (when your program is run from the command line). As it turns out, every UNIX process has an associated standard input, output, and error *stream*. In addition, UNIX provides a mechanism, known as a *pipe*, to connect these streams together.

Want to take the output from one program and feed it to the input of another? Use a pipe. Pipes are one-way only. For obvious reasons, you can't connect the output of one process to the output of another. Same with connecting an input to an input. A process's error stream is an output stream.

> **NOTE:** By convention, a program that produces useful output sends it to standard output. If it has any error or diagnostic messages, it sends those to standard error. Often these two outputs are connected to the same pipe, which means it doesn't matter which one you use because they all end up in the same place. But sometimes shells want to separate the program's regular output from its error messages and will connect those character streams to different pipes.

Before a program starts running, it is connected to a character stream of incoming bytes (standard in) and a character stream of outgoing bytes (standard output). The program reads characters from standard in and writes characters to standard output. What it doesn't do is care about what those pipes are connected to. Someone else determines that.

A command-line tool may only read from standard in, only write to standard output, both, or neither. What make sense depends on the nature of the tool.

Redirection

By connecting a process to different character streams, it's possible to reconfigure a single command-line tool to be used in different ways—without changing the tool. Connecting a command's input or output to an alternative stream is called *redirecting* its input/output (I/O). The following are the four most common character streams that a process will be connected to:

- Keyboard (input) or window (output)
- A file
- Nothing at all
- Standard in/out of another program

The Interactive Character Streams

The first type of connection is the default when running your command in Xcode or from the shell. If you don't redirect your command's input or output, its input will be connected to the keyboard and its output will be connected to the console window.

Anything you type on your keyboard appears on your program's standard in as characters. Anything your program outputs to standard output appears in the console pane or Terminal window. You've already seen the latter countless times. You'll try out the keyboard in the next project.

Pipes to Files

The second option occurs when your program's standard in or out is redirected to a file. This is very common. The file acts as either a pre-determined source of characters (when connected to standard in) or as a repository for characters (when connected to standard output). If you want the output of a command to be saved as a file, instead of simply appearing in the Terminal window, you use one of the redirection operators (such as > or >>) to connect its standard output to a file.

You did that when you installed your first command line tool. Normally, the output of the `echo` command goes to the Terminal window. You saw this with the command `echo $PATH`. But when you were reconfiguring the bash shell, you redirected the output of the `echo` command to the `.bash_profile` file like this:

```
echo 'PATH="$PATH:~/bin"' >> ~/.bash_profile
```

To redirect a tool's output you can use either > or >>. The > operator redirects a tool's standard output to a file. The file is overwritten with whatever the tool outputs. Nothing appears in the Terminal. For example, if you want to save a long directory listing of the current directory to a file on your desktop named `Dir.txt`, issue this command in the Terminal:

```
ls -l > ~/Desktop/Dir.txt
```

The >> operator is the same as >, except that if the file already exists it isn't erased; whatever the tool outputs is appended to the end of the existing file. You did this with the `echo` command so that, on the off chance you already had a `.bash_profile` file, the existing file wasn't deleted first.

Note that >> and `~/.bash_profile` are not arguments of the echo tool. That is, they don't appear in its `argc`/`argv` parameters. The redirection operators are recognized by the shell and are used to configure the tool's standard in and standard output before the tool is even started.

The shell's < operator will redirect a file to the command's standard in. You can redirect both the input and output in the same command.

Null

Your program's standard in or out may not be connected to anything at all. When your program tries to obtain characters from standard in, it will get nothing. Anything it sends to standard output will pass into oblivion.

UNIX even has a pseudo-file that represents nothing, named `/dev/null`. The `null` file isn't a regular file. It's a connection to a built-in driver that produces nothing when read and discards everything written to it. It's the character stream equivalent of a black hole. You can intentionally connect a command to this black hole using a redirection operator:

```
ls > /dev/null
```

> **NOTE:** Pseudo-files are file system objects that appear to be regular files but are actually connections to special processes inside the operating system. Writing to a pseudo-file might send the information to a driver, a physical device, or (as in the case if `/dev/null`) to nothing at all.
>
> All of the "files" in the `/dev` ("devices") directory are pseudo-files.

Other Processes

Finally, your program's standard in or out can be connected directly to the standard output or in (respectively) of another process, and this is where the command line gets really interesting. Take a look at this command:

```
ls | wc
```

You know the `ls` command does, but what this command outputs certainly isn't a directory listing:

```
       9       9      69
```

So what happened? In the shell, the | (vertical bar) character is called the *pipe* operator, so named because it creates a pipe that connects the standard output of the left command to the standard in of the right command. The `wc` ("word count") command is tool that reads a file or character stream and counts the number of lines, words, and characters it contains. This output tells you that there were 9 lines, 9 words, and 69 characters in the output produced by `ls`.

Note that you didn't see the output of the `ls` command. The characters it sent to its standard output were transferred directly to the standard in of the `wc` command. The `wc` command read those characters, counted them, and the results were output to its standard output, which wasn't redirected and appeared in the Terminal window.

> **NOTE:** The wc command is typical of most command-line tools in that it will either do its job on the files passed to it as arguments, or on standard input if no files are named. The command `wc ~/Desktop/Dir.txt` will count the characters in the `Dir.txt` file, while the command `wc` will count the characters on its standard input.

The shell lets you combine, and recombine, tools to accomplish all sorts of tasks. As a simple example, consider the `ls` command. The `ls` command (by default) sorts the names of the files and directories into ASCII order. As you already know, the ASCII values for the upper case letters are smaller than those for the lower case letters. This causes `ls` to produce the following list:

```
Desktop
Documents
Downloads
Movies
Music
Pictures
Public
bin
```

The problem is that `bin` is after `Public`. `ls` does not think "B" comes after "P" in the alphabet. Instead, this ordering occurs because the ASCII value of "b" is larger than the ASCII value of "P."

Here's another example. This time the output of the `ls` command is piped to the `sort` command, which has a lot of options for sorting things into the desired order:

```
ls | sort --ignore-case
bin
Desktop
Documents
Downloads
…
```

The `sort` command reads the lines from standard input, sorts them according to the criteria specified by the arguments, and outputs the sorted list to its standard output. Now your folder names are sorted into alphabetical (rather than ASCII value) order.

THE TERSENESS OF THE COMMAND LINE

UNIX commands are traditionally terse. They came from a time where the command line was the computer's only interface. Programmers spent all day typing hundreds, if not thousands, of commands. The shorter the commands, the more work they could get done—also, CRT displays weren't that big.

If you were an experienced UNIX geek, the following command would make perfect sense:

```
sort -fdr
```

For the rest of us, we'd have to go to the `sort` command's man page to find out what the `-f`, `-d`, and `-r` options meant. Because programmers don't (thankfully!) spend all day at the command line anymore, the trend for super-short commands has reversed. Many commands now have verbose synonyms for their options. The command

```
sort --ignore-case --dictionary-order --reverse
```

is identical to the previous one, and much easier to understand without a manual. Similarly, command names themselves are getting longer and more descriptive. Newer commands like `system_profiler` are appearing alongside old ones like od ("octal dump," if you must know).

Namer.xcodeproj

Let's start with a simple program that reads something from standard input. Open the Namer project. You'll find it in the 09.02 - Namer folder.

Namer will ask you to type your first name on the keyboard. Once you've typed your first name and pressed Return, the program will use your name to create a custom welcome message. Then Namer will tell you how many characters long your name is. How useful!

To run Namer, select **Run** from the **Product** menu. A console window will appear, prompting you for your first name, like this:

```
Type your first name, please:
```

Type your first name, and then press Return. You should see something like what's shown in Figure 9-11. Let's take a look at the source code that generated this output.

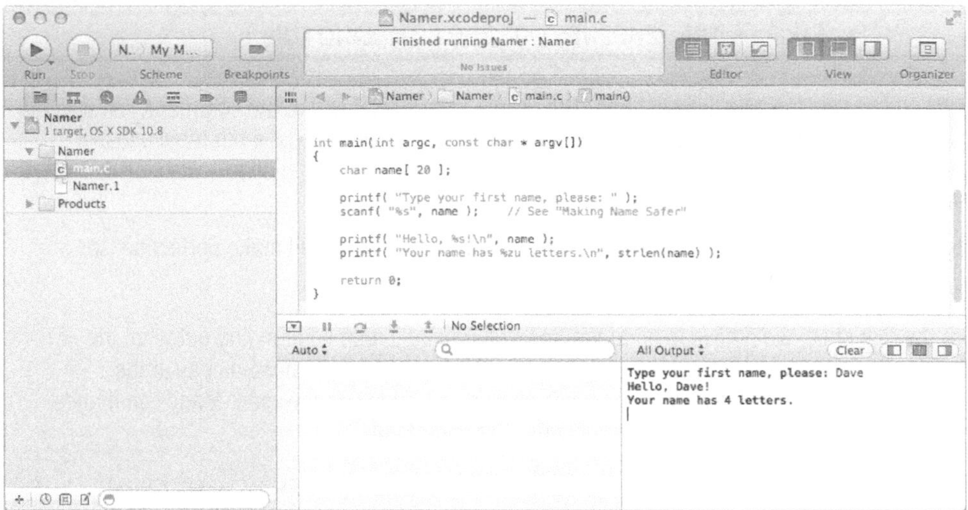

Figure 9-11. *The output, and input, of the Namer program*

Stepping Through the Namer Source Code

At the heart of *Namer* is a Standard Library function called scanf(). scanf() is the flip side of printf(). Where printf() takes variable values you already have, formats them, and sends them to standard output as characters, scanf() reads characters from standard input, converts them to values, and stores the results in variables that you can use.

This code will read in an int from standard input:

```
int    myInt;
scanf( "%d", &myInt );
```

The %d tells scanf() to read an int from the character stream. Notice the use of the & before the variable myInt. This passes myInt's address to scanf(), allowing scanf() to change myInt's value.

Namer starts off with a pair of #includes. <string.h> gives you access to the Standard Library function strlen(). From <stdio.h> you're going to get your old friend printf(), and now scanf(), too.

```
#include <stdio.h>
#include <string.h>
```

To read in a text string, you have to first declare a variable to receive the text characters. Namer uses an array of characters for this purpose:

```
int main (int argc, const char * argv[])
{
    char    name[ 20 ];
```

The array name is big enough to hold a 19-byte text string. When you allocate space for a text string, remember to save 1 byte for the NUL that terminates the string.

The program starts by printing a prompt. A prompt is a text string that lets the user know the program is waiting for input.

```
    printf( "Type your first name, please: " );
```

The Input Buffer

Before we get to the scanf() call, you should understand how the computer handles input from the keyboard. When the computer starts running your program, it automatically creates a big array of chars for the sole purpose of storing keyboard input to your program. This array is known as your program's input buffer. The input buffer is carriage-return based. Every time you hit a carriage return, all the characters typed since the last carriage return are appended to the current input buffer.

When your program starts, the input buffer is empty. If you type this line using your keyboard

```
123 abcd
```

and follow it with a carriage return, the input buffer will look like Figure 9-12. The computer keeps track of the current end of the input buffer. The space character between the "3" and the "a" has an ASCII value of 32. Notice that the Return key is also translated into a carriage return character (13) and added to the input buffer.

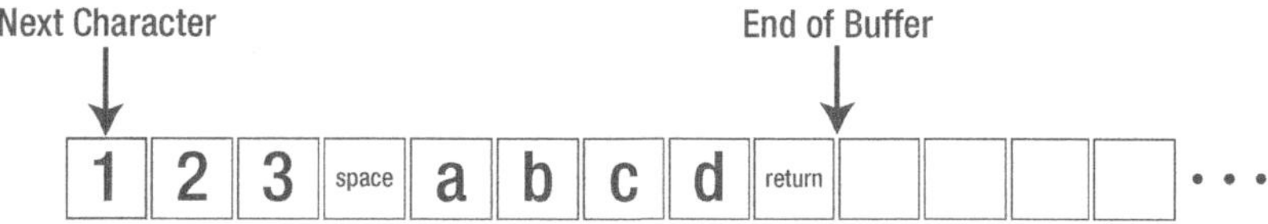

Figure 9-12. *Standard input buffer after typing a line on the keyboard*

Given the input buffer shown in Figure 9-12, suppose your program called scanf(), like this:

```
scanf( "%d", &myInt );
```

Since you asked scanf() to scan an integer, it starts at the beginning of the input buffer and reads only characters that would be characters of an integer (that is, digits and possible a positive or negative sign), one at a time, until it hits any character that isn't part of an integer. The scanner will also skip over any whitespace before the number (or most anything else it's scanning). In this example, it scans the characters "1," "2," and "3." It stops when it hits the space character because a space can't appear in the middle of an integer number.

After the scanf(), the input buffer looks like Figure 9-13. Notice that the characters read by scanf() were removed from the input buffer and that the rest of the characters slid over to the beginning of the buffer.

> **NOTE:** Software engineers call this a *first in, first out* (FIFO) buffer because, as the name implies, the first character written into the pipe will be the first character to be read from the pipe. All UNIX pipes are FIFOs.

Once it stops reading characters, scanf() translates the characters "1," "2," and "3" into to the numeric value 123, and stores that value in the variable myInt.

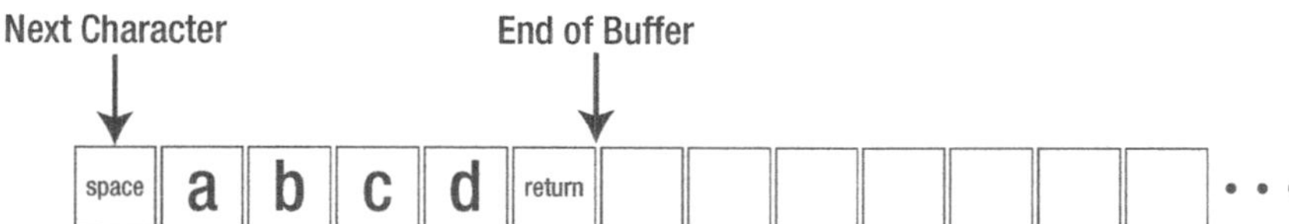

Figure 9-13. *Input buffer after scanning "%d"*

If you then typed the following line

```
3.5 DM
```

followed by a carriage return, the input buffer would look like Figure 9-14. At this point the input buffer contains two carriage return characters. To the input buffer, a carriage return is just another character. To a function like scanf(), the carriage return is both whitespace and a line break.

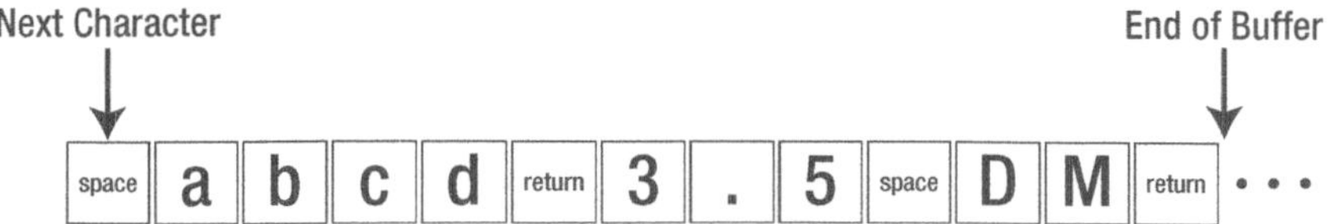

Figure 9-14. *Standard input buffer after typing a second line*

> **NOTE:** If you forgot what whitespace is, it's all of the characters you don't see (tab, space, newline, return) but are still considered text.

On with the Program

Before we started the discussion on the input buffer, `main()` had just called `printf()` to prompt for the user's first name:

```
printf( "Type your first name, please: " );
```

Next, it called `scanf()` to read the first name from the input buffer:

```
scanf( "%s", name );
```

Since the program just started, the input buffer is empty. `scanf()` will wait until characters appear in the input buffer, which will happen as soon as you type some characters and press Return. Type your first name, and press Return.

> **NOTE:** As mentioned earlier, `scanf()` will (typically) ignore leading whitespace characters in the input buffer. If a line contains nothing but whitespace, the entire line will be ignored. For example, if you type a few spaces and tabs and then press Return, `scanf()` will continue to sit there, waiting for some real input. Try it!

Once you type your name, `scanf()` will copy the characters, a byte at a time, into the `char` array pointed to by name. Remember, because `name` was declared as an array, `name` points to the first of the 20 bytes allocated for the array.

If you type in the name "Dave," `scanf()` will place the four characters "D," "a," "v," and "e" in the first four of the 20 bytes allocated for the array. Next, `scanf()` will set the fifth byte to a value of `'\0'` (NUL) to terminate the string properly (see Figure 9-15). Since the string is properly terminated by the `'\0'` in `name[4]`, you don't really care about the value of the bytes `name[5]` through `name[19]`.

Next, you pass name on to `printf()`, asking it to print the name as part of a welcome message. The `%s` tells `printf()` that `name` points to the first byte of a zero-terminated string. `printf()` will step through memory, one byte at a time, starting with the byte that name points to. `printf()` will print each byte in turn until it hits a byte with a value of `'\0'`. The NUL character marks the end of the string.

```
printf( "Hello, %s!\n", name );
```

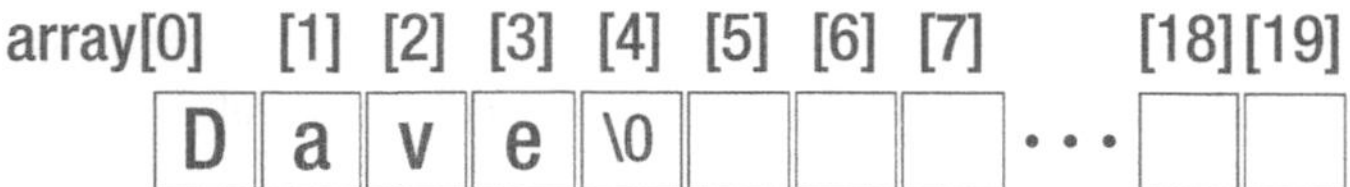

Figure 9-15. *Name array after the string "Dave" is copied to it*

> **NOTE:** If `name[4]` didn't contain a zero, the string wouldn't be properly terminated. Passing a non-terminated string to `printf()` is a sure way to confuse `printf()`. `printf()` will step through memory one byte at a time, printing a byte and looking for a zero. It will keep printing bytes until it happens to encounter a byte set to `'\0'`. Remember, C strings must be terminated!

The next line of the program calls another Standard Library function, called `strlen()`. `strlen()` takes a pointer as a parameter and returns the length, in bytes, of the string pointed to by the parameter. `strlen()` depends on the string being zero-terminated. Just like `sizeof()`, `strlen()` returns a value of type `size_t`, so you use a format specifier of `%zu`.

```
    printf( "Your name is %zu characters long.", strlen( name ) );

    return 0;
}
```

The Problem with Namer

So far, the program looks great. Namer seems to run just fine. What's the problem?

Imagine what would happen if you typed a 20-character, or longer, name in response to the console prompt. We realize that very few of you have a name that long, but just bear with us. The `name` array is only long enough to hold a 19-character name, reserving one byte for the string terminating `NUL`. `scanf()` doesn't know how big your `name` array is, so it doesn't know when to stop copying characters. When `scanf()` receives data too long for its `char` array, it keeps copying bytes anyway, even if it means stepping off the end of the array. When `scanf()` writes that 21st character in an array defined to have a length of 20, where does that extra byte go? No place good.

Figure 9-16 shows what happens when you run Namer, typing in the follow for a name:

```
qwertyqwertyqwertyqwertyqwertyqwertyqwertyqwerty
```

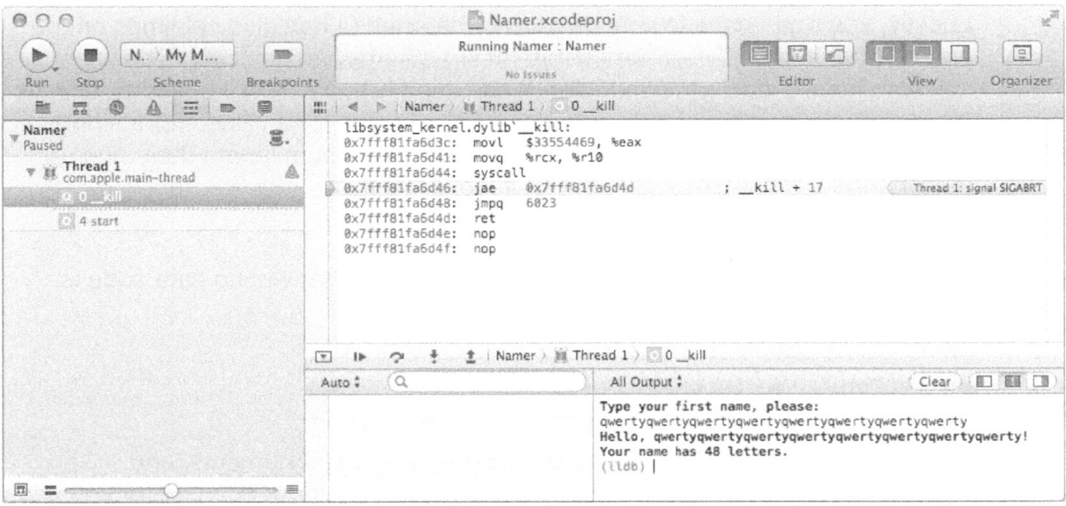

Figure 9-16. *Program crash due to buffer overflow*

Making Namer Safe

So how do you fix Namer? Just as with the Overflow project in Chapter 8, there are three approaches: allocate the buffer that's always big enough for the data, make sure the data is never too big to fit in the buffer, or make sure the data never overflows the buffer.

You can't use the first solution here because it's a Catch-22; you have to allocate the `name` array *before* you call `scanf()` to read the input buffer, and you can't find out how long the name in the input buffer is until `scanf()` returns.

The second approach isn't practical either. You can't force the user to limit themselves to a 20, 50, or even 60,000 character name. No matter how big you make the buffer, someone could feed your program a string that's one character longer than that.

So the third approach looks like your best (only) option. One solution would be to use a function other than `scanf()`, as you did in the Overflow project. There you replaced the `strcpy()` and `strcat()` functions with their `strlcpy()` and `strlcat()` counterparts, which were safer. For reading a string from standard input, you could use a function like `fgets()`. `fgets()` reads one line of characters from an input stream and copies them to a `char` array. And just like `strlcpy()` and `strlcat()`, one parameter is the maximum size of the destination array—`fgets()` promises to never copy more characters than will fit.

Luckily, you don't have to change much. The `scanf()` can also set limits on the size of what it scans. Just like their `printf()` counterparts, `scanf()` specifiers can also have a *field width* modifier. When used with a `scanf()` specifier, it limits the maximum number of characters `scanf()` will read for a value. For a string conversion, that pretty much translates into the maximum length the string will be. Change the `scanf()` statement so it looks like this:

```
    scanf( "%19s", name );
```

Now your program is as safe as houses. Remember that writing safe code is easier than fixing unsafe code.

Pointer Arithmetic

We know this chapter is all about command-line tools, arguments, and character streams, but we have a very special lesson about pointers for you. It's a feature of C called *pointer arithmetic*. It's really handy when dealing with character strings one character at a time, which makes this the perfect place to talk about it.

C allows you to add and subtract integer values to the value of a pointer. A pointer is, after all, just an integer that represents an address of a byte in memory. But when you add or subtract a pointer and an integer, C treats that arithmetic very differently than it does when you add or subtract two integers.

Let's start with some basics about comparing pointers, and then we'll "do the math."

Comparing Pointers

This might seem blindly obvious to you, or maybe you didn't even think about it, but you can compare two pointers for equality or inequality. The first one is simple:

```
int array[ 10 ];
int *aPointer;
int *bPointer;
aPointer = &array[2];
bPointer = &array[2];
if ( aPointer == bPointer ) {
    ...
```

If `aPointer` and `bPointer` point to the same memory address, the `if` expression is true. What might not be obvious is that you can compare pointers for inequality too:

```
aPointer = &array[1];
bPointer = &array[7];
if ( aPointer < bPointer ) {
    ...
```

Elements in an array are always allocated in successive memory locations, having progressively higher addresses. So the address of the second element in any array will always be higher (greater than) the address of the first element. Now we'll explain why that obvious piece of information is so important.

Pointer Addition

C allows you to add an integer value to a pointer value. The result of the expression is another pointer. Here's an example:

```
aPointer = &array[1];
bPointer = aPointer + 1;
```

When you add a number (integer) to a pointer (address), C doesn't merely add the integer value of the number to the integer value of the memory address. C treats every pointer as a reference to an "element" in memory, just as every index of an array (`array[0]`, `array[1]`, `array[2]`, and so on) addresses one element of that array.

In this example, `aPointer` points an `int`. Let's pretend that this `int` is at memory address 2,004. The memory occupied by that `int` is 4 bytes (assuming 32-bit `int`s). Asking C to add 1 to the pointer is asking it to calculate the address of the next `int` "element" in memory. It does that by adding 4 to the pointer, because the size of an `int` is 4 bytes. The value of `bPointer` is now 2,008.

Let's try this statement:

```
bPointer = aPointer + 6;
```

Again, you're asking C to calculate the 6th element past the variable that `aPointer` currently points to. Since `aPointer` points to an `int` variable (4 bytes), it adds 24 (6•4) to the pointer's address. The address in `bPointer` is now 2,028 (2,004+6•4) and points to `array[7]`.

C treats pointers like arrays, so a pointer to a variable is (in C's mind) a pointer to the first element of an array. Adding one to a pointer calculates the address of the next "element" in that "array." You can see this in relationship shown in Figure 9-17.

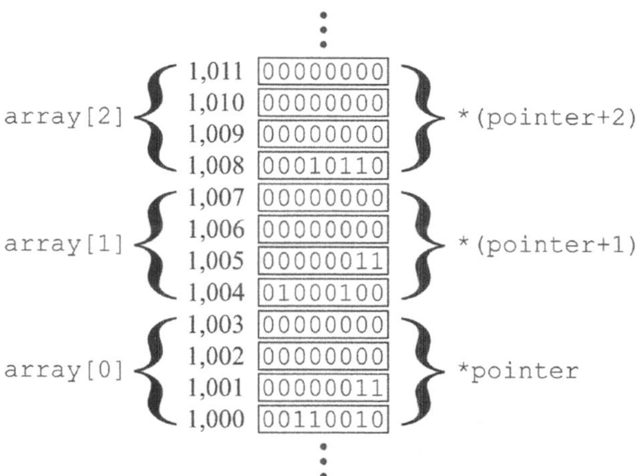

Figure 9-17. *Equivalency of array elements and pointer addition, assuming pointer==array*

Stated precisely, adding an integer to a pointer adds the value of the integer times the size of the variable type the pointer points to, to the address of the pointer. This means that when adding an integer to a pointer, the math depends on the size of the variable the pointer points to. Consider the following code fragments:

```
char *charPtr;
int *intPtr;
double *doublePtr;
charPtr += 1 // adds 1 to address in charPtr
intPtr += 1 // add 4 to address in intPtr
doublePtr += 1 // adds 8 to address in doublePtr
```

In each of these expressions, the integer 1 was added to a pointer. But the pointers all point to variables of different sizes, so the number of memory addresses added to each pointer is different.

You can also subtract integers from pointers, as well as increment and decrement them; the effect is the same. Take this snippet of code:

```
aPointer = array; // aPointer points to array[0]
aPointer += 3; // aPointer points to array[3]
aPointer -= 2; // aPointer points to array[1]
aPointer++; // aPointer points to array[2]
```

In each case, an integer was added or subtracted from a pointer. Adding or subtracting integers adjusted the address of the pointer based on the size of the variable type (`int`) of the pointer. As you've probably guessed already, when dealing with arrays of one-byte elements (like `char`), integer math and pointer math are synonymous.

Incrementing and decrementing a pointer is the same as adding or subtracting the integer 1. It's this last fact that C programmers employ a lot, and this is the expression you're going to use in the next project. But before we get to that, let's cover one more tidbit of C pointer arithmetic.

POINTER EQUIVALENCY

We've hinted at this in the past, but now you know enough about arrays, pointers, and pointer arithmetic to appreciate just how interchangeable pointers and array variables are.

We've prepared a kind of "cheat sheet" for you. Open the PointerEquivalence project that you'll find in the *09.03 - PointerEquivalence* folder. The program consists of nothing but short blocks of code that demonstrate functionally equivalent statements. Take this code, for example:

```
int i, array[ 10 ];
int *pointer, *intPtr;

pointer = array;
i = 4;

intPtr = &array[ i ];
intPtr = pointer + i;
```

The last two statements are functionally identical. Because `pointer` was set to the address of the first element in `array`, the expressions `&array[i]` and `pointer+i` mean the same thing: a pointer to the ith element of `array`.

The equivalency between array variables and pointers runs deep in C. So deep that array variable names and pointer variables are largely interchangeable. The following C code might look insane, but it is perfectly legal and will work exactly the way you think it should:

```
int x;
x = pointer[ i ];
x = *(array+i);
intPtr = &pointer[ i ];
intPtr = array + i;
```

You can use the subscript operator ([ ]) with a pointer variable, and you can use any array variable name as though it was a pointer variable pointing to the first element of that array. The only thing you can't do is

```
array = intPtr;
```

because `array` isn't a pointer variable that can be assigned a new value.

Use PointerEquivalence to study pointer and array syntax, or use it as a reference when trying to determine the best solution to a pointer problem. Read through the PointerEquivalence project carefully—line by line—until you're sure you understand every statement. Do that, and you're well on your way to C pointer mastery.

Subtracting Pointers

If a pointer plus an integer equals another pointer, than a pointer minus a pointer should equal an integer, right?

Right you are. Subtracting two pointers yields an integer, and it follows the same rules as pointer addition. The difference of two pointers is the count of elements between the two pointers. An "element" is the type of variable the pointers point to. Here's a really simple example:

```
int array[ 10 ];
int *aPointer = &array[ 1 ];
int *bPointer = &array[ 7 ];
int x = bPointer - aPointer;
```

Can you guess what x will be set to? Let's assume that the memory address of `array` is 2,000. The address of `aPointer` will be 2,004 (assuming 4-byte `int`s), and the address of `bPointer` will be 2,028. The difference between the `aPointer` and `bPointer` is 24 bytes of memory.

The variable x will be set to 6 because the difference between `aPointer` and `bPointer` is 6 `int`s (24÷4). This works for all variable types, not just `int`s. The formula C uses when subtracting pointers is the difference in byte addresses divided by the size of the variable the pointers point to. C will only let you subtract pointers to variables of the same size.

Now that you know all of these cool new tricks with pointers, let's do something with it.

WordCount.xcodeproj

Look in the *Learn C Projects* folder, inside the *09.04 - WordCount* subfolder, and open the project *WordCount.xcodeproj*. WordCount will ask you to type a line of text and will count the number of words in the text you type.

To run WordCount, select **Run** from the **Product** menu. WordCount will prompt you to type a line of text.

```
Type a line of text, please:
```

Type at least a few words of text, and end your line by pressing Return. When you press Return, *WordCount* will report its results. *WordCount* is open to all kinds of whitespace, so feel free to sprinkle your input with tabs, spaces, and the like. An example output is shown in Figure 9-18. Let's take a look at the source code that generated this output.

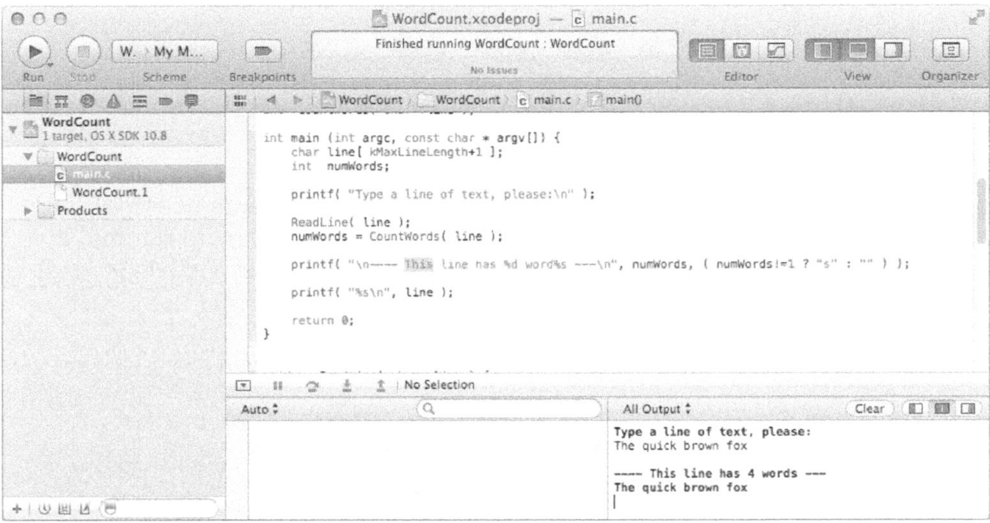

Figure 9-18. *The results of running WordCount*

Stepping Through the WordCount Source Code

WordCount starts with the usual #includes and adds a new one. <ctype.h> includes the prototype of the function isspace(), which takes a char as input and returns a non-zero number if the character is either a tab ('\t'), carriage return ('\r'), newline ('\n'), vertical tab ('\v'), form feed ('\f'), or space (' '), and returns 0 otherwise.

```
#include <stdio.h>
#include <ctype.h>
#include <stdbool.h>
```

Next is a constant, kMaxLineLength, that specifies the largest line this program can handle. 200 bytes should be plenty.

```
#define kMaxLineLength       200
```

Then the function prototypes for the two functions ReadLine() and CountWords() are defined. ReadLine() reads in a line of text and CountWords() takes a line of text and returns the number of words in the line:

```
void ReadLine( char *buff );
int  CountWords( char *line );
```

main() starts by defining an array of chars that will hold the line of input you type and an int that will hold the result of your call to CountWords():

```
int main (int argc, const char * argv[])
{
    char line[ kMaxLineLength+1 ];
    int  numWords;
```

main() prompts the user to type some text and press Return.

```
    printf( "Type a line of text, please:\n" );
```

Once the prompt is output, you pass line to ReadLine(). Remember that line is a pointer to the first byte of the array of chars. When ReadLine() returns, line contains a line of text, terminated by a '\0' character, making line a legitimate, NUL-terminated C string. You'll pass that string on to CountWords().

```
    ReadLine( line );
    numWords = CountWords( line );
```

You then print a message telling how many words there were in the line:

```
    printf( "\n---- This line has %d word%s ---\n", numWords, ( numWords!=1 ?
"s" : "" ) );

    printf( "%s\n", line );

    return 0;
}
```

CONDITIONAL OPERATOR

Are you wondering what that strange expression (numWords!=1 ? "s" : "") in the printf() argument is all about? It's called the *conditional operator*. The conditional operator is a trinary operator that takes three (3!) operands. Its general form is this:

```
condition ? true_expression : false_expression
```

It works just like an if statement, but entirely inside an expression. If the condition is true (non-zero), the whole expression becomes the value of true_expression. If the condition is false (zero), the whole expression becomes the value of false_expression. In other words, the statement describes two expressions; only one gets used, depending on the value of the condition expression.

The three expressions (condition, true_expression, and false_expression) can be any kind of C expression you want—they could even contain another conditional operator—with the following restrictions: The condition expression must be suitable for use in an if statement and true_expression and false_expression must be the same type of expression. For example, if `true_expression` was an integer, then `false_expression` must also be an integer. Remember that C will replace the whole expression with either `true_expression` or `false_expression`, so the two must be interchangeable at that position in the overall expression.

There's a long-standing debate over whether the conditional operator is pure genius or pure evil. Extremists will claim that you should never use it, while other programmers use it like ketchup. The problem is that overuse of conditional operators can make your code difficult to read. On the other hand, a well-placed conditional operator can dramatically simplify your code.

Our advice is to use it when it makes your code substantially simpler. For example, here are two alternate ways to write the `printf()` statement in `WordCount`:

```
char *plural;
if ( numWords != 1 )
    plural = "s";
else
    plural = "";
printf( "\n---- This line has %d word%s ---\n", numWords, plural );
```

A second solution is something like this:

```
printf( "\n---- This line has %d word ", numWords );
if ( numWords != 1 )
    printf( "s" );
printf( " ---\n" );
```

We think that the conditional operator used in the WordCount project made the code more concise and easier to read.

If you plan on using conditional operators, you'll almost always want to put them inside parentheses so that the left and right expressions don't get confused with what surrounds it.

This last bit of code shows attention to detail, something very important in a good program. Notice that the sentence in the first `printf()` ended with the characters "word%s." If the program found either no words or more than one word, you want it to say

This line has 0 words.

or

This line has 2 words.

If the program found exactly one word, the sentence should read

This line has 1 word.

You accomplish this by ending the word with a string format specifier (%s), that will be replaced with either the string "s" if it needs to be plural, or "" (an empty string) if not. Which string gets printed is determined by a conditional operator (read the sidebar "Conditional Operator" for more information). Got it? Let's move on.

ReadLine()

In main(), you defined an array of chars to hold the line of characters you type in. When main() called ReadLine(), it passed the name of the array as a parameter to ReadLine():

```
char        line[  ];
```

```
ReadLine( line );
```

As we said earlier, the name of an array also acts as a pointer to the first element of the array. In this case, line is equivalent to &(line[0]). ReadLine() now has a pointer to the first byte of main()'s line array.

```
void ReadLine( char *buff ) {
```

numCharsRead will track how many characters you've read so far. You'll use it to make sure you don't read more characters into line than line can hold.

```
int numCharsRead = 0;
```

This while loop calls getchar() to read one character at a time from the input buffer. getchar() returns the next character in the input buffer as an int (not a char). If there's an error, or you run out of characters to read, it returns the constant EOF. You'll learn more about EOF in Chapters 11 and 12.

The expression in the while loop contains an assignment operator, so the character value just read gets stored into c before anything else happens. That's important because you'll need to know what the character was later.

```
int c;
while ( (c = getchar()) != EOF
       && c != '\n'
       && ++numCharsRead <= kMaxLineLength ) {
```

The while loop's condition tests three things. You want the while loop to stop if there are no more characters to read from the input stream, the user pressed the Return key, or if the number of characters read has exceeded the size of your line buffer.

The first condition is tested by comparing getchar()'s return value to EOF. The second one compares the character read to the newline constant ('\n'). (You know that the value returned by getchar() has already been stored in the c variable because the && operator always evaluates the left expression before the right one.) Finally, the ++ operator is used to add 1 to the count of characters you've read so far and checks to see that you have'tt read more characters than will fit in the array.

INVERTING COMPOUND CONDITIONALS

Sometimes you need to express a conditional in the negative. For simple expressions, this is easy. If you need to test for night time, you can write `!isDaytime`. But sometimes you need to invert a compound Boolean expression. For example, what's the opposite of `isDaytime || isCloudy`? You have two choices.

The simplest is to wrap the ! operator around the whole expression. If you want an expression to be true when you *can not* go stargazing, that would be `( isDaytime || isCloudy )`. If you want an expression to be true when you *can* go stargazing, then simply negate the whole thing: `! ( isDaytime || isCloudy )`.

The second alternative is to negate the compound. In logic, there's a formula for expressing any && or || expression in the negative, as shown in table 9-2.

Table 9-2. *Inverting logical && and ||*

Regular Expression	Opposite Expression
A && B	!A || !B
A || B	!A && !B

So if you have an expression that's true when `A && B` are true, the opposite of that expression is `!A || !B`, equivalent to `! ( A && B)`. In the stargazing example, the opposite of `( isDaytime || isCloudy )` would be `( !isDaytime && !isCloudy )`. Think about it; you *can* go stargazing if it's nighttime *and* the sky is clear.

Logically, the three conditions in `ReadLine()`'s `while` loop are testing for things that will stop the loop. But the condition expression of a `while` loop must be written so that it's true for the loop to continue. There are at least two ways to write this:

```
while ( (c = getchar()) != EOF
          && c != '\n'
          && ++numCharsRead <= kMaxLineLength ) {
```

and

```
while ( ! ( (c = getchar()) == EOF
```

```
        || c == '\n'
        || ++numCharsRead > kMaxLineLength ) ) {
```

In the first form, the condition reads "run the loop if the getchar() does not return EOF, the character isn't a newline, and there's still room in the buffer." The second condition means exactly the same thing, but reads "stop the loop if getchar() returns EOF, the user pressed Return, or the buffer has run out of space." Remember that != is the opposite of ==, and <= is the opposite of >.

Humans have problems with the word "not." When our mothers tell us that we "can not have a cookie," our brains tend to ignore the "not" and the only message that gets through is "can have a cookie." Programmers have the same problem. Sometimes expressing conditions in the negative ("not daylight and not cloudy") can make code difficult to comprehend. Reformulating the condition ("not (daylight or cloudy)") can make it easier to understand.

CAUTION: Note that c is an int, not a char. getchar() returns an int variable, which is larger than a char variable. The getchar() function must return a value that represents all single byte character values (-128...127) *in addition to* a constant (EOF) that means the input stream ended. It can't do this if it returned a single byte char value, because every possible char value is already spoken for.

getchar()'s solution is to return the 256 possible char values as an unsigned int value (0...255), leaving the rest of the range of int values available to mean other things. When c is compared to EOF, two full ints are being compared and the condition can tell the difference between the EOF value of -1 and a character value of -1 (because a character value of -1 will be 255). When c is assigned to *buff, only the lowest 8 bits of data in the int are assigned to the char variable. Since the char variable is signed, a value of 255 becomes -1.

If any of this is confusing, review the section "The Long and Short of ints" in Chapter 8 and look forward to the "Conversion Rules" section in Chapter 13.

If the while loop conditional passes all of the tests, the loop's one and only statement is executed.

```
*buff++ = c;
```

You'll see this kind of statement a lot in C. It efficiently performs three operations in a single, compact, statement.

1. The address of the char variable that buff points to is obtained.

2. The value of c is stored at the char variable at that address.
3. 1 is added to the pointer buff so that it now points to the next element in memory.

The important thing to note is the use of the post-increment operator (++) to increment the pointer *after* the value of c was stored in *buff. If buff pointed to line[0] before this statement, then c would be stored in line[0] and buff would point to line[1] afterwards.

Contrast that with this statement:

```
*++buff = c;
```

Here the buff pointer is incremented before it's dereferenced. If buff pointed to line[0] beforehand, then c would get stored in line[1] because buff was changed from line[0] to line[1] *before* the assignment was made. For your program, that's not what you want. You want buff to always point to the next empty element of line. When a character is stored there, buff is incremented afterwards so it (once again) points to the next empty element in the line array.

Finally, the loop ends and you terminate whatever characters the loop stored in line with a '\0'. Remember that a C string *must be terminated by with a NUL* character or it won't be a valid string.

```
*buff = '\0';
```

To review, when the ReadLine() returns to the caller, the address passed to it will contain the characters read from the input stream, terminated with a NUL character to make it a proper C string. The string will never be more than kMaxLineLength long. It will be shorter if a newline ('\n') character is read or if there are no more characters in the input stream. Perfect! Now let's move on to CountWords().

CountWords()

CountWords() also takes a pointer to the first byte of main()'s line array as a parameter. CountWords() will step through the array, looking for non–whitespace characters. When one is encountered, CountWords() sets inWord to true and increments numWords and keeps stepping through the array looking for a whitespace character that marks the end of the current word. Once the whitespace is found, inWord is set to false again and the process repeats.

```
int CountWords( char *line )
{
    int numWords, inWord;
```

```
numWords = 0;
inWord = false;
```

When the while loop is entered for the first time, line points to the first character in the string. The loop continues as long as *line contains a character value other than NUL ('\0'). Let's start by looking just at the "outside" portion of the loop:

```
while ( *line != '\0' ) {
    … // do something with *line
    line++;
}
```

This is a great loop for processing an array of something and is very common in C. The while loop's conditional determines when the loop should stop based on the value that the pointer is pointing to now. For your purposes, you stop when you get to the NUL ('\0') character at the end of the string. At the bottom of the loop, the line pointer is incremented so that it points to the next element in the array when it repeats. Compare that code to this:

```
int i;
for ( i = 0; line[i] != '\0'; i++ ) {
    … // do something with line[i]
```

That's right, it's basically the same logic—without a pointer variable. Now let's look at the entire loop.

```
while ( *line != '\0' ) {
    if ( isspace( *line ) ) {
        inWord = false;
    }
    else {
        if ( ! inWord ) {
            numWords++;
            inWord = true;
        }
    }

    line++;
}
```

The body of the loop processes each character in the line string, one character at a time. It maintains a bool variable named inWord that will be set to false when it finds a character that is whitespace (space, tab, newline, etc.). It sets it back to true when it finds a character that is not whitespace (letters, numbers, punctuation, and everything else).

Computer scientists call this kind of logic a *state machine*. A state machine is the simplest form of machine logic (and the basis for all computers, by the way). The loop operates in one of two states: in word or not in word.

When a state machine changes from one state to another, it's called a *state transition*, and that's how this loop does its job. When the `isspace(*line)` test is false, it means that this is an "in word" character and the `else` block is executed. Before it sets `inWord` to `true`, it checks to see if `inWord` is currently `false`. If it is, it means that the previous character (the one immediately before this character) is a whitespace character, which means that this character is the beginning of a new word. When this happens, the `numWords` counter is incremented.

Now that `inWord` is now `true`, the increment statement won't be executed again until another whitespace character is found (setting `inWord` to `false`), followed by another non-whitespace character. This is sometimes called *edge logic* because `numWords` is only incremented on the "edges" between whitespace and non-whitespace characters.

If this isn't completely clear, run `CountWords` in the debugger, step through this loop, and watch how `inWord` and `numWords` change.

When `CountWords()` is finished, it returns the number of words it found in the string. Technically, it returns the number of whitespace to non-whitespace transitions it found, but that's basically the same thing.

Now that you understand this program completely, let's run it again. Choose the ***Run*** command from the ***Product*** menu. When the program starts running, click in the console pane, type a line, and press the Return key. You should see something like the output back in Figure 9-18.

> **NOTE:** The connection between your keyboard and standard input for an Xcode or Terminal window will only be active when that pane or window is active. To type characters to your command, first make sure the Xcode console window is active by clicking the mouse in the console pane.

Now let's test your program from the command line. We'll show you this to prove how versatile command-line tools can be, and to show you a handy trick for testing your program from the command line.

Testing WordCount in the Shell

When you ran WordCount in Xcode, Xcode provided a console window connected to standard output and connected your keyboard to standard input. But what if you want to quickly run your program in the shell without going through the archive and deployment steps you did at the beginning of this chapter? It turns out that there's a clever feature of the Terminal window that will make this easy.

If you just ran the WordCount program, then Xcode has recently built the executable. If not, choose the **Product ➤ Build for ➤ Running** command from the menu bar to make sure you binary executable is up to date.

Open a window in the Terminal and position it alongside the workspace window, as shown in Figure 9-16. Type the following command in the terminal—but don't press Return yet! (The last character on the line is the vertical bar, usually found above the Return key.)

```
echo 'Four score and seven years ago' |
```

Now switch back to the Xcode workspace window. In the project navigator, find the *WordCount* executable inside the *Products* group. This object represents your finished program during development and testing. Drag the WordCount program over to the Terminal window and drop it. You should see a result similar to that in Figure 9-19.

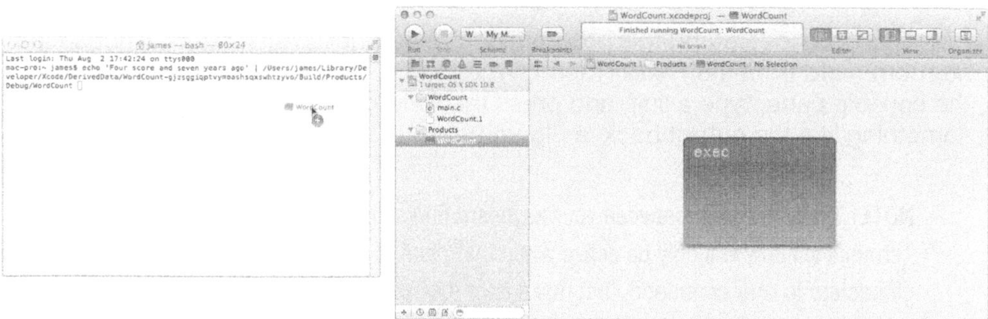

Figure 9-19. *Dropping a file into a Terminal window*

Dropping a file or folder into the Terminal window while at a command prompt will insert the absolute path of that item into your command line. It's a fantastic time saver. For example, type `cd`, drop any folder from the Finder into the Terminal window, and then press Return. Your current working directory will now be set to that folder.

> **NOTE:** Both path auto-completion and the Terminal's drag-and-drop feature will escape any special characters. A lot of characters, especially the "space" character, mean something to the shell (space separates arguments). To tell the shell that this character is part of a path name and is not a shell operator, precede the character with the "\" (backslash)—the same one you use in C string constants to tell the compiler that the next character means something special. This is called *escaping* the character.

In this case, the path inserted is the one to Xcode's magic storage where it keeps all of your project's intermediate files organized and up-to-date. Again, it's not important where this is. What's important is that it's an absolute path to the last executable Xcode built, and as such the shell will execute this program directly.

Switch back to the Terminal window and press the Return key. The shell's | (pipe) operator will execute two commands: `echo` and your `CountWords` tool. It connects the standard output of `echo` to the standard input of your tool, and both start running.

The `echo` tool sends the text of its arguments to standard output. These characters ("Four score and seven years ago\n") appear on your tool's standard input. `CountWords` now reads those words from standard input, counts them, and send its output to standard output, which appears in the Terminal window, as shown in Figure 9-20.

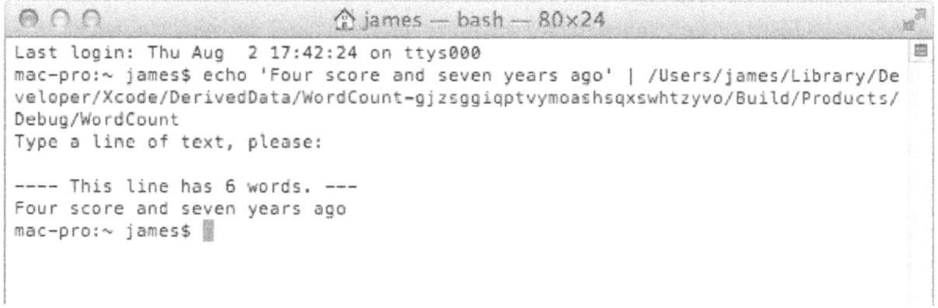

```
james — bash — 80×24
Last login: Thu Aug  2 17:42:24 on ttys000
mac-pro:~ james$ echo 'Four score and seven years ago' | /Users/james/Library/De
veloper/Xcode/DerivedData/WordCount-gjzsggiqptvymoashsqxswhtzyvo/Build/Products/
Debug/WordCount
Type a line of text, please:

---- This line has 6 words. ---
Four score and seven years ago
mac-pro:~ james$
```

Figure 9-20. *Text sent to CountWords through a shell pipe*

But why stop there? Try your command again, on its own without the `echo` command, but this time end the command with an input file redirection operator, as shown in Figure 9-21.

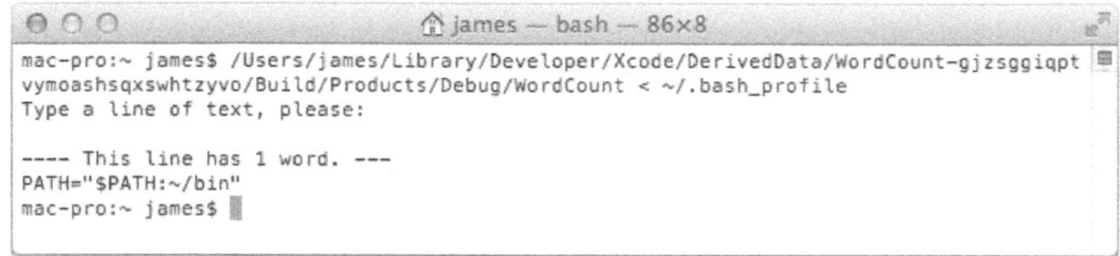

Figure 9-21. *CountWords counting the words in a file*

Without making any modifications in your command-line tool, you just repurposed it to count the words output by the echo command, and again to count the words in the first line of a file. Just as easily, the output of your program could become the input of some other tool. That's the versatility of standard input and standard output.

Before we move on, there are two things to make note of. First, your program still outputs the string "Type a line of text, please:". That's because your program doesn't know that there's no human sitting at a keyboard typing characters. It just reads the characters it gets from standard input, which is the correct way for a tool to think about the world. It's beyond the scope of this book, but command-line tools written by experienced programmers can examine properties of the standard input character stream to determine if it's an interactive source (like a keyboard) or a character stream coming from a file or another program. The tool can then adjust its behavior by, for example, only outputting the prompt string when it's getting characters from a keyboard.

The other thing that you'll notice is that when you typed "The quick brown fox" in the Xcode console pane, the words "The quick brown fox" appeared in the window after the prompt. But when you piped "Four score and seven years ago" to your tool, they didn't. That's because Xcode and the Terminal *echo* characters typed on the keyboard, meaning that the character is sent both to the program and to the window—so you can see what you're typing. Characters piped from one program to another don't go anywhere near the window. Again, experienced programmers can control the echo mode, which is how a command that prompts for a password is able to hide the characters you type on the keyboard.

So far, none of the projects in this book rise the level of "useful command line tool." Most were just exercises in C, and the last two duplicate commands already written. Your *SeeArgs* program is basically the echo command, and *CountWords* is a pale imitation of the wc ("word count") tool.

Let's finish up this chapter by writing something that's not already built into OS X. We can't say it's super-useful, but we're sure that you don't already have a program like it.

RomanNumeral.xcodeproj

In your *Learn C on the Mac* projects folder, find the *09.0X - RomanNumeral* folder and open the *RomanNumeral.xcodeproj* document. This is a command-line tool that converts its argument from decimal into roman numerals.

The program starts out with some #includes and defines some constants.

```
#include <stdio.h>
#include <string.h>
#include <stdlib.h>

#define kMinDecimalNumber        1
#define kMaxDecimalNumber        3999
#define kMaxRomanNumeralLength  15
```

The range of numbers the program can convert is limited to 1 through 3,999. It's easy to determine that the length of the converted Roman numeral will never exceed 15 characters—the longest possible result is MMMDCCCLXXXVIII (or 3,888), if you're curious. These are all established as constants for the program.

Your "number to Roman numeral" conversion function needs a prototype.

```
void NumberToRomanNumeral( int number, char *romanNumeral );
```

main()

The main() function loops through the command's arguments, converts each one from a decimal number to a Roman numeral, and outputs the results to standard output.

```
int main( int argc, const char * argv[] )
{
    int i;
    for ( i=1; i<argc; i++ ) {
        int number;
        number = atoi( argv[i] );
        if ( number >= kMinDecimalNumber && number <= kMaxDecimalNumber ) {
            char romanNumeral[ kMaxRomanNumeralLength+1 ];
            NumberToRomanNumeral( number, romanNumeral );
            printf( "%d = %s\n", number, romanNumeral );
        }
    }

    return 0;
}
```

The only function you haven't seen before is atoi(). The atoi() ("ASCII to Integer") function takes a string pointer as an argument and returns an int. If the string begins with the characters of a decimal number, it converts that to a numeric value and returns it. Otherwise, it returns 0. In other words, if you pass it the string "173" atoi() will return the integer value 173.

NumberToRomanNumeral()

Now we get to the really interesting part of the program. The NumberToRomanNumeral() function takes two parameters: an int value to convert and a pointer to a string buffer where the converted value will be stored. This function uses character arrays and pointers in ways that you haven't seen before, so let's go through it carefully.

```
void NumberToRomanNumeral( int number, char *romanNumeral )
{
    static char roman[] = "IVXLCDM";
```

The first statement defines a static character array pre-initialized to a string constant. You haven't seen this before, but when you combine an array declaration with an *array initializer*, the array's dimension is set exactly to the size needed to store the value(s). In this statement, the array will be 8 chars long.

> **TIP:** To initialize an array of something other than chars, list the values between curly braces, separated by commas. This statement will allocate an array of 6 ints and fill its elements with the values listed:
>
> ```
> int testValues[] = { -1, 0, 1, 3, 99, 276 };
> ```

The program is going to use the characters in this array in pairs. The first two characters represent the Roman numerals for 1 and 5, the next two for 10 and 50, the next two are 100 and 500, and finally 1,000; you don't need 5,000 because the function only converts numbers less than 4,000.

The numeral value is going to be used as an index into the roman array. It's initialized to 0.

```
    int numeral;
    numeral = 0;
```

A local char array is allocated to hold the Roman numeral string as it's being constructed, along with a char pointer that will be used to point to elements of that array.

```
char result[ kMaxRomanNumeralLength+1 ];
char *resultPtr;
```

The result array is initialized by setting its last element to NUL. resultPtr is then set to point to that element.

```
result[ kMaxRomanNumeralLength ] = '\0';
resultPtr = &result[ kMaxRomanNumeralLength ];
```

Typically, you deal with characters of a string starting with the beginning of an array and working up. But this program is going to build the Roman numeral representation backwards, starting with the last character and working (right to left) towards the beginning of the buffer. The one rule to remember in C is that there are no rules; use the solution that fits the problem.

Why the string is constructed backwards makes sense when you see the loop that performs the conversion. The loop runs until the value of number is zero, meaning there are no more digits to convert. It begins by isolating the one's digit of the number, dividing it by 10, and getting the remainder. If the value of number was 173, then first value of digit will be 3.

```
while ( number != 0 ) {
    int digit;
    digit = number % 10;
```

The loop is going to convert the decimal numbers from right to left (3, then 7, and finally 1). This is why the results are constructed from right to left.

Now we get to the heart of the conversion. If you don't know how Roman numerals work, it's pretty simple. Decimal digits between 1 and 9 are represented by combinations of Roman numeral characters that represent the values of 1, 5 and 10: 1 = I, 2 = II, 3 = III, 4 = IV ("one less than five"), 5 = V, 6 = VI ("one more than five"), 7 = VII, 8 = VIII, 9 = IX ("one less than ten"). The next power of ten repeats this pattern, but with different characters that represent 10, 50, and 100 (X, L, and C).

The program converts a single digit to the appropriate pattern using a switch statement.

```
        switch ( digit ) {
            case 0:
                break;

            case 3:
                *--resultPtr = roman[ numeral ];
            case 2:
                *--resultPtr = roman[ numeral ];
            case 1:
                *--resultPtr = roman[ numeral ];
                break;
```

```
        case 4:
            *--resultPtr = roman[ numeral+1 ];
            *--resultPtr = roman[ numeral ];
            break;

        case 8:
            *--resultPtr = roman[ numeral ];
        case 7:
            *--resultPtr = roman[ numeral ];
        case 6:
            *--resultPtr = roman[ numeral ];
        case 5:
            *--resultPtr = roman[ numeral+1 ];
            break;

        case 9:
            *--resultPtr = roman[ numeral+2 ];
            *--resultPtr = roman[ numeral ];
            break;
    }
```

The variations on this statement are the heart of the code:

```
*--resultPtr = roman[ numeral ];
```

Reading it from right to left, it uses the `numeral` integer to address one element of the `roman` array. This is the static array that contains the characters "I," "V," and so on. The first time through the loop `numeral` is 0, so `roman[numeral]` will be the character I.

On the assignment side of the operator is the pointer expression `*--resultPtr`. As you already know, this is a combination of a pointer dereference and a pre-decrement operator. The pointer's address is first decremented by one element, and the address is used to store the character ("I"). `resultPtr` started out pointing to the `result[15]`. After this statement, `result[14]` will contain the character "I" and `resultPtr` will point to it.

The character sequence for each number is constructed by a carefully arranged set of `case` statement labels. If the value of the digit is 1, execution jumps to the `case 1:` label, which inserts one "I" into `result`. If the value is 3, then `case 3:` label does exactly the same thing. But `case 3:` isn't followed by a `break` statement, so it falls through and executes the code for `case 2:`, which falls through to `case 1:`. The result? If the value is 3, three "I" characters are inserted into `result`.

The patterns for 5, 6, 7, and 8 work similarly, except that the value inserted for `case 5:` is `roman[numeral+1]`. The first time through the loop, numeral is 0, so `numeral+1` will address the "V" character in the array.

Cases 4 and 9 insert two characters, either the pattern "one less than five" or "one less than ten."

After the `case` statement is finished, the loop prepares for the next iteration. The first step is to divide the working number by 10.

```
    number /= 10;
```

If the starting number was 173, `number` will now be 17—essentially chopping off the last decimal digit. The next time through the loop, the value of `number` will be 17, and `digit` will be 7. The third time, both will be 1. When 1 is divided by 10, the value of `number` goes to 0 and the loop stops.

But the real magic happens with the next statement.

```
    numeral += 2;
}
```

`numeral` is the index into the static set of `roman` characters. By adding 2 to it, it shifts the set of characters used by the `switch` statements. Now `roman[numeral]` refers to "X" (ten) instead of "I" (one). On the third pass through the loop, `roman[numeral]` will be a "C" (one hundred), and so on.

As each power-of-ten decimal digit is processed by the loop, the index of numeral increases to select a matching power of ten Roman numeral.

When the loop exits, the `resultPtr` pointer points to the last character inserted into the `result` array. This is the first character of the finished string. Remember that you started by setting the last element of `result` to `NUL`, so `resultPtr` is always pointing to a `NUL`-terminated C string.

The last step is to copy the finished string to the buffer provided by the caller. This assumes that the caller has provided enough space to hold the results, which is reasonable since the maximum length of the finished string is well known.

```
strcpy( romanNumeral, resultPtr );
```

Try your program by setting some test arguments in the **Edit Scheme** dialog, as shown in Figure 9-22. When testing your program, give it a wide range of numbers that will exercise all execution paths of your program. You want to verify that it works on typical values, but you're also looking for values that might trip it up or expose a flaw in the logic.

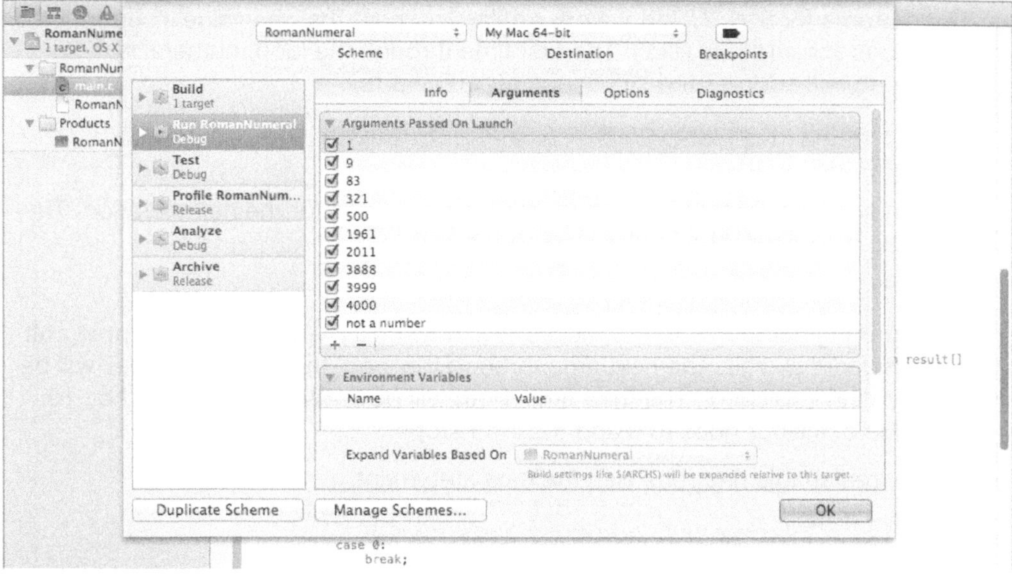

Figure 9-22. *Setting test arguments for RomanNumeral*

Run your program and you should see output like that shown in Figure 9-23.

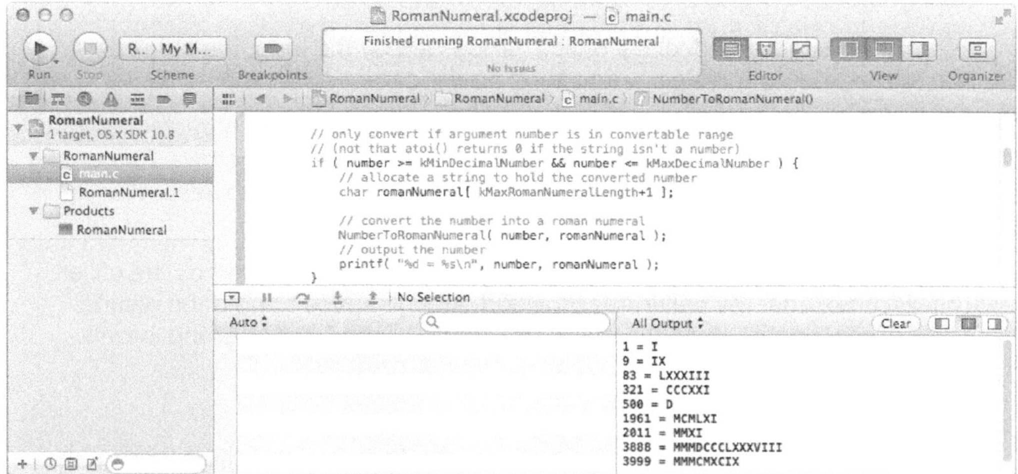

Figure 9-23. *Output of RomanNumeral test run*

If there's anything about this program that isn't crystal clear at this point, run it in the debugger. Step through each line and watch how the variables change and how the program flow through the loop and the switch statements work.

Also try out your new command in the Terminal, using any of the techniques we've shown you so far. Give it different numbers as arguments, or something that isn't a number at all.

Hang onto this project, because you're going to revisit it in a later chapter.

One Last Word About the Command-Line Interface

Before we end this chapter, we want to revisit the CLI one more time. The number of command-line tools, and what they can accomplish, is staggering. It's not a computer interface that most people learn, but those that understand it weld a powerful tool.

Just to give you a taste, what if we told you that many of the applications you use in OS X are just fronts for command-line tools? Take Apple's Disk Utility application. It can format and repair volumes, create disk images, partition drives, unmount disks, and so on. But none of these capabilities are part of the application. When you choose to repair a volume, for example, the Disk Utility application simply runs the `diskutil` command-line tool. If you look at the man pages for `diskutil`, `hdiutil`, and `pdisk`, you'll find that you can do all of these things directly from the command line. This means that you can write a shell script to do it. It also means you can log in from a remote computer and do it.

Applications like Disk Utility are called *wrappers* or shells, because they are nothing more than a GUI (graphical user interface) "wrapped" around the functionality of an existing command line tool.

When you installed Xcode, it added a whole bunch of new commands to your command line. All of the compiling, linking, and debugging that Xcode does is actually performed by command-line tools (`gcc`, `gdb`, and so on) that you can run too. Xcode even provides a command-line tool that will let you build Xcode projects from the command line, appropriately named `xcodebuild`. You can read about it using man:

```
man xcodebuild
```

Professional programmers use tools like this to automate their development. Most large applications are not produced by someone opening a project file and pressing the ***Build*** button. The developers write a shell script that checks out the final source files from a source control system, builds and archives the project using the `xcodebuild` tool, and then packages up the deployed files into a disk image, installer package, or however the program will be distributed. By automating the process, the developer won't accidently forget an important step when delivering their program to their customers.

And now that you know how to create your own command-line tools, you can make the CLI even more powerful.

What's Next?

What you accomplished in this chapter is huge. You learned how to create a finished (deployed) program that you can install and use in the OS X command line interface. You learned how commands get arguments. You also learned about standard output and standard input, how they can be redirected to other sources, and connected to other programs. Along the way you learned some really important pointer skills.

In the next chapter, you're going to expand your variable universe even more by learning how to define and use structures.

CHAPTER 9 EXERCISES

1. Modify the *SeeArgs* project so that it acts more like the Unix `echo` command: output each argument string to standard output, separated by spaces, and followed by a single newline character. Bonus points for outputting a space character only *between* multiple argument strings.
2. At the end of this code, what will the `printf()` statement output?

```
char message[] = "Leo cC ran the Man";
int x[] = { 2, 3, 5, 4 };
int y[] = { 6, 4, 1, 13 };

int i;
for ( i = 0; i < (sizeof(x)/sizeof(x[0])); i++ ) {
    char *xPtr, *yPtr;

    xPtr = message + x[ i ];
    yPtr = xPtr + y[ i ];

    char c;
    c = *xPtr;
    *xPtr = *yPtr;
    *yPtr = c;
}

printf( "%s!\n", message );
```

3. Change *WordCount* so that it continues to read, and count the words in, subsequent lines.

Chapter 10

Designing Your Own Data Structures

Chapter 8 introduced several new data types, such as `float` and `char`. We discussed the range of each type and the format specifiers used to print each type using `printf()`. Next, you explored the concept of arrays, focusing on the relationship between `char` arrays and C strings. Along the way, you discovered the `#define` statement, C's text substitution mechanism. In Chapters 7, 8 and 9, you learned a lot about pointers.

This chapter will show you how to use existing C types as building blocks to design your own customized data structures. You'll also learn how to dynamically allocate memory for those structures as you need it.

Bundling Data

There will be times when your programs will want to bundle together, or *associate*, related data. For example, suppose you are writing a program to organize your DVD collection. Imagine the type of information you will want to access for each DVD. At the very least, you'll want to keep track of the movie's title. You might also want to rate each DVD on a scale from one to ten. Finally, let's add in a comment field you can use to describe your feelings about the movie or perhaps note to whom you loaned this particular movie.

In the next few sections, we'll look at two separate approaches to a basic DVD tracking program. Each approach will revolve around a different set of data structures. One will make use of arrays (Model A) and the other a set of custom designed data structures (Model B).

Model A: Three Arrays

One way to model your DVD collection is with a separate array for each DVD's attributes:

```
#define kMaxDVDs            5000
#define kMaxTitleLength     256
#define kMaxCommentLength   256

char    rating[ kMaxDVDs ];
char    title[ kMaxDVDs ][ kMaxTitleLength ];
char    comment[ kMaxDVDs ][ kMaxCommentLength ];
```

This code fragment uses three `#defines`. `kMaxDVDs` defines the maximum number of DVDs this program will track. `kMaxTitleLength` defines the maximum number of characters in a DVD title. `kMaxCommentLength` defines the maximum number of characters in the DVD comment array.

Next, `rating` is an array of 5,000 chars, one `char` per DVD. Each of the `chars` in this array will hold a number from 1 to 10, the rating you've assigned to a particular DVD. This line of code assigns a value of 8 to DVD 37:

```
rating[ 37 ] = 8;     /* A pretty good DVD */
```

The arrays `title` and `comment` are each known as *multidimensional arrays*. A normal array, like `rating`, is declared using a single dimension. The statement of

```
float    myArray[ 5 ];
```

declares a normal (one-dimensional) array containing five `floats`, namely:

```
myArray[ 0 ]
myArray[ 1 ]
myArray[ 2 ]
myArray[ 3 ]
myArray[ 4 ]
```

This statement

```
float        myArray[ 3 ][ 5 ];
```

declares a two-dimensional array containing 15 `floats` (3 * 5 = 15), namely:

```
myArray[0][0]
myArray[0][1]
myArray[0][2]
myArray[0][3]
myArray[0][4]
myArray[1][0]
myArray[1][1]
myArray[1][2]
```

```
myArray[1][3]
myArray[1][4]
myArray[2][0]
myArray[2][1]
myArray[2][2]
myArray[2][3]
myArray[2][4]
```

Think of a two-dimensional array as an array of arrays. `myArray[0]` is an array of five `floats`. `myArray[1]` and `myArray[2]` are also arrays of five `floats` each.

Here's a three-dimensional array:

```
float       myArray[ 3 ][ 5 ][ 10 ];
```

How many `floats` does this array contain? Tick, tick, tick—got it? 3 * 5 * 10 = 150. This version of `myArray` contains 150 `floats`.

> **NOTE:** C allows you to create arrays of any dimension, though you'll rarely have a need for more than a single dimension.

Why would you ever want a multidimensional array? If you haven't already guessed, the answer to this question is going to lead us back to the DVD tracking example. Here are the declarations for your three DVD tracking arrays:

```
#define kMaxDVDs            5000
#define kMaxTitleLength     256
#define kMaxCommentLength   256

char    rating[ kMaxDVDs ];
char    title[ kMaxDVDs ][ kMaxTitleLength ];
char    comment[ kMaxDVDs ][ kMaxCommentLength ];
```

Once again, `rating` contains one `char` per DVD, while `title` contains an array of `chars` whose length is `kMaxTitleLength` for each DVD. Each of `title`'s arrays is large enough to hold a title up to 255 bytes long with a single byte left over to hold the terminating `NUL` byte. And `comment` contains an array of `chars` whose length is `kMaxCommentLength` for each DVD. Each of `comment`'s arrays is large enough to hold a comment up to 255 bytes long with a single byte left over to hold the terminating `NUL` byte.

MultiArray.xcodeproj

Here's a sample program that brings this concept to life. MultiArray defines the two-dimensional array `title` (as described previously), prompts you to type a series of DVD titles, stores the titles in the two-dimensional `title` array, and then prints out the contents of `title`.

Open the *Learn C Projects* folder, go inside the folder 10.01 - MultiArray, and open the project MultiArray.xcodeproj. Run *MultiArray* by selecting **Run** from the **Product** menu. *MultiArray* will first tell you how many bytes of memory are allocated for the entire title array:

```
The title array takes up 1024 bytes of memory.
```

To see where this number came from, here's the declaration of `title` from *MultiArray*:

```
#define kMaxDVDs          4
#define kMaxTitleLength   256

char    title[ kMaxDVDs ][ kMaxTitleLength ];
```

By performing the `#define` substitution yourself, you can see that `title` is defined as a 4-by-256 array: 4 * 256 = 1,024, matching the result reported by *MultiArray*.

After *MultiArray* reports the `title` array size, it enters a loop, prompting you for your list of favorite movies:

```
Title of DVD #1:
```

Enter a DVD title, and press Return. You'll be prompted to enter a second DVD title. Type in a total of four DVD titles, pressing Return at the end of each one.

MultiArray will then step through the array, using `printf()` to list the DVDs you've entered. If your entire DVD collection consists entirely of classic TV boxed sets and obscure anime, feel free to use our list, shown in Figure 10-1.

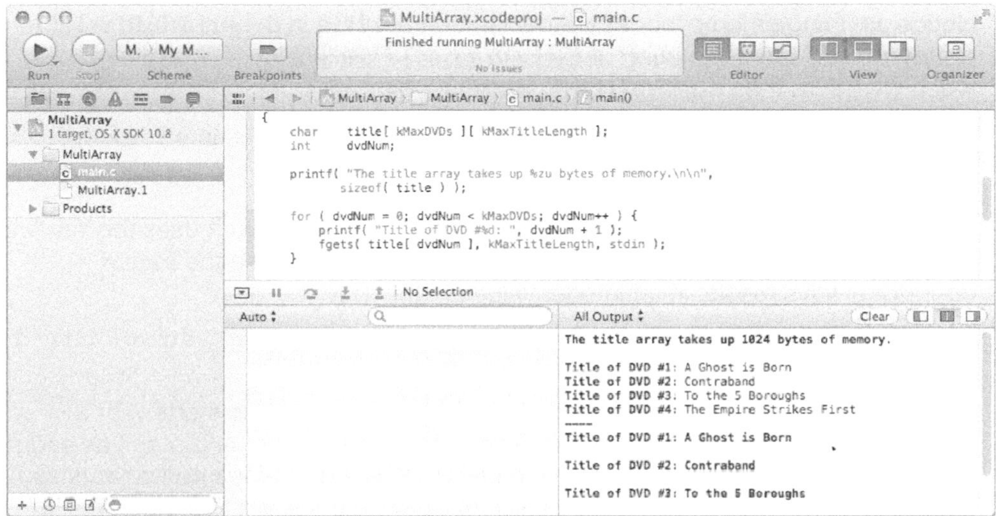

Figure 10-1. *MultiArray in action*

Let's take a look at the source code.

Stepping Through the MultiArray Source Code

MultiArray starts with a standard #include. <stdio.h> gives you access to both printf() and fgets().

```
#include <stdio.h>
```

These two #defines will be used throughout the code:

```
#define kMaxDVDs            4
#define kMaxTitleLength     256
```

Let's look at the function prototypes for PrintDVDTitle(). PrintDVDTitle() prints out the specified DVD title. Note the return type of void. This means that this function does not return a value.

```
void PrintDVDTitle( int dvdNum, char title[][ kMaxTitleLength ] );
```

main() starts off by defining title, your two-dimensional array. title is large enough to hold four movie titles. The name of each title can be up to 255 characters long, plus the terminating NUL byte.

```
int main (int argc, const char * argv[]) {
    char    title[ kMaxDVDs ][ kMaxTitleLength ];
```

Notice anything different about the declaration of title in the PrintDVDTitle() prototype and the declaration of title in main()? We'll discuss this difference when we get to the PrintDVDTitle() code in a bit.

dvdNum is a counter used to step through each of the DVD titles in a for loop.

```
int     dvdNum;
```

This printf() prints out the size of the title array. Notice that it uses the %zu format specifier to print the result returned by sizeof, because the sizeof operator always results in an integer value of type size_t.

```
    printf( "The title array takes up %zu bytes of memory.\n\n", sizeof( title )
);
```

Next, let's look at the loop that reads in the title names. dvdNum starts with a value of 0, is incremented by one each time through the loop, and stops as soon as dvdNum is equal to kMaxDVDs. Why "equal to kMaxDVDs"? Since dvdNum acts as an array index, it has to start with a value of 0. Since there are four elements in the array, they range in number from 0 to 3. If dvdNum is equal to kMaxDVDs, the loop needs to stop or it will be trying to access title[4], which does not exist. Make sense?

```
for ( dvdNum = 0; dvdNum < kMaxDVDs; dvdNum++ ) {
```

Each time through the loop, the prompt "Title of DVD #" is output to the console, followed by the value of dvdNum+1. Though C starts its arrays with 0, people like to number things starting with 1.

```
    printf( "Title of DVD #%d: ", dvdNum + 1 );
```

Once the prompt is printed, you call fgets() to read in a line of text from the console. fgets() is used because it's safe; the second parameter is the total length of the array the characters will be copied to. fgets() promises to never copy more characters than will fit in the array.

> **NOTE:** The third parameter of fgets() is a pointer to the input stream it will read characters from. Functions like printf() and scanf() always use the standard out and standard in character streams (respectively). But there are many other character streams, and functions like fgets() can be directed to use any of them using this third parameter. To direct fgets() to read from standard in, pass it the stdin constant, conveniently provided by the Standard Library.

The line of characters read from the keyboard are stored in the char array title[dvdNum]. You'll tell fgets() to limit input to the length of that char array, which is kMaxTitleLength. The last parameter, stdin, tells fgets() to read its input from standard in, as opposed to reading from a file.

```
        fgets( title[ dvdNum ], kMaxTitleLength, stdin );
    }
```

Take a look at the first parameter you passed to fgets(), (title[dvdNum]). What type is this parameter? Remember, title is a two-dimensional array, and a two-dimensional array is an array of arrays. title is an array of char arrays. title[dvdNum] is an array of chars, and thus exactly suited as a parameter to fgets().

Imagine an array of chars named blap:

```
char    blap[ 100 ];
```

You'd have no problem passing blap as a parameter to fgets(), right? fgets() would read the characters from the input buffer and place them in blap. title[0] is just like blap. Both are pointers to an array of chars. blap[0] is the first char of the array blap. Likewise, title[0][0] is the first char of the array title[0].

OK, let's get back to the code.

Once the first loop ends, it prints a dividing line. A second loop then calls PrintDVDTitle() for each DVD title. The first parameter to PrintDVDTitle() specifies the number of the DVD you want printed. The second parameter is the title array pointer.

```
    printf( "-----\n" );

    for ( dvdNum = 0; dvdNum < kMaxDVDs; dvdNum++ )
        PrintDVDTitle( dvdNum, title );
```

Finally, main() ends by returning 0:

```
    return 0;
}
```

Printing the DVD Titles

Next, the PrintDVDTitle() function begins. Take a close look at the definition of PrintDVDTitle()'s second parameter. Notice that the first of the two dimensions is missing (the first pair of brackets is empty). While you could have included the first dimension (kMaxDVDs), the fact that you were able to leave it out makes a really interesting point. When memory is allocated for an array, it is allocated as one big block. To access a specific element of an array, the compiler needs the starting address of the array, the size of each element in the array, and number of the element you want to access. It works just like pointer math: memory address = pointer + (index • sizeof(element))

```
void    PrintDVDTitle( int dvdNum, char title[][ kMaxTitleLength ] ) {
    printf( "Title of DVD #%d: %s\n",
            dvdNum + 1, title[ dvdNum ] );
}
```

In the case of `title`, the compiler allocated a block of memory 1,024 bytes long. Think of this block as four `char` arrays, each of which is 256 bytes long (4 * 256 = 1,024). To get to the first byte of the first array, you just use the pointer that was passed in (`title` points to the first byte of the first of the four arrays). To access the first byte of the second array (in C notation, `title[1][0]`), the compiler adds 256 to the pointer `title`. In other words, the start of the second array is 256 bytes further in memory than the start of the first array. The start of the fourth array is 768 bytes (3 * 256 = 768) further in memory than the start of the first array.

While it is nice to know how to compute array offsets in memory, the point we're making here is that the compiler calculates the title array offsets using the size of each element. But in this case, the "element" isn't simply an `int`, `char`, or `float`—it's another array—and the compiler doesn't know how big that array is unless you tell it.

You also might expect the compiler to use the first array dimension (4) to verify that you don't reference an array element that is out of bounds. For example, you might expect the compiler to complain if it sees this line of code:

```
title[5][0] = '\0';
```

Guess what? C compilers don't do bounds checking of any kind. If you want to access memory beyond the bounds of your array, no one will stop you. This is part of the "charm" of C—it gives you the freedom to write programs that crash in spectacular ways. Your job is to learn how to avoid such pitfalls.

To sum up: when defining an array of indeterminate size, you may leave out the dimension of the highest order array, because C doesn't care how big it is. (You should care, but C doesn't.) You must, however, supply the sizes of any arrays used as elements of that array because without that the compiler can't determine how big each element is, and if it can't do that, it can't calculate the address of an individual element.

Let's return again to the `printf()` statement inside `PrintDVDTitle()`:

```
    printf( "Title of DVD #%d: %s\n", dvdNum + 1, title[ dvdNum ] );
```

Note the two format specifiers. The first, %d, is used to print the DVD number. The second, %s, is used to print the DVD title itself. The \n at the end of the string is used to force a carriage return between each of the DVD titles.

Getting Rid of the Extra Carriage Return

If you look back at Figure 10-1, you might notice an extra carriage return after each line of output produced by PrintDVDTitle(). That's because when fgets() reads a line, it includes all of the characters on that line, including the newline character at the end of the line. (This is in contrast to scanf(), which stops when it gets to the newline character.) Under normal circumstances, the newline character is always the last character in the string buffer, so you can add this line of code (just after the call to fgets()) to get rid of it:

```
title[ dvdNum ][ strlen( title[ dvdNum ] ) - 1 ] = '\0';
```

Note that you'll need to add a #include <string.h> to the top of the file to access the strlen() function. This line of code finds the length of the string that was just typed in. The string includes a carriage return at the very end of it. You subtract one from the length, and then store a NUL character right where the carriage return sits, making the string one byte shorter.

This code isn't particularly good because it lacks some basic safeguards. You'll learn about error and range checking in a later chapter, where we'll explain what's wrong with this code. But for now, it's good enough.

Finishing Model A

In the beginning of the chapter, we described a program that would track your DVD collection. The goal was to look at two different approaches to solving the same problem. The first approach, Model A, uses three arrays to hold a rating, title, and comment for each DVD in the collection:

```
#define kMaxDVDs             5000
#define kMaxTitleLength      256
#define kMaxCommentLength    256

char    rating[ kMaxDVDs ];
char    title[ kMaxDVDs ][ kMaxTitleLength ];
char    comment[ kMaxDVDs ][ kMaxCommentLength ];
```

Before you move on to Model B, take a closer look at the memory used by the Model A arrays:

- The array rating uses 1 byte per DVD (enough for a 1-byte rating from 1 to 10).

- The array title uses 256 bytes per DVD (enough for a text string holding the movie title, up to 255 bytes in length, plus the terminating NUL character).
- The array comment also uses 256 bytes per DVD (enough for a text string holding a comment about the DVD, up to 255 bytes in length, plus the terminating NUL character).

Added together, Model A allocates 513 bytes per DVD. Since Model A allocates space for 5,000 DVDs when it declares its three key arrays, it uses 2,565,000 bytes (5,000 • 513 = 2,565,000) for its data.

Since the program really only needs 513 bytes per DVD, wouldn't it be nice if you could allocate the memory for a DVD only when you need it? With this type of approach, if your collection only consisted of 50 DVDs, you'd only have to use 25,650 bytes of memory (50 • 513 = 25,650), instead of 2,565,000.

> **NOTE:** Memory usage is just one factor to take into account when deciding which data structures to use in your program. Another is ease of use. If you have plenty of memory available, Model A takes less time to implement and is much easier to work with. In that case, memory be damned; go for the simpler solution. The cool thing about being the programmer is that you get to decide what's best in any given situation.

As you'll see by the end of this chapter, C provides a mechanism for allocating memory as you need it. Model B takes a first step toward memory efficiency by creating a single data structure that contains all the information relevant to a single DVD. Later in this chapter, you'll learn how to allocate just enough memory for a single structure.

Model B: The Structure Approach

As mentioned, your DVD program must keep track of a rating (from 1 to 10), the DVD's title, and a comment about the DVD:

```
#define kMaxDVDs             5000
#define kMaxTitleLength      256
#define kMaxCommentLength    256

char    rating[ kMaxDVDs ];
char    title[ kMaxDVDs ][ kMaxTitleLength ];
char    comment[ kMaxDVDs ][ kMaxCommentLength ];
```

C provides the perfect mechanism for wrapping all three of these variables in one tidy bundle. A *struct* allows you to associate any number of variables together under a single name. Here's an example of a struct declaration:

```
#define kMaxTitleLength        256
#define kMaxCommentLength      256

struct DVDInfo {
    char    rating;
    char    title[ kMaxTitleLength ];
    char    comment[ kMaxCommentLength ];
};
```

This struct declaration creates a new type called struct DVDInfo. Just as you'd use a type like int or float to declare a variable, you can use this new type to declare an individual struct. Here's an example:

```
struct DVDInfo    myInfo;
```

This line of code uses the previous type declaration as a template to create an individual struct. The compiler uses the type declaration to tell it how much memory to allocate for the struct and allocates a block of memory large enough to hold all of the individual variables that make up the struct.

The variables that form the struct are known as *fields*. A struct of type DVDInfo has three fields: a char named rating, an array of chars named title, and an array of chars named comment. To access the fields of a struct, use the . operator (called the "dot" operator). Here's an example:

```
struct DVDInfo    myInfo;
myInfo.rating = 7;
```

Notice the . between the struct name (myInfo) and the field name (rating). The . following a struct name tells the compiler that a field name is to follow.

An entire struct can be copied to another struct using the assignment (=) operator, like this:

```
struct MyStruct {
    int i;
    long int l;
    float f;
} aStruct, bStruct;

aStruct = bStruct;
```

Like any other kind of assignment, the entire contents of the right operand are copied to the left operand, just as if you had manually copied each field individually, like this:

```
aStruct.i = bStruct.i;
aStruct.l = bStruct.l;
aStruct.f = bStruct.f;
```

StructSize.xcodeproj

Here's a program that demonstrates the declaration of a `struct` type, as well as the definition of an individual `struct`. Open the *Learn C Projects* folder, go inside the folder 10.02 - StructSize, and open the project StructSize.xcodeproj. Run `StructSize`.

Compare your output with the console window shown in Figure 10-2. They should be the same, or very similar. The first three lines of output show the names of the rating, title, and comment fields. To the right of each field name you'll find printed the number of bytes of memory allocated to that field. The last line of output shows the memory allocated to the entire `struct`.

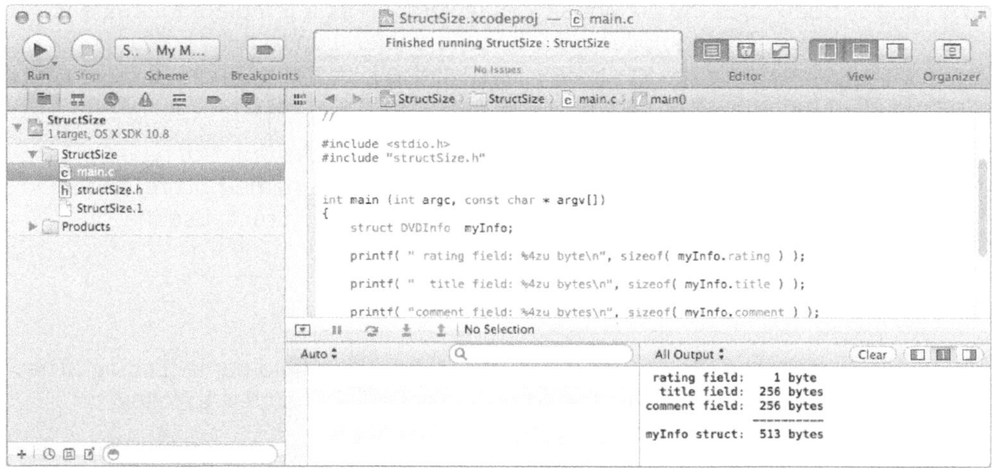

Figure 10-2. *StructSize shows the size of a* `DVDInfo` *struct.*

Stepping Through the StructSize Source Code

If you haven't done so already, take a minute to look over the source code in `main.c`. Once you feel comfortable with it, read on.

`main.c` starts off with the standard `#include` along with a new one:

```
#include <stdio.h>
#include "structSize.h"
```

The angle brackets (<>) that surround all the `#include` files you've seen so far tell the compiler to look for the `#include` file in the directories that contain *library header* files, which are C source files that are part of C's Standard Library, provided by Apple, or from other sources that came bundled with Xcode. When you surround the include file name by double quotes ("") instead (like those around "structSize.h" in this example), you are telling the compiler to look for this `#include` file in your project. These are referred to as *project headers*, to distinguish them from library headers. The quick and dirty tip to remember is you use brackets around files you didn't write and quotes around files you did.

> **NOTE:** If you use double quotes ("") in an `#include` directive and the compiler can't find that file in your project, it will fall back to searching the library headers just as if you had used angle brackets (<>) instead. Because of this, some lazy programmers use double quotes for all of their `#include` files, but that practice is discouraged.

Regardless of where it locates the `#include` file, the compiler treats the contents of the `#include` file as if it were actually inside the including file. In this case, the compiler treats <stdio.h> and "structSize.h" as if they were directly inside `main.c`. Strictly speaking, the preprocessor replaces the `#include` line with the entire contents of the included file, before control is handed off to the compiler.

> **NOTE:** As you've already seen, C `#include` files typically end in the one character extension `.h`. Though you can give your `#include` files any name you like, the `.h` extension is one you should definitely stick with. The "h" stands for "header."

Let's take a look at *structSize.h*. The simplest way is to select the file in the project navigator. For files that are part of your project, this works just fine. Another way to do this is through Xcode's Related Files pop-up menu, shown in Figure 10-3, which works for header files that you wrote as well as those that you didn't. Just above the editing pane in the workspace window, look toward the left edge of the control ribbon. There, next to the back and forward history buttons, is the Related Files menu button.

Click the button, find the Includes submenu, and select ***structSize.h*** from the menu. The editor pane will now display the *structSize.h* file. Note that this pop-up includes all included files, including (no pun intended) *stdio.h*.

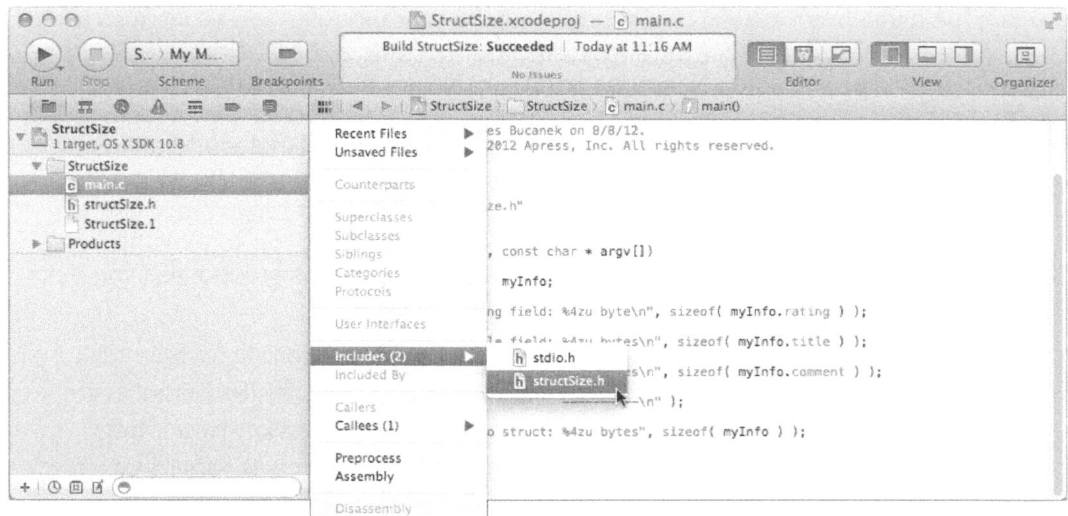

Figure 10-3. *Selecting an include file from Xcode's Related Files menu*

Now the editor is displaying the *structSize.h* file. If you look again at the Related Files menu, you'll see an Included By submenu that lists *main.c*! Xcode is constantly cross-referencing all of the files in your project, so that you can easily jump to any included header file, or see all of the source files that include the header file you're looking at.

> **NOTE:** Header files typically contain things like `#defines`, global variables, and function prototypes. By embedding these things in an `#include` file, you remove clutter from your source code file, and more importantly, you make this common source code available to other source code files via a single `#include`.

structSize.h starts off with two `#defines` you've seen before:

```
#define kMaxTitleLength    256
#define kMaxCommentLength  256
```

Next is the declaration of the `struct` type, `DVDInfo`:

```
struct DVDInfo {
    char    rating;
    char    title[ kMaxTitleLength ];
    char    comment[ kMaxCommentLength ];
};
```

By including the header file at the top of the file (where you might place your globals), you've made the DVDInfo struct type available to all of the functions inside *main.c*. If you placed the DVDInfo type declaration inside of main() instead, your program would still have worked (as long as you placed it before the definition of myInfo), but you would not have access to the DVDInfo type outside of main().

> **NOTE:** That's probably isn't all that's in the .h file. The C header file template that comes with Xcode inserts code like this whenever you create a new C header file:
>
> ```
> #ifndef ProjectName_filename_h
>
> #define ProjectName_filename_h
>
> // Your source code goes here
>
> #endif
> ```
>
> This bit of preprocessing magic lets you #include your .h file without worrying if some other file has already included it. Including it twice will likely result in duplicate definition errors. These preprocessor directives check to see if this header has already been included and, if not, allows the code to be compiled. If it has been included already, the code is ignored. If you poke around the headers of the Standard Library, you'll see this often.

That's all that was in the header file *structSize.h*. Back in *main.c*, main() starts by defining a DVDInfo struct named myInfo. myInfo has three fields: myInfo.rating, myInfo.title, and myInfo.comment.

```
int main (int argc, const char * argv[])
{
    struct DVDInfo  myInfo;
```

The next three statements print the size of the three myInfo fields. The %zu format specifier is used again to print the value returned by sizeof, but this time a minimum field width of 4 is thrown in to make all of the numbers line up neatly.

```
    printf( " rating field: %4zu byte\n", sizeof( myInfo.rating ) );
    printf( "  title field: %4zu bytes\n", sizeof( myInfo.title ) );
    printf( "comment field: %4zu bytes\n", sizeof( myInfo.comment ) );
```

This next printf() prints a separator line, purely for aesthetics:

```
    printf( "               ----------\n" );
```

Finally, you print the total number of bytes allocated to the `struct`. Do the numbers add up? They should!

```
    printf( "myInfo struct: %4zu bytes", sizeof( myInfo ) );
    return 0;
}
```

On some computers, these numbers won't always add up. Here's why: many computers follow rules to keep various data types lined up a certain way. For example, the old Motorola 68000 CPU was incapable of reading an `int` unless its address was an even number. So the compiler had to make sure that every `int`, `long int`, `float`, `double`, and `struct` would start at an even address. Conversely, a `char` or array of `char`s could start at either an odd or even address. In addition, on a 68000 machine, a `struct` must always have an even number of bytes.

This is called data *alignment*. The alignment rules, like the sizes of `int`s, vary from one CPU to the next. Even on CPUs that don't require an integer to start on an even memory address, it may be faster if it does, so the compiler may choose to align variables to addresses that are evenly divisible by 2, 4, or even 8 bytes.

If you want, you can see this right now. In the *structSize.h* file, add an `int` between the `rating` and `title` variables, like this:

```
char rating;
int fourBytes;
char title[ kMaxTitleLength ];
```

When we made this change and ran `StructSize` on our systems, the size of `myInfo` jumped from 513 bytes to 520, which is 7 bytes longer. That's because, in addition to the 4 bytes for the new `int`, the compiler inserted three unused bytes between `rating` and `fourBytes` so that `fourBytes` would start on an address that's evenly divisible by 4. This is called *padding*. On our particular CPU, this makes reading and storing the `fourBytes int` much faster—that's a good thing.

> **TIP:** In general, you shouldn't worry about alignment. How the compiler aligns, packs, and pads structures is already optimized for your particular CPU. Should it ever become an issue for your program, check the build settings and read up on the `#pragma pack()` preprocessor directive. These let you adjust the alignment rules the compiler uses.

Passing a struct As a Parameter

Think back to the DVD tracking program we've been discussing throughout this chapter. It started off with three separate arrays, each of which tracked a separate element. One array stored the rating field, another stored the movie's title, and the third stored a pithy comment.

We then introduced the concept of a structure that would group all the elements of one DVD together in a single struct. One advantage of a struct is that you can pass all the information about a DVD using a single pointer. Imagine a routine called PrintDVD(), designed to print the three elements that describe a single DVD. Using the original array-based model, you'd have to pass three parameters to PrintDVD():

```
void    PrintDVD( char rating, char *title, char *comment ) {
    printf( "rating: %d\n", rating );
    printf( "title: %s\n", title );
    printf( "comment: %s\n", comment );
}
```

Using the struct-based model, however, you could pass the information using a single pointer. As a reminder, here's the DVDInfo struct declaration again:

```
#define kMaxTitleLength         256
#define kMaxCommentLength       256

struct DVDInfo {
    char    rating;
    char    title[ kMaxTitleLength ];
    char    comment[ kMaxCommentLength ];
};
```

This version of main() defines a DVDInfo struct and passes its address to a new version of PrintDVD() (we'll get to it next):

```
int main (int argc, const char * argv[])
{
    struct DVDInfo    myInfo;

    PrintDVD( &myInfo );

    return 0;
}
```

Just as has been the case in earlier programs, passing the address of a variable to a function gives that function the ability to modify the original variable. Passing the address of myInfo to PrintDVD() gives PrintDVD() the ability to modify the three myInfo fields. Though the new version of PrintDVD() doesn't modify myInfo, it's important to know that the opportunity exists. Here's the new, struct-based version of PrintDVD():

```
void PrintDVD( struct DVDInfo *myDVDPtr )
{
    printf( "rating: %d\n", (*myDVDPtr).rating );
    printf( "title: %s\n", myDVDPtr->title );
    printf( "comment: %s\n", myDVDPtr->comment );
}
```

Notice that PrintDVD() receives its parameter as a pointer to (i.e., the address of) a DVDInfo struct. The first printf() uses the * operator to turn the struct pointer back to the struct it points to and then uses the . operator to access the rating field:

```
(*myDVDPtr).rating
```

C features a special operator, ->, that lets you accomplish the exact same thing. The -> operator is binary. That is, it requires both a left and right operand. The left operand is a pointer to a struct, and the right operand is the struct field. The following notation

```
myDVDPtr->rating
```

is exactly the same as

```
(*myDVDPtr).rating
```

Use whichever form you prefer. In general, most C programmers use the -> operator to get from a struct's pointer to one of the struct's fields.

Passing a Copy of the struct

In addition to being copied via the assignment operator (=), a struct can be included as an argument in a function call. Here's a version of main() that passes the struct itself, instead of its address:

```
int main (int argc, const char * argv[]) {
    struct DVDInfo    myInfo;

    PrintDVD( myInfo );
}
```

As always, when the compiler encounters a function parameter, it passes a copy of the parameter to the receiving routine. The previous version of PrintDVD() received a copy of the address of a DVDInfo struct (pass by reference).

In this new version of PrintDVD(), the compiler passes a copy of the entire DVDInfo struct (pass by value), not just a copy of its address. This copy of the

DVDInfo struct includes copies of the rating field plus the title and comment arrays.

```
void PrintDVD( struct DVDInfo myDVD )
{
    printf( "rating: %d\n", myDVD.rating );
    printf( "title: %s\n", myDVD.title );
}
```

When you pass a copy of a struct (pass by value), it works just like passing any other variable type. Any changes made by the function only change the local parameter—and are lost when the function returns. If this version of PrintDVD() made changes to its local myDVD struct, those changes would be lost when PrintDVD() returned.

> **TIP:** Just as you can pass a copy of an entire struct as a parameter, a function can return a copy of an entire struct. Just make the function's return type a struct.

Sometimes you'll want to pass a copy of a struct. One advantage this technique offers is that there's no way that the receiving function can modify the original struct. Another advantage is that it offers a simple mechanism for making a copy of a struct. A disadvantage is that copying a struct takes time and uses memory. Though time won't usually be a problem, memory usage might be, especially if your struct gets pretty large. Just be aware that whatever you pass as a parameter is going to get copied. Pass a struct as a parameter, and the compiler will copy the struct. Pass a pointer to a struct, and the compiler will copy the pointer.

ParamAddress.xcodeproj

There's a sample program in the *Learn C Projects* folder, inside a subfolder named 10.03 - ParamAddress, that should help show the difference between passing the address of a struct and passing a copy of the struct. Open and run ParamAddress.xcodeproj. Note that main() defines a DVDInfo struct named myDVD and prints the address of myDVD's rating field.

```
    struct DVDInfo  myDVD;
    printf( "Address of myDVD.rating in main(): %28p\n", &(myDVD.rating) );
```

As you can see, you print an address using the %p format specifier. The "p" stands for pointer. This is the proper way to print the address of a pointer in C. Here's the output of this printf() on our computer:

```
Address of myDVD.rating in main():              0x7fff5fbff7b8
```

Next, main() passes the address of myDVD as well as a copy of myDVD as parameters to a routine named PrintParamInfo():

```
PrintParamInfo( &myDVD, myDVD );
```

Here's the prototype for PrintParamInfo():

```
void PrintParamInfo( struct DVDInfo *myDVDPtr, struct DVDInfo myDVDCopy );
```

The first parameter is a pointer to a myDVD struct. The second parameter is a copy of the same struct. PrintParamInfo() prints the address of the rating field of each version of myDVD:

```
    printf( "Address of myDVDPtr->rating in PrintParamInfo(): %10p\n",
&(myDVDPtr->rating) );
    printf( "Address of myDVDCopy.rating in PrintParamInfo(): %10p\n",
&(myDVDCopy.rating) );
```

Here are the results, including the line of output generated by main():

```
Address of myDVD.rating in main():                0x7fff5fbff7b8
Address of myDVDPtr->rating in PrintParamInfo(): 0x7fff5fbff7b8
Address of myDVDCopy.rating in PrintParamInfo(): 0x7fff5fbff730
```

Notice that the rating field accessed via a pointer has the same address as the original rating field in main()'s myDVD struct. If PrintParamInfo() uses the first parameter to modify the rating field, it will, in effect, be changing main()'s rating field. If PrintParamInfo() uses the second parameter to modify the rating field, main()'s rating field will remain untouched.

HEXADECIMAL MEMORY ADDRESSES

Most programmers, the Xcode debugger, and the %p format specifier use hexadecimal notation (hex for short) when they deal with addresses. Hex notation represents numbers as base 16 instead of the normal base 10 you are accustomed to using. Instead of the 10 digits (0 through 9), hex features 16 digits: 0, 1, 2, 3, 4, 5, 6, 7, 8, 9, a, b, c, d, e, and f. Each digit of a number represents a successive power of 16 instead of successive powers of 10.

For example, the number 532 in base ten is equal to $5 \cdot 10^2 + 3 \cdot 10^1 + 2 \cdot 10^0 = 5 \cdot 100 + 3 \cdot 10 + 2$. The number 532 in hex is equal to $5 \cdot 16^2 + 3 \cdot 16^1 + 2 \cdot 16^0 = 5 \cdot 256 + 3 \cdot 16 + 2 = 1{,}330$ in base 10. The number ff in hex is equal to $15 \cdot 16 + 15 = 255$ in base 10. Remember, the hex digit f has a decimal (base 10) value of 15.

Computer engineers love hexadecimal because every two hexadecimal digits is exactly one byte, which makes it well suited for describing values stored in RAM.

C also supports a (rarely used) notation called octal. Octal numbers are base 8, using only the digits 0 through 7. In C, Octal numbers begin with a 0 digit. Thus, the constant 123 is one hundred and twenty three, while the constant 0123 is eighty three ($1 \bullet 8^2 + 2 \bullet 8^1 + 3 \bullet 8^0 = 1 \bullet 64 + 2 \bullet 8 + 3$). Octal was popular in some of the very earliest computers that uses 6-bit bytes, but when CPUs moved to 8-bit bytes it was no longer very convenient.

To write a hex constant in C, preceded it by the characters `0x`. The constant `0xff` has a decimal value of 255. The constant `0xFF` also has a decimal value of 255. C doesn't distinguish between uppercase and lowercase hex digits.

struct Arrays

Just as you can declare an array of `chars` or `ints`, you can also declare an array of `structs`:

```
#define kMaxDVDs    5000
struct DVDInfo myDVDs[ kMaxDVDs ];
```

This declaration creates an array of 5,000 `structs` of type `DVDInfo`. The array is named `myDVDs`. Each of the 5,000 `structs` will have the three fields: `rating`, `title`, and `comment`. You access the fields of the structs as you might expect. Here's an example (note the use of the all-important . operator):

```
myDVDs[ 10 ].rating = 9;
```

You now have an equivalent to the first DVD tracking data structure. Where the first model used three arrays, you now have a solution that uses a single array. As you'll see when you start writing your own programs, packaging your data in a `struct` makes life a bit simpler. Instead of passing three parameters each time you need to pass a DVD to a function, you can simply pass a `struct`.

From a memory standpoint, both DVD tracking solutions cost the same. With three separate arrays, the cost is as follows:

```
                 5,000 bytes /*rating array*/
5,000 * 256 = 1,280,000 bytes /*title array*/
5,000 * 256 = 1,280,000 bytes /*comment array*/
              -----------------
Total         2,565,000 bytes
```

With an array of structs, this is the cost:

```
5,000 * 513 = 2,565,000 bytes    /*Cost of array of 5,000 DVDInfo structs*/
```

So what can you do to cut this memory cost down? We thought you'd never ask!

Allocating Your Own Memory

One of the limitations of an array-based DVD tracking model is that arrays are not resizable. When you define an array, you have to specify exactly how many elements make up your array. For example, this code defines an array of 5,000 `DVDInfo` structs:

```
#define kMaxDVDs    5000
struct DVDInfo    myDVDs[ kMaxDVDs ];
```

As mentioned, this array will take up 2,565,000 bytes of memory, whether you use the array to track 1 DVD or 5,000. If you know in advance exactly how many elements your array requires, arrays are just fine. In the case of this DVD tracking program, using an array just isn't practical. For example, if your DVD collection consists entirely of a test DVD that came with your DVD burner and a rare bootleg of Gilligan's Island outtakes, a 5,000 `struct` array is overkill. Even worse, what happens if you've got more than 5,000 DVDs? No matter what number you pick for `kMaxDVDs`, there's always the chance that it won't prove large enough.

The problem here is that arrays are just not flexible enough to do what you want. Instead of trying to predict the amount of memory you'll need in advance, you need a method that will give you a chunk of memory the exact size of a `DVDInfo struct`, as you need it. In more technical terms, you need to *allocate* and *manage* your own memory.

> **NOTE:** Allocating your own memory, called *dynamic memory allocation*, is a very important programming skill to learn. An automatic `int` variable is invaluable in writing a `for` loop when you know you're going to need one `int` variable. But you can't declare variables if you don't know how many or what kinds you're going to need. Your program will have to wait until it reads information from a file, the user asks to create a new document, they click on a button to add a DVD, or they drop in a picture; at that point your program will have to decide what variables it will need to represent those things and allocate them. As you progress to writing more useful programs, most of your data will be dynamically allocated.

When your program starts running, your operating system (Mac OS X, Unix, and Windows are all examples of operating systems) carves out a chunk of memory for the exclusive use of your application. Some of this memory is used to hold the object code that makes up your application. Still more of it is used to hold things like your application's global variables. As your application runs, some of this memory will be allocated to main()'s local variables. When main() calls a function, memory is allocated for that function's local variables. When that function returns, the memory allocated for its local variables is freed up (sometimes called *deallocated* or *released*). This memory becomes available to be allocated all over again. It's just like recycling.

In the next few sections, you'll learn about some functions you can call to allocate a block of memory and to free that memory (return it to the pool of available memory) when you're done with it. Ultimately, you'll combine these functions with a data structure called a linked list to provide a more memory-efficient, and more flexible, alternative to the array.

Using malloc()

The Standard Library function of malloc() allows you to allocate a block of memory of a specified size. To access malloc(), you need to include the file <stdlib.h>:

```
#include <stdlib.h>
```

malloc() takes a single parameter, the size of the requested block, in bytes. malloc() returns a pointer to the newly allocated block of memory. Here's the function prototype:

```
void *malloc( size_t size );
```

The block of memory comes from a vast reservoir of memory called the *heap*. The heap consists of most of the unused addresses in your computer—those not already used by your program's code, static and automatic variables, and some miscellaneous addresses reserved by the operating system.

If malloc() can't allocate a block of memory the size you requested, it returns a pointer with the value NULL. NULL is a constant, defined to have a value of zero, used to specify an invalid pointer. In other words, a pointer with a value of NULL does not point to a legal memory address. You learned about NULL in Chapter 7. Now you'll get a chance to use it.

You might be scratching your head over malloc()'s return type, void*. C allows you to declare a pointer to void. It might appear oxymoronic (a pointer to nothing), but it turns out to be very useful. C interprets a void* as "a pointer to a variable of unknown type." It's not that the pointer points to nothing; it points to something but the compiler doesn't know what.

You can use a void pointer like any other pointer. You can assign it an address, pass it as variable, and so on. The only thing you can't do is this:

```
void *nothing;
*nothing = 1;
```

You can't assign anything to the "value" that nothing points to because the compiler doesn't know what that is. Is it an int? A float? A struct of some kind?

So what good are void pointers? Bear with us and you'll find out.

Converting the Type Returned by malloc()

Here's a code fragment that allocates a single DVDInfo struct:

```
struct DVDInfo    *myDVDPtr;
myDVDPtr = malloc( sizeof( struct DVDInfo ) );
```

In general, you'll convert the void pointer returned by malloc() to the pointer type you really want. Here's how it's typically done. The first line of code declares a new variable, myDVDPtr, which is a pointer to a DVDInfo struct. At this time, myDVDPtr doesn't point to a DVDInfo struct. You've just told the compiler that myDVDPtr is designed to point to a DVDInfo struct.

The second line of code calls malloc() to allocate a block of memory the size of a DVDInfo struct. The sizeof operator results in a size_t integer, the exactly type you need to pass as a parameter to malloc(). How convenient!

On the right side of the = operator is a void * and on the left side is a struct DVDInfo *. The compiler will normally complain if you try to assign a pointer of one type to a pointer of a different type. Consider the confusion that could result if you set a pointer to a char to the address of an int.

The compiler makes an exception for void pointers. It allows you to assign a void pointer to any kind of pointer, and any kind of pointer can be assigned to a void pointer. In effect, a void * is a wildcard pointer that can point to anything in memory. C trusts that you know what it actually points to.

So you could have used a typecast here to make this more explicit:

```
myDVDPtr = (struct DVDInfo *)malloc( sizeof(struct DVDInfo) );
```

Though this explicit typecast isn't strictly necessary, it makes your intentions quite clear and allows the compiler to step in with a warning if you've got your types mixed up. Don't worry if this is confusing. You'll learn all about typecasting in Chapter 13.

CALLOC()

An alternative to the `malloc()` function is `calloc()`. `calloc()` also allocates a block of memory, exactly the way `malloc()` does, but it fills that block of bytes with zeros before it returns. When you allocate memory with `malloc()`, the contents of the new memory are uninitialized, just like when you declare an automatic variable in a function. If you want all of the values in your new variables to be set to zero, use the `calloc()` function instead.

`calloc()` take two parameters. The second parameter is the size of the structure or variable that you want allocated, just like `malloc()`. The first parameter is the number of structures you want allocated. This makes `calloc()` particularly convenient for allocating arrays of things. For example, `calloc( 100, sizeof(int) )` allocates a block of memory big enough for an array of 100 `ints` (`int array[100]`) and sets all of those `ints` to 0.

To allocate a single something, pass 1 as the first parameter, like this: `calloc( 1, sizeof(struct DVDInfo) );`

Using the Allocated Memory Block

If `malloc()` succeeded, `myDVDPtr` points to a `struct` of type `DVDInfo`. For the duration of the program, you can use `myDVDPtr` to access the fields of this newly allocated `struct`:

```
myDVDPtr->rating = 7;
```

You need to understand the difference between a block of memory allocated using `malloc()` and a block of memory that corresponds to a local variable. When a function declares a local variable, the memory associated with that variable is temporary. As soon as the function exits, the block of memory associated with that memory is returned to the pool of available memory.

A block of memory that you allocate using `malloc()` sticks around until you specifically return it to the pool of available memory (heap) or until your program exits.

free()

The Standard Library provides a function called free() that returns a previously allocated block of memory back to the pool of available memory. Here's the function prototype:

```
void free( void *ptr );
```

free() takes a single argument, a pointer to the first byte of a previously allocated block of memory. The following line returns the block allocated earlier to the free memory pool:

```
free( myDVDPtr );
```

Use malloc() to allocate a block of memory. Use free() to free up a block of memory allocated via malloc(). You are responsible for freeing up any memory that you allocate. You create it; you free it. That said, when a program exits, the operating system automatically frees up all memory allocated by that program.

> **CAUTION:** Never put a fork in an electrical outlet. Never pass an address to free() that didn't come from malloc(), calloc(), or any other function that returns an allocated block of memory from the heap. Both will make you extremely unhappy!

Keeping Track of That Address!

The address returned by malloc() is critical. If you lose it, you've lost access to the block of memory you just allocated. Even worse, you can never free() the block, and it will just sit there, wasting valuable memory, for the duration of your program. This is called a *memory leak*.

Here are the essential rules for allocating your own blocks of memory.

1. Allocate a block of the correct size using malloc() (or any similar function) and save the pointer malloc() returns in a variable.
2. Use the returned pointer to access the variables in that block of memory however you please.
3. When you're done with it, pass the original pointer to free() so that memory block can be recycled.
4. Once you pass an address to free(), never use it again—in another call to free() or for any other purpose. If you have a pointer variable that still points to that address, set it to NULL.

> **NOTE:** One great way to lose a block's address is to call `malloc()` inside a function, saving the address returned by `malloc()` in a local variable, and then fail to call `free()` before the function exits. Your local variable goes away, taking the address of your new block with it!

There are many ways to keep track of a newly allocated block of memory. As you design your program, you'll figure out which approach makes the most sense for your particular situation. One technique you'll find useful is to place the pointer inside a special data structure known as a linked list.

> **TIP:** Modern computers have so much memory that you're likely never to notice if your program is leaking small amounts of memory. One way to check is to use any of Xcode's memory leak detection tools (and there are several).
>
> Get into the practice of occasionally profiling your program using Xcode's Instruments tool. It will analyze your program and look for all kinds of problems—like memory leaks.

Working with Linked Lists

The linked list is one of the most widely used techniques for organizing data structures in C. A linked list is a series of `struct`s, each of which contains a pointer field. Each `struct` in the series uses its pointer to point to the next `struct` in the series. Figure 10-4 shows a linked list containing three elements.

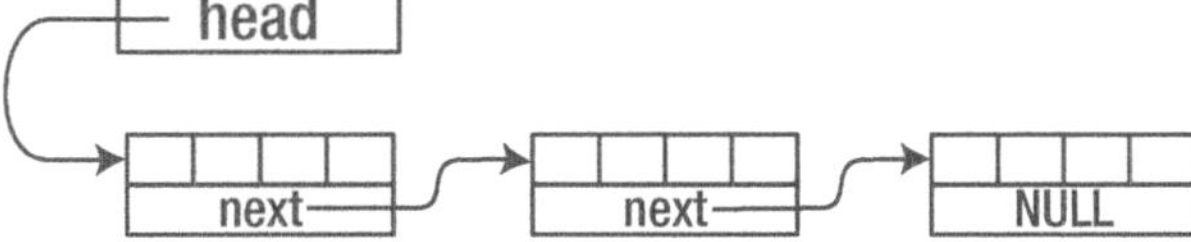

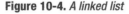

Figure 10-4. *A linked list*

Figure 10-4 shows a linked list containing three `struct`s. A linked list starts with a master pointer. The master pointer is a pointer variable that points to the first `struct` in the list, also known as the head. This first `struct` contains a field, also a pointer, which points to the second `struct` in the linked list. The second `struct` contains a pointer field that points to the third element. The linked list in

Figure 10-4 ends with the third element. The pointer field in the last element of a linked list is typically set to NULL. The last element in the list is known as the tail.

Why Use Linked Lists?

Linked lists allow you to be extremely memory efficient. Using a linked list, you can implement your DVD tracking data structure, allocating exactly the number of structs that you need—no more, no less. Each time a DVD is added to your collection, you'll allocate one new struct and add it to the linked list.

A linked list starts out as a single master pointer. When you want to add an element to the list, call malloc() to allocate a block of memory for the new element. Next, make the master pointer point to the new block. Finally, set the new block's next element pointer to NULL.

Creating a Linked List

The first step in creating a linked list is the design of the linked list struct. Here's a sample:

```
#define kMaxTitleLength       256
#define kMaxCommentLength     256

struct DVDInfo {
    char              rating;
    char              title[ kMaxTitleLength ];
    char              comment[ kMaxCommentLength ];
    struct DVDInfo    *next;
}
```

The change here is the addition of a fourth field, a pointer to a DVDInfo struct. This field is the link that connects two different DVDInfo structs together. If myFirstPtr is a pointer to one DVDInfo struct and mySecondPtr is a pointer to a second struct, this line

```
myFirstPtr->next = mySecondPtr;
```

connects the two structs. Once they are connected, you can use a pointer in the first struct to access the second struct or its fields! For example, the following line sets the rating field of the second struct to 7:

```
myFirstPtr->next->rating = 7;
```

Using the next field to get from one struct to the next is also known as *traversing* a linked list.

The next (and final) program for this chapter will incorporate the new version of the `DVDInfo` `struct` to demonstrate a more memory-efficient DVD tracking program. This program is pretty long, so you may want to take a few moments to let the dog out and answer your mail.

> **NOTE:** There are many variants of the linked list. If you connect the last element of a linked list to the first element, you create an unending *circular list*.
>
> If you add a `prev` field to the `struct` and use it to point to the previous element in the list (in addition to the next one) you've created a *doubly-linked list*. This technique allows you to traverse the linked list in two directions.

As you gain more programming experience, you'll want to check out some books on data structures. Three books well worth exploring are *Algorithms in C*, Parts 1–5 by Robert Sedgewick (Addison-Wesley 2001), *Data Structures and C Programs* by Christopher J. Van Wyk (Addison-Wesley 1990), and our personal favorite, *Fundamental Algorithms*, volume one of Donald Knuth's *The Art of Computer Programming* series (Addison-Wesley 1997).

DVDTracker.xcodeproj

DVDTracker implements Model B of your DVD tracking system, but instead of pre-allocating a huge array of `DVDInfo` structs, it's going to allocate memory only for the ones it needs as it goes. It uses a text-based menu, allowing you to quit, add a new DVD to the collection, or list all of the currently tracked DVDs.

Open the *Learn C Projects* folder, go inside the folder 10.04 - DVDTracker, and open the project DVDTracker.xcodeproj. Run *DVDTracker*. The console window will appear, showing the following prompt:

```
Enter command (q=quit, n=new, l=list):
```

At this point, you have three choices. You can type "q" and press Return to quit the program. You can type "n" and press Return to add a new DVD to your collection. Finally, you can type "l" and press Return to list all the DVDs in your collection.

Start by typing "l" and pressing Return. You should see this message:

```
No DVDs have been entered yet...
```

Next, the original command prompt should reappear:

```
Enter command (q=quit, n=new, l=list):
```

This time, type "n" and press Return. You will be prompted to enter a DVD title and comment:

```
Enter DVD Title:  The Ring
Enter DVD Comment:  Scariest movie ever!
```

Next, you'll be prompted for a rating for the new DVD. The program expects a number between 1 and 10. Try typing something unexpected, such as the letter "x", followed by a carriage return.

```
Enter DVD Rating (1-10):  x
Enter DVD Rating (1-10):  9
```

The program checks your input, discovers it isn't in the proper range, and repeats the prompt. This time type a number between 1 and 10, and press Return. The program returns you to the main command prompt:

```
Enter command (q=quit, n=new, l=list):
```

Type "l" and press Return. The single DVD you just entered will be listed, and the command prompt will again be displayed:

```
Title:   The Ring
Comment: Scariest movie ever!
Rating:  9

----------
Enter command (q=quit, n=new, l=list):
```

Type "n" and press Return to enter another DVD. Repeat the process one more time, adding a third DVD to the collection. Now, type "l" and press Return to list all three DVDs. Here's our list:

```
Enter command (q=quit, n=new, l=list):  l
Title:   The Ring
Comment: Scariest movie ever!
Rating:  9
--------
Title:   Tenacious D in the Pick of Destiny
Comment: Jack Black rocks. Kyle Gass can play.
Rating:  7
--------
Title:   Hot Fuzz
Comment: Simon Pegg sleeper - must see!
Rating:  8

----------
Enter command (q=quit, n=new, l=list):  q
```

Finally, type "q" and press Return to quit the program.

```
Goodbye...
```

Let's hit the source code.

Stepping Through the DVDTracker Source Code

main.c starts by including four different files. *stdio.h* gives you access to routines like `printf()` and `fgets()`. *stdlib.h* gives you access to `malloc()` and `free()`. *string.h* gives you access to `strlen()` and `strlcpy()`. *ctype.h* brings in `isspace()`. The fourth include file is your own *dvdTracker.h*.

```
#include <stdio.h>
#include <stdlib.h>
#include <string.h>
#include <ctype.h>
#include "dvdTracker.h"
```

dvdTracker.h starts off with two `#defines` that you should know pretty well by now:

```
#define kMaxTitleLength        256
#define kMaxCommentLength      256
```

TIP: As you make your way through the *DVDTracker* source code, you'll notice we've added some decorative comments used to mark the beginning of a section of code. For example, in *dvdTracker.h*, we've added comments to mark off areas for defines and `struct` declarations.

In *main.c*, we've done something similar to set off the beginning of each function. Each includes a short description of what the function does, what the parameters mean, and so on. You should do something similar in your own code. It'll make your code easier to read and understand later.

Next is the new and improved `DVDInfo` `struct` declaration:

```
struct DVDInfo {
    char            rating;
    char            title[ kMaxTitleLength ];
    char            comment[ kMaxCommentLength ];
    struct DVDInfo  *next;
};
```

Let's get back to *main.c*. After the `#includes` are the local function prototypes. We'll explain each function as we get to them.

```
char            GetCommand( void );
struct DVDInfo  *ReadStruct( void );
void            AddToList( struct DVDInfo *curPtr );
void            ListDVDs( void );
char            *TrimLine( char *line );
```

Next, you need two global variables to keep track of your linked list.

```
static struct DVDInfo *gHeadPtr, *gTailPtr;
```

The gHeadPtr pointer points to the first (head) DVDInfo struct in your linked list. The gTailPtr pointer points to the last (tail) struct in your linked list. A tail pointer isn't strictly necessary—you can always find the last (tail) struct in the list by starting at the head and traversing all of the links—but it makes some operations super simple, so this program will use a tail pointer.

Being defined outside of any function makes gHeadPtr and gTailPtr global variables. Remember that global variables are always initialized to zero before your program begins running, so both of these pointers will be set to NULL when main() starts.

main()

Speaking of which, let's get main() started. main() begins by defining a char named command, which will be used to hold the single letter command typed by the user.

```
int main (int argc, const char * argv[])
{
    char command;
```

Next, main() enters a while loop, calling the function GetCommand(). GetCommand() prompts you for a one character command: 'q', 'n', or 'l'. Once GetCommand() returns 'q', you drop out of the while loop and exit the program.

```
    while ( (command = GetCommand() ) != 'q' ) {
```

If GetCommand() returns 'n', the user wants to enter information on a new DVD. First, you call ReadStruct(), which allocates space for a DVDInfo struct and prompts the user for the information to place in the new struct's fields. Once the struct is filled out, ReadStruct() returns a pointer to the newly allocated struct.

The pointer returned by ReadStruct() is passed on to AddToList(), which adds the new struct to the linked list.

```
        switch( command ) {
            case 'n':
                AddToList( ReadStruct() );
                break;
```

If GetCommand() returns 'l', the user wants to list all the DVDs in a collection. That's what the function ListDVDs() does.

```
            case 'l':
                ListDVDs();
                break;
        }
        printf( "\n----------\n" );
    }
```

At the end of the loop a couple of lines are output to separate the last command from the next one. If GetCommand() returns a 'q', then the loop exits and says "Goodbye" before it ends.

```
    printf( "Goodbye...\n" );
    return 0;
}
```

GetCommand()

Next up is the GetCommand() function. GetCommand() prompts the user to type one of the commands and press return. It then reads a line of text from standard in (which will be the keyboard) and returns the first character on that line.

```
char GetCommand( void )
{
    char buffer[ 100+1 ];
    printf( "Enter command (q=quit, n=new, l=list):  " );
    fgets( buffer, sizeof(buffer), stdin );
    return *TrimLine( buffer );
}
```

The function starts by allocating a temporary string buffer to read the line. 100 characters should be more than enough. It outputs a prompt, and then uses the fgets() function to read the line into buffer. The second parameter is the size of the array, so fgets() will never try to copy more characters than there's room for.

The TrimLine() function removes any and all whitespace characters from both the beginning and the end of the line the user just typed. We'll explain how TrimLine() works a little later. The only thing you need to know right now is that it returns a pointer to the string of characters the user typed in. Since GetCommand() is only interested in the first character, the * (pointer dereference) operator is used to fetch the first character in the string array and return it to the caller.

ReadStruct()

Next up is ReadStruct(). Notice the unusual declaration of the function name:

```
struct DVDInfo *ReadStruct( void )
{
```

This declaration says that ReadStruct() returns a pointer to a DVDInfo struct.

ReadStruct() calls malloc() to allocate a block of memory the size of a DVDInfo struct. The variable infoPtr stores the pointer to the new block.

```
    struct DVDInfo  *infoPtr;
    infoPtr = malloc( sizeof( struct DVDInfo ) );
```

Next, you'll print a prompt for the DVD title and call fgets() to read a line from the input buffer. fgets() will copy the line to a temporary buffer array.

```
    char buffer[ 500+1 ];
    printf( "Enter DVD Title:  " );
    fgets( buffer, sizeof(buffer), stdin );
```

The second parameter of fgets() is the size of the buffer array in bytes. By using the sizeof() operator, you don't have to remember how many characters are in buffer; the compiler will figure it out for you. If you decide to change the dimension of buffer in the future, you can do so knowing that the call to fgets()will adjust itself accordingly.

Earlier in the chapter (in the MultiArray sample program), you discovered that fgets() leaves '\n' at the end when it reads in a line of input. Also, the user may start or end their title with superfluous space or tab characters, which you don't want to store. Space, tab, and the newline character are all whitespace characters, so we wrote a routine to strip off any whitespace from the ends of the string. This is called *trimming* a string. Again, we'll get to the details of how TrimLine() works in a moment; for now, just know that it trims off any whitespace and returns a string pointer. This pointer is passed to the strlcpy() function to safely copy the trimmed string into the title field of the struct.

```
    strlcpy( infoPtr->title, TrimLine( buffer ), sizeof(infoPtr->title) );
```

You then repeat the process to prompt for and read in the DVD title.

```
    printf( "Enter DVD Comment:  " );
    fgets( buffer, sizeof(buffer), stdin );
    strlcpy( infoPtr->comment, TrimLine( buffer ), sizeof(infoPtr->comment) );
```

Now a do-while loop starts. The loop first prompts the user to enter a number between 1 and 10. Again, fgets() and TrimLine() are used to get just the characters typed on the line. Like you did in the last chapter, the atoi() function is used to convert the string into a numeric value.

```
int num;
do {
    printf( "Enter DVD Rating (1-10):  " );
    fgets( buffer, sizeof(buffer), stdin );
    num = atoi( TrimLine( buffer ) );
}
while ( ( num < 1 ) || ( num > 10 ) );
```

The loop continues to repeat until the user types in a line of text that can be converted into a number between 1 and 10. Hopefully, they'll get it right on the first try. When they do, the loop ends and the num variable is assigned to the rating field of the new DVDInfo struct.

```
    infoPtr->rating = num;
```

Finally, and this is the exciting part, the pointer to the new struct is returned to the caller.

```
    return ( infoPtr );
}
```

When the call to ReadStruct() returns the main(), the pointer it just returned is immediately passed to AddToList().

AddToList()

AddToList() takes a pointer to a DVDInfo struct as a parameter. It uses the pointer to add the struct to the end of the linked list:

```
void AddToList( struct DVDInfo *curPtr )
{
```

The first thing it does is test to see if gHeadPtr is NULL, indicating that the list is empty. If so, then the new DVDInfo struct is the first one in the list, making it the new head.

```
    if ( gHeadPtr == NULL )
        gHeadPtr = curPtr;
```

If gHeadPtr is not NULL, the linked list contains at least one element. In that case, make the next field of the very last element on the list point to the new struct.

```
    else
        gTailPtr->next = curPtr;
```

In either case, set gTailPtr to point to the new last element in the list. Finally, make sure the next field of the last element in the list is NULL. You'll see why you want it this way in the next function, ListDVDs().

```
    gTailPtr = curPtr;
    curPtr->next = NULL;
}
```

ListDVDs()

Moving on, the ListDVDs() function is called when the user enters the 'l' command. ListDVDs() lists all the DVDs in the linked list, and the variable curPtr is used to point to the link element currently being examined.

```
void ListDVDs( void )
{
    struct DVDInfo *curPtr;
```

If no DVDs have been entered yet, you'll print an appropriate message:

```
    if ( gHeadPtr  == NULL ) {
        printf( "No DVDs have been entered yet...\n" );
```

Otherwise, you'll use a for loop to step through the linked list. The for loop starts by setting curPtr to point to the first element in the linked list and continues as long as curPtr is not NULL. Each time through the loop, curPtr is set to point to the next element in the list. Since you make sure that the last element's next pointer is always set to NULL, when curPtr is equal to NULL, you know you have been through every element in the list and you are done.

```
    } else {
        for ( curPtr = gHeadPtr; curPtr != NULL; curPtr = curPtr->next ) {
            if ( curPtr != gHeadPtr )
                printf( "--------\n" );
            printf( "Title:   %s\n", curPtr->title );
            printf( "Comment: %s\n", curPtr->comment );
            printf( "Rating:  %d\n", curPtr->rating );
        }
    }
```

The first two statements print a separator line, but only if curPtr is pointing to something other than the first DVDInfo struct in the list. The if statement outputs a separator between each DVD title, but not before the first one (or after the last one).

The next two printf()s use the %s format specifier to print the strings in the fields title and comment. Finally, the rating field is printed, and you head back to the top of the loop.

TrimLine()

The last function is the `TrimLine()` function that's been used from several places so far. The values you get from someone typing characters on the keyboard are going to be examined for command characters, copied to string fields, and converted into numbers. In all of these situations, you don't want extraneous whitespace characters at the beginning or end of the line getting in the way. When you have a routine job that needs to be performed in multiple places, that is the code that should be put in a function.

`TrimLine()` receives a pointer to a string and returns a pointer to a string.

```
char *TrimLine( char *line )
{
```

> **NOTE:** `TrimLine()` doesn't need to know the size of the array where the line is stored because it will only get smaller. There's no chance `TrimLine()` could spill over into memory it's not supposed to, so `TrimLine()` is inherently safe.

The first task it undertakes is to strip off any whitespace characters at the end of the line. Just as you've done in other programs, replacing any character in a string with a `'\0'` character terminates that string at that point, shortening it by one or more characters.

The first task is to determine the location in the array of the last character.

```
    size_t length = strlen( line );
```

The `length` value tells you how many characters are in the string and can be used to calculate the index of the last character, which is exactly what the `while` loop does:

```
    while ( length > 0 && isspace( line[length-1] )) {
        line[length-1] = '\0';
        length--;       // string is now one char shorter
    }
```

The first condition checks to see that there are still characters in the array. It's just as unsafe to access elements before the array as it is to access ones off the end of the array. If `length` is 0, the expression `line[length-1]` would access a non-existent element. Not a good thing.

The second half of the loop condition determines if the last character in the string is whitespace, using the `isspace()` function you got by including the *ctype.h* header. If it is a whitespace character, it is replaced with `'\0'`. This terminates the string and makes it one character shorter. To account for this, the `length` variable is decremented and the loop repeats.

It doesn't matter how many whitespace characters are at the end of this string—none or fifty. The loop will continue to run until they are all gone.

The second half of `TrimLine()` eliminates whitespace characters from the beginning of the string, but using a different technique. This time it starts with a pointer to the first character and increments that pointer until it points to a character that isn't a whitespace character.

```
    char *head = line;
    while ( isspace( *head ) )
        head++;
```

Now what? You might be surprised to discover that the function is finished. All it has to do is return the head pointer to the caller.

```
    return head;
}
```

The caller gets back a pointer to string that does not start, or end, with any whitespace. Note that if the first character is not whitespace, the pointer returned will be the same as the original `line` pointer.

This works because of the definition of a string in C: a pointer to an array of characters terminated by a `NUL` character. In effect, the address of every successive character in a string is a pointer to a valid string; a string that's just one character shorter than the address of the previous element.

> **TIP:** There are functions, such as `strspn()`, that do the same kind of work that `TrimLine()` does. We elected to write this code out because we're trying to teach you how C works. In day-to-day programming, however, look for library functions that already do what you want to do. In other words, don't reinvent the wheel. If something seems obvious, like sorting elements into order, it's highly likely that a routine has already been written—and you should use it. The functions in the libraries are high-quality code that have been thoroughly tested and optimized. You could spend days and still not come up with something better.

Again, if you don't follow this exactly, we encourage you to run your program in the debugger. Give it some input lines that start and/or end with a few extra spaces, and watch how `TrimLine()` does its magic.

What's Next?

This chapter covered a wide range of topics, from `defining structs` to managing linked lists. The intent of the chapter, however, was to attack a real-world programming problem—in this case, a program to catalog DVDs. This chapter showed several design approaches, discussing the pros and cons of each. Finally, the chapter presented a prototype for a DVD tracking program. The program allows you to enter information about a series of DVDs and, on request, will present a list of all the DVDs tracked.

One problem with this program is that once you exit, all of the data you entered is lost. The next time you run the program, you have to start all over again. Chapter 11 offers a solution to this problem. The chapter introduces the concept of files and file management, showing you how to save your data from memory out to your hard disk drive and how to read your data back in again. The next chapter updates *DVDTracker*, storing the DVD information collected in a file on your disk drive.

CHAPTER 10 EXERCISES

1. Each of these code fragments contains either a syntax error or a logical flaw. What is it?

   a.
   ```
   struct Link {
       name[ 50 ];
       Link *next;
       };
   ```

   b.
   ```
   struct Link {
       struct Link next;
       struct Link prev;
       };
   ```

   c.
   ```
   void StepAndPrint( char *line )
   {
       while ( *line != '\0' )
           line++;
       printf( "%s", line );
   }
   ```

2. Rewrite `TrimLine()` so that it uses the Standard Library function `strspn()` to skip over any space or tab characters at the beginning of the string.

3. Update *DVDTracker* so it maintains its linked list in order from the lowest rating to the highest rating. If two DVDs have the same rating, the order is unimportant.

4. Update *DVDTracker* to add a `prev` field to the `DVDInfo` `struct` so it maintains a doubly linked list. As before, the `next` field will point to the next `struct` in the list. Now, however, the `prev` field should point to the previous `struct` in the list. Add an option to the menu that prints the DVD list backward, from the last `struct` in the list to the first.

Chapter 11

Working With Files

Chapter 10 introduced *DVDTracker*, a program designed to keep track of your DVD collection. *DVDTracker* allowed you to enter a new DVD, as well as list all existing DVDs. *DVDTracker's* biggest shortcoming was that it didn't save the DVD information when it exited. If you ran *DVDTracker*, entered information on ten DVDs, and then quit, your information would be gone. The next time you ran *DVDTracker*, you'd have to start from scratch.

The solution to this problem is to somehow save all of the DVD information before you quit the program so it can be used again the next time you run it. This is called *persistence*. This chapter will show you how to implement persistence. It introduces the concept of files, the long-term storage for your program's data. You'll start off with the basics, learning how to open and read a file and displaying its contents in the console window. Next, you'll learn how to write data out to a file. You'll learn about a variety of file opening modes that give you more options when dealing with files, and how to selectively read and update portions of a file. Towards the end, you'll learn how files and character streams are related.

> **NOTE:** As you move on to other programming languages (such as Objective-C, Java, or C++), sophisticated development frameworks (such as Cocoa), and even other operating systems, you'll find there are many ways to work with files. Most of them are based on the concepts you'll learn in this chapter.
>
> Stay with the program! Learn the basics, and you'll find moving on to other development platforms much, much easier in the long run.

What Is a Data File?

A data file is a series of bytes residing in some storage media. Files can be stored on your hard drive, on a recordable DVD or CD, flash memory, a file server, or even on your iPod. The iTunes application is made up of a collection of files, including the actual executable, the preference files, and all the song files. Your favorite word processor lives in a file, and so does each and every document you create with your word processor.

The project archive that came with this book contains many different files. Apple's developer tools are made up of hundreds of files. Each of the Learn C projects consists of at least two files: a project file and at least one source code file. When you compile and link a project, you produce a new kind of file, an executable file. All of these are examples of the same thing: a collection of bytes known as a file.

All of the files on your computer share a common set of traits. All files reside on a *filesystem*. Every file has a name. Each file has a size, measured in bytes. The file main.c from the DVDTracker project contains about 4 thousand (4K) bytes. An HDTV movie in iTunes might take up several billion bytes.

File Basics

A file consists of a stream of consecutive bytes. The bytes in a file are organized very much like a `char` array in memory. Every byte in a file has an address, called an *offset* or *position*. The first byte of a file is always at offset 0, and the offset of the last byte is always one less than the length of the file. The position after the last byte of a file is called the *end of file* (EOF) position.

When you want to access the data in a file, you first open the file using a Standard Library function. The one you'll be using is `fopen()`, pronounced "eff-open." Once your file is open, you can read data from the file or write new data back into the file using Standard Library functions like `fgets()`, `fscanf()`, and `fprintf()`. Once you are done working with your file, you'll close it using another Standard Library function, `fclose()`.

Before we get into the specifics of opening a file, let's take a side trip to examine the rules for naming files in C.

Understanding File Names

You've already explored path and file names in Chapter 9. If any of that seems fuzzy now, consider rereading the section "Using Paths" in Chapter 9.

In OS X's native filesystem, a file or directory name can be up to 255 characters long. File names are typically uncomplicated, but OS X allows them to contain any Unicode character (except '/'). This means they are allowed to contain symbols and foreign characters. It really doesn't matter to the operating system; a file name is simply a sequence of bytes. To refer to a file you must provide that sequence of bytes.

Other filesystems may have (and often do) different rules for file names. They will have different limits on the number of characters a file name can have and what those characters can be. In the original Microsoft DOS operating system, for example, file names couldn't be more than 8 characters long! C doesn't impose these rules—they're imposed by the filesystem your program is using. So if your program reads files from a cloud server, you'll have to live within the rules for that server. If you stick to plainly named files (using only ASCII characters) of reasonable length (32 characters or less), you should be fine.

File names traditionally end with a file name extension. An extension is a `.` (period) followed by a short sequence of characters that indicate the kind of data in the file. Commonly used extensions are `txt` (plain text), `mp3` (MPEG-2 audio layer 3 encoded sound), `png` (Portable Network Graphics encoded image), and so on. A file named "Notes" that contained only ASCII characters would be named `Notes.txt`. OS X does not require you to use extensions, but it's the norm.

As you learned in Chapter 9, the / (slash) character has a special meaning and is used to separate directory and file names in a path—and is why the / character is the only one not allowed in a file name. The `.` and `..` names refer to the current and parent directory (respectively).

You also learned about the ~ path that specifies your home directory. You can't use the ~ path in most C file functions, but we'll show you how to work around that shortly.

Opening and Closing a File

Here's the function prototype for `fopen()`, found in the file `<stdio.h>`:

```
FILE *fopen( const char *name, const char *mode );
```

The `const` keyword marks a variable or parameter as read-only. In other words, while name and mode are both pointers to variables, the `fopen()` function promises not to change them. It will only use their values, but won't modify the values they point to in any way. We'll talk more about the `const` keyword in Chapter 13.

The first parameter to `fopen()`, name, tells `fopen()` which file you want to open. The second parameter, mode, tells `fopen()` how you'll be accessing the file. The three basic file modes are "r", "w", and "a", which stand for read, write, and append, respectively.

> **TIP:** The mode parameter is char *, not char. In other words, mode is a `NUL`-terminated C string, so use "r", not 'r'. Don't worry if you forget; the compiler will complain if you mix them up.

"r" tells `fopen()` that you want to read data from the file and that you won't be writing to the file at all. The file must already exist in order to use this mode. In other words, you can't use the mode "r" to create a file.

The mode "w" tells `fopen()` that you want to write to the specified file. If the file doesn't exist yet, a new file with the specified name is created. If the file does exist, `fopen()` deletes it and creates a new empty file for you to write into.

> **CAUTION:** This point bears repeating: calling `fopen()` with a mode of "w" will delete a file (along with the file's contents!) if the file already exists, essentially starting you over from the beginning of the file. Be careful!

The mode "a" is similar to "w" mode. It tells `fopen()` that you want to write more to the specified file and to create the file if it doesn't exist. If the file does exist, however, the data already there won't be deleted. Any data you write to the file is appended to the end of the file.

If `fopen()` successfully opens the specified file, it allocates a `struct` of type `FILE` and returns a pointer to the `FILE struct`. The `FILE struct` contains information about the open file, including its current mode (e.g., "r", "w", or "a") as well as the current file position.

The *file position indicator* is a pointer into the file that acts like a bookmark in a book. When you open a file for reading, for example, the file position points to the first byte in the file (position 0). When you read the first byte, the file position moves to the next byte (position 1).

It's not really important to know the details of the `FILE struct`. All you need to do is keep track of the `FILE` pointer returned by `fopen()`. By passing the pointer to a Standard Library function that reads or writes, you'll be sure the read or write takes place in the right file and at the right file position. You'll see how all this works as you go through this chapter's sample code.

Here's a sample fopen() call:

```
FILE    *fp;
if ( (fp = fopen( "My Data File.txt", "r")) == NULL ) {
    printf( "Can not open file!!!\n" );
    exit(1);
}
```

This code first calls fopen(), attempting to open the file named My Data File.txt for reading. If fopen() cannot open the file for some reason—perhaps you've asked it to open a file that doesn't exist—it returns NULL. In that case, it'll print an error message and exit.

> **NOTE:** There is a limit to the number of simultaneous open files. This limit is implemented as a #define, FOPEN_MAX, defined in the file <stdio.h>. At the time of this writing, FOPEN_MAX was defined to be 20.

If fopen() does open the file, it will allocate the memory for a FILE struct, and fp will point to that struct. You can then pass fp to routines that read from the file. Once you're done with the file, you'll pass fp to the function fclose().

```
int fclose( FILE *stream );
```

fclose() takes a pointer to a FILE as a parameter and attempts to close that file. If the file is closed successfully, fclose() frees up the memory allocated to the FILE struct and returns a value of 0. It is very important that you match every fopen() with a corresponding fclose(), particularly if you are writing to the file.

Once you've passed a FILE pointer to fclose(), that FILE pointer no longer points to a FILE struct. After calling fclose(), do not attempt to use that FILE struct pointer for anything. If the pointer variable is going to hang around, set it to NULL. If you want to access the file again, you'll have to make another fopen() call.

Reading a File

Once you open a file for reading, the next step is to read data from the file. Several Standard Library functions help you do just that. For starters, the function fgetc() reads a single character from a file. Here's the function prototype:

```
int fgetc( FILE *fp );
```

The single parameter is the FILE pointer returned by fopen(). fgetc() reads a single character from the file and advances the file position indicator one byte. If the file position pointer is already at the end of the file, fgetc() returns the constant EOF.

The function fgets(), which you made use of in Chapter 9, reads a series of characters into an array of chars. Here's the function prototype:

```
char *fgets( char *s, int n, FILE *fp );
```

You should already be comfortable using fgets(). In the previous uses, you passed stdin as the third parameter to fgets(). As it turns out, stdin is a FILE pointer automatically provided to your program when it starts. In this chapter, you'll open a file with fopen() and use fgets() to read from that file instead.

Here's an example using fopen(), fgetc(), and fclose():

```
#define kMaxBufferSize  200
FILE    *fp;
if ( (fp = fopen( "My Data File.txt", "r")) == NULL ) {
    printf( "Can not open file!!!\n" );
    exit(1);
}

printf( "File contents: " );
int c;
while ( (c = fgetc( fp )) != EOF ) {
    putchar( c );

fclose( fp );
```

This program attempts to open the file My Data File.txt for reading. If successful, it reads the characters in the file, one at a time, echoing each to standard out until it has read them all. When that happens, the next call to fgetc() returns the constant EOF, indicating that the file position indicator is now beyond the last byte of the file. It then closes the file.

The function fscanf() is similar to scanf(), but it reads from a specific file instead of standard in. Here's the prototype:

```
int fscanf( FILE *fp, const char* format, ... );
```

The first parameter is the FILE pointer returned by fopen(). The second parameter is a format specification embedded inside a character string. The format specification tells fscanf() what kind of data you want read from the file. The ... operator in a parameter list tells the compiler that zero or more parameters may follow the second parameter. Like scanf() and printf(), fscanf() uses the format specification to determine the number of parameters it expects to see. Be sure to pass the correct number of parameters or your program will get confused.

These are a few of the file access functions provided by the Standard Library. Want to look up something? Here's that link to that online Standard Library reference we keep mentioning:

`www.infosys.utas.edu.au/info/documentation/C/CStdLib.html`

Click the link to `<stdio.h>` at the top of the page. You might also want to take a look at *C, A Reference Manual* by Samuel Harbison and Guy Steele, especially Chapter 15, "Input/Output Facilities" (Prentice Hall, 2002).

In the meantime, here's an example program that uses the functions `fopen()` and `fgetc()` to open a file and display its contents.

PrintFile.xcodeproj

PrintFile opens a file named My Data File.txt, reads in all the data from the file one character at a time, and prints each character in the console window.

Open the *Learn C Projects* folder, go inside the folder 11.01 - PrintFile, and open the project PrintFile.xcodeproj.

To get PrintFile to do something useful, you'll need to supply it with a file to read. Launch the TextEdit application that came with OS X or your favorite plain text editor (it doesn't matter which). Create a new document and type something into it, as shown in Figure 11-1.

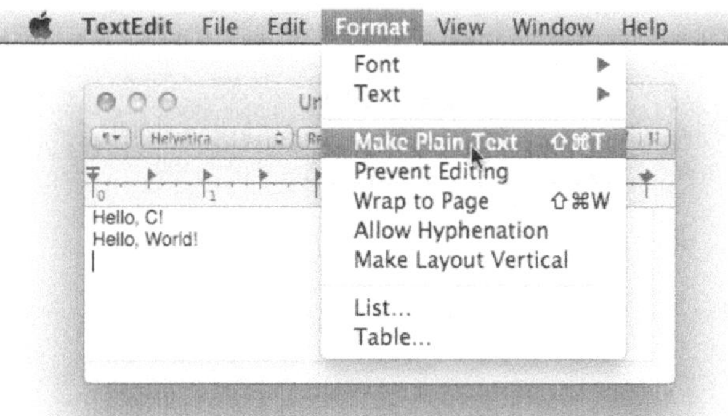

Figure 11-1. ***Creating the*** `My Data File.txt` ***file***

If you're using TextEdit, make sure you choose the ***Format* ➤ *Make Plain Text*** command so the document is saved as plain ASCII (or Unicode) characters. Choose the ***Save*** command, navigate to your *Desktop* folder, and save the file with the name `My Data File`, as shown in Figure 11-2. The application should add a `txt` extension automatically. If it doesn't, make sure the file name ends with `.txt`.

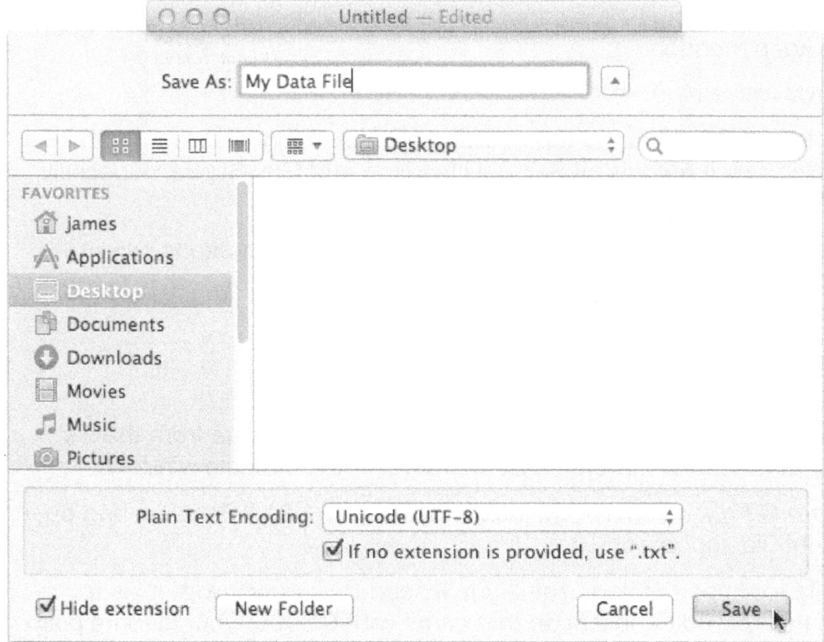

Figure 11-2. *Saving the* `My Data File.txt` *file*

> **NOTE:** The Finder may optionally hide a file's file name extension. While you see a file named "My Data File" in the Finder, the real name of the file is still *My Data File.txt*. Use the Finder's *`Get Info`* command to confirm this or to toggle the file's *Hide Extension* option.

Switch back to Xcode and run the project. Your console should look like the one in Figure 11-3.

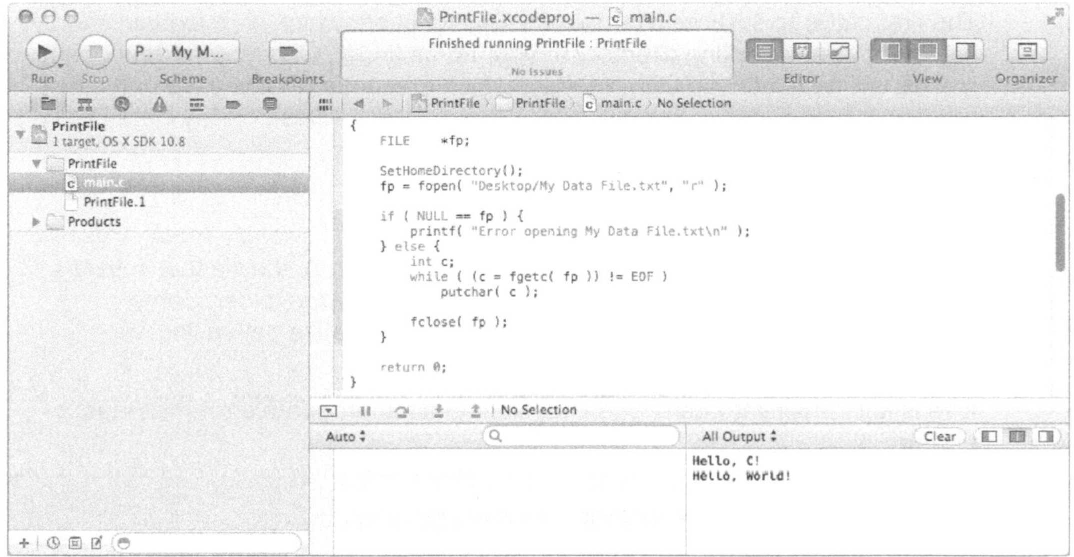

Figure 11-3. *PrintFile echoing* `My Data File.txt` *to the console*

Let's take a look at the source code.

Stepping Through the PrintFile Source Code

Open the source code file main.c by clicking its name in the project navigator. Take a minute to look over the source code. Once you feel comfortable with it, read on.

main.c starts off with some needed `#includes` and a function prototype.

```
#include <stdio.h>      // fopen(), fgetc(), fclose(), ...
#include <pwd.h>        // getpwuid()
#include <unistd.h>     // getuid()
void SetHomeDirectory( void );
```

The `<pwd.h>` and `<unistd.h>` headers, along with the `SetHomeDirectory()`, are so the program can find your home directory. Remember that we said most Standard Library functions don't recognized the ~ path? This is one way around that limitation.

`main()` defines an `fp` variable to point to the `FILE` pointer.

```
int main( int argc, const char * argv[] )
{
    FILE    *fp;
```

The first call is to SetHomeDirectory(). This function, which we'll explain shortly, sets the current working directory to your home folder. Once this is done, path names will be relative to this directory, which is exactly what is used in the next function call to fopen(). fopen() opens the file named Desktop/My Data File.txt for reading, and saves the file pointer in the variable fp:

```
SetHomeDirectory();
fp = fopen( "Desktop/My Data File.txt", "r" );
```

Because the path is a relative path (does not start with /), the file that fopen() will try to open is the My Data File.txt inside your *Desktop* folder. Some programs like to be explicit that they're specifying relative path using *./Desktop/My Data File.txt*. Both work just as well.

If fp is NULL, fpopen() can't open the file and an appropriate error message is printed.

```
if ( NULL == fp ) {
    printf( "Error opening My Data File.txt\n" );
} else {
```

If the file was opened successfully, you enter a while loop that continuously calls fgetc(), passing it the file pointer fp. fgetc() returns the next character in the file. The returned character is assigned to c. If c is not equal to EOF, putchar() is called, taking c as a parameter.

```
    int c;
    while ( (c = fgetc( fp )) != EOF )
        putchar( c );
```

putchar() prints the specified character to the console window. You could have accomplished the same thing by using printf().

```
printf( "%c", c );
```

NOTE: As you program, you'll often find multiple solutions to the same problem. Should you use putchar() or printf()? If performance is critical, pick the option that is more specific to your particular need. In this case, printf() is designed to handle many different data types. putchar() is designed to output a single character. Chances are, the source code for putchar() is simpler and more efficient than the source code for printf() when it comes to outputting one char. If performance is critical, you might want to use putchar() instead of printf(). If performance isn't critical, go with your own preference.

Once you're done, close the file by calling `fclose()`. Remember to always balance each call of `fopen()` with a corresponding call to `fclose()`.

```
        fclose( fp );
    }

    return 0;
}
```

SetHomeDirectory()

Now let's get back to that `SetHomeDirectory()` function. It's a deceptively simple bit of code, but it takes a little explaining.

First up is the `struct passwd` pointer. The `passwd struct` is defined by the Standard Library and contains fields that contain details about a user's account. These details include the user's account name, their ID, the group they belong to, their default shell, and so on. The particular field you're interested in is the `pw_dir` field; it contains the path name of the user's home directory.

```
void SetHomeDirectory( void )
{
    struct passwd *pw;
```

Given the appropriate user ID, the `getpwuid()` function will return a `struct passwd` pointer to this information for any user account on the system. You, however, are only interested in one user—the user that is currently logged in. You get that from the `getuid()` ("get user ID") function. Pass the value returned from `getuid()` to `getpwuid()`, and you now have lots of interesting information about, well, yourself!

```
    pw = getpwuid( getuid() );
```

The `chdir()` function changes the current working directory for the process. To make your home folder the current working directory, pass the `pw_dir` field to `chdir()`.

```
    chdir( pw->pw_dir );
}
```

And you're done! Those two lines of code are all that's needed to get the ID of the user that's running this program, look up some basic account information about that user, and use that information to set the current working directory to their home folder. That's pretty slick.

Writing Files

So far, you've learned how to open a file using `fopen()` and how to read from a file using `fgetc()`. You've seen, once again, that you can often use two different functions to solve the same problem. Now let's look at some functions that allow you to write data out to a file.

The Standard Library offers many functions that write data out to a previously opened file. This section will introduce three of them: `fputc()`, `fputs()`, and `fprintf()`.

`fputc()` takes an `int` holding a character value and writes the character out to the specified file. `fputc()` is declared as follows:

```
int fputc( int c, FILE *fp );
```

If `fputc()` successfully writes the character out to the file, it returns the value passed to it in the parameter `c`. If the write fails for some reason, `fputc()` returns the value `EOF`.

> **NOTE:** Calling `fputc( c, stdout )` is the same as calling `putchar( c )`. Writing a single character to standard out is such a common task that someone wrote the `putchar()` function so you don't have to write `fputc(c,stdout)` every time. These are called *convenience functions*. It's quite common to see several functions that can accomplish the same thing, but some have a less complicated set of parameters designed to make it easier to perform typical tasks. You can always switch to the more complicated function if you need to do something more unusual.

`fputs()` is similar to `fputc()`, but writes out a `NUL`-terminated string instead of a single character. `fputs()` is declared as follows:

```
int fputs( const char *s, FILE *fp );
```

`fputs()` writes out all the characters in the string but does not write out the terminating zero. If the write fails, `fputs()` returns `EOF`; otherwise, it returns a nonnegative number.

`fprintf()` works just like `printf()`. Instead of sending its output to the console window, `fprintf()` writes its output to the specified file. `fprintf()` is declared as follows:

```
int fprintf( FILE *fp, const char *format, ... );
```

The first parameter specifies the file to be written to. The second is the format specification text string. Any further parameters depend on the contents of the format specification string.

DVDFiler.xcodeproj

In Chapter 10 you ran DVDTracker, a program designed to help you track your DVD collection. The big shortcoming of DVDTracker is its inability to save your carefully entered DVD data. When you quit the program, the DVD information you entered gets discarded, forcing you to start over the next time you run DVDTracker.

The next program, DVDFiler, solves this problem by adding two special functions to DVDTracker. `ReadFile()` opens a file named DVD Data.txt, reads in the DVD data from the file, and uses that data to build a linked list of `DVDInfo` structs. `WriteFile()` writes the linked list back out to the file.

Open the Learn C Projects folder, go inside the folder 11.02 - DVDFiler, and open the project DVDFiler.xcodeproj. Check out the DVDFiler workspace window shown in Figure 11-4. Notice that this project is made up of several source files: main.c, DVDInfo.c, DVDInfo.h, DVDFile.c, and DVDFile.h. Your project can contain as many source code files as you like. Just make sure that only one of the files has a function named `main()`, since that's where your program will start.

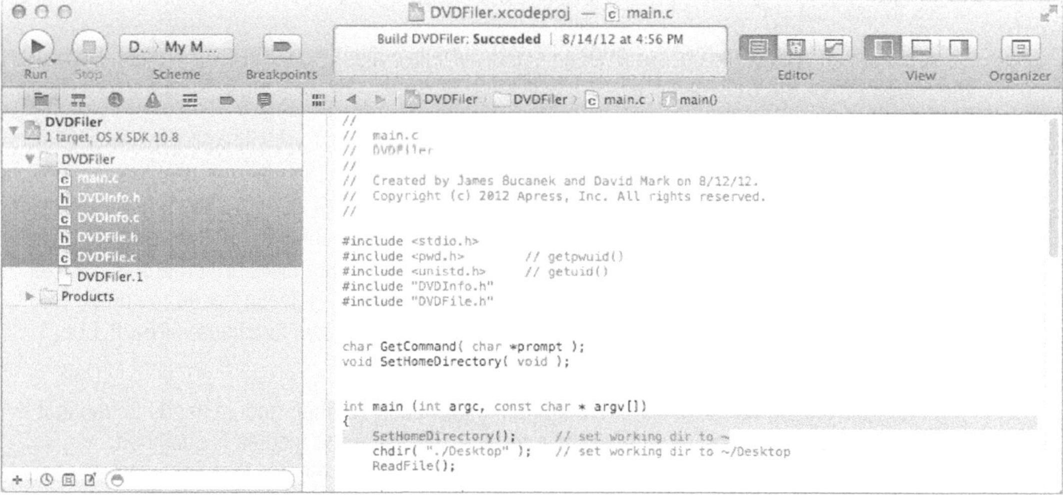

Figure 11-4. *The DVDFiler project window*

The file main.c starts out very much like the main.c from Chapter 10's DVDTracker program. Most of the functions that deal with `DVDInfo` structs are, however, curiously absent. These have been moved into the DVDInfo.c source file. A new file, DVDFile.c, contains the new functions that read and write the DVD data file. So why were these functions moved into different source files? Read the "Modular Code" sidebar to find out.

MODULAR CODE

The *DVDFiler* program has gotten just complicated enough that we decided to break it up into *modules*. As your programs get bigger, you'll want to begin organizing them so they don't get out of hand.

Programs are kind of like companies. As a business grows, it will often reorganize itself into divisions, departments, subsidiaries, and so on. That's because one person can't manage everything that's going on in a big organization. The company creates departments within itself, each of a manageable size. Department A can work with department B to accomplish things, but department A doesn't have to worry about the details of department B (who they hire, what their vacation schedule is, and so on).

Similarly, programmers organize large applications into functions, modules, objects, and frameworks. C programmers refer to each `.c` file as a *module*. Generally, a module has two parts: its *implementation* and its *interface*. The implementation is the code in the `.c` file that does the work. Its interface, usually in a matching `.h` file, is the information another module needs to use that code.

To see this in practice, look at the DVDFile.h and DVDFile.c files in the DVDFiler project. Here's the content from the DVDFile.h file:

```
extern void WriteFile( void );
extern void ReadFile( void );
```

It only contains two function prototypes: `WriteFile()` and `ReadFile()`. They are marked with the `extern` keyword to indicate that these functions are implemented in another module. If you look at the DVDFile.c source file, you'll see those two functions, but there are others as well. All of that code is part of the implementation. A function (like `main()`) doesn't need to know anything else about the code in DVDFile.c except that it contains two functions—`ReadFile()` and `WriteFile()`—that will load or save the list of DVDs.

The interface should be the minimum amount of information another module needs to use that module. Broadly speaking, the simpler the interface, the better the module is designed. Returning to the recipe analogy from Chapter 3, a well-designed module that bakes cakes should have a simple interface. It should include functions to order a cake and pick it up. There should be constants for the flavors to choose from. But the details of the cake-baking process (where the flour is purchased, the ratio of sugar and egg whites) are details that only the implementation is concerned about.

As you design your functions and modules, think of them as a bakery or any other kind of retail service. Your customer (often called the client) is the code that will be using the services of your module. The module's interface is your storefront—menu, counter, and cash register. This is all the information your customer needs. What goes on in the kitchen (mixing equipment, recipes, inventory, and so on) is the implementation. That stays hidden.

Programmers do this so they can change the details of how a module works without upsetting the rest of the program. As long as the "contract" of the interface remains the same, the implementation of the module can be safely changed without introducing new bugs. In *DVDFiler* you could, for example, change the file name of the DVD Data.txt file or its format; you could even decide to store your DVD data in an SQLite database instead of a single file. But `ReadFile()` and `WriteFile()` function will, from `main()`'s perspective, still do exactly what they do now.

The `getpwuid()` function you used in the PrintFile project is a perfect example of this kind of evolution. When UNIX was very young, the `getpwuid()` function got its data from a simple ASCII text file, no more complicated than the DVD Data.txt file you're using today. As UNIX matured, account information got more complex. Today, OS X stores its user account information in a sophisticated database that uses encryption, shadow passwords, and can even connect to other databases over a network. So while the format and location of the user account information has changed a dozen times over the past four decades (the implementation), the `getpwuid()` function (the interface) still works the same as it always has.

Exploring *DVD Data.txt*

Before you run DVDFiler, take a quick look at the file DVD Data.txt. You'll find it in the 11.02 – DVDFiler folder, although the file is not part of your Xcode project. Drag the DVD Data.txt file to your desktop using the Finder (hold down the Option key before dropping it to make it a copy). The DVDFiler application will expect to find this file in your *Desktop* folder. If you don't have a copy of DVD Data.txt don't worry, the program will still work.

Take a look at the DVD Data.txt file. You can open it using TextEdit (as you did earlier), your favorite text editor, Xcode (drag the DVD Data.txt file from the desktop and drop it into the Xcode icon in the dock), or just preview it in the Finder.

At first glance, the contents of the file may not make much sense, but the text does follow a well-defined pattern:

```
The Ring
Scariest movie ever!
9
Tenacious D in The Pick of Destiny
Jack Black rocks, Kyle Gass can play
7
Hot Fuzz
Simon Pegg sleeper - must see!
8
```

The file is organized in clusters of three lines each. Each cluster contains a one-line DVD title, a one-line DVD comment, and a one-line numerical DVD rating.

> **NOTE:** The layout of your data files is as important a part of the software design process as the layout of your program's functions. The DVD Data.txt file follows a well-defined pattern. As you lay out a file for your next program, think about the future. Can you live with one-line DVD titles? Do you want the ability to add a new DVD field, perhaps the date of the DVD's release? The time to think about these types of questions is at the beginning of your program's life, during the design phase.

Running DVDFiler

Run DVDFiler. The console window will appear, prompting you for a q, n, or l:

```
Enter command (q=quit, n=new, l=list):
```

Type "l", and press Return to list the DVDs currently in the program's linked list. If you need a refresher on linked lists, now would be a perfect time to turn back to Chapter 10.

```
Title:   The Ring

Comment: Scariest movie ever!

Rating:  9

--------

Title:   Tenacious D in The Pick of Destiny

Comment: Jack Black rocks, Kyle Gass can play

Rating:  7

--------
```

```
Title:   Hot Fuzz
Comment: Simon Pegg sleeper - must see!
Rating:  8
---------
Enter command (q=quit, n=new, l=list):
```

While Chapter 10's DVDTracker started with an empty linked list, DVDFiler starts with a linked list built from the contents of the DVD Data.txt file. The DVDs you just listed should match the DVDs you saw when you viewed the DVD Data.txt file.

Let's add a fourth DVD to the list. Type "n", and press Return:

```
Enter command (q=quit, n=new, l=list): n
-----------
Enter DVD Title: The Shawshank Redemption
Enter DVD Comment: #1 movie of all time on imdb.com
Enter DVD Rating (1-10): 10
-----------
Enter command (q=quit, n=new, l=list):
```

Next, type l to make sure your new DVD made it into the list:

```
Enter command (q=quit, n=new, l=list): l
-----------
Title:   The Ring
Comment: Scariest movie ever!
Rating:  9
--------
Title:   Tenacious D in The Pick of Destiny
Comment: Jack Black rocks, Kyle Gass can play
Rating:  7
--------
Title:   Hot Fuzz
Comment: Simon Pegg sleeper - must see!
Rating:  8
--------
```

```
Title:   The Shawshank Redemption
Comment: #1 movie of all time on imdb.com
Rating:  10
------------
Enter command (q=quit, n=new, l=list):
```

Finally, type “q”, and press Return. This causes the program to write the current linked list back out to the file DVD Data.txt. To prove this write worked, run DVDFiler one more time. When prompted for a command, type “l” to list your current DVDs. You should find your new DVD nestled at the bottom of the list. Let’s see how this works.

Creating a New Source Code File

Before you move on to the program itself, let’s take a look at the process of creating a new source code file in your project. When Xcode creates a command line tool project, it adds a single source code file, main.c. To add a new file, start by clicking the *Source* folder in the project navigator (shown on the left, behind the sheet, in Figure 11-5). This tells Xcode where you want the new file placed.

Select ***New* > *File*** from the ***File*** menu. The new file template dialog will appear, as shown in Figure 11-5. To add a C source file, select the C and C++ template group (under OS X) on the left side of the window. Then choose *C File* from the list that appears and click the *Next* button. In the next screen that appears, you’ll be asked to name the file and choose what project targets it belongs to. You’ll probably have only one target, which should be selected. When you’re good to go, click the *Create* button.

> **NOTE:** If you just added new files to the DVDFiler project, be sure to select any files you added, and press the Delete key to remove the files from the project.

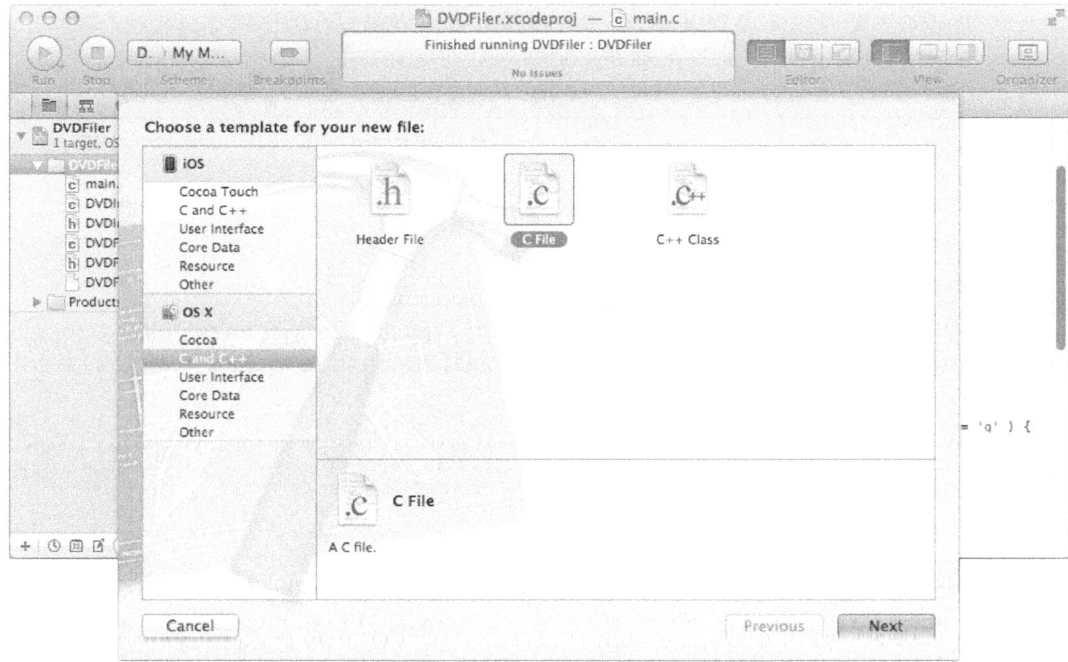

Figure 11-5. *New file template dialog*

If you want to add a header (`.h`) file to your project, repeat the same steps but choose the *Header File* template instead of the *C File* template.

We now return to the program previously in progress.

Stepping Through the DVDFiler Source Code

Now we're going to walk you through the DVDFiler source one file at a time. Since the project is broken up into modules, we'll tackle each file one at a time, describing the functions therein. So here we go.

main.c

The main.c file contains three functions: `main()`, `GetCommand()`, and `SetHomeDirectory()`. These functions are in main.c because they facilitate running the overall program, and they don't belong in either of the other two modules. Sometimes determining where a function belongs is a matter of figuring out where it doesn't belong.

main.c starts out with code you'll instantly recognize. It includes the headers it needs, including the project headers DVDInfo.h and DVDFile.h, and it declares prototypes for the other two functions.

```
#include <stdio.h>
#include <pwd.h>        // getpwuid()
#include <unistd.h>     // getuid()
#include "DVDInfo.h"
#include "DVDFile.h"

char GetCommand( char *prompt );
void SetHomeDirectory( void );
```

With the preliminaries out of the way, `main()` gets started. The first thing it does is set the working directory to your *Desktop* folder and read the contents of the DVD Data.txt file.

```
int main (int argc, const char * argv[])
{
    SetHomeDirectory();
    chdir( "./Desktop" );
    ReadFile();
```

The working directory is set in two steps. `SetHomeDirectory()` sets the working directory to your home directory. The call to `chdir()` then changes it again, this time to your *Desktop* folder. The path passed to `chdir()` can be a relative path, based on the current working directory.

We'll take a look at `ReadFile()` later.

Next, `main()` enters a loop and processes commands until the user enters the 'q' command. This is almost identical to the DVDTracker program from Chapter 10.

```
    char command;
    while ( (command = GetCommand( "Enter command (q=quit, n=new, l=list)" ) )
!= 'q' ) {
        switch( command ) {
            case 'n':
                AddToList( ReadStruct() );
                break;
            case 'l':
                ListDVDs();
                break;
        }
        printf( "\n----------\n" );
    }
```

When the loop exits (because the user quit the program), you call `WriteFile()` to write any changes made to the linked list (like a new DVD!) back out to the DVD Data.txt file.

```
    WriteFile();
```

The program says farewell and exits.

```
    printf( "Goodbye...\n" );
    return 0;
}
```

We won't go over the `GetCommand()` or `SetHomeDirectory()` functions, because they are pretty much identical to those used in the PrintFile and DVDTracker programs you've already worked through.

DVDInfo.h

Now take a look at the *DVDInfo.h* header file. It contain `#defines` and `struct` declarations that should be familiar to you.

```
#define kMaxTitleLength     256
#define kMaxCommentLength   256

struct DVDInfo
{
    char            rating;
    char            title[ kMaxTitleLength ];
    char            comment[ kMaxCommentLength ];
    struct DVDInfo  *next;
};
```

Following those definitions are the function prototype for the public functions of the `DVDInfo` module. Public functions are ones you expect other modules to call to accomplish tasks. They are marked as extern so that, when included in main.c or DVDFile.c, the compiler knows that the source for these functions are in another module.

```
extern struct DVDInfo *ReadStruct( void );
extern void AddToList( struct DVDInfo *curPtr );
extern void ListDVDs( void );
extern struct DVDInfo *NewDVDInfo( void );
extern char *TrimLine( char *line );
```

The DVDInfo.h header also declares a global variable that keeps track of the beginning of the linked list. The `extern` keyword at the beginning of the declaration tells the C compiler that the actual variable is defined elsewhere, probably in a different module. You can declare `extern` functions and variables wherever you want, but you can only define them once. In this case, the gHeadPtr is defined in DVDInfo.c. But any module that includes this header can access that global, because the compiler now knows about it.

```
extern struct DVDInfo *gHeadPtr;
```

DVDInfo.c

Now let's move on to the DVDInfo.c file. It starts with the usual includes:

```
#include <stdlib.h>
#include <stdio.h>
#include <string.h>
#include <ctype.h>
#include "DVDInfo.h"
```

Following that are the actual definitions of the gHeadPtr and gTailPtr variables.

```
struct DVDInfo *gHeadPtr;
static struct DVDInfo *gTailPtr;
```

Notice that the gTailPtr is defined to be static, and an extern declaration for it isn't included in the DVDInfo.h header. We've decided that gTailPtr should be a "private" variable, only accessible to the functions in the *DVDInfo* module. The static keyword limits the scope of this variable to this module only. Functions in other modules can't use it, even if they wanted to.

So why did we do this? Because the other modules (main.c and DVDFile.c) don't need it and we might decide to do something different in the future. If you looked at the exercise answers for DVDTracker in Chapter 10, you've already seen an alternate version of DVDTracker that doesn't use a gTailPtr variable. By making gTailPtr "private," we're free to change what it means or even get rid of it without affecting how the rest of the program works. Does that make sense? Let's move on.

Most of the remaining code in *DVDInfo* is almost identical to what's in the DVDTracker program. The functions ReadStruct(), AddToList(), ListDVDs(), and TrimLine() are only slightly changed, so we won't rehash them again here. The only thing that's really different is the new function NewDVDInfo():

```
struct DVDInfo *NewDVDInfo( void )
{
    return calloc( 1, sizeof( struct DVDInfo ) );
}
```

We found ourselves writing the statement malloc(sizeof(struct DVDInfo)) over and over. When you find yourself writing the same code again and again, consider turning it into a function that can be more easily reused. Now all of those calls to malloc() can be replaced with a call to NewDVDInfo(). In addition, we changed the implementation so that it calls `calloc()` instead of `malloc()`; now the returned `DVDInfo struct` is pre-initialized with zeros, which just seems so much more tidy. (We're going to revisit `NewDVDInfo()` in the next chapter, where you'll learn another reason why we made this change.)

DVDFile.c

Now (finally!) you get to the functions that read and write the DVD Data.txt file. You've already seen the DVDFile.h header file. This defines the interface to the *DVDFile* module, which is pretty straightforward.

```
extern void WriteFile( void );
extern void ReadFile( void );
```

Open up the DVDFile.c file and we'll step through the implementation. It starts out with these `#includes`:

```
#include <stdbool.h>
#include <stdlib.h>
#include <stdio.h>
#include <unistd.h>
#include "DVDInfo.h"
#include "DVDFile.h"
```

Most of these you've already experienced. Note that DVDFile.c includes both DVDInfo.h and DVDFile.h files. The DVDInfo.h gives the module all of the knowledge it needs to use the functions in the *DVDInfo* module as well as defining the `DVDInfo` struct and related constants. The DVDFile.h provides the prototype for the `WriteFile()` and `ReadFile()` functions. Next up are the constants.

```
#define kDVDFileName    "DVD Data.txt"
```

The only constant defined is the name of the DVD Data.txt file. Since this is defined in the `.c` file, it's a "private" constant—the other modules don't know what the file name is. This means you can change the name without affecting code in other modules.

In addition to `ReadFile()` and `WriteFile()`, there's also the `ReadStructFromFile()`, which needs a prototype.

```
static struct DVDInfo *ReadStructFromFile( FILE *fp );
```

`ReadStructFromFile()` is not intended to be called from other modules. It's only used by `ReadFile()` to create and read one record from the data file. By including the `static` keyword, you restrict the scope of this function to this module. In other words, you can't call this function from another module—even if you tried, C won't let you. By making `ReadStructFromFile()` a "private" function, you can later decide to change how it works, or even replace it with something else.

WriteFile()

WriteFile() is the first of the two big file functions. It's called by main() just before the program quits to save whatever is in the DVDInfo struct list to a file. After declaring a couple of variables, it opens the DVD Data.txt file for writing.

```
void WriteFile( void )
{
    FILE            *fp;
    struct DVDInfo  *infoPtr;

    fp = fopen( kDVDFileName, "w" );
```

The fopen() function returns a FILE pointer to the newly open, and created, file. Passing "w" for the mode parameter means you're going to rewrite this file. If the file exists, it's first deleted and replaced with a new (empty) file. If the file didn't exist, a new (empty) file is created. After fopen() returns, you know the file exists, is empty, and is ready to write data to.

The for loop steps through the linked list, setting infoPtr to point to the first struct in the list, moving it to point to the next struct, and so on, until infoPtr is equal to NULL. Since the last struct in the list sets its next pointer to NULL, infoPtr will be equal to NULL after the last struct in the list.

```
    for ( infoPtr=gHeadPtr; infoPtr!=NULL; infoPtr=infoPtr->next ) {
```

Take a good long look at this for loop statement. It contains all of the statements needed to traverse a linked list. The initialization statement starts by setting infoPtr to the first (head) struct in the list. The loop's condition statement stops when pointer to the next struct is NULL. After one DVDInfo struct has been processed, the increment statement gets the pointer to the next struct in the list, or NULL if there are no more. If everything in the statement makes sense to you, you are well on your way to becoming a C master.

Each time through the list, you call fprintf() to print the title string followed by a carriage return and then the comment string followed by a carriage return. Remember, each of these strings was NUL-terminated, a requirement if you plan on using the %s format specifier. The rating field is output using the %d specifier.

```
        fprintf( fp, "%s\n", infoPtr->title );
        fprintf( fp, "%s\n", infoPtr->comment );
        fprintf( fp, "%d\n", infoPtr->rating );
    }
```

Once you finish writing the linked list into the file, you close the file by calling fclose().

```
    fclose( fp );
}
```

One thing you'll notice is that if there are no DVD structs in the list (gHeadPtr is NULL), then WriteFile() creates an empty file; the file is created, nothing is written to it, and then it's closed.

ReadFile()

ReadFile() is the complement to WriteFile(). It's called when main() starts. It opens the file DVD Data.txt for reading. If you can't open the file—presumably because the file doesn't exist—it prints an error message and returns, leaving the list empty.

```
void ReadFile( void )
{
    FILE *fp;

    if ( ( fp = fopen( kDVDFileName, "r" ) ) == NULL ) {
        printf( "Could not open file!\n" );
        printf( "File '%s' expected to be in %s.\n", kDVDFileName, getwd(NULL)
);
        return;
    }
```

If the file could not be opened, main() outputs an informative message that includes the name of the file and what directory the ReadFile() function is expecting it to reside in. It gets the later from the getwd() ("get working directory") function.

With the file open, a while loop starts that runs as long as ReadStructFromFile() continues to return new DVDInfo structs. ReadStructFromFile() attempts to read one record from the file and uses that data to fill in a DVDInfo struct. If successful, it returns the completed DVDInfo struct, which the loop then adds to the linked list.

```
    struct DVDInfo *infoPtr;
    while ( ( infoPtr = ReadStructFromFile( fp ) ) != NULL ) {
        AddToList( infoPtr );
    }
```

ReadStructFromFile() returns NULL when it hits the end of the file. In that case, the loop stops and the file is closed again.

```
    fclose( fp );
}
```

ReadStructFromFile()

ReadStructFromFile() does all of the heavy lifting for ReadFile(). It uses a funky form of fscanf() to read in the first two DVDInfo fields. The format descriptor %[^\n]\n tells fscanf() to read characters from the specified file as long as the characters are in that set, and then to read a \n character and stop. The characters scanned by the %[^\n] specifier are copied in to a char array. scanf() always tacks on a terminating '\0' so the variable is a valid C string.

CHARACTER SET NOTATION

The square brackets inside a format specifier ([abcdef]) give you much greater control over scanf(). It's called *character set notation* and it appears repeatedly in C, the shell, and elsewhere. In its simplest form, it lists the characters in the set. A span of characters can be indicated by a range ([1-9]). Characters are then tested to see if they're either in the set or not. The set [aeiou] defines the set of common vowels. "a" is in that set, "b" isn't. The set [a-z] is all of the lowercase letters. The set [a-zA-Z0-9_] is the set of all letters (upper and lowercase), the digits zero through nine, and the underscore character. The character "7" is in that set. The character "." isn't.

The ^ (caret) is the inverse set modifier. When it's the first character in a set, it inverts the set. The set [^a-z] is every character that *is not* a lower case letter. The character "7" is in that set, "k" isn't. The set [^\n] is the set of every character that is not a newline character. Every ASCII character is a member of that set except, obviously, the newline character.

ReadStructFromFile() begins by defining a few variables. It then allocates a new DVDInfo struct, using the function defined in DVDInfo.c.

```
static struct DVDInfo *ReadStructFromFile( FILE *fp )
{
    struct DVDInfo  *infoPtr;
    int             num;
    bool            successful = true;

    infoPtr = NewDVDInfo();
```

The fscanf() statements that follow attempt to read the three lines that make up a DVD record in the DVD Data.txt file and convert those lines of text into the three field variables that make up a DVDInfo struct.

fscanf() returns the constant EOF if it attempts to read past the end of the file. The code checks the return value of each call to fscanf(). If any of them return EOF, the variable successful is changed from true to false.

```
if ( fscanf( fp, "%[^\n]\n", infoPtr->title ) == EOF )
    successful = false;
if ( fscanf( fp, "%[^\n]\n", infoPtr->comment ) == EOF )
    successful = false;
if ( fscanf( fp, "%d\n", &num ) == EOF )
    successful = false;
else
    infoPtr->rating = num;
```

Reading the rating value requires two steps. Since the rating value in the struct is a char, you can't use the %d specifier to read it directly—a %d expects an int pointer. The solution is to define a temporary int variable named num and scan in the value there. If the fscanf() is successful, store the value of num into the rating field. Maybe rating should have been an int? It's something to consider for a future version of your program.

The code then checks its success variable. If it's false, then at least one of the fscanf() calls encountered the end of the file. In this situation, the DVDInfo struct that was just allocated is freed—you don't want to create a memory leak—and the function returns NULL, indicating to the caller that the record couldn't be read.

```
if ( ! successful ) {
    free( infoPtr );
    infoPtr = NULL;
}
```

If everything went OK, the function returns the freshly allocated and filled-in DVDInfo struct to the caller.

```
return infoPtr;
```

Every function that reads data from a file (fscanf(), fgetc(), fgets(), and others) advances the file position indicator. The first time ReadStructFromFile() is called, the file position is at the beginning of the file (offset 0). After the first call, the file position will be pointing to the first character of the fourth line of the file—the title of the second DVD. Each subsequent call to ReadStructFromFile() reads one record and advances to the next one in the file, until they have all been read.

That's it! Everything needed to save your DVD collection data in a text file, and read that information back in the next time DVDFiler starts, was contained in those three functions. Congratulations, your first foray into data persistence was a success.

Fancier File Manipulation

Now that you've mastered the basics of file reading and writing, there are a few more topics are worth exploring. We'll start off with a look at some additional file opening modes.

The Update Modes

So far, you've encountered the two basic file opening modes: "r" and "w". There's also an "a" (append) mode that s like "w" (write) but doesn't erase any existing data. Each of these modes has a corresponding update mode, specified by adding a plus sign (+) to the mode. The three update modes, "r+", "w+", and "a+" allow you to open a file for both reading and writing.

A great chart in Harbison and Steele's *C: A Reference Manual* summarizes these modes quite nicely. My version of the chart is found in Table 11-1. Before you read on, take a minute to look over the chart to be sure you understand the different file modes.

Table 11-1. *Rules Associated with Each of the Basic File Opening Modes*

Mode Rules	"r"	"w"	"a"	"r+"	"w+"	"a+"
Named file must already exist	Yes	No	No	Yes	No	No
Existing file's contents are lost	No	Yes	No	No	Yes	No
Read OK	Yes	No	No	Yes	Yes	Yes
Write OK	No	Yes	Yes	Yes	Yes	Yes
Write begins at end of file	No	No	Yes	No	No	Yes

TIP: Most implementations of `fopen()`, including the one in OS X, will allow you to add an "x" to the end of the "w" or "a" modes, as in "w+x". This modifier will prevent the file from being opened if the file already exists. It's most useful when you want to use the "w" mode to write out a brand new file, but don't want to accidentally delete an existing file if one's already there.

Random File Access

So far, each of the examples presented in this chapter have treated files as a sequential stream of bytes. When *DVDFiler* read from a file, it started from the beginning of the file and read the contents, one byte at a time or in larger chunks, but from the beginning straight through until the end. This sequential approach works fine if you intend to read or write the entire file all at once. As you might have guessed, there is another model.

Instead of starting at the beginning and streaming through a file, you can use a technique called *random access*. The Standard Library provides a set of functions that let you reposition the file position indicator to any location within the file, so that the next read or write you do occurs exactly where you want it to.

Imagine a file filled with 100 `int`s, each of which was 4 bytes long. The file would be 400 bytes long. Now, suppose you wanted to retrieve the tenth `int` in the file. Using the sequential model, you would have to do ten reads to get the tenth `int` into memory. Unless you read the entire file into memory, you'll constantly be reading a series of `int`s to get to the `int` you want.

Using the random access model, you would first calculate where in the file the tenth `int` starts. Then, you'd jump to that position in the file and read just that `int`. To move the file position indicator just before the tenth `int`, you'd skip over the first nine `int` (9 * 4 = 36 bytes).

Using Random Access Functions

There are a number of useful functions you'll need to know about in order to randomly access your files. `fseeko()` moves the file position indicator to an offset you specify, relative to either the beginning of the file, the current file position, or the end of the file.

```
int fseeko( FILE *fp, off_t offset, int whence );
```

You pass your `FILE` pointer as the first parameter, a file position offset as the second parameter, and `SEEK_SET`, `SEEK_CUR`, or `SEEK_END` as the third parameter. The offset value is relative to the position indicated by the `whence` argument: `SEEK_SET` represents the beginning of the file, `SEEK_CUR` represents the current position, and `SEEK_END` represents the end of the file (in which case you'll probably use a negative offset).

DinoEdit.xcodeproj

The *DinoEdit* project is a simple example of random file access. It allows you to edit a series of dinosaur names stored in a file named *My Dinos.data*. Each name stored in *My Dinos.data* is allotted 20 characters in the file. A segment of a file that contains a value (or a group of related values) is typically referred to as a *record*. The position of each record in *My Dinos.data* is easy to calculate: multiple the record number by 20. The byte at that position, and the next 19 bytes, contains one name. Let's take *DinoEdit* for a spin.

Open the Learn C Projects folder, go inside the folder 11.03 - DinoEdit, and open the DinoEdit.xcodeproj document. Also inside that folder you'll find a My Dinos.data file. Move or copy that file to your desktop. DinoEdit will count the number of dinosaur names in the file My Dinos.data and will use that number to prompt you for a dinosaur number to edit.

```
Enter number from 1 to 5 (0 to exit, a to add):
```

> **NOTE:** If you don't have a copy of *My Dinos.data*, the program will still work, but you'll have to supply all of the names. Run the program and type "a" and Return, and then enter a new dinosaur name (up to 20 characters long), and press Return again. Repeat this three or four more times so you'll have a few names stored in the file.

Since the file My Dinos.data has five records, enter a number from 1 to 5. If you type the number 3, for example, DinoEdit will fetch the third dinosaur name from the file and ask you to enter a new name for the third dinosaur. When you type a new name, DinoEdit will overwrite the existing name with the new name.

```
Dino #3: Gallimimus
Enter new name (optional): Euoplocephalus
```

You can elect not to replace the name by pressing Return without entering in a new name.

Either way, DinoEdit will loop around prompt you to enter another dinosaur number. Reenter the same number, so you can verify that the change was made in the file.

```
Enter number from 1 to 5 (0 to exit): 3
Dino #3: Euoplocephalus
Enter new name (optional): Gallimimus
Enter number from 1 to 5 (0 to exit): 0
```

Goodbye...

It's not the most efficient dinosaur editor we've used, but it'll do. Let's take a look at the source code.

Stepping Through the DinoEdit Source Code

The file *DinoEdit.h* starts off with a few `#defines`. `kDinoRecordSize` defines the length of each dinosaur record. Note that the dinosaur file doesn't contain any carriage returns, just 100 bytes (5 * 20 = 100) of pure dinosaur pleasure!

`kMaxLineLength` defines the length of an array of chars you'll use to read in any new dinosaur names. `kDinoFileName` is the name of the dinosaur file.

```
#define kDinoRecordSize     20
#define kMaxLineLength      100
#define kDinoFileName       "My Dinos.data"
```

Now take a look at the main.c file. It starts with the usual `#includes`, along with an `#include` for DinoEdit.h so that you get to use those `#defines`.

```
#include <stdlib.h>
#include <stdio.h>
#include <sys/stat.h>
#include <string.h>
#include <stdbool.h>
#include <string.h>
#include <ctype.h>
#include <pwd.h>
#include <unistd.h>
#include "DinoEdit.h"
```

Next come the function prototypes for the functions in main.c:

```
void    SetHomeDirectory( void );
int     GetNumber( void );
int     GetNumberOfDinos( void );
void    ReadDinoName( int number, char *dinoName );
bool    GetNewDinoName( char *dinoName );
void    WriteDinoName( int number, char *dinoName );
char    *TrimLine( char *line );
```

TIP: If you ever want to find out which of the functions you call are dependent on a particular `#include` file, comment out the `#include` directive. Xcode will pretty quickly pop up error indicators next to the functions you just made it forget about.

> If you type a function and Xcode tells you it doesn't know what you're talking about, look up the documentation for that function (hold down the Option key and then double-click on the name of the function). Most man pages indicate which header file that function is defined in. Add that `#include` to your program and you are back in business.

main()

`main()` starts out by setting the working directory, so that the data file (*My Dinos.data*) will be where you expect it to be.

```
int main(int argc, const char * argv[])
{
    SetHomeDirectory();
    chdir( "./Desktop" );
```

Two variables are defined: one to hold the number entered by the user, and a second to hold the dinosaur name read from the file.

```
    int     number;
    char    dinoName[ kDinoRecordSize+1 ];
```

`main()` basically consists of a loop that first prompts for a dinosaur number at the top of the loop and processes the selection in the body of the loop.

```
    while ( (number = GetNumber()) != 0 ) {
```

`GetNumber()` prompts for a dinosaur number between 0 and the number of dinosaur records in the file. If the user types 0, you drop out of the loop and exit the program. If they type the letter "a" as a response, you allow them to add a new record to the end of the file.

If the body of the loop starts, then the user either entered a dinosaur number or an "a". The `if` statement executes if it's the former, reading one dinosaur name and printing it out.

```
        if ( number>0 ) {
            ReadDinoName( number, dinoName );
            printf( "Dino #%d: %s\n", number, dinoName );
```

The alternative is that the user entered "a", in which case `GetNumber()` will return -1 and the `else` statement will execute. This does nothing more than set the dinosaur number for the new record.

```
        } else {
            number = GetNumberOfDinos() + 1;
```

```
    }
```

GetNewDinoName() prompts the user for a new dinosaur name and captures what the user types in. GetNewDinoName() returns true if a name is entered and false if the user just presses return. If the user entered a name, you'll pass it on to WriteDinoName(), which will write the name to the file, either overwriting an existing name or creating a new record.

```
        if ( GetNewDinoName( dinoName ) )
            WriteDinoName( number, dinoName );
```

The loop continues until the user enters 0. The loop stops, main() bids the user adieu, and the program stops.

```
    }
    printf( "Goodbye..." );
    return 0;
}
```

GetNumber()

GetNumber() starts off with a call to GetNumberOfDinos(). As its name implies, GetNumberOfDinos() looks at the dinosaur file and returns the number of records in the file. It then starts a loop that prompts the user to enter a command. If the response is 0, an existing dinosaur record number, or the letter "a", the function returns 0, the record number, or -1, respectively. If it's anything else, the loop repeats until it likes the answer.

```
int GetNumber( void )
{
    int number, numDinos;

    numDinos = GetNumberOfDinos();

    do {
        printf( "Enter number from 1 to %d (0 to exit, a to add): ",
               numDinos );

        char lineBuffer[ kMaxLineLength ];
        fgets( lineBuffer, sizeof(lineBuffer), stdin );
        number = atoi( TrimLine(lineBuffer) );

        if ( number==0 && *TrimLine(lineBuffer)=='a' )
            return (-1);
    } while ( (number < 0) || (number > numDinos) );

    return number;
}
```

GetNewDinoName()

The GetNewDinoName() function is also not terribly complicated. You've used variations of this code in several earlier projects. It prompts the user to type in a dinosaur name, reads those characters into a buffer, strips off any whitespace, and copies the result to the dinoName parameter, making sure the name is not more than kDinoRecordSize characters long. (Remember that the buffer to hold a name that long must be one character longer, for the NUL termination character.) GetNewDinoName() returns true if the user typed something on the line, and false if they didn't.

```
bool GetNewDinoName( char *dinoName )
{
    char    line[ kMaxLineLength ];

    printf( "Enter new name (optional): " );
    fgets( line, kMaxLineLength, stdin );
    strlcpy( dinoName, TrimLine(line), kDinoRecordSize+1 );

    return ( dinoName[0] != '\0' );
}
```

GetNumberOfDinos()

GetNumberOfDinos() starts your file management adventure. GetNumberOfDinos() determines the number of dinosaur records by examining the overall length of the file and dividing that number by the length of one dinosaur name record. It uses a function named stat() that returns lots of information about a file and copies that into a stat struct, defined by the Standard Library.

```
int GetNumberOfDinos( void )
{
    struct stat fileStats;

    if ( stat( kDinoFileName, &fileStats ) != 0 )
        return 0;

    return fileStats.st_size / kDinoRecordSize;
}
```

If stat() was able to collect the information about the file, it copies that into the stat struct (at the address you supplied in the second argument) and returns a value of 0. If something goes wrong—most likely because the file doesn't exist—it returns some other value.

If the file doesn't exist, `GetNumberOfDinos()` returns 0 to the caller. This makes sense—no file, no dinosaurs.

If the file does exist, the total length of the file will be copied to the `st_size` field. Dividing that number by `kDinoRecordSize` calculates the total number of whole dinosaur name records in the file. The sample file that accompanies this book is 100 bytes long, meaning there are 5 (100÷20) records.

ReadDinoName()

Next up is the `ReadDinoName()` function. This function reads one dinosaur record and returns it, as a `NUL` terminated string, to the caller. It starts by defining a few variables and then opening the file for reading:

```
void ReadDinoName( int number, char *dinoName )
{
    FILE    *fp;
    off_t   positionOfRecord;

    fp = fopen( kDinoFileName, "r" );
```

The next step is to calculate the position of the desired record in the file. Your dinosaurs are numbered starting at 1, but file positions—like memory addresses, array indexes, and just about everything else in computers—start at 0. So 1 is subtracted from the number and then multiplied by `kDinoRecordSize`. If number was 1, the `positionOfRecord` will be 0 ((1-1)•20). If the number is 3, the position will be 40 ((3-1)•20), and so on.

```
    positionOfRecord = (number-1) * kDinoRecordSize;
```

Now the exciting part! The `fseeko()` function is called to set the file position indicator to the desired offset in the file. The `SEEK_SET` constant tells `fseeko()` that the offset is from the beginning of the file (position 0). If you want to jump right to a specific offset in a file, use the `SEEK_SET` constant.

```
    fseeko( fp, positionOfRecord, SEEK_SET );
```

> **TIP:** If you want to know where the file's file position indicator is currently at, call the `ftello()` function. The `rewind()` convenience function sets the file position to 0, the same as `fseeko(fp,0,SEEK_SET)`.

Now that the file position indicator is positioned at the first character of your dinosaur's name, all that's left to do is to read those characters into memory. The `fread()` function is similar to the `fgetc()` function you've already used. But instead of reading one character, it reads as many as you want. Unlike `fscanf()`

and `fgets()`, it doesn't look at the characters or try to interpret them in any way. It simply gets however many bytes you tell it to read and copies those to the memory address you pass in the first parameter.

```
    fread( dinoName, kDinoRecordSize, 1, fp );
```

The second parameter is the number of bytes (characters) `fread()` is going to copy. The third parameter is a multiplier for the second argument. If you want to read four `long ints`, for example, you can write `fread(array,sizeof(long int),4,fp)`. Since you only want one 20-character record, pass 1. The last argument is the `FILE` pointer.

After `fread()` returns, 20 bytes—starting from the position set by `fseeko()`—will have been copied into `dinoName`. To make sure `dinoName` is a properly `NUL` terminated C string, a `'\0'` character is stored in the 21st element of the array. This will make more sense when you get to the `WriteDinoName()` function.

```
    dinoName[ kDinoRecordSize ] = '\0';
```

There's nothing left to do except close the file and return to the caller.

```
    fclose( fp );
}
```

WriteDinoName()

`WriteDinoName()` opens the file for reading and writing using the "append" mode. Since you used a mode of "a+" instead of "w+", you won't lose the contents of *My Dinos.data* (in other words, *My Dinos.data* won't be deleted and re-created). Alternatively, you could have used the "r+" mode. That would have also opened it for reading and writing and wouldn't have erased it. But if the file didn't already exist, that mode would fail and you couldn't create a new dinosaur database from scratch. Some of these decisions can be tricky!

`WriteDinoName()` follows the same pattern as `ReadDinoName()`. It starts by opening the file, calculating the offset of the record, and moving the file position indicator to that offset.

```
void WriteDinoName( int number, char *dinoName )
{
    FILE    *fp;
    off_t   positionOfRecord;
    fp = fopen( kDinoFileName, "a+" );
    positionOfRecord = (number-1) * kDinoRecordSize;
    fseeko( fp, positionOfRecord, SEEK_SET );
```

The real difference is that it writes out the supplied name instead of reading it in, using the `fwrite()` function.

```
    fwrite( dinoName, kDinoRecordSize, 1, fp );
```

fwrite() takes the same parameters as fread(). The only thing that changes is the direction of the transfer.

It's really important to understand that fwrite() and fread() do not treat the bytes in dinoName as a C string, or any other kind of value. For fwrite(), the memory address you pass in the first parameter is just a sequence of bytes. What those bytes represent is entirely up to you.

In this program, those bytes represent a C string stored in a char array. If the name is 8 characters long, then those 8 characters, the terminating NUL character, and 11 unknown char values will be copied to the file. When those same 20 bytes are read back in, the dinoName array is filled with an 8 character name, a terminating NUL character, and 11 more bytes you don't care about because they're beyond the NUL character that marks the end of the string.

If the name is exactly 20 characters long, then those 20 characters will be written to the file. When you read them back into the dinoName array, only the twenty characters are transferred. That's why the ReadDinoName() function included the statement dinoName[kDinoRecordSize] = '\0' so in the special case of a 20-character dinosaur name, the array will still contain a properly terminated C string.

Which brings us to some questions that you might have about those 11 unknown characters. Should you care what their values are? They could be any value, but since nothing beyond the NUL character is important to your C string, their values don't matter. So why do we write them? It's important because of the way fseeko() works. If you started at position 0 and wrote just the 8 characters and the NUL, your file would be 9 characters long. When you write the next dinosaur name, your program will try to seek to position 20, but it can't because your file is only 9 characters long. fseeko() can't seek beyond the end-of-file (EOF) position of the file. So you must write these extra bytes so the file's length is always an even multiple of 20.

Now that you understand all of that, let's wrap up the WriteDinoName() function. The only thing left to do is close the file and return.

```
    fclose( fp );
}
```

Wrap Up

Finally, there's the TrimLine() function, which you've seen before. And that's the entire *DinoEdit* program. It's quite a bit different than earlier programs, and it uses files in a completely different way. So let's take this opportunity to talk about that file and other ways to use `fread()` and `fwrite()`.

Text vs. Data Files

You probably noticed that the file extension of the *My Dinos* file is `data` instead of `txt`. That's because it isn't a text file. A text file contains nothing but ASCII or Unicode characters. You can open it, and likely edit it, using any text file editor such as TextEdit or Xcode.

The *My Dinos* file is different. You can't open *My Dinos* and edit it like a text file. It's a file format that you created. You've used the generic `data` extension to indicate to the world that this file contains data that is not organized in a standarized format, like text or JPEG. As you learned in the `WriteDinoName()` function, the bytes between names might not even be valid characters. Programmers call these *junk* or pad bytes.

Sometimes it's really useful to look at the data in your files. But since My Dinos.data isn't a text file, how do you do that? It turns out that there's a handy command line tool for doing just that. Are you really surprised?

The `hexdump` command will format the raw bytes of any file and output them to standard out as hexadecimal digits. Actually, it can output data in all kinds of ways, but one hex number per byte is the default. Our favorite `hexdump` switch is `-C`. This switch outputs each byte both as a hexadecimal value and (if possible) the corresponding ASCII character. Figure 11-6 shows the My Dinos.data file being "dumped" in the Terminal window.

```
james — bash — 80×24
Last login: Fri Aug 17 16:00:38 on ttys000
mac-pro:~ james$ hexdump -C ~/Desktop/My\ Dinos.data
00000000  54 2d 52 65 78 00 00 00  00 00 00 00 00 00 00 00  |T-Rex...........|
00000010  00 00 00 00 42 61 72 6e  65 79 00 00 00 00 00 00  |....Barney......|
00000020  00 00 00 00 00 00 00 00  47 61 6c 6c 69 6d 69 6d  |........Gallimim|
00000030  75 73 00 00 00 00 00 00  00 00 00 00 56 65 6c 6f  |us..........Velo|
00000040  63 69 72 61 70 74 6f 72  00 00 00 00 00 00 00 00  |ciraptor........|
00000050  41 70 61 74 6f 73 61 75  72 75 73 00 00 00 00 00  |Apatosaurus.....|
00000060  00 00 00 00                                       |....|
00000064
mac-pro:~ james$
```

Figure 11-6. *Hexdump of My Dinos.data*

The file offsets, shown on the left column in Figure 11-6, are also in hexadecimal. So offset 00000020 is actually 32 (2•16+0) in decimal. That's why the second dinosaur name ("Barney") appears to start at offset 00000014, because that's actually offset 20 (1•16+4) in the file.

Working with Endians

So far in this book, the only thing you've written and read are single-byte characters. Characters are very portable because they're self-contained: a character is a character no matter where it goes.

We alluded to the fact that `fread()` and `fwrite()` don't regard the pointer they are given as a specific kind of variable (`char` array, `int`, `struct`, and so on). To `fread()` and `fwrite()`, the buffer pointer is just a sequence of bytes in memory. What those bytes represent is entirely up to you to decide.

There are subtle issues that arise when you start writing more complex variables, like `int`s and `struct`s, using `fwrite()` to a file that might be read back on a different computer. Data written to file has *persistence*. It has to make sense not only to your computer, but other computers, and even computers that haven't been built yet. We've already warned you that other CPUs have different lengths of `int`s and pointers, but they can also differ in how the bytes in an `int` are organized.

There are generally two ways to organize the bytes in an `int`. If you go all the way back to Chapter 4, in the section "Bytes and Bits," you learned that an `int` value is stored as individual bits. Each bit represents one power-of-2. A multi-byte `int` is stored in successive bytes. A 64-bit `int`, for example, is stored in eight bytes. The first byte stores the bits 0 through 7, the second byte stores the bits 8 through 15, and so on, up to the last byte that stores the bits 56 through 63. The complication is that some CPUs store the low bit byte in the first address of the `int`, and some CPUs store the high bit byte in the first address of the `int`.

Which "end" of the integer holds the first byte defines the CPU's *endianness*. (Try saying that quickly, three times.) When the first address of an `int` stores the least significant bits (bits 0-7) of the number, it is called *little-endian* byte order. When the first address of the `int` stores the most significant bits of the number, it is called *big-endian* byte order.

Figure 11-7 shows the same integer number (1,234) stored in a four byte `int` located at address 836. On the left, the value is stored on a CPU that uses little-endian order. On the right, the CPU uses big-endian order.

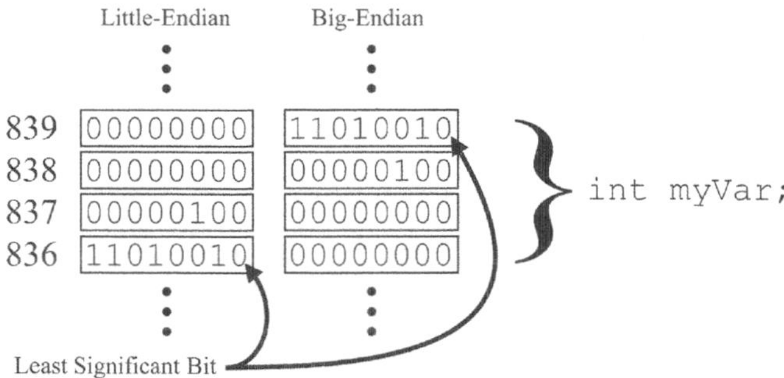

Figure 11-7. *The value 1,234 stored in little-endian and big-endian order*

If you wrote this integer to a file on a little-endian computer using `fwrite()`, and then read it in using `fread()` on a big-endian computer, the number would change from 1,234 to 3,523,477,504. This is probably not what you want. There are two techniques to make sure your number makes sense to other computers.

The first is to use the fixed-width integer types we told you about in Chapter 8. These will ensure that the length of the integer you write to a file will be the same size no matter what CPU is running your program.

The other is to use the byte-order swapping functions supplied by the operating system. Here's a code fragment that uses both techniques to safely write an integer value to a file so it always has the same size and byte order:

```
#include <libkern/OSByteOrder.h>
...

int myInt;
...

int32_t safeInt;
safeInt = OSSwapHostToBigInt32( myInt );
fwrite( &safeInt, sizeof(safeInt), 1, fp );
```

This code uses a byte-swapping function to rearrange the order of the bytes in the variable `myInt` from whatever order your CPU uses to big-endian order and then stores it in a known-width integer variable. The 4 bytes of that variable are then written to the file. The number that's in the file will always be in big-endian order no matter what the native ("host") order of your CPU is.

To read that number back from the file, reverse the process, like so:

```
int32_t safeInt;
fread( &safeInt, sizeof(safeInt), 1, fp );
myInt = OSSwapBigToHostInt32( safeInt );
```

The functions defined in `<libkern/OSByteOrder.h>` are supplied by OS X (rather than the Standard Library). OS X supplies a rich set of byte-swapping functions that are easy to understand, and we like that. The functions names are almost self-explanatory. The `OSSwapHostToBigInt32()` swaps the byte order of the 32-bit integer argument from the host byte order to big-endian order. The `OSSwapBigToHostInt32()` function reverses the process. These functions are all "smart"; they'll only reorder the bytes if you're running on a little-endian CPU. If your CPU uses big-endian byte ordering already, these functions don't change anything.

We're going to finish up this chapter by giving the RomanNumeral project from Chapter 9 a tune-up. In the process, you're going to learn a little more about writing command-line tools and some interesting facts about what it means to be a "file."

Making RomanNumeral a Better Tool

In Chapter 9 you wrote a command-line tool that would convert decimal number arguments into Roman numerals. Now you're going to make that tool even more useful—well, as useful as a Roman numeral converter can be.

Most command-line tools that process files use a well-known convention for getting the data it's going to work on. If one or more arguments passed to the program are paths to files, the tool processes those files and exits. If there are no command-line arguments, then the program processes the characters from its standard in character stream instead. Check the man pages for tools like `cat`, `sort`, `grep`, and others. They all work this way.

When you design your command-line tool to behave this way, it becomes a flexible member of the command-line community. It can be directed to perform its magic on existing files, or become one step in a chain of commands that's transforming a data stream. Consider the command

```
MyTool ~/Desktop/MyFile.txt | sort --unique
```

This command directs `MyTool` to do whatever-it-does on the file MyFile.txt. The results are piped from `MyTool`'s standard out to the `sort` tool's standard in. Because `sort` wasn't given any file arguments, it sorts the output of `MyTool`. Contrast that with this command:

```
sort --unique ~/Desktop/MyFile.txt | MyTool
```

This time the `sort` tool reads MyFile.txt and outputs the sorted results to `MyTool`. Instead of reading a file, `MyTool` reads its standard in and outputs the results. Depending on what `MyTool` does, the results could be strikingly different.

Stepping Through RomanNumeral.xcodeproj

Open the *RomanNumeral.xcodeproj* project for Chapter 11. You'll find it in the *11.04 - RomanNumeral* folder. We'll only cover the differences between this project and the one in Chapter 9. If you have questions about what didn't change, refer back to the description of the first version.

The new version starts out with two additional `#include` directives.

```
#include <stdbool.h>
#include <ctype.h>
```

In addition to the existing `NumberToRomanNumeral()` function, there are two new ones.

```
void PrintUsageAndExit( void );
void ReplaceNumbersInStream( FILE* stream );
```

main()

The `main()` function has been almost completely rewritten. It starts by looping through the arguments passed to it from the command line.

```
int main( int argc, const char * argv[] )
{
    int i;
    for ( i=1; i<argc; i++ ) {
```

Remember that `argv[0]` is the path to the tool, and not an argument, so the loop ignores that. Next it checks for the existence of a particular string.

```
        if ( strcmp( argv[i], "-h" ) == 0 )
            PrintUsageAndExit();
```

The `strcmp()` function takes two string pointers and returns 0 if the two are identical. It's the string equivalent of a comparison operator. If it does return 0, then the user passed "-h" as one of the arguments. Your program looks for that switch and prints out a usage message and stops.

Many command-line tools will output a so-called *usage message* whenever the arguments it gets don't make sense, there's some kind of problem, or it is asked to. The usage message should contain a very brief explanation of how the tool should be used and what arguments it understands. It's also common that a command will recognize a switch (typically `-h`, for "help") that will output its usage message so the user can read it.

If the argument isn't the -h switch, main() tries to convert it to a number. If successful, it converts the decimal number to a roman numeral and prints that, just like the version from Chapter 9.

```
        int number;
        number = atoi( argv[i] );
        if ( number != 0 ) {
            if ( number >= kMinDecimalNumber && number <= kMaxDecimalNumber ) {
                char romanNumeral[ kMaxRomanNumeralLength+1 ];
                NumberToRomanNumeral( number, romanNumeral );
                printf( "%d = %s\n", number, romanNumeral );
```

If the argument appears to be a number, but isn't in the range of numbers the program can convert, it prints the usage message and stops.

```
            } else {
                PrintUsageAndExit();
            }
```

Now you're at the business end of the program. If the argument wasn't the -h switch, and it wasn't a number, assume it's a file and try to open it.

```
        } else {
            FILE* fp = fopen( argv[i], "r" );
            if ( fp != NULL ) {
                ReplaceNumbersInStream( fp );
                fclose( fp );
```

If the argument is a path to a file that can be opened, the file is opened and passed to the ReplaceNumbersInStream() function. This function does most of the work for the tool, and we'll get to it in a moment.

If the file couldn't be opened, then the argument wasn't a path to readable text file. In that case, you again output the usage message and exit.

```
            } else {
                PrintUsageAndExit();
            }
        }
    }
```

Once the loop works through all of the arguments, one at a time, it stops and the code checks for one more condition. If no arguments were passed on the command line, the ReplaceNumbersInStream() function is run anyway, but this time it's passed the stdin constant.

```
    if ( argc == 1 )
        ReplaceNumbersInStream( stdin );
```

So if the user types numbers or file paths as arguments to the command, those numbers and files are converted. If they don't enter any arguments, the tool looks to standard input as the source of data. With that, the `main()` function is complete.

```
    return 0;
}
```

PrintUsageAndExit()

The `PrintUsageAndExit()` function is very straightforward.

```
void PrintUsageAndExit( void )
{
    fprintf( stderr, "Usage: RomanNumeral [ -h ] [ number | file ... ]\n" );
    fprintf( stderr, "\t-h      prints this message and exits\n" );
    fprintf( stderr, "\tnumber  between %d and %d\n", kMinDecimalNumber,
kMaxDecimalNumber );
    fprintf( stderr, "\tfile    file echoed to stdout, replacing decimal
numbers\n" );
    fprintf( stderr, "\tif no arguments are specified, replaces decimal numbers
in stdin\n");
    exit( 1 );
}
```

It's traditional that error and usage messages are sent to the standard error stream, not the standard output stream. That's why `PrintUsageAndExit()` uses `fprintf(stderr,`… instead of `printf(`….

ReplaceNumbersInStream()

Now you're at the heart of the program, `ReplaceNumbersInStream()`. It starts out with a `while` loop that's going to read every character in the input stream.

```
void ReplaceNumbersInStream( FILE* stream )
{
    int c;
    while ( (c=fgetc(stream)) != EOF ) {
```

It looks at each character to determine if it's a decimal digit. It does this using the `isdigit()` function.

```
        if ( isdigit( c ) ) {
```

If it is a digit, your program assumes that this is the first character in an integer number. It will use `fscanf()` to convert those digits into a numeric value, but before it does that it calls a very unusual function.

```
            ungetc( c, stream );
```

The problem with character streams is this: the only way to figure out if you want to do something with the next character is to read it, and once you've read it, it's no longer in the stream. If you decide it's not a character you want to process, you're stuck—the character has already been read. `ungetc()` lets you undo the last (and only the last) `fgetc()`, essentially putting the last character read back into the stream as if you'd never read it. With the first digit of the number back in the stream, you can now use `fscanf()` to scan the next integer number from the stream.

```
        long long int number;
        fscanf( stream, "%lld", &number );
```

The number read is now checked to see if it's one that your program can convert (remember that `NumberToRomanNumeral()` can only convert numbers between 1 and 3,999). If it can, the number is converted and output to standard out. The effect is that the number scanned is replaced by its Roman numeral equivalent.

```
        if ( number >= kMinDecimalNumber && number <= kMaxDecimalNumber ) {
            char romanNumeral[ kMaxRomanNumeralLength+1 ];
            NumberToRomanNumeral( (int)number, romanNumeral );
            printf( "%s", romanNumeral );
```

If the number can't be converted, the same number is echoed.

```
        } else {
            printf( "%lld", number );
        }
```

Notice that the number scanned is a `long long int`. That's in case the number encountered in the stream is a really big one, it won't get messed up because it wouldn't fit in a regular `int`.

Finally, there's the `else` clause for the original `isdigit()` decision. If the character read from the stream isn't a digit, it gets echoed verbatim and the loop goes back around and gets the next character.

```
        } else {
            putchar( c );
        }
    }
}
```

Now that you've seen all of `ReplaceNumbersInStream()`, let's review what it does. It reads all of the characters in a stream. All characters that aren't numbers get output, unchanged, to standard out. Any sequence of characters that appears to be a number is converted from decimal to Roman numerals, assuming the value of the number is within an acceptable range. If not, the decimal number is output (unchanged).

This kind of logic is called a *filter* or a *transformation*. It looks for patterns in the incoming character stream. If it finds what it's looking for, it changes it somehow. Everything else gets passed through unchanged.

Putting RomanNumeral Through Its Paces

You're going to reuse the trick from Chapter 9 to quickly test your new command-line tool from the Terminal window.

1. Build the *RomanNumeral* project (Product ➤ Build for ➤ Running).
2. Open a Terminal window and position it next to the project workspace window.
3. Open the *Products* folder in the project navigator and drag the *RomanNumeral* file into the Terminal window.
4. Type several numbers (this example uses 97, 431, and 1995) and press Return.

Your modified *RomanNumeral* tool will run and convert the three arguments, as shown in Figure 11-8. This is no different than the tool you built in Chapter 9.

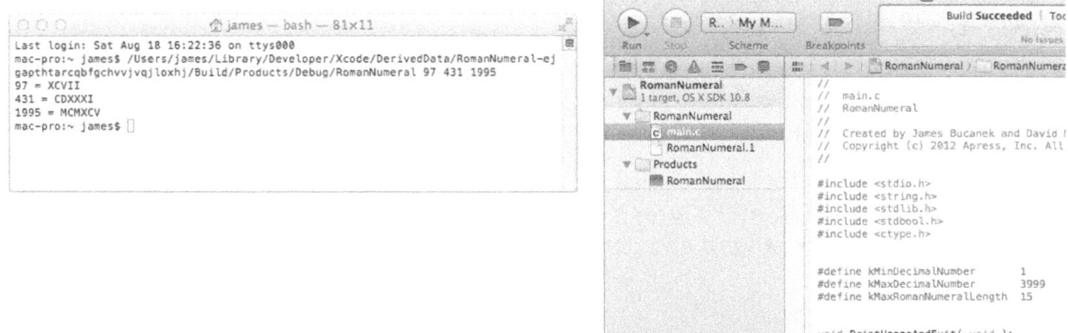

Figure 11-8. ***Testing the modified RomanNumeral project in the Terminal***

Repeat the first three steps to run your tool again, but this time specify a file that contains some numbers. When we gave the program the argument `~/Desktop/DVD\ Data.txt`, this is the output we saw (note that we shortened the path to the `RomanNumeral` tool in the book so it's easier to read):

```
mac-pro:~ james$ /some/path/to/RomanNumeral ~/Desktop/DVD\ Data.txt
The Ring
Scariest movie ever!
IX
Tenacious D in The Pick of Destiny
Jack Black rocks, Kyle Gass can play
VII
Hot Fuzz
Simon Pegg sleeper - must see!
VIII
…
```

Instead of trying to convert the argument "~/Desktop/DVD\ Data.txt" in a Roman numeral, the program read the file and converted all of the numbers it found there into Roman numerals. For this file, it was the rating value (1-9) given to each movie that got changed.

One last bit of fun. In the Terminal window, start a line with this

```
ls -l ~ |
```

and then drag your *RomanNumeral* tool into the Terminal window again. This will create a command that pipes the output of the `ls -l` ("list directory") command to the standard in of your *RomanNumeral* tool. Press Return to see the results.

```
mac-pro:~ james$ ls -l ~ | /some/path/to/RomanNumeral
total 0
drwx------+ XV james  staff   DX Aug XVII XV:LI Desktop
drwx------+  VI james  staff   CCIV Jul XXVII XI:XXXIII Documents
drwx------+  IV james  staff   CXXXVI Jul XXV XXII:XXVIII Downloads
drwx------@ XLIII james  staff  MCDLXII Aug X XVI:XXXIX Library
drwx------+  III james  staff   CII Jul XXV XXII:XXVIII Movies
drwx------+  III james  staff   CII Jul XXV XXII:XXVIII Music
drwx------+ XVI james  staff   DXLIV Aug XVIII XVIII:XXX Pictures
drwxr-xr-x+  IV james  staff   CXXXVI Jul XXV XXII:XXVIII Public
drwxr-xr-x   III james  staff   CII Jul XXVII XI:XXXV bin
```

How hilarious is that? All of the numbers in your home folder's directory listing were replaced with Roman numerals! This is UNIX for gladiators.

But seriously, we had you update the RomanNumeral project for a couple of reasons. The first was to make this über-useful program play well with the other command-line tools, and so that it acts more like a well-rounded command—complete with a usage message and a help switch.

The other, more important, reason is so you'd get a taste of using file objects (yes, we used the word "object") interchangeably.

File System Objects

What's really remarkable about the `ReplaceNumbersInStream()` function is that there is only one. This single function takes one `FILE` pointer parameter and uses it to read the characters in a file, or a character stream, or even your keyboard, and then translate that information and send the results to standard out.

This works because UNIX is built around the philosophy that "everything is a file." Thus, an open `FILE` pointer could refer to a regular file, a directory, a character stream, a pipe from another program, your keyboard, the console pane in Xcode, a Terminal window, or a network communications socket. The beauty here is that no matter what it is, if you want to send one character to that file/pipe/console/window/socket you call `fputc()`.

> **NOTE:** Don't believe us? Run your *RomanNumeral* program again, from the command line or Xcode, by itself without any arguments. It will start running and pause, waiting for you to type something since your keyboard is now connected to its standard in. Start typing words and numbers, pressing Return in between, and see what happens.

This kind of interchangeability is called *abstraction*, and it's a key concept in object-oriented programming. It's great for programmers because you don't have to write four different versions of `ReplaceNumbersInStream()`—one that reads from a file, one that reads from a pipe, one that reads from your keyboard, and one that reads from a network port. You write one function that reads from a `FILE` and then you pass it any kind of open `FILE` you can get your hands on.

Well, almost. The one thing you need to know about abstraction is that just because all of these different things can be represented by a `FILE`, it doesn't mean they all act exactly the same. Each `FILE` has a set of properties that limit what you can do with it.

Some properties are implicit. For example, the standard input character stream connected to your program is the reading-end of a FIFO pipe. You can read one or more characters from that pipe using functions like `fgetc()`, `fgets()`, `fscanf()`, and plain old `fread()`. What you can't do is try to send it characters using functions like `fputc()` or `fprintf()`. You can't write characters to standard input or read characters from standard output.

Other properties of a `FILE` can be specified. When you open a file for reading only (mode "r"), you can't use any function that would write bytes to that file, such as `fputc()` or `fprintf()`. Conversely, if you opened a file for writing only (mode "w"), you can't read anything from it.

Knowing these limitations lets you design functions that work on a variety of input and output sources. Your `ReplaceNumbersInStream()` function is designed so that it will work on any input source that supplies a sequence of characters. Thus, it works for files, pipes from other programs, and your keyboard. The functions in `DinoEdit` that randomly read and replace sections of a file would, however, not work if you tried to use `stdin` or `stdout`.

What's Next?

You learned about files and streams. You now know how to create, open, and close a file. You then moved on to reading and writing files and you explored the file opening modes. Finally, you learned all about random file access. Along the way you learned how to set the current working directory, get the length of a file, and a little about making a well-behaved command-line tool.

Chapter 12 is going to look at what could go wrong and what you should do about it.

CHAPTER 11 EXERCISES

1. Can you find the syntax error or logical mistake in each of these code fragments?

   a.
```
FILE *fp;
fp = fopen( "w", "My Data File.txt" );
if ( fp != NULL )
    printf( "The file is open." );
```

b.
```
int myData = 7;
FILE *fp;
fp = fopen( "My Data File", "r" );
fscanf( "Here's a number: %d", &myData );
```

c.
```
FILE *fp;
char *line;
fp = fopen( "My Data File.txt", "r" );
fscanf( fp, "%s", &line );
```

d.
```
FILE *fp;
char line[100];
fp = fopen( "My Data File", "w" );
fscanf( fp, "%s", line );
```

2. Write a program that reads in a text file with the following format:

- The first line in the file contains a single number. Call it x.
- All subsequent lines contain a list of x numbers, separated by spaces or tabs.

For example, if the first number in the file is 6, all subsequent lines will have six numbers per line, like this:

```
6
100 200 300 400 500 600
```

There is no limit to the number of lines in the file.

After reading in each line of numbers, it should echo those numbers to standard out, separated by tab characters. It should keep reading and printing lines until it hits the end of the file.

You can print each number as you encounter it or, for extra credit, allocate an array of `int`s large enough to hold one line's worth of `int`s and then pass that array to a function that prints an `int` array.

Chapter 12

Handling Errors

You've learned a lot about C. You've learned about arrays, pointers, dynamically allocating memory, and accessing files. Along the way, we've hinted at some of the pitfalls you have to look out for: not storing values outside the dimension of an array, not using uninitialized pointers, checking `fgetc()` for `EOF`, and so on. But we haven't really been doing this in any systematic way

Error handling is a general term for writing code so it still works when unexpected things happens. And believe us, unexpected things will happen. Your code isn't battling for survival in the inevitable zombie apocalypse, but your program does need to defend itself from erroneous values, unexpected circumstances, and (yes) even hackers. And like the hero in *Zombieland*, you can survive by following a few simple rules.

The rules we've developed for you are based on *programming best practices*. Best practices are guidelines—born of experience and research—that help you write better programs. There are entire books dedicated to this subject. Instead of going into the theory and history, we've chosen a simple set of rules to get you started. They encompass some good habits that might not be obvious to new programmers, but will generally reduce the number of bugs in your program, both now and in the future. As you gain more programming experience, you'll learn the rationale behind these rules and even circumstances where they might not apply. But for now, we want you to follow these rules. We're sure they'll get you started in the right direction.

But before we get to those rules, let's talk about what happens when things go wrong.

Murphy's Law

> *Anything that can go wrong will go wrong.*
>
> \- Edward Murphy, Jr.

Forget everything you've heard about Murphy's Law. The real Murphy's Law has nothing to do with the perverseness of the universe or buttered toast's ability to land, wrong-side-down, on your carpet.

Major Edward A. Murphy, Jr. was an aerospace engineer who worked on safety-critical systems for the United States Air Force. While the exact origins of his law are somewhat murky, his famous proclamation sums up an extremely important principle of engineering: if there is any possibility that some element of an event will fail, then it *will* fail if that event is repeated often enough.

Pouring a glass of iced tea seems like a safe and repeatable task. It might have an error rate of less than 1:100,000. In other words, if you pour 100,000 glasses of iced tea, 99,999 of those will go flawlessly and one won't—the tea misses, you knock over the glass, or whatever. That sounds like phenomenally good odds. You could easily go your entire life, pouring one or two glasses of iced tea every day, and never have a mishap.

Now take a group of 10,000,000 people pouring a single glass of iced tea each day. With an error rate of 1:100,000 there will be, on average, over 100 spilled glasses of tea every day—*every day!* Murphy's law tells us that, unless there is absolutely zero chance that something can go wrong, then no matter how remote that chance, if you continue to do that thing, and wait long enough, it will (eventually) go wrong.

What does that have to do with programming? If there's a possibility that something can go wrong, then given enough time and enough repetitions, that thing will go wrong. It could be an index that is beyond the dimension of an array. It could be a file that is missing or contains data you weren't expecting. If your code is not written to anticipate and deal with those potential problems, one day your program will behave badly. It could crash, stop working, act strangely, freeze, or even destroy important data.

Take the *DVDFiler* program you wrote in the last chapter. Imagine a hard drive glitch that caused a bad bit of data to be written to the first record in the *My DVD Data.txt* file. If the wrong amount of data was written to that first record, the remaining DVD records would all be read incorrectly. Once that happened, when the data was written back out, it would wipe out your entire database of DVD titles! Now the chances of that are slim, but remember Murphy's Law. If there was only a one-in-a-million chance that the first record of the file was messed up somehow, that sounds pretty reliable. But if you sell your DVD cataloguing program to 10,000,000 happy Mac users, odds are about 10 of them will be sending you really angry messages—every day!

As you program, you need to consider what could go wrong and code defensively so that if something does go wrong, your program will still work (within reason), or at least fail gracefully, do something predictable and not cause more problems. Programs that recover gracefully from the unexpected are said to be *fault tolerant*, and that's your goal for this chapter. Here are the rules.

Rule #1: Never Assume

Making assumptions leads to poor programming. Code that depends on an assumption is setting itself up for a fall should that assumption turn out to be erroneous one day. Remember Murphy's Law; if your code depends on an assumption, and there's any possibility that the assumption could be wrong, then your code will eventually fail.

So what is an assumption? An assumption is any fact about a value or variable that your code depends on being true to function properly. As long as the fact is true, your code will function as you intended it. But as soon as that fact is no longer true, who knows what will happen?

Assumptions About Variables

Here's a simple example of an assumption we already told you to avoid. In the *DVDTracker* program in Chapter 10, the `ReadStruct()` function prompts the user to enter a DVD title and then copies the reply into a `DVDInfo struct`.

```
char buffer[ 500+1 ];
printf( "Enter DVD Title:  " );
fgets( buffer, 501, stdin );
strlcpy( infoPtr->title, TrimLine( buffer ), 256 );
```

This code makes a couple of assumptions. The `fgets(buffer,501,stdin)` statement assumes that the `buffer` array is at least 501 characters long. Now that is not a terrible assumption to make because the declaration for `buffer` is only two lines earlier. You can easily see that `buffer` is defined as `char buffer[ 500+1 ]`.

Let's say that one day in the distant future you decide to change the size of the `buffer` to 300+1. If you make that change, you should also change the 501 in fgets() to 301 or fgets() might write beyond the end of your buffer. Remember Murphy's Law—except this time it applies to you, not your program. If you write your code so that you must remember to update two things to keep it working, then one day you're going to forget to make both changes and your previously working program will now have a bug in it.

Instead, write the code like this:

```
char buffer[ 500+1 ];
…
fgets( buffer, sizeof( buffer ), stdin );
```

This code removes the assumption you made about the size of buffer. Instead, you get the actual size of the array from the compiler, so no matter what dimension you change buffer to, the fgets() function will still be safe. One day you could even decide to declare buffer using a variable dimension (so that it is a difference size every time the function runs) and the call to fgets() will still be safe!

The last line of code also makes an assumption:

```
strlcpy( infoPtr->title, TrimLine( buffer ), 256 );
```

It assumes that infoPtr->title is a char array that is 256 characters long. If you go find the declaration of struct DVDInfo in dvdTracker.h, you can confirm that this is true.

```
#define kMaxTitleLength 256
struct DVDInfo
{
    char  rating;
    char title[ kMaxTitleLength ];
    …
```

But this definition is in another file. It would be really easy to change the declaration of kMaxTitleLength and forget to go through all of your other source files looking for any code that assumed it was still 256. You can make the code a little better by writing it like this:

```
strlcpy( infoPtr->title, TrimLine( buffer ), kMaxTitleLength );
```

This code, at least, no longer assumes that kMaxTitleLength is 256. But it still assumes that title is declared as char title[kMaxTitleLength]. If title changed to char title[kSomeOtherLength], then (again!) your code in *main.c* would be broken. The safest statement you can write is

```
strlcpy( infoPtr->title, TrimLine( buffer ), sizeof( intoPtr->title ) );
```

Again, you use the compiler to remove any assumptions from your code. Now, no matter how title is defined, the call to strlcpy() will behave itself.

Check Ranges

Another trap programmers fall into is assuming that a particular variable is always within a reasonable range. What "reasonable" is depends on the code, but it's very tempting to write your code for the values that work and forget about the values that won't.

Here are two good examples from the *Factor* project from Chapter 7, both of which are in the `Factor()` function. Let's start with the value of the number parameter.

```
bool Factor( int number, int *firstFactorPtr, int *secondFactorPtr )
{
    int factor;
    for ( factor = sqrt(number); factor > 1; factor-- ) {
        if ( (number % factor) == 0 ) {
            break;
        }
    }
```

This looks like perfectly safe code. Given any number, the loop will look for a factor of number (greater than 1) and stop. So what's the problem?

The problem is that `number` is an `int`. An `int` can also be zero or negative. The `sqrt()` function doesn't work for 0 or negative numbers. In those cases, the value that ends up getting stored in `factor` could be really whacky. On our computer, when `number` was -1, `factor` was set to some crazy value like -2,147,483,648. If `number` is 0, `factor` will likely be 0 and the `number%factor` expression will terminate your program with a "divide by zero" exception. Yikes!

So how do you protect your program from out-of-range values? There are three techniques. The first is a little timid, but legitimate: verify that the value will never be out of range. That sounds simple, doesn't it? It's usually a little more difficult than you might think. For a function like `Factor()`, we suggest a plan of action like this:

- Make the `Factor()` function `static` so that it can't be called from another module.
- Verify that every place in your program you call `Factor()` can't possibly pass it a 0 or negative value.
- Add comments to the `Factor()` function that warn any programmer using it that `number` must be a value greater than 0 or bad things will happen.

This kind of solution is usually reserved for when the code needed to protect your program is cumbersome or would be unacceptably slow. Neither of those is really the case here, so let's move on to the second technique.

The second solution is to have Factor() protect itself from bad values. Add the following code to the beginning of Factor():

```
bool Factor( int number, int *firstFactorPtr, int *secondFactorPtr )
{
    if ( number < 1 )
        return false;
    ...
```

Now Factor() is as safe as houses. You can pass it any integer value possible and it won't crash the program or return any unexpected values. It won't find the factor of any number less than 1, but it won't do anything stupid either.

We'll describe the third technique at the end of this section. For now, let's continue to worry about the values that get passed to your functions.

Tolerate All Possible Values

Sometimes the acceptable values for a variable aren't a simple range—such as greater than 1 or less then 100. The values a function is designed to deal with are called its *domain*. Any values outside its domain may have undesirable results. As a rule, you want your function to behave itself regardless of whether its values are inside or outside its domain.

Defining what values are acceptable is entirely up to you, the designer of the function. While you're still looking at the Factor() function, consider the other two parameters, firstFactorPtr and secondFactorPtr. Towards the end of the function is this code:

```
    *firstFactorPtr = factor;
    *secondFactorPtr = number / factor;
```

If the value of either firstFactorPtr or secondFactorPtr was NULL, your program would crash. How would you prevent that from happening? You could use the technique you just used for number and simply prevent the function from doing anything if either pointer is NULL:

```
    if ( number<1 || firstFactorPtr==NULL || secondFactorPtr==NULL )
        return false;
```

While that satisfies the letter of rule #1, it misses the spirit. Not having the function do anything useful if either of the return value pointers are NULL is a bit harsh. After all, number could still be valid and the purpose of the Factor() function—to find two factors of number—could still be performed.

Instead, let's replace the assignment statements with something a bit more tolerant:

```
if ( firstFactorPtr != NULL )
    *firstFactorPtr = factor;
if ( secondFactorPtr != NULL )
    *secondFactorPtr = number / factor;
```

This code is a lot more genial and (surprise!) more flexible. If number is within range, the function will still perform its calculation. If either of the two return value arguments are NULL, then that respective value is not returned to the caller—but the function still does its job. This now means that you can call Factor() to get both factors, neither, or just one by selectively passing NULL for the pointer arguments.

Allowing a parameter to be NULL to indicate that there is no value, or you don't want a value returned, is a common pattern in C functions. It makes its *usage pattern*—the ways in which your function can be used—more flexible. More importantly, it means your function doesn't assume that a valid pointer is always supplied.

Now let's jump to the *MultiArray* project from Chapter 9. In this first example of storing DVD information in arrays, we mentioned that the fgets() function will include the newline character in the string it returns. When this code executes, it could leave a newline at the end of each string:

```
for ( dvdNum = 0; dvdNum < kMaxDVDs; dvdNum++ ) {
    printf( "Title of DVD #%d: ", dvdNum + 1 );
    fgets( title[ dvdNum ], kMaxTitleLength, stdin );
```

We also told you that you could add the following code to remove that newline:

```
title[ dvdNum ][ strlen( title[ dvdNum ] ) - 1 ] = '\0';
```

Can you see what's potentially wrong with this code? What if the string returned by fgets() is empty? (It can happen.) The strlen() function will return 0 and the variable title[dvdNum][-1] will be set to '\0'. That's bad.

In this example, the domain of the strings you want to clean up includes only those strings that end in a single newline character. That means two things: the string should be at least one character long and the last character should be a newline. To be safe—and not write NUL values to invalid memory locations—you should at least test the length of the string, like this:

```
size_t titleLength = strlen( title[ dvdNum ] );
if ( titleLength>=1 )
    title[ dvdNum ][ titleLength-1 ] = '\0';
```

It's also possible that the last character of the string isn't a newline. This can happen if there are more characters on the line than the buffer size passed to `fgets()`. To be extra tolerant, you need to see if the last character is a newline before obliterating it, like this:

```
size_t titleLength = strlen( title[ dvdNum ] );
if ( titleLength>=1 && title[ dvdNum ][ titleLength-1 ] == '\n' )
    title[ dvdNum ][ titleLength-1 ] = '\0';
```

This is tolerant code! It does what it's supposed to do (remove the extraneous newline character from the end of the line), yet won't do anything bad (writing `NUL` bytes to other variables) or stupid (deleting a legitimate character from the line).

So by now you should be getting the idea. Don't make assumptions about the value of variables that aren't under your complete control. Determine the domain of your function—what kinds and ranges of values it is designed to work with—and make sure it does that. But also make sure it's prepared to deal with any values outside of that domain. What you do with out-of-domain values is up to you, but try to write your code so it does the best it can.

We mentioned a third technique for dealing with assumptions. Let's look at that now.

Assert Your Assumptions

So far you've tried to protect the `Factor()` function from crashing your program by (a) making sure it is never passed a value outside its domain or (b) adding code to protect the function from out-of-domain values. The second method is safer, but it might require you to add a lot of code to check for invalid values—values that you're pretty sure should never happen.

This leaves you torn between adding potentially useless code to the function and laying awake at night worrying that your function is going be thrown outside to be chased by zombies, with no way to defend itself. As other parts of the program get changed, as other programmers get involved, as more and more code calls your `Factor()` function, the guarantee that it will never be passed a value of 0 gets slimmer and slimmer. But is the only solution to code the function so it can handle any value?

As it turns out, there is another option. The C99 standard includes a facility called *assertions*. An assertion is a way for you, the programmer, to state what your assumptions are. If you assume that number will never be 0 or negative, you write that as an assertion in your code, like this:

```
bool Factor( int number, int *firstFactorPtr, int *secondFactorPtr )
{
    assert( number >= 1 );
```

That's all you have to write. If the expression in the assertion is true (number is greater or equal to 1), then the code continues on. If not, the program terminates and outputs a message to the standard error stream:

```
Assertion failed: (number >= 1), function Factor, file
/Users/james/Documents/Projects/Factor/Factor/main.c, line 37.
```

Terminating your program might seem a bit extreme, but allowing Factor() to run with number set to 0 is equally hazardous.

Think of assertions as a promise, or guarantee, that the number parameter will never be less than 1. It strikes a balance between merely assuming that number will never be less than 1 and adding a lot of code to protect against something that should not happen in the first place.

Assertions are usually lightweight, so feel free to add them wherever you want. They are particularly useful for testing things like array indexes before you use them.

```
int someIndex;
char string[ 100 ];
...
assert( someIndex>=0 && someIndex<sizeof(string) );
if ( string[ someIndex ] == 'X' ) {
    ...
```

This code says, "I've looked through all of the code and someIndex should never, ever, be outside the dimension of the string array. I've declared my assumption in an assert statement that will stop the program if that assumption ever proves to be wrong."

C assertions are used a lot during development and allow programmers sleep at night. If your program runs at all, then you know that all of your assertions were true.

Assertions do add code to your functions, so you might be wondering how they are different from adding code like this:

```
    if ( number < 1 ) {
        fprintf( stderr, "number should never be less than 1\n" );
        exit( 1 );
        }
```

Technically, there is no difference at all. The `assert` macro adds code your function that tests the condition. If the condition is false, it calls a function that outputs a message to standard error and terminates your program. But the `assert` macro has a hidden talent; you can turn it off.

You get the `assert` macro by including the `<assert.h>` Standard Library header, like this:

```
#include <assert.h>
```

If you *only* include the `<assert.h>` header, then all of the `assert` statements in your code will behave the way we've describe. If, however, you define the `NDEBUG` preprocessor macro *before* you include the `<assert.h>` header, like

```
#define NDEBUG
#include <assert.h>
```

all of the assert statements in your code disappear (to the compiler). The `assert` statements don't generate any code, they don't make any decisions, and they'll never terminate your program. They are also no longer protecting any of your code, but at this point you're pretty sure it doesn't need protecting.

The idea is to use assertions during development and testing. You can sprinkle your code with hundreds of assertions that you're sure should all be true. You then put your program through its paces, testing every function and possible data value you can think of. If an `assert` terminates your program, then you immediately know which assumption was wrong. You may need to modify your assumptions, or change the code so the assumption is true again. When you're done, your program should run without tripping any `assert` statements.

When your program is "clean" you can turn off all of the assertion code by defining the `NDEBUG` macro and recompiling your project. It's the same program, just without the safety net.

You should now understand what we mean by an "assumption," why assumptions pose a hazard to your programs, and the tradeoffs involved in either living with them or trying to protect your code from them. Let's move on to the next rule.

Rule #2: Stay Alert

You can't know if the zombies are coming if you're kicking back listening to your iPod with your eyes closed. Similarly, you won't know if functions are failing if you ignore their return values. Numerous projects in this book have ignored return values. We did this to keep things simple and so you could focus on the lessons at hand. Now you're ready. So let's start paying attention to return values from now on.

Pay Attention to Return Values

In the *PrintFile* project from Chapter 11, you first saw the `SetHomeDirectory()` function. It called two functions: one to get information about the current user and a second to change the current working directory.

```
void SetHomeDirectory( void )
{
    struct passwd *pw;
    pw = getpwuid( getuid() );
    chdir( pw->pw_dir );
}
```

Under normal circumstances, this code should always work. The `getpwuid()` should always return the account information for the currently logged-in user (which, after all, has to exist or the user couldn't have logged in). And since every user account has a home directory, the call to `chdir()` should always be successful. At least that's true 99.999% of the time. Now go back and read Murphy's Law again.

It's extremely unlikely, but it's entirely possible that the user ID for the current process isn't the logged-in user. It's also possible that the account record for the user can't be retrieved. It's also possible that the home directory of the account is invalid, has been renamed, or could be inaccessible. Is any of this likely? No. Is it possible? Absolutely.

Let's rewrite `SetHomeDirectory()` so it is much more robust. The first order of business is to pay attention to the values returned by `getpwuid()` and `chdir()`.

```
int SetHomeDirectory( void )
{
    struct passwd *pw = getpwuid( getuid() );
    assert( pw!=NULL );     // the current user should always be valid
    return chdir( pw->pw_dir );
}
```

First up is to check that the pointer returned from `getpwuid()` is not `NULL`. According to the documentation for `getpwuid()`, it returns a pointer to a `struct passwd` if successful, or `NULL` if not. Let's say that you've decided that, as the developer, the circumstances under which `getpwuid()` could fail are too obscure to worry about. On the other hand, if it does happen, you want to know about it and prevent the program from continuing with an invalid `pw` pointer. The `assert` statement is the perfect solution.

> **NOTE:** The call to `getuid()` can't fail, so Murphy's Law doesn't apply. Every Unix process has a user ID. If it didn't, it wouldn't be running. If it's not running, it can't call `getuid()`.

The code also pays attention to the `chdir()` return value. The documentation for `chdir()` says that if `chdir()` is successful, it will return a value of 0, and a negative value if it fails. The question is, what to do about it?

You've decided that `SetHomeDirectory()` doesn't really know what to do if `chdir()` is unsuccessful. Remember that you've used `SetHomeDirectory()` in several projects. In some programs, not being able to set the working directory to the user's home directory would be a showstopper. For other applications, it might be nothing more than an inconvenience. Instead of doing something with `chdir()'s` return value, you're going to pass the buck to the caller. The return value of the function has been changed to `int`, and the success (or failure) of `chdir()` is returned to the caller.

Now the caller can decide what to do if the working directory can't be changed. The caller might even choose to ignore it, but it won't because `SetHomeDirectory()` ignored it.

errno

The caller of your new `SetHomeDirectory()` should now pay attention to the returned value. This will let it know when `SetHomeDirectory()` is unsuccessful, but not *why* it was unsuccessful. The answer to that question can be found in the `errno` variable.

`errno` is a global variable defined by the Standard Library that stores an integer code describing the problem encountered by the last Standard Library function call that failed. Most Standard Library functions that return a success/fail indication set the specific reason for the failure in `errno` before they return.

If `chdir()` was not successful, the program should do something about it. `chdir()` is a pretty simple routine and is usually successful. But it still might not work if

- The directory named in the path doesn't exist.
- The current user doesn't have permission to read the directory named in the path.
- The path is invalid (not a properly formed directory path).

Depending on what went wrong, the program might decide to do different things. For example, if the directory is missing, the program could try to create one so it does. To find out what went wrong with chdir(), look at the value of errno:

```
if ( chdir( path ) != 0 ) {
    switch ( errno ) {
        case ENOENT:
            fprintf( stderr, "path '%s' does not exist\n", path );
            break;
        case ENOTDIR:
            fprintf( stderr, "path '%s' is not a directory\n", path );
            break;
        case EACCES :
            fprintf( stderr, "you do not have permission to access '%s' \n",
path );
            break;
        default:
            perror( "chdir() failed" );
        }
    }
```

You should only examine the value of errno after a Standard Library call fails. The value of errno is meaningless if the call succeeds. In other words, this code is wrong:

```
chdir( path );
if ( errno == EACCES ) {
    …
```

So which Standard Library functions set errno when they fail? That answer is in the documentation. A function that sets errno will state that fact in its documentation. It should also list the possible errno values that it might set and what those codes mean to that function. In OS X, the function chdir() lists seven possible errno codes: EACCES, EFAULT, EIO, ELOOP, ENAMETOOLONG, ENOENT, and ENOTDIR. You can find a list of the most common errno values on Apple's web site (https://developer.apple.com/library/mac/#documentation/Darwin/Reference/ManPages/man2/intro.2.html) and in the "intro" man page through the Xcode documentation browser.

> **NOTE:** errno is usually not a simple variable. When you write code, you treat it as if it was a variable that can only be examined. But in most operating systems, errno is a macro that expands to a function call that retrieves the error code of the last call that failed. While this normally does not affect your code, it does mean that you can't

> do certain things that you could with a regular variable. You can't, for example, get the address of the errno variable (&errno).

errno is only valid until the next Standard Library call. If you plan to refer to it again later, you should save it in another variable.

A couple of handy functions when dealing with errno are perror() and strerror(). perror() is a convenience function that writes a message to stderr along with a description of the current errno value, translated into the your local language. In the previous code example, if chdir() failed and set errno to ELOOP, the function perror("chdir() failed") will output this message to stderr:

```
chdir() failed: Too many levels of symbolic links
```

The message parameter passed to perror() is optional; you can print just the error code description using perror(NULL). perror() is handy if you just want to dump a description of the current errno value to the error output stream.

If you want to do a little more with errno, the strerror() function will translate the error code into a readable description and return that as a string pointer. You can then use that to format a more comprehensive message, or whatever else you decide. strerror()'s one parameter is the errno code to translate, so it isn't dependent on the current value of errno.

The definition of errno, and the constants for all of its possible values, is in <errno.h>. The prototype for perror() is in <stdio.h>. You'll find strerror() defined in <string.h>. For even more error display functions, check out the err(), warn(), and related functions defined in <err.h>.

Rule #3: Have an Escape Plan

When there are zombies around, you don't want to go any place where you could get backed into a corner. Effectively handling errors also means having a clear escape plan for every contingency. The path your code takes when it's doing its job is just as important as the path it takes when it can't.

There are many ways to accomplish this. The goals for effective error handling are

- Don't uglify your code.
- Handle errors consistently.

Adding extraneous code tends to obscure your code's real purpose and makes it difficult to read. So you'll want to use clearly recognizable, and easy to follow, coding patterns for error handling. You also want to make sure every possible error is handled consistently, so some unexpected error (or combination) doesn't leave your code trapped in a loop somewhere.

In this section we'll teach you six coding patterns for handling errors. The first few are demonstrated in an updated version of the *DVDFiler* project you wrote in Chapter 11 named *DVDFiler2*. It also includes some of the enhancements we've already shown you. You'll find the project document in the 12.01 - DVDFiler2 folder.

Follow the Success

The first error-handling pattern is one we call the "follow the success" pattern. Here's a sketch of what it looks like:

```
DoSomething();
if ( successful ) {
    DoSomethingElse();
    if ( successful ) {
        DoAThirdThing();
        if ( successful ) {
            // be happy
        }
    }
}
// Handle success or failure here
```

The basic principle is to test the success or failure after each step in the process using an `if` statement. If successful, the `if` statement performs the next step, and so on.

This pattern has the advantage that it is easy to follow the code, especially the successful path. All of the error handling code is grouped towards the end of the function, which is also convenient and easier to read. Let's rewrite the `ReadStructFromFile()` function using this error handling pattern.

Starting at the beginning, a new `assert` statement makes sure this function is never called with a `NULL` file pointer.

```
static struct DVDInfo *ReadStructFromFile( FILE *fp )
{
    assert( fp != NULL );
```

The local variables are declared and a new `DVDInfo struct` is allocated.

```
    struct DVDInfo  *infoPtr;
    int             scanResult;
    infoPtr = NewDVDInfo();
```

Note the new scanResult variable. You're going to use it to examine and save the result of each fscanf() call. If an fscanf() is successful (returns 1), the next fscanf() is performed, until the entire DVD record has been read from the file.

```
scanResult = fscanf( fp, "%[^\n]\n", infoPtr->title );
if ( scanResult == 1 ) {
    scanResult = fscanf( fp, "%[^\n]\n", infoPtr->comment );
    if ( scanResult == 1 ) {
        int num;
        scanResult = fscanf( fp, "%d\n", &num );
        if ( scanResult == 1 ) {
            infoPtr->rating = num;
        }
    }
}
```

If any of the fscanf() calls were not successful, then scanResult will be something other than 1 at the end of this code. You can then use it to determine if the entire operation was successful or not.

```
if ( scanResult != 1 ) {
    if ( scanResult != EOF ) {
        fprintf( stderr, "Invalid data near offset %lu, %d: %s\n",
                (long unsigned int)ftello(fp),
                errno,
                strerror(errno) );
    }
    free( infoPtr );
    infoPtr = NULL;
}
```

There are two kinds of failures that you're interested in knowing about. If any fscanf() function returned EOF, that means the entire file has been read. All you want to do is stop and return NULL to the caller. While EOF is a "failure" for the fscanf() function, it isn't a "failure" for your function; it's exactly what you expect to happen once the file has been completely read.

If the returned value is anything else, then fscanf() encountered something unexpected. It could be incorrectly formatted data in the file or a file error of some kind. It doesn't matter. Output a message that a problem occurred, approximately where in the file, and stop reading.

The final statement will return either the successfully read DVDInfo struct (if scanResult was 1) or NULL (if scanResult was anything else).

```
    return intoPtr;
}
```

While this is a pretty simple pattern to follow, it has one significant disadvantage. If you have more than a few steps to accomplish, your code keeps getting indented more and more to the right, until it start spilling off the right edge of your edit pane. That can make your code cumbersome to read and edit. So this pattern is really good for simple functions that need to perform a few steps and check for errors.

Sometimes you need to handle each step differently. To do so, use `else` statements to catch and handle individual failures. A sketch of that pattern looks like this:

```
DoSomething();
if ( successful ) {
    DoSomethingElse();
    if ( successful ) {
        DoAThirdThing();
        if ( successful ) {
            // be happy
        } else {
            // DoAThirdThing() failed
        }
    } else {
        // DoSomethingElse() failed
    }
} else {
    // Do Something() failed
}
```

Now let's rewrite `ReadStructFromFile()` again using an alternate version of this style to make the code even simpler.

Early Return

The "early return" pattern uses a `return` statement after all of the successful branches have been taken, and immediately returns the successful result to the caller. Using this pattern, the main block of code in `ReadStructFromFile()` now looks like this:

```
    scanResult = fscanf( fp, "%[^\n]\n", infoPtr->title );
    if ( scanResult == 1 ) {
        scanResult = fscanf( fp, "%[^\n]\n", infoPtr->comment );
        if ( scanResult == 1 ) {
            int num;
            scanResult = fscanf( fp, "%d\n", &num );
            if ( scanResult == 1 ) {
                infoPtr->rating = num;
                return infoPtr;  // <-- success!
            }
        }
    }
```

Notice the `return infoPtr` statement in the last block of code? If all of the `fscanf()` functions were successful, then the only thing left to do is to return that to the caller. None of the remaining code in the function is ever executed. This simplifies the code at the end of the function, which now only deals with the failures; it doesn't first have to check to see if there was a failure or not.

```
if ( scanResult != EOF ) {
    // output failure message here
}
free( infoPtr );
return NULL;
```

Your code looks pretty simple now. It's easy to read, and it has an escape path for all possible errors. Let's move on to other functions and try out some other error handling patterns.

Skip Past Failure

The "skip past failure" pattern is really the opposite of the "follow the success" pattern. In this style, a variable is used as a flag to indicate when a problem has occurred. Once that flag is set, all the remaining actions are skipped over. A sketch of this pattern looks like this:

```
bool problemOccurred = false;

if ( DoSomething() == ERROR )
    problemOccurred = true;

if ( ! problemOccurred )
    if ( DoSomethingElse() == ERROR )
        problemOccurred = true;

if ( ! problemOccurred )
    if ( DoThirdThing() == ERROR )
        problemOccurred = true;

if ( ! problemOccurred ) {
    // everything was successful
} else {
    // a problem occurred
}
```

Each step is evaluated for success. If one fails, the failure flag is set. Once set, none of the other actions in the function are performed because each one checks the failure flag first. The execution skips over the remaining steps until it gets to the error handling code towards the end of the function.

The flag can be anything. It could be a Boolean variable, such as problemOccurred, but is often an error variable that is set to 0 and remains 0 as long as no failures have been encountered. This is the style you're going to use to rewrite the WriteFile() function.

The new WriteFile() starts out just as it did in the past, but it also declares (and sets to 0) an error variable.

```
void WriteFile( void )
{
    FILE            *fp;
    struct DVDInfo  *infoPtr;
    int             error = 0;
```

As each step of the function is performed, the success of that step is reviewed. If a problem occurs, the error code is saved in error. This tells any subsequent steps that there was a problem.

```
    fp = fopen( kDVDTempName, "w" );
    if ( fp == NULL )
        error = errno;
```

Every step after that follows the same pattern: if there have been no problems up to this point, perform the step and determine if something went wrong.

```
    for ( infoPtr=gHeadPtr; infoPtr!=NULL; infoPtr=infoPtr->next ) {
        if ( ! error )
            if ( fprintf( fp, "%s\n", infoPtr->title ) < 0 )
                error = errno;
        if ( ! error )
            if ( fprintf( fp, "%s\n", infoPtr->comment ) < 0 )
                error = errno;
        if ( ! error )
            if ( fprintf( fp, "%d\n", infoPtr->rating ) < 0 )
                error = errno;
    }
```

After writing (or not) all of the DVD records, the file needs to be closed. Notice that this step isn't dependent on whether a problem occurred or not. It's your job to close the file whether you were successful in writing it or not. If there's a problem closing the file, however, you definitely want to remember that.

```
    if ( fp != NULL ) {
        if ( fclose( fp ) != 0 )
            error = errno;
    }
```

Finally, report if the whole operation succeeded.

```
    if ( error )
        fprintf( stderr, "Could not write DVD data file: %s\n", strerror( error
) );
}
```

> **NOTE:** Even though the `error` variable is an `int`, it is being used as a flag and, therefore, that is how it is being treated in the `if` statements. Remember that an expression is true if it's non-zero and false if it's zero. As long as the value of `error` remains set to zero, the error flag is false (no error yet). As soon as an error value is assigned to it, it becomes true (an error has occurred).

This is the style of error handling that Apple recommends. It's popular because it's pretty straightforward to read and no matter how many steps your function has, the code doesn't keep getting indented to the right.

You can sometimes combine this with the "early return" style. A sketch of that style looks like this:

```
if ( DoSomething() == ERROR )
    return errno;
if ( DoSomethingElse() == ERROR )
    return errno;
if ( DoThirdThing() == ERROR )
    return errno;
```

This is a very simple and readable style. It doesn't work for the `WriteFile()` function because there are things that have to be done before the function returns. Specifically, the file has to be closed using `fclose()`. To use this style, every error handing block would have to close the file before returning and that's a lot of duplicated code to maintain. Programmers call these kinds of tasks *housekeeping*. If your function doesn't have any housekeeping, the early return style is clean and simple.

You don't have to slavishly follow these patterns verbatim. We'll have you rewrite the `for` loop in `WriteFile()` one more time, this time in a much more compact form. Try it this way:

```
    for ( infoPtr=gHeadPtr; infoPtr!=NULL && !error; infoPtr=infoPtr->next ) {
        if (    fprintf( fp, "%s\n", infoPtr->title ) < 0
            || fprintf( fp, "%s\n", infoPtr->comment ) < 0
            || fprintf( fp, "%d\n", infoPtr->rating ) < 0 ) {
            error = errno;
        }
    }
```

If you look at this code carefully, you'll discover that it follows the same pattern as the previous version. But instead of using a bunch of `if` statements, it exploits the minimal evaluation feature of the `||` and `&&` operators.

If the first call to `fprintf()` returns a negative value, the expression `fprintf(...) < 0` is true, and neither of the other two expression are evaluated. For a function call, "never evaluated" means "is never called." If the first `fprintf()` returns a non-negative value (meaning it succeeded), then the expression (the next `fprintf()`) on the right side of the `||` is evaluated, and so on.

The end result is that if any of the `fprintf()` calls fail, the statement `error = errno` is performed and the loop stops. Notice that the term `&& !error` was added to the condition of the loop. As long as all of the `fprintf()` calls are successful, the loop continues until the entire linked list is written.

Deciding how to write your error handing code is a matter of taste. If you find the earlier version easier to read and understand, stick with that. If you find the latter version completely understandable, you may enjoy the more compact version. Now let's move on to the next strategy.

Percolate Errors Up

We showed you the "percolate errors up" pattern earlier, but we'll repeat it briefly here. Sometimes a function that observes an error simply doesn't know what to do about it. The simplest solution is to turn the success or failure of all of its individual steps into success or failure for the whole function, and pass the final verdict back to the caller. You already did this with `SetHomeDirectory()`:

```
int SetHomeDirectory( void )
{
    struct passwd *pw = getpwuid( getuid() );
    assert( pw != NULL );
    return chdir( pw->pw_dir );
}
```

This new version of `SetHomeDirectory()` returns 0 if successful and some other number if not. The caller should observe the results and take appropriate action. To accommodate the changes in `SetHomeDirectory()`, modify the code in `main()` to handle any problem:

```
if ( SetHomeDirectory() != 0
        || chdir( "./Desktop" ) != 0 ) {
        perror( "Could not chdir to ~/Desktop" );
        exit( 1 );
    }
```

This new code either successfully sets the working directory to ~/Desktop or it stops the program from running.

Speaking of harsh, sometimes it's appropriate for individual functions to take drastic actions on their own, which brings us to the next pattern.

Exit, Stage Left

Some errors defy a graceful recovery. There's no point in writing code to handle them, or percolating the error up to the caller; the caller can't do anything about them either. In the *DVDFiler* project, the NewDVDInfo() function is one such example. If the NewDVDInfo() function can't allocate the tiny bit of memory required to store a single DVDInfo struct, then your program is in serious, serious, trouble, and it should be put out of its misery.

```
struct DVDInfo *NewDVDInfo( void )
{
    struct DVDInfo *newInfoPtr;

    newInfoPtr = calloc( 1, sizeof( struct DVDInfo ) );
    if ( newInfoPtr==NULL ) {
        fprintf( stderr, "Out of memory!\n" );
        exit( 1 );
    }

    return newInfoPtr;
}
```

The new version of NewDVDInfo() checks for a successful allocation and calls exit() if it fails. In other words, if NewDVDInfo() can't allocate a new DVDInfo struct, then it just won't return.

This is why you don't have to check the return value of NewDVDInfo() anywhere in your program. It's impossible for it to return a NULL value. Murphy's Law doesn't apply.

NOTE: You could have written this code too:

```
newInfoPtr = calloc( 1, sizeof( struct DVDInfo ) );
assert( newInfoPtr != NULL );
return newIntoPtr;
```

As long as assertions are enabled, this would have the same effect. But remember that the purpose of assert statements are as an aid to debugging and testing. Ideally, you should be able to turn them off one day. If you did turn assertions off, then NewDVDInfo() could now return a NULL pointer and the assumption you made that it can't will now be false.

The lesson is, don't use assert statements to make decisions or handle errors. Make assertions about things that should always be true.

The Long Jump

The last error-handling pattern is a rather advanced one, and if you feel like skipping to Rule #4 now and coming back to this later, we'll completely understand. The problem programmers have with all of this error checking and handling stuff is that it gets in the way of writing the code they really want to write. In a perfect (programming) world, what you really want to write is

```
DoSomething();
DoSomethingElse();
DoThirdThing();
// be happy
```

and then somewhere else you can write the code to take care of things if they go wrong.

There's a technique called *exception handling* that allows you to do just that using a pair of magic functions named setjmp() and longjmp(). You use them by splitting up your code into two blocks. The first block contains the code that does the work. This is called the *try* block. The second block of code gets executed only if there's a problem in the try block. This is called the *exception* or *catch* block.

Let's rewrite the ReadFile() function using setjmp() and longjmp(). You can find this version of the project in the 12.02 - DVDFiler3 folder. You start off by declaring a special variable that will be used to coordinate the code flow.

```
static jmp_buf readJump;
```

This is a module-wide global because both ReadFile() and the functions it calls will need it. Next, ReadFile() gets started.

```
void ReadFile( void )
{
    FILE *fp = NULL;
    int  error;
```

The next statement is where the magic happens. The setjmp() function creates a kind of bookmark for the CPU that remembers exactly where the program is when you called it. It immediately returns 0. A 0 value means the bookmark was created and the code can begin doing whatever it was going to do.

```
    if ( ( error = setjmp( readJump ) ) == 0 ) {
```

The code that you write next is the try block: the code that you want to perform. If anything goes wrong, call the `longjmp()` function with a non-zero error code.

```
        if ( ( fp = fopen( kDVDFileName, "r" ) ) == NULL )
            longjmp( readJump, errno );

        struct DVDInfo *infoPtr;
        while ( ( infoPtr = ReadStructFromFile( fp ) ) != NULL ) {
            AddToList( infoPtr );
        }

        fclose( fp );
```

Notice that there's not a lot of error checking in this code, and no error handling at all. That's because if this code is successful (no errors), it just runs and exits the code block, as easy as walking down the street.

Next is where the magic happens. If any code calls `longjmp()`, then the program's execution jumps directly back to the point where `setjmp()` was originally called—it does not pass go, it does not collect $200. `setjmp()` returns (again!), but this time the return value is the error code you passed to `longjmp()`. The second time through, the `if` statement is false (because the error code returned is not zero) and the `else` block of the `if` statement executes. This is where all of your error handling goes.

```
    } else {
        if ( fp == NULL ) {
            printf( "Could not open file!\n" );
            printf( "File '%s' should be in %s.\n", kDVDFileName, getwd(NULL) );
        } else {
            fprintf( stderr, "Invalid data near offset %lu, %d: %s\n",
                    (long unsigned int)ftello(fp),
                    error,
                    strerror(error) );
            fclose( fp );
        }
    }
}
```

The real power of `longjmp()` is that calls to it aren't limited to the function where `setjmp()` was called. You can call `longjmp()` in any function your function calls or any functions they call. This rewrite continues with the `ReadStructFromFile()` and a new function named `ReadOneField()`.

The ReadStructFromFile() starts out simply enough.

```
static struct DVDInfo *ReadStructFromFile( FILE *fp )
{
    assert( fp != NULL );

    struct DVDInfo  tempInfo;
    int             num;
```

This version differs from the past versions in that instead of calling fscanf() directly, the fscanf() calls have been wrapped up into a new function named ReadOneField(). If ReadOneField() returns true, then the value was read successfully. If it returns false, then the end of the file (EOF) was encountered. In the latter case, you want to return NULL to the caller.

```
    if ( ! ReadOneField( fp, "%[^\n]\n", tempInfo.title ) )
        return NULL;
    if ( ! ReadOneField( fp, "%[^\n]\n", tempInfo.comment ) )
        return NULL;
    if ( ! ReadOneField( fp, "%d\n", &num ) )
        return NULL;
    tempInfo.rating = num;
```

Another feature of this modified ReadStructFromFile() is that the values are read into a temporary struct and then copied into a dynamically allocated memory block only when success has been determined. This simplifies the housekeeping in case there was an error (which will make sense in a moment).

```
    struct DVDInfo  *infoPtr;
    infoPtr = NewDVDInfo();
    *infoPtr = tempInfo;

    return infoPtr;
}
```

Now you get to the ReadOneField() function. This function attempts to read one value from the data file.

```
static bool ReadOneField( FILE *fp, const char *scanFormat, void *varPtr )
{
    int scanResult;
    scanResult = fscanf( fp, scanFormat, varPtr );
```

If successful, the value is copied to the pointer in the varPtr parameter and it returns true.

```
     if ( scanResult == 1)
        return true;
```

If the scan encountered the end of the file (EOF), then it return false.

```
    if ( scanResult == EOF )
        return false;
```

If there was any other kind of problem, the `longjmp()` function passes the error code all the way back to the `ReadFile()` routine.

```
    longjmp( readJump, errno );
}
```

`longjmp()` takes care of all of the work in percolating up any problems encountered. It doesn't matter how deep you are in `if` statements, loops, or function calls, the `longjmp()` function cuts through all of that and jumps immediately to the `setjmp()` call, all the way back in `ReadFile()`.

This also demonstrates Apple's recommended use of exceptions. Notice that the normal "error" of `EOF` is not handled through `longjmp()`. Apple's philosophy is that errors that you expect to handle in the normal course of business (file not found, end of file, and so on) should be handled using one of the earlier error handling patterns. Exceptions should be reserved for (pardon the pun) exceptional errors: events that represent serious problems or are completely unexpected.

The `WriteFile()` function in *DVDFiler3* was also rewritten to use `setjmp()` and `longjmp()`, so take a look at that function to see a second example of using `longjmp()`.

EXCEPTION HANDLING IN OTHER LANGUAGES

The idea of exception handling is new enough that it's not part of the C language. But it's a very powerful technique that can really untangle a lot of knotty error handling. Languages that came after C (C++, Java, C#, Objective-C) all recognized the power of exception handling, and those languages all have exception handling syntax built right into the language. For example, in Objective-C you can write

```
@try {
    DoSomething();
    DoSomethingElse();
    DoThirdThing();
} @catch( id whatWentWrong ) {
    // Handle errors here
}
```

We'll be honest: using exceptions in other languages is a lot easier than using `setjmp()` and `longjmp()` in C. But the concept and benefits are the same, and it's an important lesson that you can take with you to other languages.

In closing, let us say that there are many ways to structure your error handling code. These are the most popular, but by no means the only ways to do it. As long as your error handling code sticks to the principles of good design (doesn't uglify your program and deals with all possible errors), you should be fine.

Now let's look at getting out in front of problems before they occur.

Rule #4: Anticipate Problems

Why wait around for the zombies to find you when you could seek them out and stop them from coming after you? Error handling isn't entirely reactionary (only dealing with problems after they happen). Consider being proactive: design your code to anticipate problems and mitigate their impact.

Let's take a look again at *DVDFiler*. The `WriteFile()` function opens a file for writing, writes the records, and closes the file. If anything goes wrong, it logs the error and returns. What could be better than that?

The problem with `WriteFile()` is this: if the existing file was perfectly fine, the function starts out by deleting it. If anything goes wrong while writing the new file, much (if not all) of the information about your DVDs will be lost! Wouldn't it be better if you could write the new file *before* deleting the old one? That way, if anything goes wrong, the original file is still intact.

The technique of writing a temporary file and then using it to replace the original is called as *safe save*, and it's used by a multitude of applications. Let's modify *DVDFiler* to work that way. Open the *DVDFiler4* project in the 12.03 - DVDFiler4 folder. In the DVDFile.c module, add a `#define` for a temporary file name.

```
#define kDVDTempName     "DVD Data.temp"
```

The initial part of the `WriteFile()` function will be exactly the same, except that it will use the temporary filename instead.

```
void WriteFile( void )
{
    FILE            *fp;
    struct DVDInfo  *infoPtr;
    int             error = 0;

    fp = fopen( kDVDTempName, "w" );
    if ( fp == NULL )
        error = errno;

    for ( infoPtr=gHeadPtr; infoPtr!=NULL && !error; infoPtr=infoPtr->next ) {
        if (    fprintf( fp, "%s\n", infoPtr->title ) < 0
            || fprintf( fp, "%s\n", infoPtr->comment ) < 0
```

```
            || fprintf( fp, "%d\n", infoPtr->rating ) < 0 ) {
            error = errno;
        }
    }

    if ( fp != NULL ) {
        if ( fclose( fp ) != 0 )
            error = errno;
    }
```

At the end of this code, the entire DVD data file has been written to the temporary file. If everything went OK, error is still 0.

The next task is to replace the original file with the new one. This is a two-step process. First, you delete the original file and then change the name of the temporary file to the original one.

```
    if ( ! error ) {
        unlink( kDVDFileName );
```

The `unlink()` function is that Standard Library's "delete file" function. Its odd name alludes to removing an object from the file system's "tree" of directories and files. Notice that you ignored the error returned by `unlink()`. There are three possible outcomes for `unlink()`:

1. The file was successfully deleted.
2. The file wasn't deleted because it didn't exist.
3. The file wasn't deleted because of some other problem.

Surprisingly, none of these outcomes affect your program. If the file was deleted, that's great! That's exactly what was supposed to happen. If the file wasn't deleted because it wasn't there in the first place, that's OK too. It just means the program is writing the file for the first time.

If some other problem (access permissions or whatever) prevented the file from being deleted, that means that the next step (renaming the temporary file) will fail because the file name already exists. In this last case, you'll catch the problem when the `rename()` function fails and deal with it there.

The last step is to rename the temporary file so it has the name of the DVD data file.

```
        if ( rename( kDVDTempName, kDVDFileName ) != 0 ) {
            error = errno;
            unlink( kDVDTempName );
    }
```

If successful, the newly written file will take the place of the previous DVD data file, and you're done! If unsuccessful, capture the error code for reporting and then blindly delete—that is to say, ignoring any errors since you can't do anything about them—the temporary file.

Now your `WriteFile()` function is substantially more robust. If everything goes smoothly, it overwrites you data file of DVD titles. But if things go south, the original file of DVD information will still be saved.

Rule #5: Pick Your Battles

You don't have to slavishly handle every error the world throws at your program. As you design your error handling, consider the impact each failure will have on your program's behavior and what possible courses of action your program could take. Even in the final *DVDFiler* project, not every return value is examined. At the end of the `ReadFile()` function is this statement:

```
fclose( fp );
```

At this point in the program, `ReadFile()` has successfully opened the file and read every data record it can. If an error occurs closing the file, what can *DVDFiler* do about it?

The answer is "nothing." `ReadFile()` has successfully accomplished everything it was written to do. If some obscure error occurs now, it really doesn't matter.

So while error checking and handling is generally a good thing, consider why you're doing it and what you'll do with that information. And if the answer is "not much," you might not need any at all!

What's Next?

You've come a long way since Chapter 1! You've learned all of the C basics—variables, types, functions, parameter passing, pointers, arrays, structs, if statements, and loops. Along the way you've learned about C strings, the file system, the preprocessor, variable scope, modular programming, error handling, and creating command line tools.

Congratulations, you can now officially call yourself a C programmer. That's not to say that's all there is to learn about C. The next chapter covers an eclectic collection of some of the more advanced C topics. In it you'll learn about type conversion and casting, recursion, and other nifty facts and tricks. See you there.

CHAPTER 12 EXERCISES

1. What's the (error handling) flaw in this code?

```
bool ReadNumberFromFile( FILE *fp, int *value )
{
    if ( fscanf( fp, "%d", value ) == EOF )
        return false; // no more numbers
    else
        return true; // value successfully read
}
```

2. Each of the following code fragments makes at least one potentially disastrous assumption. Write an `assert` statement to ensure that assumption is always true.

   a. `if ( dvdInfoPtr->rating != 0 ) {`

   b. `if ( ( total / count ) > mean ) {`

   c.
   ```
   if ( argc < 2 ) {
       fprintf( stderr, "%s: requires at least one
   argument\n", argv[ 0 ] );
       ...
   ```

   d.
   ```
   char *copyOfString = malloc( strlen( str ) + 1 );
   strcpy( copyOfString, str );
   ```

   e. `array[ index ] += 1;`

3. What is Murphy's Law?

Chapter 13

Advanced Topics

Congratulations! By now you've mastered most of the fundamental C programming concepts. This chapter will fill you in on some useful C programming tips, tricks, and techniques that will enhance your programming skills. Some are additional features of the C language while others are advanced programming techniques. You'll start with a look at type conversion, C's mechanism for translating one data type to another.

Type Conversion

In a few places along your journey to learning C, you've assigned one type of variable to another. You've assigned an `int` variable to a `char`. In other places you passed an argument value that had a slightly different type than the function's parameter type. As an example, in the `Factor()` function, you passed an `int` argument to the `sqrt()` function, even though `sqrt()` expects its parameter to be a `double`.

When you do this, the compiler has to translate one type of value into another. This is called *type conversion*. You probably didn't think twice about this, which is fine, because C usually does the right thing automatically. But since there will be times when you need a bit more control over your type conversion, let's take a closer look at this process.

You will often find yourself converting a variable of one type to a variable of another type. For example, this code fragment

```
float f;
int i;
f = 3.5;
i = f;
```

```
printf( "i is equal to %d\n", i );
```

causes the following line to appear in the console window:

```
i is equal to 3
```

Notice that the original value assigned to `f` was truncated from 3.5 to 3 when the value in `f` was assigned to `i`. This truncation was caused when the compiler saw an `int` on the left side and a `float` on the right side of this assignment statement:

```
i = f;
```

The compiler automatically converted the `float` to an `int`. As you already know, an `int` only stores whole integers so the fractional portion of the number (.5) was discarded. In general, the right side of an assignment statement is always translated to the type on the left side when the assignment occurs. In this case, the compiler handled the type conversion for you. This is called an *implicit conversion*. Implicit conversions occur whenever the compiler believes it can reasonably convert the value for you.

Another place implicit conversions occur are in function arguments. If you supply one type of value (an `int`) but the parameter type is another (a `float`), the compiler will do its best to convert the argument value to the parameter's type. In the following code, two implicit conversions occur:

```
int a, b;
a = 5;
b = exp2( a );
```

The `exp2()` function returns the number 2 to the power of the given argument ($b = 2^a$). Here's the function's prototype:

```
double exp2( double e );
```

As you can see, neither the function's return value nor the parameter is an `int`. The compiler converted the integer value of 5 into a floating point value (5.0) and passed that to the function. The function returned a floating point value (32.0), which was converted back to an integer before being assigned to b.

The `exp2()` function will do just what you expect it to for any reasonable integer value: `exp2(10)` will return 1,024, `exp2(32)` will return 4,294,967,296, and so on.

Another hidden source of type conversion occurs in expressions. Binary arithmetic and comparison operators require that both operands be the same type. In the following code, the compiler has to convert one of the two variables so it matches the type of the other:

```
int i = 99;
double d = 98.7;
if ( i == d ) {
    ...
```

The compiler tries to promote up—performing the safest conversion it can. In this particular situation, it will convert the `int` into a `double` and then compare the two `double` values (`99.0==98.7`) for equality.

There's a kind of "trickle down" effect when you mix types in an expression. The result of all arithmetic operators will be the same type as its operands. The result of this expression

```
i - d
```

will be a `double`. The `i` is converted to a `double` so the - (subtraction) operator had two `double` operands, and the result of subtracting two doubles is a `double`.

Conversion Rules

The compiler will attempt to convert any integer or floating point variable into the needed type automatically. Assign a `char` to a `long double` and the compiler will perform whatever numeric conversion is necessary so that `long double` has the same logical value the `char` did.

Most of the time implicit conversion works silently and doesn't cause any problems. But there are some cases in which this automatic conversion could cause you some headaches, so let's look at the rules the compiler uses and why it might matter to you. These aren't the exact rules the compiler uses, but it's close enough to give you an idea of how things get done.

1. Any `int` can be safely converted to a longer `int`.

A `long int` can be safely converted to a `long long int`. A `short int` can be safely converted to an `int`, `long int`, or `long long int`. In the following code, it doesn't matter what the value of c is, all of the variables will have the same value:

```
char c; short int si; int i; long int li; long long int lli;
lli = li = i = si = c;
```

When converting to longer integer types, the compiler guarantees that the new value will always be the same number.

2. Any `int` can be successfully converted to a shorter `int`, only if the value will fit in the shorter representation.

The int value 999 (32 bits) can be converted to a short int (16 bits), but not a char (8 bits). When an int is converted to a shorter representation, only the least significant bits of the value are preserved. Here's an example:

```
unsigned int i = 999;
unsigned char c = i;
```

Only the lowest eight bits of the number 999 (11 1110 0111 in binary) are assigned to the unsigned char, becoming 231 (1110 0111).

3. When a signed integer is converted to an unsigned integer—or vice versa—of the same length, the bits of the value remain the same, but the number will change if the new type cannot represent that number.

We covered this awhile back, but it bears repeating.

```
unsigned char uc = 231;
signed char sc = uc;
```

Converting the unsigned char value of 231 (1110 0111 in binary) into a signed char will become -25 (1110 0111 in two's complement binary).

4. A unsigned integer can always be safely converted to a signed integer that has a longer representation.

This is sort of a corollary to the first and third rules. It's always safe to convert an unsigned integer to a signed integer if the signed integer's representation is longer, like this:

```
unsigned int ui;
signed long long int slli = ui;
```

No matter what value is stored in ui, that assignment statement always works.

5. Any floating point value can be safely converted to another floating representation that is longer.

Similar to the rule for ints, the C language guarantees that you can convert a shorter floating point value to a longer floating point value with no change in the value.

```
float f; double d; long double ld;
ld = d = f;
```

No matter what value f contains, all of these variables will contain the same number.

6. When a floating point value is converted to another floating point value that is shorter, the new value will be the closest approximation the new type can represent.

We already covered this extensively in Chapter 8. Shorter floating point numbers don't have as much precision as longer ones. When you assign a longer floating point to a shorter one, the compiler does its best to find a number as close to the original that the new type can represent.

7. Converting a floating point value to an integer removes the fractional portion of the value and converts the whole number portion to an integer.

Success will depend on the integer type being long enough to represent the whole number portion of the floating point value. In essence, the floating point value is truncated and turned into a `long long int`. The rest of the conversion follows the rules for converting a `long long int` to a smaller (or unsigned) integer type.

> **TIP:** Remember that floating point to integer conversion never rounds up or down; the fractional portion of the floating point value is just stripped off. This code
>
> ```
> double d = 4.999;
> int i = d;
> ```
>
> will assign the value 4 to `i`, not 5. If you want to round up or down, check out the functions `round()`, `ceil()`, and `floor()`.

Conversion Warnings

Depending on your build settings, the compiler may warn you about some conversions that it feels are suspect. It will be particularly keen to point out situations where you assign or compare signed and unsigned integers, or when you assign or compare 64-bit integers with 32-bit integers. Both are common sources of bugs.

You can suppress these warnings by exerting explicit control over the conversion of numeric values. You do this using a typecast.

Typecasting

You can tell the compiler to convert any type into any other (convertible) type using a *typecast*. A typecast is the type you want the value converted to, surround by parentheses, immediately before the value. Here's an example:

```
(long int)n
```

This expression converts the value of the variable n to a long int. It doesn't matter what n is. It could be an int, a char, a unsigned long long int, a float, or a long double. If it's physically possible to convert the value of n into a long int, the compiler will do that and the result of that expression will be a long int.

Typecasting is really handy in a variety of circumstances. First, it lets you control the type conversion performed by the compiler. Using typecasting to control conversion is called an *explicit conversion*.

Modifying the code used earlier, you can control implicit conversion like this:

```
int i = 99;
double d = 99.0;
if ( i == (int)d ) {
```

In this code, instead of automatically converting i to a double (so both sides of the == operator are double), the d variable is forced to become an int. Now the compiler looks at both operands and sees that both are ints, no implicit conversion is necessary, and the == operator compares two ints.

You can put a typecast in front of any expression you want. The compiler will do its best to convert it to that type before evaluating it in the larger context of the statement or expression.

The typecast is an operator. It doesn't change the basic rules that other C operators live by. If the earlier code was changed to

```
if ( i == (long int)d ) {
```

the compiler would look at the type of the operand on the left (an int) and the type of the operand on the right (a long int) and would implicitly convert the left int into a long int so that == is comparing two long ints. This results in two conversions: d gets converted to long int (explicit conversion), and i gets converted to a long int (implicit conversion). You can't use typecasting to change the rules of C operators, but you can use them to nudge them in the direction you want.

> **NOTE:** Technically, a variable type in parentheses immediately before any value is called a *cast operator*. The term "typecast" doesn't appear anywhere in the C language standard, but it's such a common term among programmers that we use it here.

Programmers often use typecasts to explicitly declare the conversions they know are required. It's superfluous (since the compiler must perform the conversion anyway), but it's a way for the programmer to document that they know what conversions are needed and they're OK with it. This would not be uncommon code for an experienced C programmer:

```
int a, b;
a = 5;
b = (int)exp2( (double)a );
```

Type A, obsessive programmers have even been known to cast the return value of functions that they intentionally ignore as (void), just to point out that they are ignoring the function's returned value:

```
(void)printf( "I don't care how many characters were output to stdout.\n" );
```

Typecasting Pointers

Typecasting can also be used to change the meaning of pointers. This notation casts the variable myPtr as a pointer to an int:

```
(int *)myPtr
```

C does not consider two pointers to different types to be compatible. In other words, a pointer to a char and a pointer to an int are incompatible and won't be implicitly converted. The code

```
int *iPtr;
char *cPtr;
iPtr = cPtr;
```

will cause a compiler error. It just doesn't make sense to the compiler. A pointer either points to an int or it points to a char. An address that points to a char shouldn't be assigned to a variable that points to int because that fundamentally changes the meaning of the value at that address.

The exception to the rule is the void* type, which is compatible with any specific pointer type.

> **NOTE:** Interestingly, typecasting pointers never involves any actual conversion. All pointers are the same, no matter what they point to. Typecasting pointers is entirely a matter of semantics. The compiler is trying to protect you from doing something that doesn't make any sense (treating an `int*` as if it were a `char*`), but changing a pointer from one pointer type to another doesn't change the value or the representation of the pointer.

When you typecast a pointer to a different type of pointer, you're telling the compiler that you know what you're doing and that the variable at that address is, in fact, compatible with the type that you say it is. That's a lot of power, so please make sure you're right.

For example, typecasting pointers could allow you to link together `structs` of different types. For example, suppose you declared two `struct` types, as follows:

```
struct Dog {
    struct Dog *next;
};
struct Cat {
    struct Cat *next;
};
```

By using typecasting, you could create a linked list that contains both `Cats` and `Dogs`. Imagine the source code you'd need to implement such a linked list.

```
struct Dog myDog;
struct Cat myCat;
myDog.next = &myCat; // <--Compiler error
myCat.next = NULL;
```

In the first assignment statement, a pointer of one type is assigned to a pointer of another type. `&myCat` is a pointer to a `struct Cat`. `myDog.next` is declared to be a pointer to a `struct Dog`. The compiler won't let you do that. To make this code compile, you need a typecast.

```
struct Dog myDog;
struct Cat myCat;
myDog.next = (struct Dog *)(&myCat);
myCat.next = NULL;
```

Another way to do this would be to exploit the wildcard `void*` type. Here's a new version of the `Dog` and Cat code:

```
struct Dog {
    void *next;
};
struct Cat {
    void *next;
};
struct Dog myDog;
struct Cat myCat;
myDog.next = &myCat;
myCat.next = NULL;
```

This code lets `Dog.next` point to a `Cat struct` without a typecast, because the next field is a void pointer, which basically translates into "a pointer to anything." The void pointer should only be used when the pointer is truly generic, because it removes so many of the compiler's normal safety checks. An explicit type makes it quite clear what is going on. In our previous example, anyone looking over our code would easily be able to tell that we were forcing a `Dog` to point to a `Cat`. In the void pointer example, the difference in type is far less obvious. Use type and typecasting intentionally. Make both part of your program design.

const Modifier

Several chapters back we promised to explain what the `const` modifier meant, and we mean to keep that promise now. The `const` ("constant") type modifier means that the variable's value is immutable (big word for "cannot be changed").

At first glance that seems oxymoronic; a variable that "can't be changed" isn't much of a "variable" is it? And you're right. Nevertheless, C does allow you to declare a constant variable like this:

```
const int ci = 3;
```

Attempting to assign or modify the value of `ci` in any way will generate a compiler error:

```
ci = 4; /* <-- syntax error */
```

But that's not where the `const` modifier is really useful. It's really useful in combination with pointers, and that's where you'll see it used most often. Here are a couple of examples.

This next declaration creates a pointer to a `const char` array:

```
const char* message;
```

In reality, it doesn't mean that the characters message points are *incapable* of being changed. What it means is that they *shouldn't* be changed. Any attempt to change those chars via this pointer (*message = '\0') will generate a compiler error.

The following function prototype declares a pointer to a DVDInfo struct that should not be modified. It's common to use the const qualifier on a pointer parameter that will only be used to get information from the variable the pointer points to and should never modify the value it points to.

```
void PrintDVDTitle( const struct DVDInfo *dvdInfoPtr );
```

By declaring this parameter const struct DVDInfo, any attempt by the function to change the DVDInfo struct via the pointer (dvdInfoPtr->rating = 3) is an error. When you see const in a function prototype, it's the function's ways of saying, "I will use this pointer only to get information, I won't change anything it points to." That can be very useful information to know.

You can assign a regular pointer to a const pointer, but you can't assign a const pointer to a regular pointer. The compiler considers this an "escalation of privileges," since you are assigning the address of something that shouldn't be changed to a pointer that is perfectly fine with changing it. If you must do this, you'll have to use a typecast.

```
const char *message = "fixed message";
char *greeting;
greeting = (char*)message;
```

Also be careful of where the const keyword goes. This declaration probably doesn't mean what you think it does:

```
char const *message = "fixed message";
message[ 0 ] = 'F'; /* allowed */
message = NULL; /* <-- syntax error */
```

This statement declares a pointer that you *cannot* change, which points to a char that you *can* change. The compiler is perfectly happy with the second assignment statement. The third one is a syntax error. We're pretty sure that's not what you want. Put the const keyword directly before the thing that shouldn't change. In this example, the const should be before the char (the char values shouldn't change), not before the * (the pointer can change).

Creating Your Own Types

The typedef statement lets you use existing types to create brand new types you can then use in your declarations. You'll declare this new type just as you would a variable, except that you precede the declaration with the keyword typedef. The name you declare will become the name of a new type. Here's an example:

```
typedef int *IntPointer;
IntPointer myIntPointer;
```

The first line of code creates a new type named IntPointer. The second line declares a variable named myIntPointer, which is a pointer to an int.

You've been using typedefs since the beginning of this book. The types size_t and off_t, for example, are typedefs defined by the Standard Library.

typedefs add semantic information (meaning) to your variable declarations. They also create a central place where you can modify all of those declarations at once. Let's say you have a program that performs user commands, and you decide to represent a command value as a char. You can create a typedef like this:

```
typedef char Command;
```

Now you can use the new Command type everywhere in your program where you store, pass, or manipulate a "command" value.

```
Command myCommand, *lastCommandPtr;
Command getCommand( void );
void PerformCommand( Command command );
```

Your code is now much more descriptive. The purpose and meaning of the myCommand and lastCommandPtr variables, the return value of getCommand(), and the parameter to PerformCommand() are now obvious.

> **TIP:** Do you want to quickly see how a custom type is defined? Hold down the Command key and then click on any type name in your source. Xcode will jump to header file where that type is defined.

If in the future, you decide that a "command" value should be an int instead of char, all you have to do is change one line of code.

```
typedef int Command;
```

Every Command variable, parameter, and expression in your entire program now becomes an int.

struct typedefs

typedefs are commonly used to simplify the declaration of structs (and as you'll soon see, enums and unions too). Throughout this book you've used the syntax

```
struct DVDInfo
```

to refer to the definition of the DVDInfo structure. It's much more common for programmers to define a structure using a typedef, like this:

```
typedef struct DVDInfoTag {
    char rating;
    char title[ kMaxTitleLength ];
    char comment[ kMaxCommentLength ];
    struct DVDInfoTag *next;
} DVDInfo;
```

This statement defines a new type, named DVDInfo, which is the type struct DVDInfoTag. You can now declare structures and pointers to the structure like this:

```
DVDInfo oneDVD;
DVDInfo *gHeadPtr;
void AddToList( DVDInfo *newInfo );
```

The keyword phrase struct DVDInfoTag can still be used, and the two are interchangeable. The DVDInfoTag is called the structure's *tag*. If you're using a typedef to define the struct, and you don't need to refer to the struct before the typedef is complete, then the tag can be omitted. If you omit it, the only way to refer to this struct is through its typedef name.

Which brings up an interesting quirk of the C language.

Forward References

C uses a one-pass compiler. It reads your source code one statement at a time, compiles that, and moves on. That means it must know everything it needs to compile each statement before it gets to it. This is why you always put #include and function prototypes at the beginning of each file.

An obscure problem that arises is the need to refer to a struct that hasn't been defined yet. This is called a *forward reference*.

C allows you to refer to structs (and unions, and enums) that you haven't defined yet using its tag. In other words, you can use a type like struct PlayerTag as a type *before* that struct has been defined. The limitation is that you can only use what the compiler knows about the struct so far (which isn't much). Since none of the fields of the struct are defined yet, you can't declare struct variables, get the struct's size, or access any of its fields. But you can declare a pointer to it—a pointer will be the same no matter what the structure turns out to be—and you can use it in typedefs and typecasts. Here's an example:

```
typedef struct CoachTag Coach; // <-- forward reference to struct CoachTag
typedef struct PlayerTag Player; // <-- forward reference to struct PlayerTag

struct CoachTag {
    Player *firstPlayerPtr; // <-- forward reference to struct PlayerTag
}; // <-- struct CoachTag is now fully defined

struct PlayerTag {
    Player *nextPlayerPtr; // <-- forward reference to struct PlayerTag (it's
not finished yet)
    Coach *coachPtr;
}; // <-- struct PlayerTag is now fully defined

void AnyFunction( void )
{
    Coach coach;

    coach.firstPlayerPtr = calloc( 1, sizeof(Player) );
    coach.firstPlayerPtr->coachPtr = &coach;
}
```

The Coach struct has a field that points to a linked list of players, and each player has a pointer back to their coach. Without forward references, you can see how it would be impossible to declare these types.

Enumerated Types

Similar to typedefs, the enum statement lets you declare a new type known as an *enumerated type*. An enumerated type is a set of named integer constants and a variable to store those values. A series of examples will make this clear.

```
enum Weekdays {
    Monday,
    Tuesday,
    Wednesday,
    Thursday,
    Friday
};
enum Weekdays whichDay;
whichDay = Thursday;
```

This code starts off with an enum declaration. The enum is given the tag Weekdays and consists of the constants Monday, Tuesday, Wednesday, Thursday, and Friday. The second line of code uses this new enumerated type to declare a variable named whichDay. whichDay is an integer variable that can store any of the Weekdays constants, as evidenced by the last line of code, which assigns the constant Thursday to whichDay.

Here's another example:

```
enum Colors {
    red,
    green = 5,
    blue,
    magenta,
    yellow = blue + 5
} myColor;
myColor = blue;
```

This code declares an enumerated type with the tag Colors and variable of that type named myColor. Notice that initializers accompany some of the constants in the Colors list. When the compiler creates the enumeration constants, it numbers them sequentially, starting with 0. In the previous example, Monday has a value of 0, Tuesday has a value of 1, and so on until you reach Friday, which has a value of 4. In this case, the constant red has a value of 0. But the constant green has a value of 5. Things move along from there, with blue and magenta having values of 6 and 7, respectively. Next, yellow has a value of blue+5, which is 11. This code also declares an enumeration variable named myColor, which is then assigned a value of blue.

You can declare an enumerated type without a tag if you're only interested in the constants:

```
enum {
    chocolate,
    strawberry,
    vanilla
};
int iceCreamFlavor = vanilla;
```

This code declares a series of enumeration constants with values of 0, 1, and 2. You can assign the constants to an int, as was done with iceCreamFlavor. This comes in handy when you need a set of integer constants but have no need for a tag name.

TIP: One nifty feature of using enums is that the compiler will catch switch statements that forget one of the values. If you write

```
switch ( iceCreamFlavor ) {
    case chocolate:
        …
    case vanilla:
        …
}
```

the compiler will let you know that you forgot to include a case for `strawberry`.

enums can also be declared using a `typedef`, like this:

```
typedef enum {
    Animal,
    Vegetable,
    Mineral
} Category;
Category question = Vegetable;
```

enum values are typically interchangeable with `int`s. Technically, the compiler only guarantees that an enum variable will be long enough to store all of the constants in the list, so `Category` could be as small as a `char`.

Unions

C offers a special data type, known as a union, which allows a single variable to disguise itself as several different data types. unions are declared just like `struct`s. Here's an example:

```
union Number {
    short int i;
    float f;
    char *s;
} myNumber;
```

This declaration creates a type named `union Number`. It also creates an individual variable named `myNumber`. If this were a `struct` declaration, you'd be able to store three different values in the three fields of the `struct`. A `union`, on the other hand, lets you store one and only one of the `union`'s fields in the `union`. Here's how this works.

When a `union` is declared, the compiler allocates the space required by the largest of the `union`'s fields, sharing that space with all of the `union`'s fields. If a `short int` requires 2 bytes, a `float` 4 bytes, and a pointer 8 bytes, `myNumber` is allocated exactly 8 bytes. You can store a short int, a float, or a char pointer in myNumber. The compiler allows you to treat myNumber as any of these types. To refer to myNumber as an int, refer to

```
myNumber.i
```

To refer to myNumber as a float, refer to

```
myNumber.f
```

To refer to myNumber as a char pointer, refer to

```
myNumber.s
```

You are responsible for remembering which form the union is currently occupying.

> **CAUTION:** If you store a pointer in myUnion by assigning a value to myUnion.s, you'd best remember that fact. If you proceed to store a float in myUnion.f, you've just trashed your pointer. Remember, there are only 8 bytes allocated to the entire union.
>
> In addition, storing a value as one type and reading it as another can produce unpredictable results. For example, if you stored a float in myNumber.f, the field myNumber.i would not be the same as (int)(myNumber.f).

One way to keep track of the current state of the union is to declare an int to go along with the union, as well as a #define (or enum!) for each of the union's fields.

```
#define kUnionContainsInt 1
#define kUnionContainsFloat 2
#define kUnionContainsPointer 3
union Number {
    short int i;
    float f;
    char *s;
} myNumber;
int myUnionTag;
```

If you are currently using myUnion as a float, assign the value kUnionContainsFloat to myUnionTag. Later in your code, you can use myUnionTag when deciding which form of the union you are dealing with.

```
if ( myUnionTag == kUnionContainsInt )
    DoIntStuff( myUnion.i );
else if ( myUnionTag == kUnionContainsFloat )
```

```
    DoFloatStuff( myUnion.f );
else
    DoPointerStuff( myUnion.s );
```

Why Use Unions?

In general, unions are most useful when dealing with two data structures that share a set of common fields but differ in some small way. For example, consider these two struct declarations:

```
struct Pitcher {
    char name[ 40 ];
    int  team;
    int  strikeouts;
    int  runsAllowed;
} ;
struct Batter {
    char name[ 40 ];
    int  team;
    int  runsScored;
    int  homeRuns;
} ;
```

These structs might be useful if you were tracking the pitchers and batters on your favorite baseball team. Both structs share a set of common fields, the array of chars named name and the int named team. Both structs have their own unique fields as well. The Pitcher struct contains a pair of fields appropriate for a pitcher, strikeouts and runsAllowed. The Batter struct contains a pair of fields appropriate for a batter, runsScored and homeRuns.

One solution to your baseball-tracking program would be to maintain two types of structs, a Pitcher and a Batter. There is nothing wrong with this approach. As an alternative, however, you can declare a single struct that contains the fields common to Pitcher and Batter, with a union for the unique fields, like so:

```
typedef enum {
    kMets,
    kReds
} TeamID;

typedef enum {
    kPitcher,
    kBatter
} PlayerType;

typedef struct {
    int strikeouts;
    int runsAllowed;
```

```
} Pitcher;

typedef struct {
    int runsScored;
    int homeRuns;
} Batter;

typedef struct {
    PlayerType type;
    char name[ 40 ];
    TeamID team;
    union {
        Pitcher pStats;
        Batter bStats;
    } u;
} Player;
```

Here's an example of a Player declaration:

```
Player myPlayer;
```

Once you create the Player struct, you can initialize the type field with one of either kPitcher or kBatter:

```
myPlayer.type = kBatter;
```

You can access the name and team fields like this:

```
myPlayer.team = kMets;
printf( "Stepping up to the plate: %s\n", myPlayer.name );
```

Finally, you can access the union fields like this:

```
if ( myPlayer.type == kPitcher )
    myPlayer.u.pStats.strikeouts = 20;
```

The u was the name given to the union in the declaration. Every Player you declare will automatically have a union named u built into it. The union gives you access to either a Pitcher struct named pStats or a Batter struct named bStats, both of which occupy the same memory. The previous example references the strikeouts field of the pStats field.

unions aren't used very often, but they do provide an interesting alternative to maintaining multiple data structures. Try them. Write your next program using a union or two. If you don't like them, you can return them for a full refund.

Recursion

Some programming problems are best solved by repeating the same process. For example, to learn whether a number is prime (see Chapter 6) you might step through each of the even integers between 2 and the number's square root, one at a time, searching for a factor. If no factor is found, you have a prime. The process of stepping through the numbers between 2 and the number's square root is called *iteration*.

The Iterative Approach

In programming, iterative solutions are fairly common. Almost every time you use a `for` loop, you are applying an iterative approach to a problem. An alternative to the iterative approach is known as *recursion*. In a recursive approach, instead of repeating a process in a loop, you embed the process in a function and have the function call itself until the process is complete. If that sounds a little weird, hang in there. It will make perfect sense soon.

Suppose you wanted to calculate 5 factorial (written 5!). The factorial of a number is the product of each integer from 1 up to the number, for example:

```
5! = 5 • 4 • 3 • 2 • 1 = 120
```

Using an iterative approach, you might write some code like this:

```
#include <stdio.h>

int main (int argc, const char * argv[])
{
    int i, num;
    long int fac;
    num = 5;
    fac = 1;
    for ( i=1; i<=num; i++ )
        fac *= i;
    printf( "%d factorial is %ld.\n", num, fac );
    return 0;
}
```

> **NOTE:** If you are interested in trying this code, you'll find it in the *Learn C Projects* folder, under the subfolder named *13.01 - Iterate*.

If you ran this program, you'd see this line printed in the console window:

```
5 factorial is 120.
```

As you can see from the source code, the algorithm steps through (iterates) the numbers 1 through 5, building the factorial with each successive multiplication.

A Recursive Approach

Problems that lend themselves to a recursive solution have one thing in common: a job that can be subdivided into one or more smaller jobs that are just like the larger one.

The factorial problem fits this description. The factorial of 3 is 3 • 2 • 1. The factorial of 4 is 4 • 3 • 2 • 1. So the factorial of 4 can be rewritten as 4•3! (4 times the factorial of 3). Similarly, the factorial of 5 is 5 • 4!, and so on.

A function can calculate the factorial of 5 by calling itself to calculate the factorial of 4 and then multiplying that result by 5. When the function is called to calculate the factorial of 4, it repeats the process: calling itself to calculate 3! and then multiplying that by 4. Here's a recursive function that calculates a factorial:

```
long int Factorial( long int num )
{
    if ( num > 1 )
        num *= Factorial( num - 1 );
    return( num );
}
```

`Factorial()` takes a single parameter, the number whose factorial you are trying to calculate. `Factorial()` first checks to see whether the number passed to it is greater than 1. If so, `Factorial()` calls itself, passing 1 less than the number passed into it. This strategy guarantees that, eventually, `Factorial()` will get called with a value of 1.

> **CAUTION:** Any recursive function needs a *terminating condition*: some indication that it's reached the end of the work to be done and can stop calling itself. If there's a bug in its terminating condition, the function may continue to call itself indefinitely, causing the program to run out of stack space and crash. Programmers call this an *infinite recursion* bug.

Figure 13-1 shows this process in action.

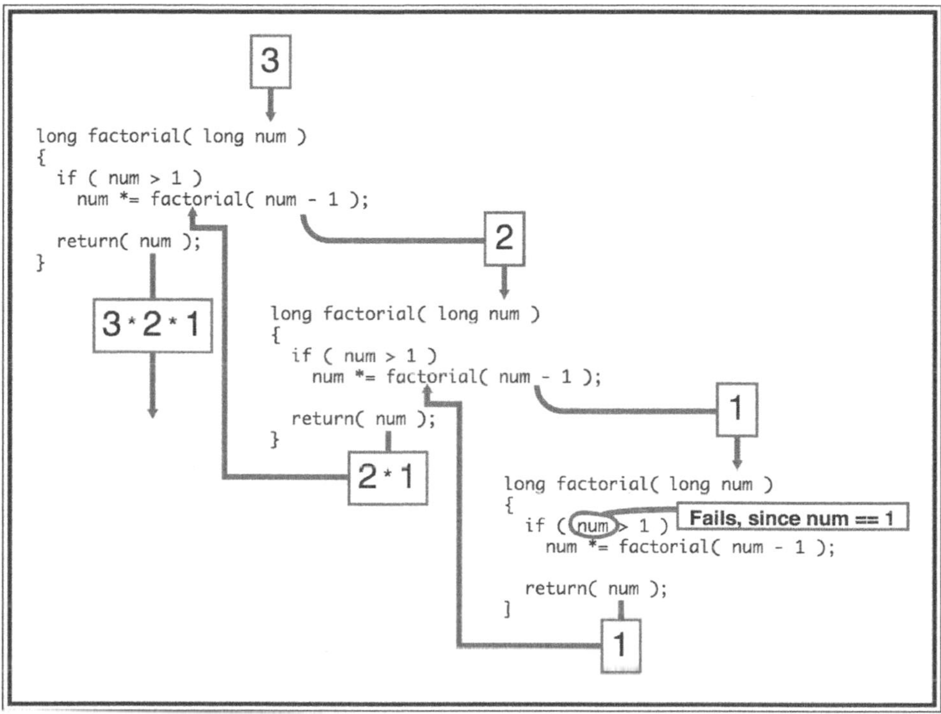

Figure 13-1. *The recursion process caused by the call Factorial(3)*

The process starts with a call to `Factorial()`:

```
result = Factorial( 3 );
```

Take a look at the leftmost `Factorial()` source code in Figure 13-1. `Factorial()` is called with a parameter of 3. The `if` statement checks to see if the parameter is greater than 1. Since 3 is greater than 1, the following statement is executed:

```
num *= Factorial( num - 1 );
```

This statement calls `Factorial()` again, passing a value of `n-1`, or 2, as the parameter. This second call of `Factorial()` is pictured in the center of Figure 13-1.

> **NOTE:** It's important to understand that this second call to `Factorial()` is treated just like any other function call that occurs in the middle of a function. The calling function's variables are preserved while the called function runs. In this case, the called function is just another copy (called an *instance*) of `Factorial()`.

This second call of Factorial() takes a value of 2 as a parameter. The if statement compares this value to 1 and, since 2 is greater than 1, executes this statement:

```
num *= Factorial( num - 1 );
```

This statement calls Factorial() yet again, passing num-1, or 1, as a parameter. The third call of Factorial() is portrayed on the rightmost side of Figure 13-1.

The third call of Factorial() starts with an if statement. Since the input parameter was 1, the if statement fails. Thus, the recursion termination condition is reached. Now, this third call of Factorial() returns a value of 1.

At this point, the second call of Factorial() resumes, completing the statement:

```
num *= Factorial( num - 1 );
```

Since the call of Factorial() returned a value of 1, this statement is equivalent to

```
num *= 1;
```

leaving num with the same value it came in with, namely 2. This second call of Factorial() returns a value of 2.

At this point, the first call of Factorial() resumes, completing the statement:

```
num *= Factorial( num - 1 );
```

Since the second call of Factorial() returned a value of 2, this statement is equivalent to

```
num *= 2;
```

Since the first call of Factorial() started with the parameter num taking a value of 3, this statement sets num to a value of 6. Finally, the original call of Factorial() returns a value of 6. This is as it should be, since 3 factorial = 3 • 2 • 1 = 6.

The recursive version of the factorial program is in the *Learn C Projects* folder, under the subfolder named *13.02 - Recurse*. Open the project and step through the program line by line. Pay particular attention to the stack in the debug navigator, as shown on the left in Figure 13-2. Notice the multiple copies of the Factorial() function on the stack. Each call to Factorial() pushes a new function onto the stack.

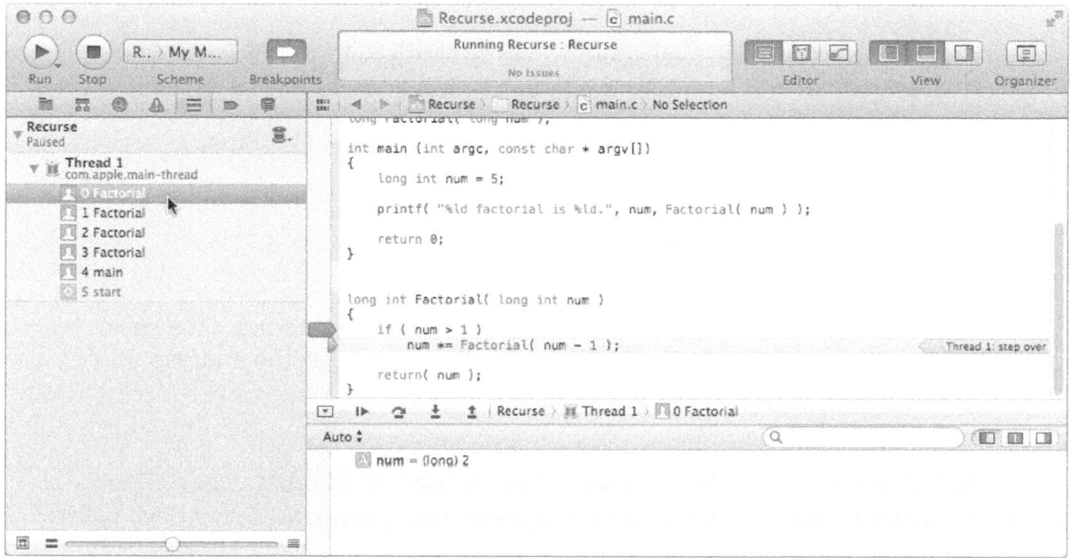

Figure 13-2. *Stepping through the Recurse project*

Function Pointers

Function pointers are next on the list of advanced topics. Function pointers are exactly what they sound like: pointers that point to functions. Up to now, the only way to call a function was to place its name in the source code, like so:

```
MyFunction();
```

Just as every variable has an address in memory, every function has an address too. You can store that address in a variable and then use that variable to call the function. Here's an example:

```
int (*myFuncPtr)( float );
```

This line of code declares a function pointer named `myFuncPtr`. `myFuncPtr` is a pointer to a function that takes a single parameter, a `float`, and returns an `int`. The parentheses in the declaration are all necessary. The first pair ties the * to `myFuncPtr`, ensuring that `myFuncPtr` is declared as a pointer. The second pair surrounds the parameter list and distinguishes `myFuncPtr` as a function pointer.

TIP: Function pointer declarations in C are notoriously ugly and hard to read. Most programmers use a `typedef` to simplify the situation. By defining the `typedef`

```
typedef int (*AFuncPtrThatTakesFloatReturnsInt)( float );
```

you can now declare the `myFunctPtr` variable with much less fuss:

```
AFuncPtrThatTakesFloatReturnsInt myFuncPtr;
```

Suppose you had a function called `DealTheCards()` that took a `float` as a parameter and returned an `int`. This line of code assigns the address of `DealTheCards()` to the function pointer `myFuncPtr`:

```
myFuncPtr = DealTheCards;
```

Notice that the parentheses were left off the end of `DealTheCards()`. This omission is critical. If the parentheses were there, the code would have called `DealTheCards()`, returning a value, and tried to store that value in `myFuncPtr`. You may also have noticed that the & operator wasn't used. When you refer to a function without using the parentheses at the end, the compiler knows you are referring to the address of that function.

Now that you have the function's address in the function pointer, there's only one thing left to do—call the function. Here's how it's done:

```
int result;
result = (*myFuncPtr)( 3.5 );
```

This line calls the function `DealTheCards()`, passing it the parameter 3.5 and returning the function value to the `int` result. C also allows for a shortcut syntax that allows you to call the function this way too:

```
int result;
result = myFuncPtr( 3.5 );
```

In our opinion, this latter form is a bit easier on the eye.

You can do a lot with function pointers. You can create an array of function pointers; call a different function each day of the week. You can pass a function pointer as a parameter to another function. This is a powerful technique that allows you, or someone else, to create a generic solution where the details of the specific solution are provided by a function passed via a pointer. You obtain the address of that function and pass it to the generic solution, which then turns around and calls the function. We'll show you an example of that in the "Standard Library" section later in this chapter.

For your enjoyment, there's a function-calling project in the Learn C Projects folder, inside the 13.03 - FuncPointer subfolder. The program is pretty simple, but it should serve as a useful reference when you start using function pointers in your own programs.

The Remaining Operators

If you go back to Chapter 4 and review the list of operators shown in Table 4-1, you'll likely find a few operators you are not yet familiar with. Most of the ones we've missed were designed specifically to set the individual bits within a byte. For example, the | operator (not to be confused with its comrade, the logical || operator) takes two values and ORs their bits together, resulting in a single value. This operator is frequently used to set a particular bit to 1.

Check out this code:

```
short int myShort;
myShort = 0x0001 | myShort;
```

This code sets the rightmost bit of `myShort` to 1, no matter what its current value. This line of code, based on the |= operator, does the exact same thing:

```
myShort |= 0x0001;
```

The & operator takes two values and ANDs their bits together, resolving to a single value. This operator is frequently used to clear a bit. Clearing a bit sets its value to 0.

Check out this code:

```
short int myShort;
myShort = 0xfffe & myShort;
```

This code sets the rightmost bit of `myShort` to 0, no matter what its current value. It might help to think of 0xfffe as 1111111111111110 in binary.

This line of code, based on the &= operator, does the exact same thing:

```
myShort &= 0xFFFE;
```

The ^ operator takes two values and XORs their values together. It goes along with the ^= operator. The XOR (exclusive or) is a Boolean operation that results in a 0 bit if both operand bits are the same, and a 1 bit if they're different. XOR gets its name from that fact that it works just like the OR operation (results in a 1 if either operand is 1), but "excludes" the case where both bits are 1.

The ~ (bitwise not) operator is a unary operator that turns all the one bits into zeros and all the zero bits into ones. It works exactly like the ! (not) operator, but on the individual bits of the value.

The &, |, ^, and ~ operators are summarized in Table 13-1.

Table 13-1. Truth Table for &, | , ^, and ~ Operators

A	B	A & B	A | B	A ^ B	~A
1	1	1	1	0	0
1	0	0	1	1	0
0	1	0	1	1	1
0	0	0	0	0	1

The previous examples assumed that a `short int` is 2 bytes (16 bits) long. Of course, this makes for some implementation-dependent code. Here's a more portable example. This code sets the rightmost bit of `myShort`, no matter how many bytes are used to implement a short:

```
short int myShort
myShort = (~1) & myShort;
```

You could also write this as follows:

```
myShort &= (~1);
```

The last of the binary operators, <<, >>, <<=, and >>= are used to shift bits within a variable, either to the left or to the right. The left operand is usually an unsigned variable, and the right operand is a positive integer specifying how far to shift the variable's bits.

For example, this code shifts the bits of `myShort` 2 bits to the right:

```
unsigned short int myShort = 0x0100;
myShort = myShort >> 2;          /* same as myShort >>= 2; */
```

`myShort` starts off with a value of 0000000100000000 and ends up with a value of 0000000001000000 (in hex, that's 0x0040). Notice that zeros get shifted in to make up for the leftmost bits that are getting shifted over, and the rightmost bits are lost when they shift off the end.

CAUTION: The right bit-shift operators are designed to work with unsigned values only. If you right-shift signed values, your CPU might fill in with 0 bits or duplicate the most significant bit (called a *signed shift*). C doesn't dictate one or the other, so read your compiler's documentation—or avoid doing that.

The last operator we need to cover is the , (comma) operator. The , operator gives you a way to combine two expressions into a single expression. The , operator is binary, and both operands are expressions. The left expression is evaluated first, and the result is discarded. The right expression is then evaluated, and its value becomes the value of the expression.

Here's an example:

```
for ( i =0, j=0; i<20 && j<40; i++, j+=2 )
    DoSomething( i, j );
```

This `for` loop is based on two variables instead of one. Before the loop is entered, `i` and `j` are both set to 0. The , operator allows you to put two expressions (`i=0` and `j=0`) where normally only one expression goes.

The loop continues as long as `i` is less than 20 and `j` is less than 40. Each time through the loop, `i` is incremented by 1 and `j` is incremented by 2.

To use the , operator in a function's parameter list, you must surround it by parentheses so it isn't confused with the commas used to separate arguments, like this:

```
MyFunction( i, (j-=2, j*j) );
```

The function `MyFunction()` is called with two arguments. The first argument is the value of `i`. The second argument begins by subtracting two from `j` and updating its value. The updated value of `j` is then squared and the result is passed as the second argument.

TIP: Using the , (comma), = (assignment), or ?: (conditional) operators in expressions can make your code hard to read and understand. All can be used to get out of sticky coding situations, but we would discourage you from using them unless you have to.

Getting More From The Libraries

There is a lot more to the Standard Library than what we've covered in this book—a lot more. And there are many more libraries beyond the Standard Library. As a newly minted C programmer, your first assignment is to dig into the C Standard Library and learn to use the functions you find there. Wikipedia has an excellent road map at `http://en.wikipedia.org/wiki/C_standard_library`.

A good place to start is with the functions declared in `<string.h>`. Read about the difference is between `strcmp()` and `strncmp()`. Wander around. Get to know the Standard Library very well. Whenever you need functionality, first turn to the Standard Library. Do not reinvent the wheel!

To give you a taste of the kinds of problems that have already been solved for you, let's take a look at some of the collection functions in both the Standard Library and Core Foundation.

Sorting with the Standard Library

A very common programming problem is how to sort a collection of items into a particular order. Let's say you have a large DVD collection. You might want to sort them into alphabetical order by title. Or maybe you want to sort them into order of rating, so your favorites are listed first. You'd like that sorting function to be fast and efficient, but you're probably not keen on taking a college-level course on data algorithms to learn about the dozens of different sorting methodologies that have been developed over decades.

A much easier solution is to turn to the Standard Library, which has a variety of sorting functions written for you. This is high-quality sorting code that embodies the best-known algorithms and optimizations. So let's see how you'd use them to sort your DVDs.

One of the fastest sorting techniques is called the "quick sort" algorithm. The Standard Library function `qsort()` will perform a quick sort. The problem with any sorting function is that it has to know how to compare two items in an array to determine what order they should be in. The authors of the Standard Library certainty couldn't anticipate you creating a `DVDInfo` structure or wanting to sort your collection by title. So how does a function like `qsort()`—that knows nothing about your data—implement a sort that's going to compare and reorder your data? The answer is function pointers.

The `qsort()` function takes a parameter that's a function pointer. That function is expected to take two pointers as parameters and return an `int`. The return value tells qsort() if the elements referred to by the pointers are in the correct order or not.

The beauty of this arrangement is that the qsort() function doesn't need to know anything about what it's sorting. All it needs to know is that you're going to supply it a function that will tell it if two elements in the array are in the correct order, and it takes care of the rest. So let's put qsort() to work sorting DVDs.

SortDVDs.xcodeproj

Find the *13.04 - SortDVDs* projects folder and open the *SortDVDs.xcodeproj* document. *main.c* starts out with the usual #includes.

```
#include <stdio.h>
#include <stdlib.h>
#include <string.h>
```

Next, you declare a DVDInfo structure. This is slightly different than the one you've used in earlier programs, but the principles are the same.

```
typedef struct {
    const char  *title;
    const char  *country;
    int         rating;
} DVDInfo;
```

The next bit of code declares an array of DVDInfo structs and fills in their fields. It does this using a complex initializer.

```
static DVDInfo testArray[] = {
    { "A Monster in Paris",     "France",           8 },
    { "Space Dogs",             "Russia",           5 },
    { "Wallace & Gromit",       "United Kingdom",   9 },
    { "A Bug's Life",           "United States",    9 },
    { "Despicable Me",          "United States",    7 },
    { "Planet 51",              "Spain",            6 }
};
```

Just as you can add an initializer to a simple variable declaration (int i = 0), you can initialize arrays and structures by separating the individual elements or fields with commas and surrounding the entire list with curly braces. In this example, you have an array of structs, so each element of the array (someType array[] = { *element0*, *element1*, *element2* }) is itself a struct initializer ({ *fieldA*, *fieldB*, *fieldC* }).

If you supply an array initializer, you can leave the dimensions of the array blank; C will determine the size of the array based on how many elements are listed. Which is why the next #define statement exists.

```
#define kNumberOfDVDs (sizeof(testArray)/sizeof(DVDInfo))
```

You could count the number of `structs` in the `testArray`, but then you'd have to remember to update that number if you later added a new one to the list. Instead, just let the compiler tell you how many `DVDInfo structs` are in `testArray` using the `sizeof` operator.

Following the data declarations are the local function prototypes. We'll explain each of these shortly.

```
void PrintTestArray( void );
int CompareDVDTitles( const void* l, const void* r );
int CompareDVDCountries( const void* l, const void* r );
int CompareDVDRatings( const void* l, const void* r );
```

main()

`main()` starts out by calling the `PrintTestArray()` function. It's a simple function the prints out the DVD information in `testArray`, one per line.

```
int main(int argc, const char * argv[])
{
    printf( "Original order:\n" );
    PrintTestArray();
```

It's called once to show you the order of the items in the array before anything is changed. Here's the output:

```
Original order:
Title                   Country         Rating
A Monster in Paris      France          8
Space Dogs              Russia          5
Wallace & Gromit        United Kingdom  9
A Bug's Life            United States   9
Despicable Me           United States   7
Planet 51               Spain           6
```

Now comes the fun part. The `qsort()` function sorts an array of *anything* into order, determined by the logic in the function passed via the last argument.

```
    qsort( testArray, kNumberOfDVDs, sizeof(DVDInfo), CompareDVDTitles );
```

The first three arguments describe your array: the address of the array, the number of elements in the array, and the size of each element. The last argument is a function pointer that will compare any two elements of the array. The function must expect two pointer parameters and return an int, like this:

```
int CompareTwoElements( const void* leftElement, const void* rightElement )
```

The two void * parameters can point to any two elements of the array. They are void pointers because qsort() doesn't know what they are and doesn't care. The function must compare the two elements—so obviously, it knows what they are—and will return 0 if the two are equal, a negative number if they are in order (left is before right), or a positive number if they are out of order (right should be before left). The function you passed is CompareDVDTitles(), which compares the title field of two DVDInfo structs. That's all that's needed to sort this array into title order.

You can verify that qsort() did its job by printing out the array again.

```
printf( "\nTitle order:\n" );
PrintTestArray();
```

When the array is printed this time, the order is different.

Title order:

Title	**Country**	**Rating**
A Bug's Life	**United States**	**9**
A Monster in Paris	**France**	**8**
Despicable Me	**United States**	**7**
Planet 51	**Spain**	**6**
Space Dogs	**Russia**	**5**
Wallace & Gromit	**United Kingdom**	**9**

You can continue to reorder the array by supplying different sorting functions. In the following statements, the array is sorted again, this time into order of country.

```
printf( "\nCountry order:\n" );
qsort(testArray,kNumberOfDVDs,sizeof(DVDInfo),CompareDVDCountries);
PrintTestArray();
```

This code produces the following output:

Country order:

Title	**Country**	**Rating**
A Monster in Paris	**France**	**8**
Space Dogs	**Russia**	**5**

```
Planet 51               Spain           6
Wallace & Gromit        United Kingdom  9
Despicable Me           United States   7
A Bug's Life            United States   9
```

The array is sorted one final time, into rating order, and output again.

```
printf( "\nRating order:\n" );
qsort(testArray,kNumberOfDVDs,sizeof(DVDInfo),CompareDVDRatings);
PrintTestArray();
```

```
Rating order:
Title                   Country         Rating
A Bug's Life            United States   9
Wallace & Gromit        United Kingdom  9
A Monster in Paris      France          8
Despicable Me           United States   7
Planet 51               Spain           6
Space Dogs              Russia          5
```

PrintTestArray()

The `PrintTestArray()` does exactly what it says, and isn't anything you haven't seen before. Here's the source for it:

```
void PrintTestArray( void )
{
    printf( "%-24s %-16s %s\n", "Title", "Country", "Rating" );
    unsigned int i;
    for ( i=0; i<kNumberOfDVDs; i++ )
        printf( "%-24s %-16s %d\n",
                testArray[i].title, testArray[i].country, testArray[i].rating );
}
```

CompareDVDTitles()

The `qsort()` function is doing all of the complicated work, but it couldn't do its job without the help of a comparison function. Your first comparison function is `CompareDVDTitles()`, which compares the `title` field of two `DVDInfo` structs.

```
int CompareDVDTitles( const void* l, const void* r )
{
    const DVDInfo *leftDVDPtr = l;
```

```
    const DVDInfo *rightDVDPtr = r;
    return strcmp( leftDVDPtr->title, rightDVDPtr->title );
}
```

That's all there is to it, and it's all the code you have to write in order to turn the generic `qsort()` function into something that can sort an array of `DVDInfo` `structs`. The real fun is in supplying different sorting algorithms, so let's look at the next one.

CompareDVDCountries()

Just like the `CompareDVDTitles()` function, this function compares two strings. The only difference is that it compares the `country` field of the two `DVDInfo` `structs` instead of the `title`.

```
int CompareDVDCountries( const void* l, const void* r )
{
    const DVDInfo *leftDVDPtr = l;
    const DVDInfo *rightDVDPtr = r;
    return strcmp( leftDVDPtr->country, rightDVDPtr->country );
}
```

Are you getting the hang of this? Let's try a slightly more complicated case.

CompareDVDRatings()

The final sort comparison function compares the ratings of two `DVDInfo` `structs`.

```
int CompareDVDRatings( const void* l, const void* r )
{
    const DVDInfo *leftDVDPtr = l;
    const DVDInfo *rightDVDPtr = r;
    int result = rightDVDPtr->rating - leftDVDPtr->rating;
    if ( result != 0 )
        return result;
    return CompareDVDTitles( l, r );
}
```

There are two things to note about `CompareDVDRating()`. First, the `result` value is calculated by subtracting the left rating value from the right rating value. This returns a positive number if the right rating is greater than the left rating. Remember that returning a positive value indicates that the two elements are out of order.

The "natural" order would be to sort the DVDs from lowest to highest rating (by subtracting the right rating from the left). This function reverses the order of the DVDs (so it's in highest to lowest rating order) by inverting the returned value.

You can do this with any sorting function. One way to sort your DVDs into reverse alphabetical order (Z to A) would be to pass `qsort()` this function:

```
int ReverseDVDTitles( void *l, void *r )
{
    return 0 - CompareDVDTitles( l, r );
}
```

TIP: The code `return CompareDVDTitles( r, l );` would also create a reverse sorting function.

The other thing that's interesting about `CompareDVDRatings()` is that it worries about the case where the ratings of the two DVDs are the same (`result` is 0). If the ratings are the same, the two elements are considered equal. `qsort()` doesn't guarantee the order of elements that are equal, except that they will next to each other in the array. For an explanation, see the sidebar "Stable and Unstable Sorting."

To make `qsort()` sort all of the DVDs into a predictable order, the `CompareDVDRatings()` function implements a sub-sort. If the primary fields being compared (`rating`) are equal, the comparison is performed on a secondary field (`title`, in this case). This causes all DVDs with the same rating to be in alphabetical order in the list.

STABLE AND UNSTABLE SORTING

Sorting algorithms can be divided into two groups: *stable* and *unstable*. Both sort items into ascending order, but differ in how they order items that are equal. As an example, look at the list of DVDs after they were sorted into title order: "A Bug's Life" came before "Despicable Me." After they were sorted by country, however, "Despicable Me" is now before "A Bug's Life."

That's because, during the country sort, both of these records were equal because both are from the United States. `qsort()` is an unstable sort; it doesn't guarantee the order of equal elements. Sometimes "A Bug's Life" will be before "Despicable Me," and sometimes it won't.

A stable sort, by contrast, guarantees that the order of equal elements will stay the same after the array is reordered. So if "A Bug's Life" was before "Despicable Me" before it was sorted by country, they will still be in the same (relative) order afterwards.

When using stable sorting, you can sort the array into title order, sort it again into country order, and you'll know that all of the titles from the same country will be in alphabetical order. To accomplish the same using an unstable sort, you must create a comparison function that performs sub-sorting, like that shown in `CompareDVDRatings()`. Stable sorting algorithms tend to be slower.

So now you know how flexible functions like `qsort()` can be and just how much work they can save you. Well, maybe you don't know, so we'll tell you: an optimized quick sort algorithm requires about a page of dense, complex, C. We could have written an entire chapter just on the quick sort. You accomplished the same with just a few lines of code.

Now let's move on to the Core Foundation library. This is another C library, but this one comes from Apple.

Collections in Core Foundation

OS X includes the Core Foundation *framework* (another kind of library) that provides you with hundreds of powerful C functions. Unlike the Standard Library, Core Foundation is much more object-oriented. In an object-oriented world, most data is in opaque (you don't know what's inside) blobs of data that you pass around by pointer. Each blob is called an *object*, and the pointer is called a *reference*. We discuss this a little more in the next chapter, but you don't need to know anything about objects for this excursion.

> **NOTE:** The Core Foundation uses the term *type* to describe a set of properties shared by multiple objects. Most object oriented programming languages use the term *class*. It's the same concept, just different names.

The Core Foundation framework provides, among other things, a number of different collection solutions. A collection is container (like an array) that can hold other bits and blobs of data. They are much more flexible than the C arrays and structures you've used so far. Core Foundation provides five kinds of collections:

- *Array:* An array is, conceptually, like a C array, except that you don't have to pre-allocate enough room to hold all of the elements. As you add more elements, the array makes room for them. You can also insert and remove elements from the middle of the array; all of the remaining elements are moved down (or up) as needed. There are also functions to sort and search the array.
- *Dictionary:* A dictionary is a form of associative array. Instead of addressing each element (value) using an integer index, each element is associated with a key. The key can be any value you choose. You define what the keys are and what the values are, and the dictionary uses one to find the other. For example, you could create a dictionary that maps an imdb.com movie ID (key) to a DVDInfo struct (value) in your DVD collection. Give the dictionary an imdb.com movie ID, and it will tell you if you have that DVD and what it is.
- *Set:* A set is an unordered collection of values, and it acts very much like its mathematical counterpart. You can't directly request an individual element in a set (by index or key), but you can determine if a value is in the set. A value can only be added to a set once. That is, a value is either in the set or it's not.
- *Bag:* A bag is like a set, but you can add the same value multiple times. Think of a bag of marbles. You can put one aggie and three steelies in a bag. Even though all three steelies are the same "value," they count as three elements in the bag.
- *Tree:* A tree organizes values into a hierarchy. The files on your hard drive form a hierarchy. Each folder can contain files and folders, which can contain files and folders, which can contain files and folders, and so on. If you have something like that in your program, you can use a tree to organize it.

The collections supplied by Core Foundation are, like the Standard Library sort functions, a generalized solution that you customize by supplying it with a set of functions. A collection requires several user-supplied functions to do its job. These are all bundled together in a struct that constitutes a kind of "personality module" for the collection. Let's see how this works by using a set collection to keep track of your favorite DVDs.

FavoriteDVDs.xcodeproj

Locate the *13.05 - FavoriteDVDs* folder and open the *FavoriteDVDs.xcodeproj* document. This project shares some code that's identical to the SortDVDs project, so we're only going to discuss the differences. It starts out the same, but it includes one new #include:

```
#include <CoreFoundation/CoreFoundation.h>
```

This includes the headers for the entire Core Foundation library. Unlike the Standard Library (which is broken up into many small header files), this single header includes most of the Core Foundation functions at once.

To use any Core Foundation functions, you must link your program to the Core Foundation framework. If your project's template didn't include CoreFoundation.framework, then you'll need to add it to your project. Select the *FavoriteDVDs* project in the project navigator (the top-most icon). The project and target settings will appear in the editor pane, as shown in Figure 13-3.

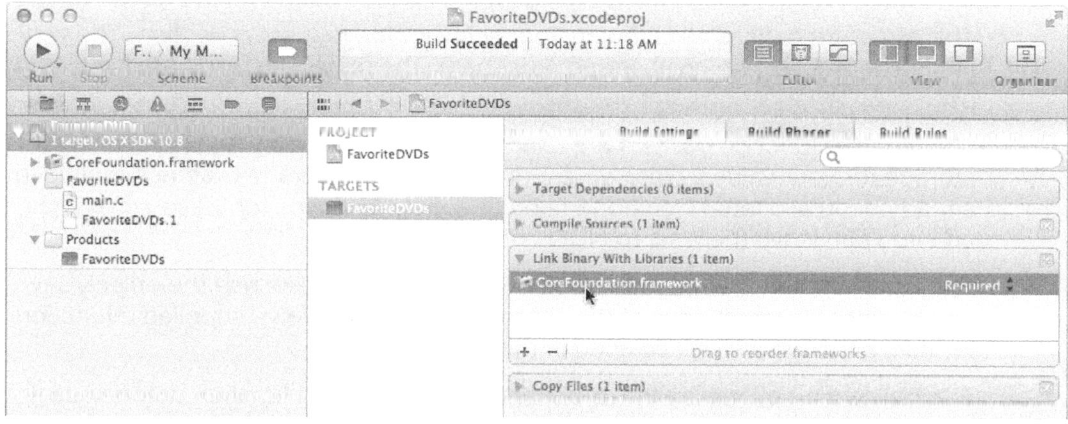

Figure 13-3. *Adding the CoreFoundation framework to a project*

Select the target, and then the target's Build Phases. Locate the *Link Binaries with Libraries* section, expand it, and click the + button to add a new framework. Navigate the list and select *CoreFoundation* from the list of frameworks. Click *Add* and your project is now ready to use any Core Foundation functions. Click back on main.c to return to your source code.

FavoriteDVDs continues on, defining DVDInfo and a testArray[], exactly the way SortDVDs did. Now come the functions that define how your set collection will behave. First, define the prototypes for your functions.

```
static CFStringRef FavoriteSetItemDescription( const void *value );
static Boolean FavoriteSetCompareItems( const void *value1, const void *value2
);
static CFHashCode FavoriteSetItemHashCode( const void *value );
```

These are the three functions you have to supply Core Foundation to have a set collection work with custom values. Your set will store pointers to C strings as values. We'll explain exactly how each function works later on.

Next, you define a `CFSetCallBacks` struct and fill it in with pointers to your functions.

```
static CFSetCallBacks FavoriteSetCallBacks = {
    0,
    NULL,
    NULL,
    FavoriteSetItemDescription,
    FavoriteSetCompareItems,
    FavoriteSetItemHashCode
};
```

This structure defines all of the custom behavior for your set collection. The very first value is a version number and must be 0. The remaining fields are the five user-supplied functions, but you don't always need to define all five.

The first two function pointers are used to automatically allocate and deallocate storage for your values. Since you're going to use pointers to C strings that have already been allocated, you don't need to supply functions for these behaviors and you can leave them set to NULL.

The third function is used when the collection wants to describe the object, say when printing a description of the set to standard out. We've supplied a function for this, although it won't be used in this program.

The last two functions are the important ones. The fourth function determines if two values in the set are equal. This is how the set determines if a value is already in the set or not. The last function generates a hash code for the value. We'll explain what that is a little later, too.

For now, just know that this block of function pointers is the "glue" that turns the Core Foundation set collection functions into ones custom made to work with your kind of data. So let's create a set and use it!

main()

`main()` starts out by creating a mutable set. "Mutable" means you can change the contents of the collection, which is definitely what you want here.

```
int main(int argc, const char * argv[])
{
    CFMutableSetRef favorites;
    favorites = CFSetCreateMutable( NULL, kNumberOfDVDs, &FavoriteSetCallBacks
);
```

The function `CFSetCreateMutable()` creates the set. The first parameter is a memory allocation function, which should always be NULL. The second is a hint to the set collection on how many elements this set is expected to hold. For small collections, this value doesn't matter much. For really large ones, letting the framework know ahead of time that it's going to store a boatload of elements can make it more efficient.

The last argument is the key: it's the `CFSetCallBacks struct` you defined earlier, filled with the custom functions you want this set collection to use. With the set created, it's ready to use. Start by adding two DVD titles to the set.

```
    CFSetAddValue( favorites, testArray[0].title );
    CFSetAddValue( favorites, testArray[3].title );
```

The `CFSetAddValue()` function adds a value to a set. The value must be what your custom callback functions expect. In this case, your callback functions are designed to store and compare C strings, so the values are C string pointers.

Adding a value to a set adds it to the set only if that value isn't already in the set. So it doesn't matter how many time you add "Space Dogs" to the set. Only the first call to add "Space Dogs" adds it to the set. Subsequent calls determine that "Space Dogs" is already in the set and does nothing else.

Now the code loops through the DVDs, printing them out. As each DVD is printed, it uses the set to determine if this DVD is a favorite or not.

```
    printf( "Fav Title\n" );
    unsigned int i;
    for ( i=0; i<kNumberOfDVDs; i++ ) {
        char fav = ' ';
        if ( CFSetContainsValue( favorites, testArray[i].title ) )
            fav = '*';
        printf( " %c  %s\n", fav, testArray[i].title );
    }
```

The `CFSetContainsValue()` function returns `true` if the given value is in the set or `false` if it isn't. The loop uses this information to determine if it will print a '*' next to your favorite DVD titles. Here's the output of the program:

```
Fav Title
 *  A Monster in Paris
    Space Dogs
```

```
   Wallace & Gromit
*  A Bug's Life
   Despicable Me
   Planet 51
```

Ignoring our obvious obsession with animated insects, the code was able to determine which DVDs were our favorites without adding a new field to DVDInfo.

Now let's look at the three callback functions that made this possible.

FavoriteSetItemDescription()

The description function is only used when you request a "description" of an item in the collection. This program doesn't do that, so this function is never called. Nevertheless, it's good practice to supply a description function for custom collections. This one works by simply converting the C string into a Core Foundation string object.

```
static CFStringRef FavoriteSetItemDescription( const void *value )
{
    return CFStringCreateWithCString( NULL, value, kCFStringEncodingASCII );
}
```

FavoriteSetCompareItems()

The next function is one that's critical to getting the set to work. This is the function the set will call when it needs to determine if two values are equal. Since both values are C strings, you can pass this off to the strcmp() function to do the work. strcmp() returns 0 if the strings are equal, so the == operator is used to turn that result into the "is equal" or "is not equal" return value the set is expecting.

```
static Boolean FavoriteSetCompareItems( const void *value1, const void *value2 )
{
    return ( strcmp(value1,value2) == 0 );
}
```

FavoriteSetItemHashCode()

The last function you need to supply is called a hash code function. Sets, dictionaries, and bags all use *hash tables* to speed up the process of finding a value in the collection. See the "Hash Tables" sidebar if you're interested in learning more about them.

HASH TABLES

Hash tables are a technique for searching large collections of values quickly.

Arrays are notoriously slow to search, and the time required to search one increases with the size of the collection. If array A had 100 elements and array B had 10,000 elements, it would take (on average) a hundred times longer to find an element in array B than array A.

One technique is to first sort the array into order. Then you can use a *binary search* to more quickly find a value. By assuming the array is sorted, a binary search will start by checking the middle element of the array. If that element is before the value it's looking for, the search knows that none of the elements before the middle can be the value. It then checks the middle element of the upper half and repeats the process, each time eliminating half of the remaining elements, until it narrows in on the one value it was looking for. The Standard Library's `bsearch()` function implements a binary search for you.

A binary search can reduce the time needed to search a collection dramatically. For an array with 10,000 elements, the number of tests drops from 5,000 to just 11 or 12 (on average). But—and this is a big "but"—it requires that the collection be in sorted order, which itself can be a very time consuming activity.

Enter, hash tables. They have the almost magical ability to reduce the search time to almost nothing, and the size and order of the collection doesn't matter. A hash table can find an element in an unsorted collection of 10,000,000 elements almost as fast as in one with only 10.

Hash tables accomplish this feat by assigning an integer number to each value, called a *hash code*. The hash codes for two identical values will always be the same. The hash codes for two values that are not equal are highly likely to be different (but they don't have to be). A large array of pointers is created and filled with pointers to each element in the collection. The index of each pointer is that element's hash code. To find any element matching a value, the hash code for that value is generated, that number is used as an index into the hash table, the pointer element at that index is fetched, and the value it points to is compared with the original value. If they match, you found the value. If not, you didn't. It's quick, simple, and efficient.

We've oversimplified hash tables some. We could spend the rest of this chapter going into the details, but we couldn't do better than the hash table Wikipedia page at `http://en.wikipedia.org/wiki/Hash_table`, which we encourage you to peruse.

The key to using a hash table is to assign every value a hash code, which is an integer number. Two values that are equal *must* return the same hash code. Two value that aren't equal could have the same hash code, but the collection is more efficient if they don't. So the idea is to write a formula that will generates different codes for almost any two values but must return the same code for two values that are equal. Here's the hash code function for this set:

```
static CFHashCode FavoriteSetItemHashCode( const void *value )
{
    CFHashCode code = 0;
    unsigned int bitShift = 0;
    const char* c = value;
    while ( *c != '\0' ) {
        code += ( ((CFHashCode)*c) << bitShift );
        if ( ++bitShift >= (sizeof(CFHashCode)-sizeof(char)) * 8 )
            bitShift = 0;
        c++;
    }
    return code;
}
```

This code adds the ASCII value of each character to the code variable, shifting the bits of each successive character one more bit to the left (essentially multiplying it by the next power of 2). If `bitShift` gets close to shifting the bits of the `char` past the end of the `CFHashCode` integer, it's reset to 0 and starts over again.

The end result is that the bits of each character get smeared across the bits of the `CFHashCode` integer. Both character value and order affect the final value, so the strings "tar" and "rat" will return different hash codes.

You're done. That's all the code it takes to create a set that stores C strings. Core Foundation arrays, dictionaries, and other collections all work in a similar manor. Whip up a set of callback functions that define the kind and behavior of the data you want to store there, and let the array, dictionary, or set handle all of the details.

> **NOTE:** If you want to store Core Foundation type objects (`CFType`, `CFString`, `CFNumber`, and so on) in a collection, you don't have to do any work at all. The `kCFTypeSetCallBacks` constant already contains a set of functions for storing, describing, comparing, and hashing Core Foundation objects in a set. There are similar constants for arrays, dictionaries, bags, and trees.

By now, you should have a taste of what the Standard Library and Core Foundation framework can do for you.

What's Next?

You learned about a variety of topics in this chapter. You started with type conversion and typecasting and then moved on to unions. You learned about recursion and function pointers. You found out about the rest of the C operators. Finally, you took a field trip to sorting, collections, and the world of object-oriented programming.

Chapter 14 answers the question, "Where do you go from here?" Do you want to learn to create programs with that special Mac look and feel? Ready to start writing iOS apps? Would you like more information on data structures and C programming techniques? Chapter 14 offers some suggestions to help you find your programming direction.

CHAPTER 13 EXERCISES

1. What's the syntactic or logical flaw in each of the following code fragments?

a.
```
struct Dog {
    struct Dog *next;
} ;
struct Cat {
    struct Cat *next;
} ;
struct Dog myDog;
struct Cat myCat;
myDog.next = (struct Dog)&myCat;
myCat.next = NULL;
```

b.
```
int *MyFunc( void );
typedef int (*FuncPtr)();
FuncPtr myFuncPtr = MyFunc;
```

c.
```
union Number {
    int   i;
    float f;
    char  *s;
};
Number myUnion;
myUnion.f = 3.5;
```

d.
```
struct Player {
    int  type;
    char name[ 40 ];
    int  team;
    union {
        int   myInt;
        float myFloat;
    } u;
} myPlayer;
myPlayer.team = 27;
myPlayer.myInt = -42;
myPlayer.myFloat = 5.7;
```

e.
```
int *myFuncPtr( int );
myFuncPtr = main;
*myFuncPtr();
```

2. For each of the following descriptions, choose a Core Foundation collection that you think would best fit the data. The choices are array, dictionary, set, bag, or tree.

   a. The names of the days of the week (Sunday, Monday, Tuesday, and so on).

   b. b. URLs that you want to visit later.

   c. The taxonomical name of organisms, organized by species, genus, family, order, class, phylum, and so on.

   d. Gym locker numbers assigned to members. Given a member's name, find the locker number they are assigned.

   e. Raffle entries, recorded by name. A person can buy more than one chance to win the raffle, which will enter them multiple times.

Chapter 14

Where Do You Go from Here?

Now that you've mastered the fundamentals of C, you're next step is to dig into the specifics of Mac programming. As you ran the example programs in the previous chapters, you probably noticed that none of the programs sport the look and feel that make a Mac program a Mac program. For one thing, all of the interaction between you and your program focuses on the keyboard and the console window. None of the programs take advantage of the mouse. None offer color graphics, pull-down menus, buttons, checkboxes, scrolling windows, or any of the thousand things that make OS X applications so special. These things are all part of the Mac user interface.

In short, the book has, so far, only taught basic C programming on a Mac computer. This is fundamentally different from creating programs that have a Mac GUI interface. That's the next logical step in the process, and that's what this chapter is about.

The Mac User Interface

The user interface is the part of your program that interacts with the user. So far, your user interface skills have focused on writing to and reading from the console window using functions such as `printf()`, `scanf()`, and `getchar()`. The advantage of this type of user interface is that each of the aforementioned functions is available on every machine that supports the C language. Programs written using the standard library are extremely portable.

On the down side, console-based user interfaces tend to be limited. With a console-based interface, you can't use an elegant graphic to make a point. Text-based interfaces can't provide animation or digital sound. In a nutshell, the console-based interface is simple and, at the same time, simple to program. OS X's graphical user interface (GUI) offers an elegant, more sophisticated method of working with a computer.

Learning Objective-C

Your Mac programs just wouldn't be the same without windows, drop-down and pop-up menus, icons, buttons, and scroll bars. You can and should add these user interface elements to your programs. Fortunately, the set of Apple developer tools you downloaded and installed at the beginning of this book includes everything you need to build world-class applications with all the elements that make the Mac great!

The key to working with these elements lies in understanding Objective-C and Cocoa. The Objective-C language is a superset of C. This means that everything you just learned about C will work in Objective-C! There are a number of excellent resources available for learning Objective-C. One of them is just a mouse click away.

Choose the `Documentation and API Reference` command from the Xcode Help menu. This will open Xcode's documentation browser. In the search field, type in "Programming Objective-C" and press *Return*. In the list of results, locate two documents: *Programming with Objective-C* and *The Objective-C Programming Language*. Start with the first if you want to get a feel for what Objective-C has to offer. Jump to the second if you want to start learning the language. If you've never done any object oriented programming, the second document has a link to the *Object Oriented Programming with Objective-C* guide, which is a great primer on the advantages of objects.

We love these documents. They are very well written and detailed, and best of all, they're free! Take a few minutes to read through the first few pages. If you feel comfortable with the language and the tone, you've found your path to learning Objective-C.

If this document makes your eyes glaze over and you start to feel a bit queasy, there are plenty of other ways to learn Objective-C. If you like the experience you had reading this book, check out its companion book from Apress called *Learn Objective-C on the Mac* by Mark Dalrymple and Scott Knaster (2009). Mark and Scott are two of the smartest people we know, and they do an excellent job explaining the concepts behind the Objective-C language.

Because that book was written as a sequel to this one, you should feel right at home.

What's Objective-C got that regular old C doesn't? In a word, objects. Just as a struct brings variables together under a single name, an object can bring together variables as well as functions, binding them together under a single class name.

Objects are incredibly powerful. Every part of the Mac user interface has a set of objects associated with it. Want to create a new window? Just create a new window object and the object will take care of all the housekeeping associated with maintaining a window. The window object's functions will draw the contents of the window for you, perhaps communicating with other objects to get them to draw themselves within the window.

There are pull-down menu objects, icon objects, scrollbar objects, file objects, even objects that can organize other objects. If you can imagine it, there's probably a set of objects that will help you build it.

Learning Cocoa and Cocoa Touch

Learning Objective-C will teach you the mechanics of working with objects. Once you get that down, you can turn your attention to Cocoa or Cocoa Touch, Apple's object libraries. Cocoa is an extensive collection of objects that will allow you to implement pretty much every aspect of the Mac OS X experience. Cocoa Touch is a collection of objects that will allow you to create exciting mobile applications for iOS devices like the iPod Touch, iPhone, or iPad.

As you might expect, Apple's developer tools contain some excellent Cocoa documentation. Back in the documentation browser, search for "Cocoa" and locate the article "Introducing Cocoa," if your interested in creating OS X applications. If you're goal is rock the iOS world, a good place to start is the "iOS Technology Overview." All of this excellent documentation can be found right in your Documentation browser, and you can't beat the price.

As the names suggest, the Cocoa and Cocoa Touch libraries share a lot in common. Learn one, and you've already learned half of the other.

A Bit of OS X Code

Our editors are hounding on us to get this last chapter submitted, but we can't resist showing you a bit more—just three more projects—and then we'll let you go. These are just to give you a taste of where you're heading.

Fire up Xcode, and choose ***New ➤ Project*** command from the **File** menu. When the new project assistant appears, select the *Command Line Tool* template, and click *Next*. Type in "TastOfObjC" for the *Product Name*. For this project, change the *Type* from *C* to *Foundation* (see Figure 14-1), and click the *Next* button. Choose a location and click *Create*.

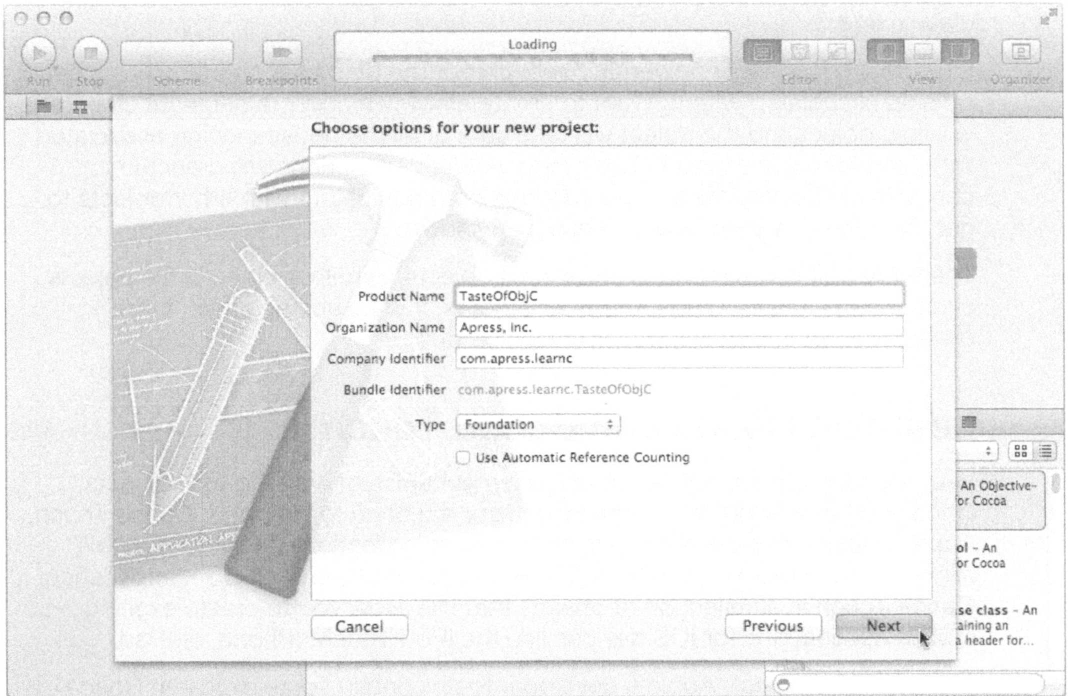

Figure 14-1. *Creating a Foundation tool project*

When the project appears, select ***Run*** from the ***Product*** menu. Once the build is complete, bring up the console. You should see something that looks like this:

```
2012-08-26 19:12:35.347 TasteOfObjC[580:303] Hello, World!
```

That's it. This project is the starting point for your next big adventure—mastering Objective-C. You'll find that your Objective-C output looks much the same as your C output. All your programs will run in the console window. The difference? You'll be building and using objects. This is the perfect platform for learning the mechanics of programming with Objective-C before you add Cocoa to the mix.

Speaking of Cocoa, let's build a Cocoa project, since we're here. Back in Xcode, choose ***New ➤ Project*** command from the ***File*** menu. When the New

Project assistant appears, select *Application* in the OS X section. This time select the *Cocoa Application* template, and click the *Next* button. Name the project "TasteOfCocoa" and click the *Create Document-Based Application* option. The rest of the options don't matter for this demonstration.

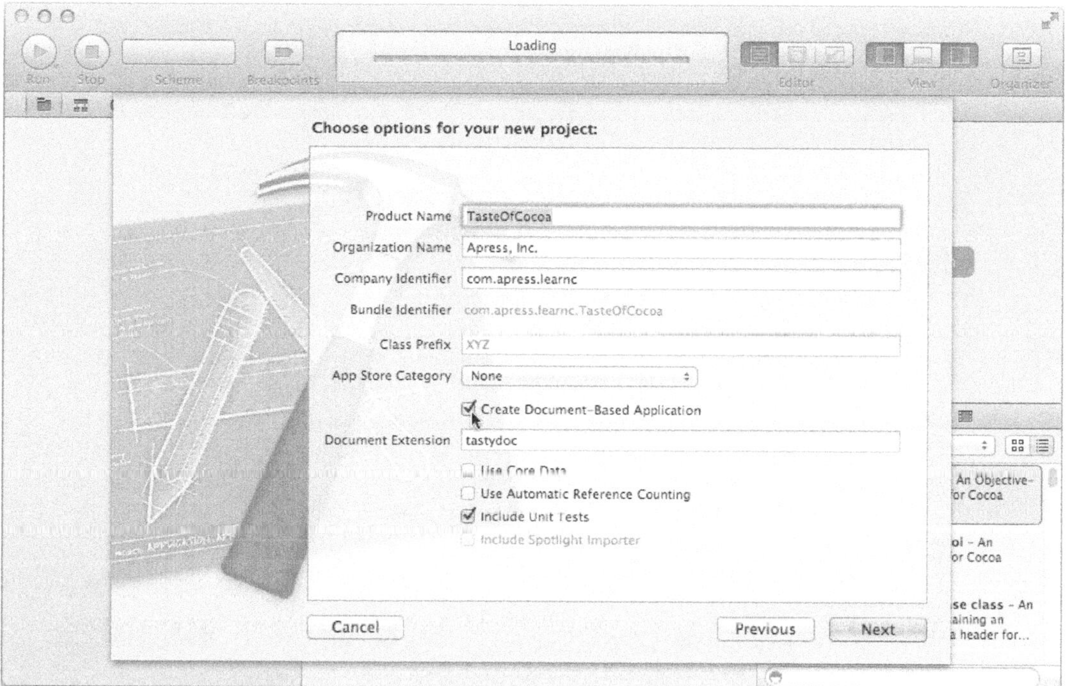

Figure 14-2. *Creating a new Cocoa application project*

When the project appears, select *Run* from the *Product* menu. After a few seconds of intense compiler action, a new application will launch. You'll be able to tell the new application is running because a window similar to the one shown in Figure 14-3 will appear. In addition, a new application icon with the name `TasteOfCocoa` will appear on the dock, toward the right side, and a menu named *TasteOfCocoa* will appear in the menu bar, just to the right of the Apple menu.

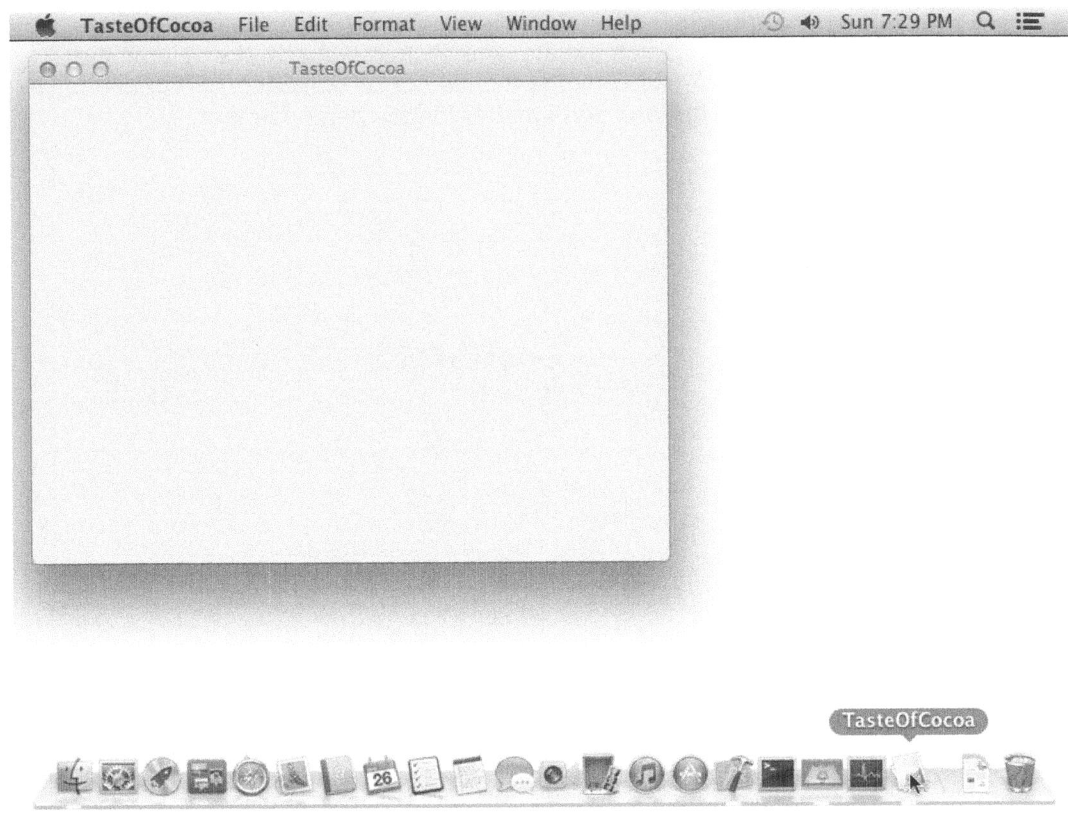

Figure 14-3. *A simple Cocoa application*

`TasteOfCocoa` is a real-life Cocoa application. Try resizing the window. Select ***New*** from the ***File*** menu, and a new window will appear. You can open and close as many windows as you like. Try the ***Format ➤ Font ➤ Show Fonts*** command, or the ***Format ➤ Font ➤ Show Colors*** command. For a laugh, choose the ***TasteOfCocoa ➤ About TasteOfCocoa*** command. This is the "Hello, World!" of Cocoa applications.

A Quick iOS App

It's pretty obvious that you can create OS X applications using OS X and Xcode, but what about those iOS devices? Xcode provides everything you need to create, test, and debug applications for Apple's mobile operating system too. Let's take a quick peek at how that works.

Once again, and we swear for the last time, choose ***New*** ➤ ***Project*** from the ***File*** menu. When the New Project assistant appears, select *Application* in the *iOS* (not the OS X!) section. On the right you'll see a lot of possible iOS templates, as shown in Figure 14-4. Select the *Utility Application* template, and click the *Next* button. Name the project "TasteOfiOS". Make sure the *Use Storyboards* option is turned off and click the *Next* button.

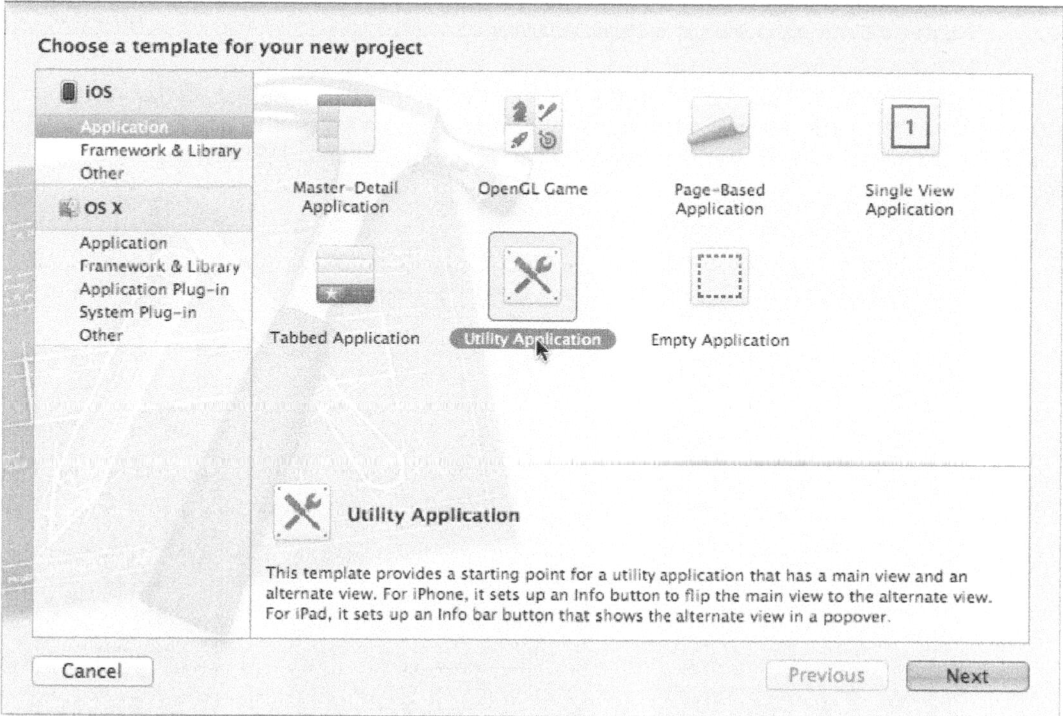

Figure 14-4. *Creating an iOS app*

To help you quickly code and debug iOS applications, Xcode includes an iOS device simulator. That's right. You're Mac can pretend to be any iOS device. It's theoretically possible (although not recommended) that you could create, debug, and deliver an iOS app without ever touching an actual mobile device.

Find the *Scheme* control in the toolbar and change it to ***iPhone 6.0 Simulator***, as shown in Figure 14-5.

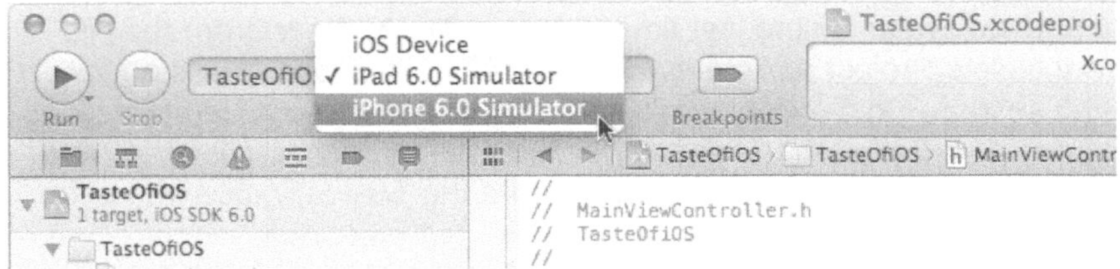

Figure 14-5. *Changing Scheme to iPhone Simulator*

Now press the Run button in the toolbar or choose the ***Product* ➤ *Run*** command. An iPhone interface will appear on your screen, shown on the left in Figure 14-6. It's the iOS project you just created running in a simulated iPhone.

Figure 14-6. *iPhone simulator*

The Utility Application template creates a simple one-screen iOS app with an auxiliary view accessible through an "info" button. Click the *i* in the lower right corner of the screen and watch the app flip to its auxiliary view, as shown in the middle of Figure 14-6. (If you run this in the iPad simulator you get a slightly different interface.)

You can even quit the app by clicking the home button. After your app quits, the simulator goes back to the springboard (shown on the right of Figure 14-6). Click your app to launch it again, just as you would on a real iPhone.

Just a Touch of Objective-C

Quit the simulator and go back to the `TasteOfiOS` project. Click the *`MainViewController.h`* file in the project navigator, as shown in Figure 14-7, and take a quick look at it. Now do the same with *`MainViewController.m`*.

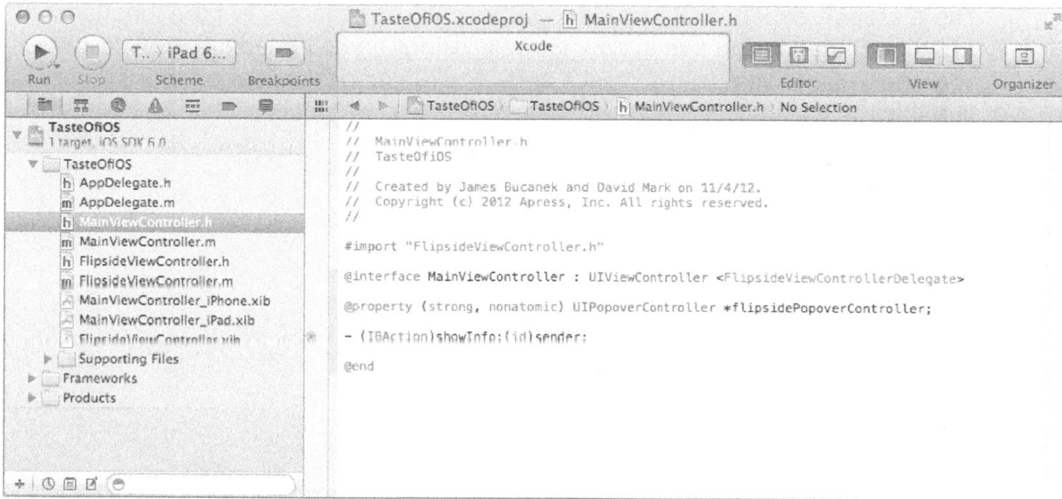

Figure 14-7. *MainViewController.h source*

What you're reading is Objective-C, and it doesn't look much like the C that you've learned in this book. Remain calm. There's a perfectly logical explanation, and you'll soon discover you know a lot more about this code than you think you do.

Most modern object-oriented languages (Java, C#, C++) are "C-like" languages. That is, they kind of look and work like C, but they're not C. If you already know C, then that's great; you have a leg up on learning these languages because you only need to learn what's different from C, which saves some time. But they're not C, and a lot of the details are different.

Objective-C is an extension to C, not a look-alike. Objective-C adds new syntax to the C language, but doesn't change anything about C itself. That's important, because—unlike those other languages—it means that *everything* you've learned in this book will apply to Objective-C. You just have something new to learn beyond it.

So that the Objective-C extensions aren't confused with existing C, they are quit distinct from regular C syntax. Objective-C adds a few so-called "at" keywords, like `@interface`, `@property`, `@class`, `@end`, and so on. And Objective-C functions (called methods) are called by placing them between brackets, like this: `[object myFunction]`. Just about everything else (that is, anything not starting with an "@" sign or between brackets) is plain old C.

The primary tool of the object-oriented programmer is the class. A class is just like a `struct`, except that it binds together not just variables but the functions (methods) that act on that `struct` as well. Using C, you already learned to bind together related values in a `struct` and write functions that act on that `struct`, like this:

```
struct DVDInfo {
    const char *title;
    const char *comments;
    int rating;
    struct DVDInfo *next;
};
struct DVDInfo *NewDVDInfo( void );
void AddDVDToList( struct DVDInfo *dvdInfoPtr );
...
struct DVDInfo *myDVD = NewDVDInfo();
myDVD->rating = 9;
AddDVDToList( myDVD );
```

C programmers do this because it's just good programming. Objective-C adds new syntax that makes this easier to write, helping you keep your code neat and tidy. Here's the same concept written using an older form of Objective-C (so you can see the similarities):

```
@interface DVDInfo : NSObject {
    NSString *title;
    NSString *comments;
    int rating;
    DVDInfo *next;
}
- (DVDInfo*)next;
- (void)addToList;
@end
...
DVDInfo *myDVD = [DVDInfo new];
myDVD->rating = 9;
[myDVD addToList];
```

As you can see, a class looks and works very much like a struct. The methods (functions) that work on this object (`struct`) are declared as part of the class, defined between the `@interface` and `@end` keywords.

Objective-C puts the object front and center in the method calling syntax, so your focus becomes the object and what messages (functions) you want that object to perform. While this looks radically different than how C works, behind the scenes the computer ultimately does the same work: it calls a function (`addToList`) and the first (invisible to you) parameter is a pointer to your `myDVD` object—exactly the way the `AddDVDToList()` function works. Isn't that clever?

Modern Objective-C departs a little further from the C `struct` syntax, but the results are still very similar. Here's the final version of the `DVDInfo` class declaration, written in Objective-C 2.0:

```
@interface DVDInfo : NSObject
    @property (strong) NSString *title;
    @property (strong) NSString *comments;
    @property int rating;
    @property (readonly) DVDInfo* next;
    - (void)addToList;
@end
...
DVDInto *myDVD = [DVDInfo new];
myDVD.rating = 9;
[myDVD addToList];
```

So don't be spooked by the odd syntax. Objective-C is really just some additional tools that will help you write even better C, keep your data organized, and take care all kinds of details (like allocating and freeing memory) for you. Trust us, you're going to love it.

Go Get 'Em

Well, that's about it. We hope you enjoyed reading this book as much as we enjoyed writing it. Above all, we hope you are excited about your newfound programming capabilities. By learning C, you've opened the door to an exciting new adventure. You can move on to Objective-C and Cocoa, tackle web programming with PHP, enter the Windows universe with C#, or explore the cross-platform capabilities of Java. There are so many choices out there, and they are all based on C.

Go on out there and write some code. And keep in touch!

Appendix

Answers to Exercises

This appendix features the answers to the exercises in the back of each chapter. Chapter 3 was the first chapter to feature exercises, so that's where we start.

Chapter 3

1. This screenshot shows the error we got when we changed `SayHello() ;` to `SayHello(;`.

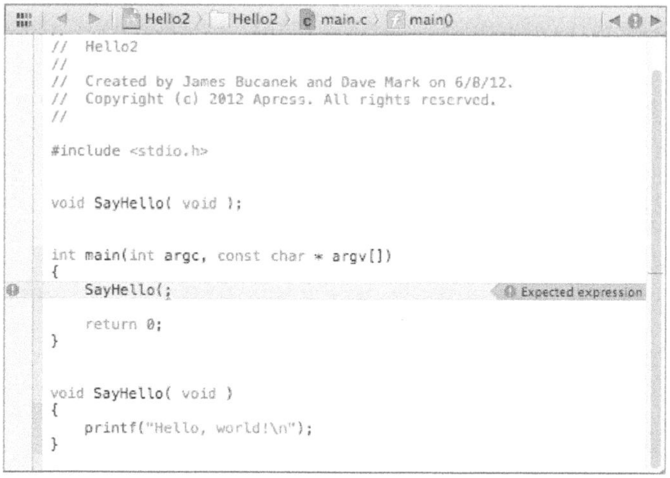

```
Hello2 > Hello2 > main.c > main()

//  Hello2
//
//  Created by James Bucanek and Dave Mark on 6/8/12.
//  Copyright (c) 2012 Apress. All rights reserved.
//

#include <stdio.h>

void SayHello( void );

int main(int argc, const char * argv[])
{
    SayHello(;                                  Expected expression

    return 0;
}

void SayHello( void )
{
    printf("Hello, world!\n");
}
```

2. This screenshot shows the error we got when we changed `main` to `MAIN`. The linker fails because every program must have a function named `main()`, and now yours doesn't.

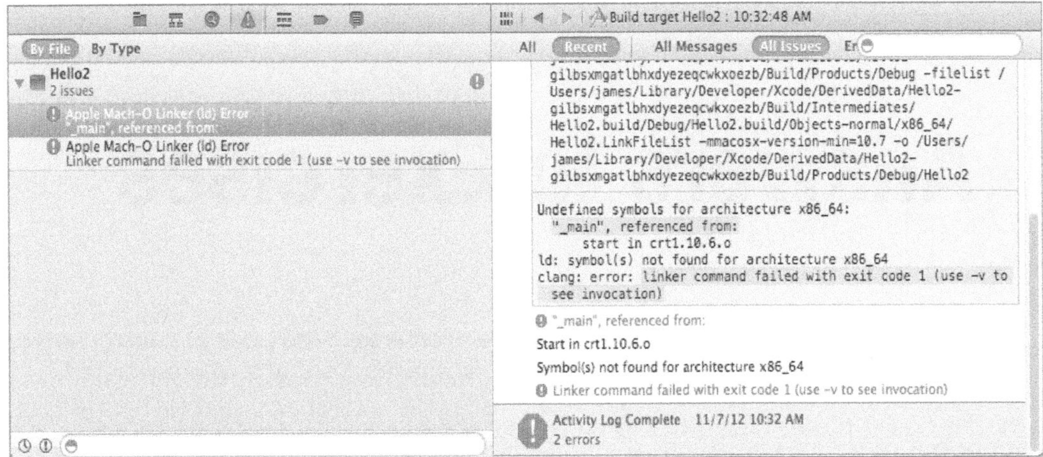

3. This screenshot shows the error we got when we deleted the left curly brace that opens the `main()` function.

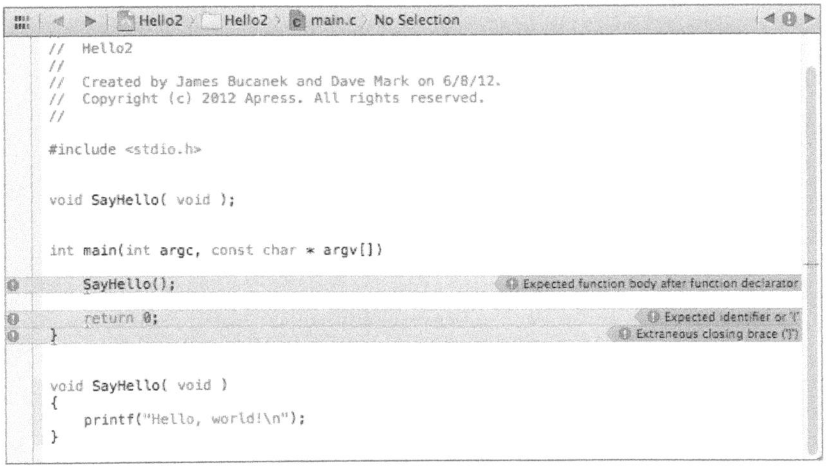

Hello2 › Hello2 › main.c › No Selection

```
//  Hello2
//
//  Created by James Bucanek and Dave Mark on 6/8/12.
//  Copyright (c) 2012 Apress. All rights reserved.
//

#include <stdio.h>


void SayHello( void );


int main(int argc, const char * argv[])

    SayHello();                 Expected function body after function declarator

    return 0;                   Expected identifier or '('
}                               Extraneous closing brace ('}')


void SayHello( void )
{
    printf("Hello, world!\n");
}
```

4. This screenshot shows the errors we got when we changed the case of the SayHello() function prototype.

```
Hello2 > Hello2 > main.c > SAYHELLO()

//  Hello2
//
//  Created by James Bucanek and Dave Mark on 6/8/12.
//  Copyright (c) 2012 Apress. All rights reserved.
//

#include <stdio.h>

void SAYHELLO( void );

int main(int argc, const char * argv[])
{
    SayHello();        Implicit declaration of function 'SayHello' is invalid in C99

    return 0;
}

void SayHello( void )        Conflicting types for 'SayHello'
{
    printf("Hello, world!\n");
}
```

Chapter 4

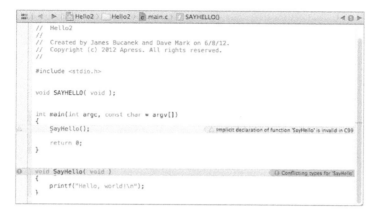

1. Find the mistake in each of the following code fragments:

    a. The quotes around "Hello, World" are missing.

    b. The comma between the two variables (myInt and myOtherInt) is missing.

    c. =+ should be +=.

    d. The second parameter to printf() is missing. Each format specifier in the first string must be matched with an appropriate variable in the parameter list.

    e. Here's another runtime error. This time, you are missing the %d in the first argument to printf(). This won't cause any problems (the myInt value is simply ignored), but it's probably not what you intended.

    f. This time, you've either got an extra \ or are missing an n following the \ in the first printf() parameter.

    g. The left-hand and right-hand sides of the assignment are switched. The variable being assigned is always on the left.

    h. The declaration of anotherInt is missing. The compiler doesn't know what anotherInt is.

2. Compute the value of `myInt` after each code fragment is executed:

    a. 70

    b. -6

    c. -1

    d. 4

    e. -8

    f. 2

    g. 14

    h. 1

Chapter 5

After stepping through the `Hello3` project:

1. The debugger stopped at breakpoints a total of four times.
2. The debugger stopped before the `printf()` statement three times, once for each time the debugger stopped at breakpoints a total of four times.
3. The `main()` function executed once, and the debugger stopped for the breakpoint in `main()` once. The `SayHello()` function was executed three times, and the debugger stopped for the breakpoint in that function each time, for a total of four breaks.

Chapter 6

1. What's wrong with each of the following code fragments?

    a. An `if` statement's expression must be surrounded by parentheses.

    b. We increment `i` inside the for loop's expression and then decrement it in the body of the loop. This loop will never end!

c. The `while` loop has parentheses but is missing an expression.

d. The do statement should follow this format:

```
do
    statement
while ( expression ) ;
```

e. Each case in this switch statement contains a text string, which is illegal. Also, case default should read default.

f. The `printf()` will never get called because if `i` is less than 20, then it can't possibly be equal to 20.

g. This is probably the most common mistake made by C programmers. The assignment operator (=) is used instead of the logical equality operator (==). Since the assignment operator is perfectly legal inside an expression, the compiler won't find this error. This is an annoying little error you'll encounter again and again!

h. Once again, this code will compile, but it likely is not what you wanted. The third expression in the `for` loop is usually an assignment statement—something to move `i` toward its terminating condition. The expression `i*20` is useless here, since it doesn't change anything.

2. Look in the folder *06.E2 - NextPrime2*.

3. Look in the folder *06.E3 - NextPrime3*.

Chapter 7

1. Predict the result of each of the following code fragments:

    a. The final value is 25.

b. The final value is 512. Try changing the `for` loop from 2 to 3. Notice that this generates a number too large for a 2-byte short to hold. Now change the `for` loop from 3 to 4. This generates a number too large for even a 4-byte int to hold. Be aware of the size of your types!

c. The final value is 1,024.

2. The expression `isPrime` is not recognized, because the scope of a variable ends with the block of code it was declared in.

3. Look in the folder *07.E3 - Factor2*.

Chapter 8

1. What's wrong with each of the following code fragments?

    a. The char type defaults to signed, so c can only hold values from -128 to 127. It would be better to use an int.

    b. Use `%f`, `%g`, or `%e` to print the value of a float, not `%d`. Also, the variable being printed is `f`. It should be `myFloat`.

    c. A character constant is surrounded by single quotes, not double quotes. The text string `"a"` is an array composed of two characters: `'a'` and the terminating `'\0'` char. The variable `c` is only a single byte in size. Even if `c` were 2 bytes long, you couldn't assign a pointer to an integer. Try copying the text one byte at a time into a variable large enough to hold the text string and its terminating zero byte.

    d. Once again, this code uses the wrong approach to copying a text string. Also, even if the characters in the string were correctly copied into `c`, the `c` array is not large enough to hold that text string and its zero byte.

    e. A `#define` directive is not a C statement and does not end with a semicolon (unless you want a semicolon to be included in the replacement text).

f. The #define of kMaxArraySize must come before the first non-#define reference to it.

g. This array definition (char c[kMaxArraySize]) creates an array ranging from c[0] to c[kMaxArraySize-1]. The reference to c[kMaxArraySize] is out of bounds.

2. Look in the folder *08.E2 - Dice3*.

3. Look in the folder *08.E3 - Overflow*.

Chapter 9

1. Look in the folder *09.E1 - SecArgs2*.

2. "Learn C on the Mac!" If you want to step through the program, look in the folder *09.E2 - Message*.

3. Look in the folder *09.E3 - WordCount2*.

Chapter 10

1. What's wrong with each of the following code fragments?

   a. The keyword struct before Link is missing in the declaration of the next field.

   b. You can't declare a field of a struct to be a copy of itself. It's more likely that these should be pointers to similar structs, in which case the correct syntax is struct Link *next.

   c. While this is perfectly valid C code, it will never output anything. The while loop advances the line pointer until it points to a '\0' character. It then prints this value using printf(), but since line always points to a '\0' nothing is output.

2. Look in the folder *10.E2 - DVDTracker2*.

3. Look in the folder *10.E3 - DVDTracker3*.

4. Look in the folder *10.E4 - DVDTracker4*.

Chapter 11

1. What's wrong with each of the following code fragments?

   a. The arguments to `fopen()` are backwards. The first argument is the path to the file, and the second is the mode.

   b. The first parameter to `fscanf()` contains a prompt, as if you were calling `printf()`. The first parameter of `fscanf()` is the `FILE` pointer.

   c. `line` is declared as a `char` pointer instead of as an array of chars, the pointer is uninitialized, and no memory was allocated for the string being read in by `fscanf()`. Also, since `line` is a pointer, the `&` in the `fscanf()` call shouldn't be there.

   d. This code is fine except for two problems. The file is opened for writing, yet we are trying to read from the file using `fscanf();` this will fail. Also, there is no protection against reading more than 99 characters into the line array.

2. Look in the folder *11.E2 - FileReader*.

Chapter 12

1. The `fscanf()` function returns the number of values successfully scanned, or `EOF`. The `if` statement only tests for `EOF` and assumes the conversion was successful otherwise. The correct test should be `if ( fscanf(fp,"%d",value) != 1 )` to determine if the conversion was successful or not.

2. Write an `assert` statement to ensure each assumption is true.

   a. `assert( dvdInfoPtr != NULL );`

   b. `assert( count != 0 );`

   c. `assert( argc >= 1 );`

   d. `assert( str != NULL ); assert( copyOfString != NULL );`

   e. `assert( index >= 0 && index < sizeof(array) );`

3. Anything that can go wrong, will go wrong.

Chapter 13

1. What's wrong with each of the following code fragments?

   a. In the next-to-last line, the address of `myCat` is cast to a `struct`. Instead, the address should be cast to a pointer to a `struct` (`struct Dog *`).

   b. The `typedef` defines `FuncPtr` to be a pointer to a function that returns an int. `MyFunc()` is declared to return a pointer to an `int`, not an `int`.

   c. The declaration of `myUnion` is missing the keyword `union`. Unless you use a `typedef`, `union`s and `struct`s are declared using a tag. A tag must always be used in conjunction with the `union` or `struct` keyword. Here's the corrected declaration: `union Number myUnion;`

   d. The `Player union` fields must be accessed using `u`. Instead of `myPlayer.myInt`, refer to `myPlayer.u.myInt`. Instead of `myPlayer.myFloat`, refer to `myPlayer.u.myFloat`.

   e. First, `myFuncPtr` is not a function pointer and not a legal l-value. As is, the declaration just declares a function named `myFuncPtr`. This declaration fixes that problem `int (*myFuncPtr)( int );`. Next, `main()` doesn't take a single int as a parameter. Besides that, calling `main()` yourself is a questionable practice. Finally, to call the function pointed to by `myFuncPtr`, use either `myFuncPtr();` or `(*myFuncPtr)();`, instead of `*myFuncPtr();`.

2. Choose a Core Foundation collection that best fits the data.

a. Array. The names of the week are a sequence which one would naturally address using a day number (0 for Sunday, 1 for Monday, and so on).

b. Set. URLs that you want to visit don't have any particular order, and you don't want them duplicated in the collection if you add the same URL more than once.

c. Tree. The organization of species forms a hierarchy, which is perfectly suited for trees.

d. Dictionary. A dictionary can easily map locker numbers (the value) with member names (the key).

e. Bag. Like set, a bag stores unordered values. Unlike a set, a bag can contain duplicate values. This permits a person's name to be added to the bag more than once, and thus be entered into the raffle more than once, improving their odds.

Index

D

F

G

H

I, J

P